Legacy

Jayne Olorunda

Dedicated to Mum, thanks for everything.

In memory of Abayomi Olorunda a.k.a 'Max'

Foreword.

Mum was once a strong, determined person or so I was told. Personally, I found her quite flighty, almost silly although she did make me laugh. Granted she had her moments when she was sensibility itself but these moments were glimpsed rarely, now they are so few and far between that I wonder if I imagined them. Mum always had some ridiculous stories and strange little ways; when it comes to the past Mum's accuracy is scrupulous, yet when she talks about the present she confuses names, numbers and even addresses. She often told me that we had been cursed, that made me laugh the most; until now.

In the winter of 2010, Mum was placed in a secure mental health unit where she could no longer harm others and more importantly herself. It was during this time that I began to wonder about Mum's tales. I began to question my scepticism, my persistent doubts, because surely no one could attract as much bad luck as Mum and my family.

Mum always loved to tell me about her youth, the fun she had had and the happiness that she experienced. She would tell me about my childhood and that of my sisters. Her stories were so vivid that I felt I was seeing what she saw and experiencing what she had experienced. She had a gift, a God given talent that allowed her to bring the spoken word to life. Anyone who listens to a true storyteller rely their craft becomes a captive listener and for a time I was in the front row, her main audience. As I grew older Mum's tales became more and more frequent and to my shame more and more irrelevant. I was constantly urging her to look forward and stop looking back, to say goodbye to yesterday.

I now care for Mum and try to maintain as stable a life as possible. It is ironic that I once a cynic, have come to see Mum's accounts of yesteryear as my way forward; necessary if I am to ever understand me, where I came from and who I am. Unexpectedly, Mum's story now holds the key to my present and the answers to why my family is such a strange little gathering. It explains the circumstances that led to us being unable to fit into any boxes.

Not fitting in has always been the route of our problems, for my family could be described as neither black nor white, not really Catholic, and not really Protestant, not really working class, yet not really middle class. Hence the dilemma; we fitted in nowhere,

Mum raised us in a no man's land. She did her best to get us out, but she never managed to steer us away from that place. She tried with all her might to follow the signposts to stability, happiness and security, but fate always intervened and gave them a little twist. No matter what direction she turned was wrong, her best intentions steered us deeper and deeper into nowhere.

Often she would reach out to a passer-by, asking and even screaming at them for help, but they were busy. Times had moved on and every one of them turned their back on her, leaving her there in that no man's land with no-one but her three children for company. Her children found life in no man's land difficult; those that left could not be blamed. I would never leave; I would never leave Mum alone in that cold place.

In their teens most children are passed houses, cars, knowledge or the family dynasty. I was left with no dynasty only that of picking up the pieces from a soiled legacy. The legacy of a man I did not know, whose existence and death had set in motion a chain of events that had such momentum they had taken on a life their own.

Last year the British Queen, the figurehead of the UK met Martin McGuiness, the former commander of the IRA. Publically they shook hands to show how much Northern Ireland has moved on. To the outside world and those who went unscathed in the troubles, this historic handshake represented the current beliefs of the population. Yet what of the silent masses? The three thousand plus dead and countless injured? As foes became friends the widows, the widowers, the orphans, the brother less, the sister less and the maimed were pushed into Northern Irelands closet, the door was marked '**The Past'** and categorically closed. How did the occupants of the closet feel? Did the handshake reconcile their pain, did it bring back their dead, their lost limbs or minds, and did it heal their broken hearts? Or did they wonder as they watched the scene unfold, what was it all about? Countless lives wasted, seemingly atoned for with a simple shaking of hands.

For those like Mum who were left behind, there will never be peace; they carry their losses with them each and every living day. All the handshakes in the world cannot erase her memories nor undo the tattoo etched permanently yet invisibly across her psyche. All the victims have a story to tell; this is the story of just one victim and her unique family. A victim who fought against all to marry, who gave up on everyone and everything she knew to pursue her heart.

I will try to tell her tale as I see it, I will piece together stories she imparted to me and the stories from my memory to describe how it all unfolded. This is my account of Mum's story. What follows is my view of events.... (Some names have been changed only those of non-essential characters).

Prologue

Date: **15th January 1980**

Time: **18.06**

Location: Europa Station Belfast.

The station swarmed with rush hour crowds. Around her commuters rushed to and from their trains. Gabrielle was invisible to them, so was 'IT'. A few minutes earlier she had been just another face in the crowd. Now she was alone with the exception of one companion, *terror*.

'IT' had come out of nowhere and stood less than six inches from her, its darkness infiltrating her every pore. All light, all happiness, any joy she had ever been exposed to evaporated. 'IT' had captured her in its web, wrapping her in strand after strand of its sinister silk.

Feebly, Gabrielle recited every prayer that she could remember and when her memory failed her, she beseeched the heavens to take this thing away from her. Her pleas went unanswered and she stood there powerless.

Gabrielle tried to scream but no words came. She contemplated running but her limbs were motionless. Even the simple gesture of averting her eyes from IT's penetrating gaze, became impossible. She was paralysed, her defenceless body forcing her to remain on the spot.

'IT' opened its mouth and words, lots of words tumbled out. It spoke in a language that Gabrielle had never heard before or hoped to hear again.

Its menacing tones were infused with hatred and malice. Only its finale was spoken in a human tongue, six words that shook Gabrielle to the core, "I curse you and your family".

Instinct told her that she had encountered a being that represented all things evil. She had just been exposed to something that was not of this world.

In a green cloud 'IT' was gone back to the nowhere it had appeared from. Gabrielle dropped to her knees relieved at its departure and waited for the waves of terror to leave her. Her moment in darkness had seemed a lifetime. It was 18.06, no time had passed. *Had she imagined the episode?*

She glanced at the ground where 'IT' had stood. Sure enough 'IT' had left an ominous souvenir, some sort of green pendant. Then this thing *had* happened. Reassured that her sanity was still intact, she looked at the commuters the people all around her, they would be shaken too. What had they made of this thing? Yet their faces registered no shock, they were simply the ordinary faces of ordinary commuters in a busy train station.

Gabrielle's ordeal had been invisible to them and so had 'IT'.

Part One

Go placidly amid the noise and haste, and remember what peace there may be in silence.

As far as possible without surrender be on good terms with all persons.

Speak your truth quietly and clearly; and listen to others, even the dull and ignorant; they too have their story.

Avoid loud and aggressive persons, they are vexations to the spirit.

If you compare yourself with others, you may become vain and bitter; for always there will be greater and lesser persons than yourself.

Enjoy your achievements as well as your plans.

Keep interested in your career, however humble; it is a real possession in the changing fortunes of time.

Exercise caution in your business affairs; for the world is full of trickery.

But let this not blind you to what virtue there is; many persons strive for high ideals; and everywhere life is full of heroism.

Be yourself.

Especially, do not feign affection.

Neither be critical about love; for in the face of all aridity and disenchantment it is as perennial as the grass.

Take kindly the counsel of the years, gracefully surrendering the things of youth.

Nurture strength of spirit to shield you in sudden misfortune. But do not distress yourself with imaginings.

Many fears are born of fatigue and loneliness. Beyond a wholesome discipline, be gentle with yourself.

You are a child of the universe, no less than the trees and the stars;

you have a right to be here.

And whether or not it is clear to you, no doubt the universe is unfolding as it should.

Therefore be at peace with God, whatever you conceive Him to be,

and whatever your labors and aspirations, in the noisy confusion of life keep peace with your soul.

With all its sham, drudgery and broken dreams, it is still a beautiful world. Be careful.

Strive to be happy.

© Max Ehrmann 1927

Chapter One

They say the grass is always greener on the other side and for Gabrielle's father never a truer phrase was uttered. Standing with him at the garden gate looking over the field beyond it, she would listen to him reminisce of when the country was one. He would pick her up on his broad shoulders and point just past the field to his beloved Ireland; for there and only there, was the grass truly green.

He loved to regale her with his family history of how they had come from Co. Mayo, bringing their 'Protestant' name with them. When probed about this as he often was, he would scratch his head and inform his audience that in Co. Mayo his name was not a Protestant name, in Mayo it was the most Catholic name of them all. A more inquisitive person would ask her father about his unique colouring, something she often pondered over, for it was certainly true that he did not have an Irish complexion. Her father's hair was dark as the night and his skin a rich mahogany even in the harshest of winters. Yet her father would convince anyone who enquired that in Co. Mayo, all the natives were as dark as him. Her father convinced not only himself, but everyone he met that he was an Irishman through and through and with a conviction as firm and deep set as his, he was rarely doubted.

Gabrielle entered the world in 1951, a time of hope and prosperity. Born and raised in the border town of Strabane, she had an idyllic, carefree childhood. As the eldest of a large family she was fortunate to relish in being the only child for six years.

Then, the only thing she hated was school. Every day she was encouraged out the door with a little aid from her mother's constant companion, 'the stick'. Unfortunately, 'the stick' was to cross the generational gap and became an integral part of my childhood too!

For Gabrielle everything about school unsettled her, the huge grey crumbling building, the dank dingy corridors and most of all the wrinkled, torturous gargoyles called 'nuns' who roamed them. The gargoyles were responsible for providing the then only cloud on her otherwise blue sky of a life. The gargoyles and their beloved dunce's cap, a great big red and blue striped hat emblazoned with 'I am a dunce' became the bane of her childhood. Gabrielle spent most of her school days facing the front of the class, shamefacedly modelling the gargoyles carefully crafted couture.

Gabrielle had many friends, however her very best friend was a little Jack Russell terrier called Patch. Wherever Gabrielle went Patch followed, they were a twosome adored by the adults around them. This situation changed when Gabrielle reached the age of six, when her cosy *only child* bubble was burst.

It happened on an ordinary summer's day, she and Patch were playing when her mother casually informed her that the stork would be coming soon. The stork would bring her a little brother or sister. Now she wonders if a childish remark from her may have had some part in the storks visit. She remembers her mother entertaining guests whilst she was happily drawing in the corner. She wasn't normally privy to adult conversations, so as all children do when given the chance she soaked up every enticing little morsel. The women were talking about their husbands and sharing their beds; apparently it was a necessity to do this when you were married. If you didn't undertake the arduous task of sharing a bed, then children would never be granted. Gabrielle was utterly perplexed by the conversation as for as long as she could remember, her mother shared a bed with her. Questions began to form in her little mind; how on earth was *she* made then? Her internal dilemma and no doubt external facial contortions were obviously visible to all, as very soon one of the ladies noticed her exertion and asked,

"Gabrielle what's wrong?"

Gabrielle pondered briefly and answered

"If Mummy and Daddy are married, why does Daddy sleep across the hall?" She further explained "When he thinks I'm asleep he gets all upset and calls for Mummy to join him, she calls him a dirty auld brute and tells him to get into his bed". Gabrielle's mother now a deep shade of scarlet bristled whilst the other ladies burst into raucous laughter; ever since her mother shared a bed with her father!

Unfortunately, for Gabrielle that summer's visit was not to be the first visit from the horrid stork, if she could have clutched that loathsome bird then and there she would have wrung its neck, plucked and stuffed it.

Instead in the absence of the elusive stork, she sought the gypsies. They were never far from the doors of the town, regularly peddling anything from mats, to books and if you were very lucky they even took goods off your hands. Gabrielle hoped she would be very lucky, as *she* was about to offer them a whole new market , *she* would offer them her baby brother or sister and she wouldn't even set a price; as far as she was concerned they could have this little irritation for free!

Not even the gypsies were interested.

She would just have to get the used to the idea of sharing her mother, father, grandmother, aunties, and uncles with this new little creature. She was not happy as like any only child who is '*blessed*' with a new sibling, she suspected that as soon as the new arrival came her life would change; no longer would her every whim be catered to, from now on she would have to share. This thought did not sit comfortably.

Sure enough the bloody stork came to her house delivering a little brother and a few years later delivering a sister. For the next twenty years it delivered another and yet another until her little house was full and she was well and truly dethroned. The storks delay between visits created an age gap, one that prevented Gabrielle from feeling close to her siblings. With the exception of her brother, she was in her teens when most of them were born. Perhaps this caused the fiercely independent streak that overshadowed her future and the future of those who would follow.

Chapter Two

The arrival of Gabrielle's siblings ushered in a period of austerity. With more and more mouths to feed and backs to clothe, family life settled into a routine of mundanity. Her mother took up dressmaking to cut down on the clothing bills and baking to maximise the food supplies. Her father worked longer and harder than ever before.

Gabrielle was usually put in charge of the children a task she hated, so much so that when the weather was dry she took the yard brush and brushed the screaming little horrors out to the garden! Life became a case of economising, nothing was ever wasted in their house and everything was shared. Even the meals took on a feeling of routine with each day being assigned a particular dinner. If you were to ask Gabrielle now this very moment, she can still memorise her meal pattern; Monday remains of Sundays roast, Tuesday cabbage and bacon, Wednesday stew and so on until they reached Sunday (not to mention Friday when they enjoyed 'Fenian Steak'). This pattern continued throughout her years at home as did the most unbearable pattern of all; cleaning.

Every Saturday, Gabrielle was to wake up to not only to her daily dose of thick porridge but the prospect of an entire day of scrubbing, brushing, washing and polishing. In her childhood a clean home was revered and no stone was left unturned. This was a tradition she brought into adulthood and enforced on her own children. I remember Mum used to make us start at the top of the house and work our way down, when this was finished Mum just like her mother before her would check on our work; running her finger along surfaces, lifting our mattresses to check on the bed and opening doors to ensure that even the door seams were gleaming. If we neglected to clean even the tiniest particle we could rest assured Mum's keen eye would find it and as always we would be made to start again. Mum could not tolerate a dirty house, over the years she instilled the conviction that a person could be judged by their home into each of us. I wonder now if this belief was what plunged her into the state of mind that would attempt to destroy her later in life; she judged herself by her own standards.

During Gabrielle's teenage years Saturday night was just another night. While most young people were planning trips to the cinema, walks around town or even a stolen kiss Saturday night for her meant red raw fingers and an aching back. After cleaning all she was capable of doing was crawling into her bed. Her mother had teenage control down to a fine art. Until Gabrielle's late teenage years she didn't have time or the energy to even contemplate a social life.

Little Patch's demise came when she was just thirteen. Gabrielle was sent to the town's chemist to get baby supplies, when she was faced with her first glimpse of tragedy. Being sent to the chemist was a routine request, one she loved as she benefitted from half an hour's independence and a walk around the town. On this particular day she and Patch set off through the field and over the bridge, they didn't rush their journey instead they meandered at a leisurely pace taking in all the sights and sounds of their home town. They went to the chemist, made their purchases and began to make their journey home.

When they got to the bridge, they picked up their pace; they had already taken more than the half hour she was allowed, if she wasn't home soon her mother would come looking for her. When she got halfway over the bridge, a loud horn startled her and broke the tranquillity that had until then surrounded her. She turned quickly in its direction, seeing a car drive away. What she saw shattered her tiny world; little Patch lay in a bloody heap on the other side of the road. She could see that he had lost a lot of blood and remembers dropping the chemist bag, neither looking left nor right as she flew across the road to his side. Her speed made no difference as already her first friend was dead. He was so still and small, his little head crushed on the left side, she knew he would never, could never wake. She petted him and called him over and over until she couldn't see through her tears, but Patch was still. She watched horrified as the blood flowing from his lifeless body slowed and settled into a stagnant puddle around him, soaking into his once gleaming white coat, and drying on his face. That was the first time Gabrielle felt pain and to her it was the worst pain imaginable, she couldn't do a thing. Her insides grew heavy and her heart swelled in pain as she sat beside Patch and watched death take him away from her.

Gabrielle never forgot the death of little Patch for it shook the foundations of her world.

Sudden death would come back to her again one day, this time more shocking than she could ever imagine and once again she would be powerless to stop it. That day in Gabrielle's thirteenth year was one of the saddest days in her childhood but a minuscule taster of what was to come......

Chapter Three

The most dominant element of Gabrielle's early life was the influence of the Catholic Church. Her parents were staunch Catholics and like the rest of the small town spent each Sunday and any day of religious significance 'kissing the altar' rails. For Gabrielle the unfortunate part of their adherence to the Roman Catholic convictions was that she was made to join them. Every Sunday was Mass day, when the entire family donned their Sunday bests with the rest of the town and walked to Mass, never did they miss a day. No matter how sick anyone was, they were well enough to go to Mass. Gabrielle's compulsory and non-negotiable attendance at Mass felt like a prison sentence especially in her teens. Even if illness had taken her, she firmly believed that she would have been wheeled to Mass on her deathbed rather than be permitted to damage her mortal soul by missing one service. On top of the weekly Mass on Saturdays, they also had confession and during the week they usually had at least one visit from Father Converey.

To have a priest as a regular caller to one's home was a great honour, it was one thing that her parents did not take lightly. When Father Converey called it was like the Great Lord himself had graced them with his presence, the best china came out, the children were dismissed and the conversation became closed and serious. Even if they passed a priest on the street they were made to bless themselves and say "Hello Father" in such a respectful manner that they just stopped short of genuflecting. Nothing was more important to her parents than the church, the priest embodied this great organisation and what he said went. They lived their lives according to Roman Catholic dogma, something Gabrielle took for granted as they recited the nightly rosary and fasted for a saint's day. It was only as she grew older that she decided that such a strong and unquestioned devotion was not for her.

Strabane, which was once home to both Catholics and Protestants gradually became almost entirely Catholic. As news trickled through the grapevine of Protestant families being removed from Catholic towns and Catholic families being removed from Protestant towns, her neighbours began to doubt their safety. Protestant families and neighbours moved out one by one over the years. Their confidence was eroded and worn so thin that they left the town. They moved away and joined larger more Protestant towns and cities across the North. By Gabrielle's early teens all that remained in the once mixed town was an increasingly bitter Catholic enclave.

It was during her teenage years that Gabrielle began to question her upbringing, to doubt the preaching's of the church and to formulate her own opinions on Ireland North and South. She bravely began to question these teachings, to test her mother on her iron resolve that her take on life was correct. She began to assert her independence, to formulate her own viewpoints being careful to ensure that they were on opposing angles to her mother's and more importantly that they shunned the Church.

In her late teens Father Converey spent most of his Mass preaching on the evils of the mini skirt. In protest to his outburst she proudly flaunted her mini and paraded up and down the street. She ensured that all the neighbours witnessed her modern fashion sense and saw how little regard she had paid to Father Converey. Arriving home that night, Gabrielle was met by the stick and was told to apologise to the Sacred Heart picture that permanently loomed above her mother's chair. She was dispatched to bed without so much as a 'God Bless'. Rather than be ashamed, on the contrary she stomped to bed; well shuffled as her skirt, all two inches of it did not allow for much movement!

In her room she went straight to her satchel, pulling out pen and paper and composed a letter to the 'Sunday Independent'. She stated the case for mini's, modernity whilst lambasting the church, its preaching's and it's dinosaur of a Pope. She posted her rant first class the very next morning.

Immediately after posting the letter she regretted it but she doubted her treachery would ever be discovered. A week later she was shocked to find that her rant had been published!

She talks of how it was father Converey who 'outed' her, so much for following the Lord's teachings! He called around that evening slamming the letter on the table, then instructed her mother to deal with her daughter and promptly left. Her mother was understandably incandescent with rage, 'the stick', the Sacred Heart and a few choice obscenities came out that night. For the next few years Gabrielle continued to test her mother with her elaborate antics; the stick would come out often. By way of avoidance she began to spend more and more time with her kindly grandmother, often staying overnight and generally avoiding home and 'the stick'.

Chapter Four

Gabrielle had always wanted to be a nurse. In the late sixties career choices for girls were limited and when faced with the alternatives nursing was definitely the best option. Nowadays girls can leave school and study for anything they like; choices are so vast that for many it is as difficult to decide on a career plan as it is to actually embark on a career! Yet back then by all accounts the choices for girls consisted of getting married on leaving school and not many would relish that idea, to become a teacher (for Gabrielle this would have been fine if children were removed from the equation!). The remaining options for her and most of her generation was to become a civil servant or a bank clerk neither prospect held much appeal.

Luckily for her a further option glimmered in the distance, to become a nurse. As far as she was concerned there was no choice, the other options were repugnant. She had been an avid follower of Doctor Kildare, read far too many hospital based Mills & Boons and even studied Florence Nightingale for her O-Levels! The culmination of these led her to believe that a more glamorous, worthy career for a young woman just didn't exist. She romantically pictured herself waltzing up and down the wards in a commanding yet feminine uniform, leaning over the bedsides of the infirm and whispering teams of endearment. She would be surrounded by movie star handsome doctors and work all over the world.

She focused on passing her exams and getting all the experience she could in order to gain a much coveted place in the local Derry hospital to begin her training. She spent two years volunteering with the St John's Ambulance Core and in her spare time read up on biology and anatomy so that by the time she was offered a place on the course she was brimming with confidence and well equipped.

Gabrielle's parents were pleased with her choice, her Fathers chest puffed out with pride at the very thought of his little girl entering into such a noble profession. Her mother who had herself aspired to become a nurse was also overjoyed. Her mother didn't tell her this but Gabrielle had heard her mention it at every available opportunity. Should the conversation be about autumn leaves or the price of butter, her mother somehow managed to manipulate the topic around to her daughter's acceptance into nursing.

To embark on her studies Gabrielle required what seemed like an impossible amount of supplies, the hospital had sent a long and expensive list. She would need everything from thick nursing textbooks, standard nursing shoes, a nursing coat, and even a fob watch. It was with great reluctance that Gabrielle presented this list to her parents she knew they could not afford even one of these items, yet alone the entire list.

On seeing their stunned faces as they read the list she was besieged with guilt. Rather than ask her struggling parents to pay for such a quantity of items she decided to be a martyr and tell them that nursing wasn't for her. She stoically told them about an office job she had seen advertised in Derry and how much it appealed to her. She laughs as she remembers conjuring up as much excitement as she could as she talked about learning to type and take important phone calls.

Only a few days later her mother was to ask her to go material shopping with her as she was making up some dresses for her little sisters and needed to choose an attractive yet hardwearing fabric. Gabrielle was still inwardly glum at having given up on her dream but she re-pasted her happy face on and agreed to accompany her. First they went to the material shop, where her mother selected the various materials and bits and bobs that she would require. Followed by a trip to the general store, when her mother surprised her and instead of walking their usual route to the food supplier, they went upstairs and in the direction of the shoe department. Her mother made small talk with the shopkeeper and then asked a question that took her breath away.

"Do you stock any suitable nurses' shoes?"

Gabrielle was speechless and looked at her mother wide eyed, where she quite casually replied,

"Well you're going to need them."

Gabrielle had never been as grateful to her parents as she was that summer when they somehow managed to buy all of her supplies. She will never forget their generosity.

She remembers being so overwhelmed that she had to blink back the tears as her mother patted her shoulder and said "make us proud". She doesn't know where her parents obtained the money from as it was never mentioned. All she knew was that by some miracle come September, she was fully kitted out and ready to embark on her training.

Gabrielle would go on to suffer three years of gruelling nursing training a time of laughs, horror, fun and tears. To a country girl the hospital was huge, an endless maze of corridors swamped with doctors, nurses and patients. She describes hospital life as a world within a world, an insular bustling environment that she yearned to be a part of. Yet one obstacle stood between Gabrielle and her full immersion into that world; three years of rigorous training.

The figurehead of that obstacle was the Matron who oversaw all the trainee nurses. Nothing got past her. She inspired terror in them all Gabrielle portrays her as an unkind, strict and demanding woman who ensured all of the trainees were put through their paces, constantly testing them and pushing them to their limits and beyond. Matron was to make each of them start at the bottom scrubbing floors and lockers with pungent disinfectant, serving food to patients and getting used to the reality of life on the wards. She loved to allocate them to 'slush room days' and reinforce to them every day that they were the lowest of the low. This was aided by the qualified nurses who delighted in barking as many orders at them as Matron.

Gabrielle's time was split between equally between the ward and the classroom. She dreamt of the serenity of the classroom and of being away from the constant wailing of "nurse, nurse" and Matrons perverse commands.

Chapter Five

The training was rigorous and at times Gabrielle felt that it was insurmountable but the good times outweighed the bad. During her training she lived in the nurse's home where life was more bearable. She enjoyed the camaraderie with the girls and despite the strict curfew of ten o'clock each night (unless on duty) they had fun. Twice a week, when Matron's watchful eyes finally closed and the lights went out, the girls would creep out of the nurse's home and escape into Derry.

They would tiptoe downstairs and climb out the kitchen window always ensuring that it was pulled down just enough so it appeared closed. If anyone was caught going in or out after this time they would be suspended or worse. The young nurses who had gone before them had kindly tipped the girls off about the kitchen window; so far everyone had managed to escape. The Matron did a final check of the corridors of the home around half ten locking all doors and windows and switching off the lights. The kitchen window with its loose handle was the exception to her search, in Gabrielle's three years in the nurses home the Matron never once checked beyond the kitchen door and of course the fridge lock.

The Matron's unusual lapse was to the girls gain; they were free to enjoy themselves dancing, drinking and following the infamous show bands until the wee small hours (often reporting to the wards having had no sleep at all!).

There comes a time when all girls grow up, even country girls and it was during these wild days that Gabrielle proudly admitted to discovering cigarettes, booze and men. She boasts at having made it her point to regularly sample all three! Gabrielle smoked twenty a day (still does), drinking and dating as often as she could. She was determined to enjoy her youth and freedom. The girls suspected that Matron, a small joyless woman had an inkling that the girls were going out after curfew yet she simply lacked the proof. Despite her vigilance and almost daily security checks she never discovered their exit route. Without proof there was little she could do with regards to her suspicions.

Hospital life meant that Gabrielle met people from all around the world, especially men! Many young doctors came to work and study at the hospital and by the time she was twenty she had dated Protestants, Indians, Spaniards, Italians and young men from as far afield as Egypt and India. She could even boast of having dated an officer from the British army and a policeman. Life in Derry immersed her into a world that was a million miles away from her strict upbringing; a world that would never have been possible had she stayed in her insular home town. She was never silly enough to mention her antics at home. Even then she was savvy enough to know that tolerance of anything other than a Catholic, a good Irish Catholic at that would never be granted.

Gabrielle's training involved a rotation where she worked in various different areas of the hospital from theatre, to A&E and paediatrics until she was competent in them all. Everything seemed to be going reasonably well until Gabrielle was faced with the challenge of the labour ward. She had an idea that she wouldn't enjoy this particular rotation, but knew that in order to pass she would have to endure it.

Gabrielle went with a hopeful and cautiously optimistic mind to begin her first day on the labour ward, where she was met with a woman who was in the final stages of labour. The woman's hair was wet with sweat and glued to her red and purple face. She appeared utterly inhuman as she frantically pushed the child out, puffing and panting, her legs akimbo with untold fluids dripping out of what seemed like every private orifice. The image disgusted Gabrielle, so much so that something strange happened, her stomach heaved and she threw up. If this was the miracle of life, then life didn't offer much! She had seen so much during her training, people's inners, vomit, burns, diarrhoea, pus and countless other horrors. Yet none had the same effect on her as watching that woman giving birth.

After being sick she took to her two size fives and ran, she never wanted to see such a display again. She was well and truly traumatised.

When she had gained a good distance from the hospital, she stopped running, smoked three cigarettes in a row and waited until the shaking subsided. Unsure of what to do she recalls racking her brain for a plan because she knew she would never darken the doors of that foul cesspit again. What seemed like eons passed until she decided that there was only one thing to do; *go back to her old rotation on the recovery ward and act like nothing happened!* If she kept her head down and went on with her usual work, she naively believed that no one would question her presence.

How wrong she was!

Within an hour of escape from the labour ward she sensed that she was being watched. She quickly clambered behind a locker and ducked her head down. It was too late. Gabrielle was caught. A voice that sent shivers down her spine boomed down the corridor,

"Nurse Caulfield!"

With those words her stomach lurched. "Oh God", she was in a living hell. She unfolded herself from her hiding place and forced an answer.

"Yes, Matron" she whimpered

"My office please" Matrons clipped tones replied.

Gabrielle was now sweating as profusely as the woman on the labour ward. Her legs felt like jelly as she manoeuvred them in the direction of Matron's office. She could barely tap the door her hands were shaking so much,

"Come in" barked Matron.

Gabrielle stepped in to the stuffy smoke filled office and approached the desk. Matron didn't even look up from her writing, her chubby fingers gripping the pen to the point of strangulation, the only indication that she was aware of Gabrielle's presence.

"Nurse Caulfield, why are you not on the maternity ward? Why am I faced with you this morning?" she demanded.

This was it after two years of hard slog it was over, the cretin would expel her. Gabrielle answered with the only excuse she had,

"Matron I didn't like it" she faltered, already aware of how feeble her words would sound.

"*You* didn't like it?"

Gabrielle nodded unable to meet her steely eyes.

"*YOU* didn't like it" she roared, in a mixture of bemusement and disgust.

"How dare you! How *dare* you! Since when can a nurse pick and choose her duties, this is not a holiday camp" (More a concentration camp, thought Gabrielle).

"That ward is a vital part of your training, it is not about *like*" Matron sneered.

Gabrielle, who always had an answer regardless of the situation, was for once gobsmacked. She was so caught up in her own world that she could barely listen to the Matron's rant. She could see Matrons brow furrowed and could hear key words, "disappointment, disgrace, and specimen"; she could see Matron's spittle but was too concerned with the ramifications of her actions. It was at the moment when Matron scraped her chair back and stood in front of her, her rotund body rigid with outrage as she muttered the word 'suspended' that Gabrielle woke up.

Gabrielle felt her blood run cold; the room began to spin.

"Collect your belongings and leave, I will be in touch when I have made my decision."

Still gobsmacked words still eluded her she simply turned and left the office. She was in trouble. She was suspended until further notice until Matron decided on what further course of action she would take.

This time it took four cigarettes to compose herself, there was nothing she could do now. She would either be allowed to finish her training or not. The only positive that came from that day's development was the fact that she would never have to set foot in the labour ward again. Or so she thought; as fate would have it she would have to endure the labour ward not as a nurse but as a patient three more times in all.

She called her father and told him she was given a week's leave; her hours were on a rota basis so he wasn't surprised at her having given no warning regarding her days off. It was a risky step for Gabrielle to take, as there would be no way of knowing if a week was long enough because Matron had given her no indication of how long the suspension would last. One thing she was sure of was that Matron would let her stew; she would not rush to put her out of her misery. She craftily omitted to mention to her father that she might never need returned back to the nurse's home. She would impart that information when she had heard definite confirmation, but for now she was going to try and enjoy her unexpected unearned break!

It was to be exactly a week to the day that she returned home when an ominous looking letter arrived. It was etched with the hospitals official stamp instantly Gabrielle knew its contents revealed her future. Of course in her home there was never any privacy, she grew up surrounded by an endless stream of visitors and family. This is a sharp contrast to my childhood where very few, if any, got past our door.

Aware of being watched by a full house Gabrielle managed to keep herself composed and casually tore the thick envelope open. She was aware of her mother watching her from the side of her eye; she had never had a letter from the hospital in her two years of training. So she knew that her spectator was wondering what she had done now. Well she wasn't going to enlighten her.

"What are you all gawping at" she raged.

She knew her mother would call her up on this rudeness later, but right now she didn't care. For now her outburst ensured everyone in the room had averted their eyes and went on with their tedious conversation.

Gabrielle scanned the contents of the letter quickly being careful not to re attract any attention to herself. It seemed that she had had a reprieve and was due back on the ward the following Monday! Better still she was due at A & E and the labour ward was not mentioned.

She was triumphant as her little protest had been successful!

The suspension had been the longest time Gabrielle had been separated from her work and it forced her to admit that she actually missed it. She would return to Derry and work harder than ever and she would be diligent, obedient and dedicated. She would prove to Matron that she was a worthy contender to her now ardently craved title of 'nurse'.

The journey back to the hospital would have followed the river Foyle it was a journey I was to take several times in my childhood. I'm sure her view was much the same as mine on approaching the city. She would have passed the Waterside's now familiar railway station, its row upon row of terraces, children playing out, neighbours on doorways gossiping and of course the steaming windows of the many pubs.

Back then Derry was an industrial, hardworking city but overall a happy one. A real sense of community prevailed. Looking over her shoulder she would have seen the river Foyle's waters parting the city in two, with the hills of Donegal looming in the background creating a picturesque scene. Unlike me, Gabrielle was glad to be there; she fitted in.

When the old gasworks wall would have scaled her vision she would have known that in less than a mile she would be back at the nurse's home. Now Gabrielle could get back to work and normality. The suspension only made her see what she had almost lost.

Chapter Six

Gabrielle arrived early because she remembers whiling the day away in the communal room. Although it was 1970, TV was still a real treat and the fact that the nurse's home had one was an attraction for all the girls. She greeted the few girls who were in the room with a nod and turned her attention to the TV.

Something about what was on attracted Gabrielle and meant that it wasn't long until she was completely engrossed. The English journalist was reporting all the way from America and was covering the plight of the African Americans. Equal rights had been granted in many states but prejudices were still commonplace. The TV switched to show a picture of the late Dr. Martin Luther King, and she listened intently to what he was saying. From Gabrielle's stance the Americans struggles seemed implausible, yet civil rights and the injustices faced by these people were never far from the news. She just couldn't comprehend why anyone would make such a distinction between human beings, why one race felt they had the right to demean another. She listened actively to see if any explanation was proffered, unsurprisingly there was none. There never would be.

When Gabrielle was growing up she remembers seeing a person of colour in Strabane, she can't recall much about them except for the fact that they were so attractive. She pleaded with her family in the months leading up to her fifth Christmas for a black baby doll. When that Christmas came, no black baby doll arrived. She was so disappointed that none of her other presents held any appeal. Santa was a bad man he had let her down and ruined her Christmas. However, one kindly aunt's efforts were to prove successful in pacifying her. Her aunt promised her that someday she would have a real black baby. It was as if her aunt had a crystal ball.

Gabrielle's work meant encountering people from all over the world; she couldn't imagine creating a distinction between people. She could never be an American. Her dislike for Americans and their hatred was the only real political conviction of her youth.

That day she discreetly studied one of her fellow students from the corner of her eye. Modupe was a pretty girl, stalwartly studious and excruciatingly quiet. The result was that Gabrielle didn't know her very well. She knew that Modupe was from Africa, and her parents had sent her here to complete her nursing training. She surveyed her for a while trying to ascertain these differences that the Americans claimed to see. Yet everything about her was exactly the same as her white counterparts. The only difference she could see was that her skin colour was darker. She marvelled at how so many people believed that having darker skin somehow made a person inferior and would have continued to do so had Modupe not noticed her appraisal and stared openly back.

Embarrassed she flushed, looked away and gave up on her train of thought. It wouldn't be long until such thoughts would keep her awake at night.......

Chapter seven

After the fiasco of the labour ward Gabrielle was placed in A&E and loved it. She loved not knowing who or what would come through the swinging doors; she loved the buzz. She describes her days as being adrenalin fuelled and hectic. To her this was what nursing was all about, not watching women debase themselves pushing out goo covered babies.

During training Gabrielle's home life remained constant, her mother asking about her studies and enquiring if she had met any young men. Luckily her mother was usually bent over the sewing machine so couldn't see Gabrielle's face as she lied and said she hadn't met any. Her siblings ran in and out from the back garden, the noise was piercing as they played whatever new game they had invented. Gabrielle was relieved to be living away from this madness, children babbling and shrieking incessantly gave her a headache. Every time she went home she vowed never to succumb to having children of her own. She always felt that that no one should ever be expected to put up with noisy children. Not to mention endure the miracle of life.

One evening an unannounced caller gave away her talk of never having had a boyfriend in Derry. She was almost ready to prepare for bed when a knock came to the door, assuming it was the gypsies or worse the priest she let her father answer it. This was a mistake because her father was to invite the caller in and it certainly wasn't the gypsies, or the priest. It was a boy she had been dating in Derry and had told no one at home about.

Her father had sent this boy to the sitting room. It was a room that they seldom used except when they had their best company. Whoever he was had obviously impressed.

Her father told her that her visitor was,

"A lovely chap, very posh, called Harry"

Gabrielle went puce at the very mention of his name; she hoped her parents didn't notice. Her mother rose and wiped away the threads from her sewing off her dress,

"Gabrielle go and greet your guest" she ordered.

As she walked into the living room she found Harry sitting awkwardly on the settee,

"Hello" she said feigning surprise "what brings you here?"

"I decided it was high time I met your family" said Harry making her cringe.

As if on cue her mother walked into the room.

"Hello" she said in her authoritative voice reserved for visitors or trouble, "I'm Gabrielle's mother, pleased to meet you"

Harry jumped to his feet and went over to shake her mother's hand.

Gabrielle was delighted with Harry's show of manners because she knew her mother would appreciate it.

"Harry Thornton, pleased to meet you Mrs Caulfied"

"Have a seat John's just preparing some tea"

"Thank you" he answered sitting back down on the settee.

"You have a beautiful home Mrs Caulfield" he remarked. Gabrielle wasn't convinced that her boyfriend's comments were genuine. After all he came from a family of Doctors and lived in one of the most affluent areas of Derry. Whilst Gabrielle's home was tastefully decorated, fashionable and clean she doubted it would impress Harry.

"Gabrielle didn't let us know she had plans so I can only apologise for not expecting you" her mother said.

"That's entirely my fault Mrs Caulfield we actually didn't have any plans. I just decided to call on the off chance that Gabrielle would be free. It's so rare to get a weekend off these days."

"Really Harry? May I ask what line of work you're in?" Her mother enquired.

"I'm a doctor; I work in Altnagelvin as well"

"I see" said her mother "so you're obviously very busy, well we're delighted you could take the time to call"

"Gabrielle, why don't you go and help your father, Harry would you rather tea or coffee?"

"Coffee please if it's not too much trouble".

Mum remembers hurrying to the kitchen to find her father rattling and banging plates,

"What's keeping you?"

"Just checking to see what biscuits we have"

"Do you need a hand?"

"No, no, you go up to your guest. I've found some shortbread"

"Grand thanks for your help"

"Gabrielle, one more thing he seems a nice lad, I just wondered if he's................"

She didn't let him finish, she already knew what her father was getting at,

"For God's sake, if you must know he's Protestant!" she said storming off.

Doctor or not now she knew now that her parents would not be impressed. She suppressed a fleeting thought that they didn't have any shortbread and made her way back into the living room.

"Aye that's what I thought" Mumbled her Dad.

She joined her mother and Harry in the living room where the conversation was flowing. Being the woman she was her mother had a keen interest in current affairs and she was glad to have someone to discuss them with.

"Gabrielle, we're just talking about the situation in Derry"

The British army were a considerable presence in the city but it wasn't anything Gabrielle was particularly interested in.

She was already bored and let them resume their conversation.

Finally her father came in carrying a tray with four cups and saucers, milk and sugar.

"Gabrielle will you do the honours?" he asked.

"I'm just going to get some biscuits, shortbread okay for you Harry?"

"It's my favourite Mr Caulfield' "Harry replied.

"Grand," her father eyes twinkling went to fetch the shortbread.

Two minutes later her father returned with the plate of shortbread.

He approached Harry first.

Harry's face registered shock but immediately recovered, thus drawing Gabrielle's attention to the plate.

To her absolute horror when she looked at it she didn't see any shortbread instead a plate filled with tiny chunks of roughly cut stale bread. If this wasn't bad enough, rather than use the plates they had reserved for guests or even their own everyday plates it was clear that her father had gotten this 'plate' from the local skip. It was a mass of cracks and chips with filthy brown marks clinging to its edges and to top it all off was sopping wet. Gabrielle was mortified and still cringes as she recounts the tale; even more so when Harry obviously not wanting to offend took a piece.

Her mother was silent. Clearly she was horrified too but quickly regained her composure.

All of a sudden Harry jumped up,

"I do apologise, Mr and Mrs Caulfield, Gabrielle, but I've just realised I have an appointment". Looking flustered he swiftly added "I really must go".

With that he got up and made towards the door.

"That's a shame" her father said feigning disappointment, "I'll see you out, maybe you'll come for a good Irish dinner the next time?"

That was the first and last time Dr Thornton ever called for Gabrielle (or within a five mile radius of her home!).

Boyfriends came and went over the years, if they were Protestant and met her father they usually went. Her father had his unique disposal methods and each poor young man was sent away red faced.

Gabrielle's father came from an idealistic world, he despised snobs to him no one person was better than another. A person was distinguished by how they conducted their life and how close to God they were (in a Catholic way). A person should always be judged on their decency, honesty and integrity. A sense of humour also helped, but if none existed then so long as the other three were in abundance it could be sacrificed.

Chapter Eight

Gabrielle had come from a cosseted world; the safe familiar walls of the hospital reinforced this. But even she couldn't help observing how much life was changing in Derry. The city was rapidly becoming awash with armed soldiers, navy and police. A cloud of tension hung in the air even on the calmest days. She was no longer comfortable using her free time to explore the city and tended to stay close to the nurses home.

It was in Gabrielle's final year of training that a civil rights movement had called a march on the streets of Derry. She didn't know it then but she was about to become involved in a historic day. The marchers came out to protest at the perceived inequalities experienced by the Catholic people of Derry. It was conducted in the fashion of civil rights marches that had gone before in America and would highlight the Catholic people's struggles.

The general consensus at the time was that Catholics in Northern Ireland did not get equal rights in housing, education and jobs. Gabrielle didn't doubt their argument but had never felt subject to any form of inequality; so unlike most of her contemporaries she would not be joining the March. From an early age it had been instilled in her that a good education would carry one anywhere. She saw that all her friends had gone on to university and all of them herself included were in the process of gaining entrance into one profession or another. She hadn't experienced any inequalities nor had anyone she knew.

Gabrielle had never stood back to examine the wider picture. Growing up in an almost solely Catholic area meant that schools and houses were good; they never had to share these with another community. Catholics in other areas that were not as segregated as hers perhaps felt differently. Gabrielle was solidly ambiguous towards the plight of these people and suspected that little would change that.

Almost twenty years after the Catholic civil rights movement Gabrielle spoke to a colleague from a Protestant background that had grown up in the Shankill area of Belfast. By all accounts her upbringing was similar to Gabrielle's except for the inequalities, not on Gabrielle's part however. It seemed her colleague had lived in inferior government housing, had limited prospects of work and had grown up in a situation of abject poverty and little aspiration.

Inequalities were across the board, they were a matter for the working classes; a class that Gabrielle was determined never to be a part of. If only she knew.

Keen to witness the march Gabrielle's mother suggested they go for tea in the City Hotel. The hotel overlooked the marcher's route and would allow them to get a good view as it passed. Nothing on this scale had happened before in the North West and her mother wanted to say that she had seen it. So on that freezing Sunday; Gabrielle was accompanied by both her parents on her journey to Derry. That day was to become known as 'Bloody Sunday'.

Gabrielle remembers her father taking the familiar journey extra cautiously. All along the road little patches of ice danced in front of the car, on each sighting he would mutter, "black ice, it's the most dangerous thing drivers face". Her Mother as usual rolled her eyes and tutted. His slow driving was one of the many things she chastised him about. On this occasion she claimed that they would have been quicker walking!

When they eventually reached Derry anticipation radiated from the very pavements the air was charged with positivity. It seemed that thousands of people had taken to the streets to join the march. Gabrielle and her parents were simply there to observe. Strict instructions were given to her father to collect them from the hotel in precisely an hour and a half. This would allow plenty of time to watch the march unfold. No real consideration was given to what her father would do in that time, even now Gabrielle cannot remember. She can only assume that he went home.

They were fortunate to get a window seat at the hotel. They sipped their coffees ensconced in the comfort of the lavish lobby. From here they watched as the march passed.

Gabrielle saw the marchers carry huge banners emblazoned with slogans demanding equal rights. The street was lined with Saracens. To some it may have looked ominous but to the people of Derry it didn't; heavily armed streets were now familiar. They watched the passage of the March in silence as it made its way towards the Bogside.

It didn't seem long until the chants of the demonstrators were overtaken by gunfire and angry screams. Gabrielle immediately knew that something was wrong, the sirens began to blare as more and more military swarmed the streets. She had never seen anything equal to this before and shock surged through her. The voices around them in the hotel became raised and some people rushed out. Inside the hotel mirrored the streets outside; pure pandemonium.

Within minutes the news that shooting had broken out got through to them. Wails of a new siren different to that of the police siren, confirmed that people were injured. The noise was deafening as the screams of the ambulance competed against the Saracens making an eerie tune.

Even as a trainee Gabrielle knew protocol and she would be expected to report to the hospital. She gathered up her belongings and prepared to leave. Sure enough just as she was fastening her coat the radio began to call for any medical personal to make their way to the hospital.

Outside she saw ambulances, police and people race by. It was like a warzone, she did not dare imagine what would confront her when she made it to the hospital.

When her father came to collect them from the hotel, he looked shaken yet his face was alight with relief when he glimpsed them.

He had obviously been worried, another indicator that something very wrong was unfolding outside. Her parents were clearly unsure whether she should offer her services but she convinced them that protocol meant that she had little choice.

On reaching the hospital Gabrielle was confronted with complete and utter carnage. That day they dealt with twelve gunshot victims. This was made all the worse as in addition to the gunshot victims one poor young man had been suffocated in the skirmish that ensued. It was Gabrielle's first experience of such wounds but over the next few years she would become as familiar with gunshot victims as she would be with fractures.

She soon became immersed in a new brand of nursing; one that her training had not prepared her for. She was to become accustomed to rubber bullets forcing eyes out of sockets, shootings, kneecappings, tarring and featherings and the ultimate carnage - bomb victims. Her patients would range from armed police, to innocent civilians and even IRA men all of whom she was expected to treat in a moment's notice. In work Gabrielle was no longer shockable as she had learned to expect anything and everything.

Being so young it didn't take long before Gabrielle began to wish for an easier post, even the labour ward would be an improvement on this. Yet she can proudly say that despite wanting an easier post, she did her level best for all the people she treated, those who were innocent and of course the instigators. When I ask her how she could do that she simply replies that she was a nurse, it was not for her to judge any individual. She was there simply to treat, God could do the rest. The smells, sights and sounds of those years were a far cry from the glamorous career she had envisaged and a premonition of her own glimpse into hell.

It was the bomb victims who stayed with her, they were so charred their bodies were unrecognisable; the percentage of burns so high that sometimes even pain relief was futile. She inwardly grieved with their families; no one should have had to endure such suffering. She can close her eyes even now and be transported to those dark days in A&E; the smells once again assailing her nostrils, the mutilation of innocence seizing her sight, the anguished wails of the bereaved assaulting her ears. She will forever carry a little piece of their torment with her alongside her own.

In those days she was determined not to let these atrocities remain in the foremost regions of her mind. Yet they stayed with her somewhere. In Mum's recent tales she can recount each and every experience, she never forgot them. I think she found a convenient little shelf in her brain and alongside Patch, Matron and anything else that could harm her she stored them there and continued with her day to day living. Unfortunately for Gabrielle someday all the horror would come to the forefront of her mind and the shelf it was placed on would collapse.

Chapter Nine

During this time Gabrielle met and became engaged to a nice, local Catholic boy. I often wonder how she would have fared if things had worked out. That I will never know. So far advanced were the wedding plans that the venue was booked, the flowers organised and invitations sent. She had even booked the honeymoon.

It transpired two weeks before her big day that this wedding was not meant to be. Gabrielle called at her fiancés home to discuss the seating arrangements at the hotel. She hadn't given any notice (as she normally would) because she was so intent on getting this wedding right.

Gabrielle walked into his house and was surprised that he didn't even enquire as to who was there. Flippantly she looked for him downstairs. Not finding him, she sought him upstairs. She barged into his bedroom about to make him work through her crucial seating plan when she instinctively knew that something was amiss. As her eyes adjusted to the darkness her seating plan was no longer relevant; she saw what she had never wanted to see. Her fiancé was not alone; she could see the outline of another body lying next to him, could smell a sweet cloying perfume and saw the discarded clothes strewn around the room. On seeing Gabrielle he was immediately on his feet, his nudity confronting her, yet he had the audacity to claim "It's not what you think". Gabrielle rarely gave anyone a second chance and her fiancé was not to be the exception. She turned on her heel and walked out of his room, his house and his life for good. To top it all off after several attempts to contact her the cretin even went on the honeymoon – courtesy of Gabrielle!

For the next few months Gabrielle was so devastated that she didn't set foot outside. She stayed at home and cried, wallowing in her betrayal. Her friends tried everything to rouse her, but nothing would work. She was heartbroken, humiliated and nothing would bring her round. In the aftermath of her failed engagement her life became a cycle of work, work and more work. Work allowed her to escape thinking about the cancelled wedding. It allowed her to escape the stares and the sympathy. A jilted bride was always a good gossip point.

Eventually though her maudlin had to end. She began tentatively taking steps out, even having nights out again, though always careful to avoid men. One of her friends at the time noticed Gabrielle's stalwart avoidance of the opposite sex and decided to set her up on a blind date. Her friend would not take no for an answer, so after much cajoling Gabrielle reluctantly agreed. She was to go to a party at her friend's house and was promised that her 'perfect man' would be there.

Not expecting much from this mystery man she arrived at the party that night yet she saw nothing outstanding; the same old clones. Northern Ireland never offered much to Gabrielle by way of its men folk, which was one of the reasons she had expected little from her 'date'. She took a few drinks and was about to chastise her friend for dragging her to this silly party, when the back door opened and in walked a tall dark handsome creature, of course accompanied by a typical Northern Irish man. Her friend nudged her as if she thought that the new addition to the room had escaped her. Gabrielle simply prayed that the pasty Northern Irish man who accompanied the tall dark stranger was not the man her friend had in mind for the blind date.

Unlike the other excuses for men present, this dark man exuded dapperness; he held himself so proudly and confidently that to her he was the essence of class. He wore a clearly expensive suit and a heavy cashmere overcoat, he was tall and lean and he was completely and utterly gorgeous. This man was by no means classically good looking, yet he was unique and so, so attractive. His skin was a dark brown, almost black and he wore his hair shaved close. On seeing his chocolate brown eyes, Gabrielle didn't know it then, but she was smitten. This man was obviously older than most of her counterparts too old for her. She imagined he must have been at least thirty!

As sure as she had noticed him he had noticed her and it wasn't long until he approached and began making conversation. Gabrielle doesn't remember what they spoke about but she does remember that his accent was strange, guttural, nothing like the sing song feminine accents of the men she was accustomed to. On further investigation she soon established that he came from Nigeria, and his name was Max. He lived in Belfast but had travelled to Derry tonight in order to meet his friend who had accompanied him. He had practically been forced to attend this party.

Despite finding Max attractive, Gabrielle was still refusing to entertain any man. Should Omar Sharif have thrown himself at her right then and there she would have refused him. So, even when Max asked her out her out she firmly refuted his offer. The party ended later that night and as far as Gabrielle was concerned that was the last she would see of the handsome stranger called Max.

As fate conspired this was not the case, it seemed Max was in love, he was also a man who rarely gave up on what he wanted. Max wanted Gabrielle. For the next few weeks and months

Gabrielle received flowers, weekly letters and phone calls. This was a man who would not take no for an answer. She tried to put his stubborn refusal down to a cultural barrier, she even went so far as to learn how to say "no go away" in Nigerian, yet her efforts were wasted. The fact that she had made clear to him after each of his advances that she wasn't interested irritated her. Who did this eejit think he was? His self-assurance and denial of rejection grated on her and she began ignoring all of his offerings concluding that he would give up eventually.

Chapter Ten

By the summer of 1973, Gabrielle had spent five years in Altnagelvin; three as a trainee and two as a qualified nurse. She could never say she was bored, but like most young people she felt the urge to spread her wings and move to pastures new. She considered working in both Belfast and Dublin and was surprised when the first hospital she had applied to offered her an interview. Belfast City Hospital had vacancies and she became set on gaining one.

A major barrier stood in her way, the interview date fell in the middle of the month. This was not the ideal time for her, her salary was long gone. Gabrielle was notorious for spending every penny within a week of payday and living even less than frugally for the remaining days of the month. She barely had enough money to pay the bus fare for the two hour journey to Belfast. Yet she wanted the job, she wanted a change. Maybe it would be worth starving for two weeks until her next payday to travel to Belfast. Always conscious of her figure Gabrielle felt that two weeks on a meagre diet would do wonders! She resigned herself to a fortnight of bread and coffee and made her plans to attend the interview. Her main regret was that she couldn't have made a day of going to Belfast and enjoying a quick shop as well. Gabrielle supposed if she was successful in the interview she would shop in Belfast all the time, so one missed shopping opportunity wouldn't be the end of the world.

With that Gabrielle determined to get the bus and give the best interview she had ever given. Even though the bus journey was long, she wasn't bored for a second of it. She always loved to travel and this was further than she had ever gone. Gabrielle spent most of the journey peering out the window at the many small towns they passed through. Towns that were now littered with sectarian graffiti destroying their otherwise friendly facades.

She arrived in Belfast early as she had no idea where the city hospital was located, she would have to ask for directions and in a city this size, she would no doubt have to ask more than once. Luckily enough she found the hospital without too much difficulty and made it in ample time for her interview. Her youthful ego meant that she was confident and prepared and with the exception of her stomach rumbling, she left the hospital secure in the knowledge that she had done enough to be offered the post.

Gabrielle had been so concerned with preparing for the interview that she had forgotten to bring lunch with her; now that the interview was over she was painfully aware of her growing hunger. She knew she couldn't afford to stop off at any of the cafes and restaurants she passed to refuel, well without offering to wash the dishes! Nor could she pop into a shop and buy even a snack. It would take at least four hours to get home and she wallowed at the thought of not having a bite until then. She continued to walk down the Lisburn road towards the bus depot. By now she was so full of self-pity at her self imposed fast that when she heard her name called it took a while to register. Hunger had her every thought. She supposed meeting someone she knew so far from home was a good reason to distract her even momentarily from the hunger pangs. She stopped and turned around to see who would know her here in Belfast.

Standing in front of her, showing off his pearly whites was Max. Once again Gabrielle was taken aback by his attractiveness. He looked so very exotic standing there in his crisp white shirt, peaking out behind a summer suit. In her mind he belonged more on the streets of a chic city rather than on the streets of Belfast.

Impressed as she was she inwardly groaned, she was not in the mood for small talk especially when she was wasting away. Her hunger was making her feel light headed and her stomach ached. Her mood instantly changed when her ears and stomach extracted from his mundane small talk three magic words that would seal her fate and mine, "There's a nice little restaurant across the road, how about we catch up over lunch?"

Part Two 1973 – 1980

"Belfast Belfast wonderful town doesn't matter if your skin is brown", Boney M

Chapter Eleven

Gabrielle's prediction was right. As expected she had succeeded in gaining the post in Belfast. Within six weeks of her interview she was firmly installed in the recovery unit at the City Hospital. She enjoyed the challenges of the job and soaking up the sense of community that this huge hospital encouraged amongst its staff. The only thing she had not considered was where she was going to live. Finding a home was a time consuming pursuit at the best of times, but when working full time and coping with so many changes, the prospect was not one she was eager to embrace. Gabrielle decided against trawling this alien city for a suitable flat and took up residence in the nurse's home.

The nurse's home offered an opportunity to make friends, avail of cheaper accommodation and reside within walking distance from the hospital. Living in the home would give Gabrielle time to explore the city and gain her bearings. Gabrielle decided that when she was more sure of her surroundings she would begin searching for somewhere of her own. For now, the accommodation on offer was more than comfortable, the rooms were bright and airy and the shared facilities clean and modern.

Gone were the curfews and rules of her training. As a qualified nurse the nurse's home was exactly as described; a home. She often looked at the pale and drawn faces of the trainees who lived in the student building next door and couldn't help but feel a little pity for them. She understood their plight. Yet at the same time a little voice inside wanted to gloat. In hospital hierarchy she was their superior and the thought filled her with a wily pride.

Gabrielle's initial excitement at moving to Belfast was blemished slightly by the warnings of her colleagues. Already they had cautioned her on the 'no go areas', volatile areas where trouble was guaranteed and incessant. She absorbed every shred of advice and began crossing out the areas deemed dangerous on her little map of the city. When she got the chance to explore she would make a point of avoiding every area that had been mentioned. After two or three conversations however; it seemed an altogether easier option to list the areas she could safely go!

Gabrielle could barely find an area on her map that wasn't crossed out. By the time she had heeded every warning her map resembled a distorted treasure map. Any pirate would have been devastated on finding it; for the multitude of crosses on the map did not mark plunder and riches, instead they signified danger. When she finally found areas clear of crosses she was left with two or three 'mixed' or quiet areas to explore.

Gabrielle was soon to discover that even these 'safe' places were not altogether immune from the violence, they too experienced shootings and bombings; on a less frequent level granted, but nevertheless the unrest had infiltrated the entire city. In the end she threw caution to the wind and vanquished her list. If she needed to go somewhere then she would. If an area regardless of having crosses had shops then she would venture there.

In those early days in Belfast it seemed that everywhere she looked there was an armed soldier either on patrol, kneeling between gateposts or fences or standing on street corners. Gabrielle really didn't have any opinion towards them. She was blissfully ambivalent, until one day she was rushing out the door and tripped over one. From that point onwards Gabrielle saw them as health hazards! The colossal bump on her shin that the encounter left her with ensured that she became as watchful of the soldiers as they were of her. Yet all things considered she could endure the bomb warnings, she could turn a blind eye to the intimidating sectarian graffiti and even the growing number of soldiers. For Gabrielle craved city life, if these things were the downside then she would just have to accept them.

On one of her days off a colleague offered to take her 'into town' luckily for her it was the end of the month so she had money to spend. She gladly availed of the offer. They travelled into town on the bus and were offloaded directly opposite the historical building that was the City Hall. Belfast city centre revolved around one main street that was intersected by a few small streets. With the exception of new shopping centres it still remains like this today. On Gabrielle's first outing to the city centre she wanted to see every little street. Purse at the ready she was almost as armed as the soldiers and police! She fully intended to stock up her wardrobe and couldn't wait to enter the large shops that at home she had only read about. Her friend led her in the direction of the main street, Royal Avenue. On approach Gabrielle was astounded at the sight that met her because before she could even enter the street she would have to go through security.

Barriers large and menacing blocked entry to the entire city centre, the only way in was to pass through an armoured hut.

People lined up to gain entrance and one by one in single file they passed through security. Here bags were searched and pockets were emptied. Gabrielle wasn't in the least bit daunted, the only feelings she had were those of frustration. The security hut meant that her much anticipated shopping trip would be delayed; patience was never and never has been one of Gabrielle's virtues. She would have to stand and wait in line for God knows how long. As usual when she was flummoxed she said a quick aspiration to the Holy Virgin Mary. This time she beseeched her to ensure that no one in front of her presented a threat. If they did then her wait would be extended even more and she only had one day off! The Holy Virgin Mary must have heard her because before long they had cleared security and were able to make their way to the first shop.

Gabrielle viewed security as an irritating inconvenience which was to become a stark contrast to her attitude of a few years later.

The searching was repeated in the next shop and the next, until she grew accustomed to it. By shop number four Gabrielle automatically opened her bag on entrance. In future she would plan her shopping trips not by hours or even by her favourite shops, but by which shops had the least security. Her time off was precious and she could see this constant searching becoming an annoyance. She began to wonder if it was worth all this hassle simply to buy a few dresses. But when she looked down Royal Avenue and wondered through CornMarket, she saw shop upon shop lining the streets. Gabrielle determined there and then that a few little searches wouldn't come between her and all this!

In those days it became habit for Gabrielle and no doubt the bulk of women in Northern Ireland to ensure their handbags were tidy and pockets empty before going shopping, an untidy handbag or full pockets only served to cause delays.

Gabrielle never did tour the city as she had planned, she preferred to spend any free time whiling away her days in the relative safety of the Lisburn Road or in the Fort Knox that was the city centre. The minute amount of news she listened to or read reiterated the same pattern day after day bomb, riots or shootings. Remarkably some of the news which she routinely disregarded must have subliminally entered her head, for as time went on and the troubles worsened she gained a healthy apprehension and rarely ventured into the unknown. This combined with her dire sense of direction always kept her within close proximity to the hospital.

Staying close to the hospital was never a chore her instincts were right; a change of environment was exactly what she needed. Within walking distance from the hospital was an array of shops, restaurants and bars flourished. These were thronged with students from the local Queens' University who despite their surroundings, were keen to experience the seventies. Their colourful clothing, long hair and flares brightened the entire area and lightened the atmosphere in the otherwise guarded and forlorn city. Their proximity to the nurse's home kept the girls surrounded by a charged, vibrant ambience that pulsed with youthful energy, making the city a fun place to be.

Chapter Twelve

The move to Belfast stimulated a fresh burst of life in Gabrielle and she looked forward to each new day. Her colleagues were a sociable bunch of girls and it wasn't long before she felt right at home in the big city. Her days passed in a whirl of laughter, learning and contentment and she wished she had made the move to Belfast months earlier.

It would be fair to say that Gabrielle could not attribute all of her fervour to her wonderful new job and friends, a much stronger compulsion fuelled her exhilaration. Max.

Gabrielle was totally consumed with love for Max. Since he had bought her that lifesaving lunch two months earlier, she had really gotten to know him. No longer did she reject his advances on the contrary she positively sought them. Much to the confusion of the girls in Derry, she had suddenly become available to take his calls and reply to his letters. Luckily for her he never questioned how busy she had once claimed to be. If he had asked the only truthful answer Gabrielle could have furnished him with would have been that she was busy, very busy in fact. Busy avoiding him!

Since that lunch everything had changed, they even met up in Derry once or twice. Yet one hundred miles separated them and this was a distance that seemed futile. Max lived in Belfast and Gabrielle would have moved heaven and earth to have been near him. The fact that she chose to move to Belfast rather than Dublin was no coincidence. During that first lunch any initial reservations she had regarding his perceived arrogance and ego evaporated. He single handedly restored her confidence in the male species.

On talking with Max she found a genuine, sensitive, assured and proud man. His stunning appearance simply secured the deal. She was sold. For the first time ever she could identify with the multitude of love songs and films she had been exposed to. Now they had true meaning, she knew without a doubt what all the fuss was about. Gabrielle was in love and her gut told her that she had found her soul mate. Her mother had always said when you meet the right one you will know, she was right on this point, because when Gabrielle was with Max she just knew. All that had gone before was simply child's play and she thanked God for being jilted, for her Fathers shortbread and the effectiveness of his whole host of male disposal efforts!

Within months of meeting they were spending every second of their free time together, yet somehow for Gabrielle it never seemed enough. If she had one day off she wanted two, two days she wanted three, going so far as to wish that she could somehow cut herself in half so that she could be with him all the time. The rest of her could carry on with work, visit home and conduct the dreary necessities of life. It was perfect, they were perfect and right then her life was perfect.

Chapter Thirteen

As always where there is light and beauty there is darkness and ugliness. For a dark shadow stalked Gabrielle and Max, wherever they went it went. It introduced Gabrielle to bitterness and acrimony, to the repulsive side of humanity. The shadow's name was racism and it continues to stalk my family to this very day. The shadow manifested itself in many different guises, from the upper and middle class 'polite' insult, to casual remarks from colleagues, right through to loud insults from aggressive and blatant strangers. Regardless of its form and the different mouthpieces it exploited, its perpetrators all looked the same. Their indignant faces would be twisted with bitterness; their hatred consumed all their features. They became warped and grotesque, as they regarded Gabrielle and Max with eyes that exhibited the depths of contempt that lurked inside.

When they were dating Gabrielle made light of any causally thrown comments, stares and malevolent remarks. Hours were spent laughing them off or rolling her eyes mockingly. Sometimes Gabrielle even managed to make Max laugh, mocking their persecutors in secret whispers and sarcasm. Sometimes they even tried to pre-empt the comments, they could almost tell by the individual how their comments were going to form before they had even been uttered.

Despite this a pattern emerged that would continue for the rest of her life. When she would lie down at night in the restless hours waiting for sleep, her mind would revisit the incidents of that day. She would explore them over and over again, trying to make sense of them, she never succeeded. She would contemplate the nature of those who could do such things. She could never and would never consider these individuals as human. Were these creatures blind? Could they not see the beauty that she saw? The kindness? The generosity of spirit? Gabrielle was always a deep thinker and when unsavoury events occurred she became introverted and would linger on events far longer than any mind could cope with. Perhaps it was this aspect of her personality, the fact that she cared so much that led to her problems in later life.

It was at times when Gabrielle experienced blatant racism that she was ashamed to be white, ashamed to have even the smallest strand of DNA in common with these monstrosities. Thinking back to her youthful views on the American people, she realised that her own people were not any different.

On one occasion Gabrielle and Max had decided to go for a quiet meal and had chosen a popular Belfast eatery. When they walked through the door the hustle and bustle of the busy restaurant instantly stopped, all eyes were on them. The silence that ensued makes me think of a rowdy cowboy in an old western at the moment when he saunters into a saloon bar demanding a duel with the town's hero. Gabrielle and Max were the rowdy cowboys to these people; they perceived them, Max in particular as a stranger - a threat. It would not have surprised me from the description of that night if tumbleweed had blown along the restaurant floor in front of them!

Max surely must have felt the atmosphere yet acted like nothing was amiss and escorted them to their seats. It was only when couples came in after them that Gabrielle noticed a maître de clamouring to welcome the new arrivals. He boasted of the specials whilst selecting prime seating for them. Gabrielle and Max waited and waited for a menu which arrived with a kindly slam on the table, Max's slam was given with additional force.

No kindly maître de recited the specials to them.

After waiting a further forty minutes for their order to be taken, Gabrielle grew increasingly agitated and pleaded with Max to allow them to leave. Max refused stubbornly insisting that they waited. Gabrielle was in no doubt angry, not only with the restaurant but also with Max; it was a miracle that they didn't argue. By this stage all who arrived after them had been served, some were even ordering desert.

As the situation unfolded around them Gabrielle was learning that Max was a proud man; he did not easily align himself with defeat, so it was with a heavy heart that she suppressed her anger and waited with him. When almost an hour had passed and still no food arrived, Max made his way to the maître de while Gabrielle looked on discreetly. After he had spoken to the maitre de Max turned to return to the table.

It all happened so fast; the maître de extended his right foot and hooked it around Max's ankle. Max immediately fell to the floor with an agonising thud.

Gabrielle heard bone collide with the hard ground. The maître de and the kitchen staff laughed, the other diners simply looked on. Gabrielle ran to him and this time he needed no pleading on her part to leave the restaurant.

As they left Gabrielle saw the maître de wipe their unused table; a bottle of disinfectant in hand.

Many other deplorable incidents occurred in those months, too numerous to detail. It is suffice to say that Max's handling of these, never complaining yet never quite accepting, only made Gabrielle admire him more.

It wasn't all doom and gloom on the social scene however, as a couple they had good friends, friends who restored Gabrielle's faith in humanity and the people she lived amongst. Her friends were predominantly from the hospital background. They were surrounded by a multitude of different races in their everyday life so they didn't bat an eyelid at Max. Nor did they flinch at Gabrielle and Max's relationship. Max's friends came mainly from his work. Gabrielle thought they were boring accountants', bookish nerds but Max was clearly fond of them so by default she was too. They went to many parties and in an unspoken agreement between them only frequented familiar and safe places. They became regulars at the 'Egg' bar, where if even a derogatory stare was thrown in their direction the staff would immediately remove the offender (s).

Their friends were also to become protective of Max; they like Gabrielle were utterly perplexed by the attitudes emerging around them. To Max's accountancy friends he was a strong contender in the race for the coveted title of 'chartered' accountant. To Gabrielle's medical friends he was simply 'Gabrielle's Max'. All of them saw beyond Max's skin colour, seeing him for what he was; a professional young man, fun, mannerly and a great conversationalist.

After only a year together the couple became engaged, it was no surprise to their friends and congratulatory cards and gifts were showered upon them. Gabrielle's parents knew that she was dating someone and she looked forward to greeting them with the news. Max was going away for a training session the following week so Gabrielle planned a trip home. She would use this visit to seize the opportunity to announce her good news.

In their regular telephone conversations her mother had told Gabrielle of the antics in her home town, she seemed thoroughly disheartened by it all. She spoke of the increase in IRA activity and of how she would not stand for such inexcusable behaviour. She was outraged, she claimed that no battle was ever won through bloodshed, talking was what was needed.

"What kind of an outfit preys on young men, with their whole lives in front of them" her mother would lament.

Her mother's account of the situation at home seemed so bleak that Gabrielle knew a spoonful of good news would be just the tonic. Her mother would then have something to take her mind of events and something new to concentrate on. Gabrielle cemented the arrangements for visiting that very weekend.

For once Gabrielle actually looked forward to going home; she wanted to see the delight of her mother and father. By now all the girls that she had grown up with were happily married. Some were even on child number three! Yet she was twenty three and still residing in the exclusively female nurse's home. Gabrielle was worried that her parents doubted her sexuality!

When the weekend finally arrived Gabrielle took the bus home ensuring that she had the previous night's mass sheet safely ensconced in her handbag. Her mother liked to question her on her church attendance. Gabrielle discovered that collecting a mass sheet from the chapel and memorising it was enough to convince her that she was continuing in the Catholic life she had been lumbered with. Having not attended one mass service since moving to Belfast she had no intentions of starting now, she even went so far as to time her arrival home to coincide with the end of Sunday mass. She would simply say she had attended the night before. Belfast was so busy that the sacred Sunday mass was also held on Saturdays to ensure that all the devout got a chance to bask in the joys of boredom! This tradition remains until this very day.

Gabrielle would stay at home until Wednesday so she could get a good break and catch up on all the news. She was quite sure though that the upcoming wedding would outshine any news that they could throw at her. She also had an ulterior motive for her extended stay at home. Max's training would last until Wednesday, so he wouldn't be back in Belfast until then. There was little point in her being there without him. Without him Belfast would be a lonely place. A lesson she would one day learn, it's a pity her older self didn't heed her younger self's opinions, instead Gabrielle would chase the source of her happiness and one day return.

As the bus chugged along the road to Strabane, she took the two hour opportunity to memorise the previous night's mass.

Chapter Fourteen

As usual when Gabrielle arrived home she found that home life continued as normal. Her siblings still managed to eradicate any promise of silence, her father was still working long shifts and her mother was still holding throne. Gabrielle liked the sense of normality that home gave her regardless of what was going on in the world outside, behind that little front door nothing ever changed. The routines of her childhood were still practised, the same visitors still called and the teapot was always on. There is comfort in familiarity and after a hectic week on the wards this was exactly what she sought.

As it was Sunday they were having their Sunday roast and would all dine together at the table. For the remaining six days of the week the children ate at the 'children's' table a small collapsible table reserved strictly for them and their spillages.

The formality of today's dinner was lost on Gabrielle. She was positively bursting with excitement, eager to broadcast the news of her up and coming nuptials. She had so far flaunted her engagement ring in more faces than enough. To her disappointment no one noticed. The children were so concerned with avoiding the dreaded 'stick' that they concentrated solely on being good. Her mother was too busy pontificating and of course dissecting every blessed word the priest had uttered in the earlier mass. Her father was holding court with anyone who would listen. The result was that her huge sparkling diamond and sapphire ring went unnoticed. Blind as bats the lot of them she thought. She knew that for now she was fighting a losing battle, so concentrated less on the ring and instead on finding the perfect moment to reveal her news.

Over dinner, talk inevitably lingered on the current political situation and the rise in sectarian activity. Her mother expressed her unhappiness with Gabrielle's choice of Belfast as a home, stating that safety should be everyone's prime consideration.

"Innocent people get caught out too you know, do you think they would care about anyone who stood in their way'" her mother demanded.

Her father on the other hand, at the mention of innocents shot or murdered, shook his head at the very thought,

"No lives worth a blade a grass," he said,

Gabrielle's father firmly believed that if Ireland was ever to be united it should be done peacefully.

As the mood at the table became more and more sombre, Gabrielle knew that it was time to interject with her good news. She waited until the subject of Belfast was raised again before seizing her opportunity.

It was one of her little sisters who opened the conversation asking about the shops, cinemas and restaurants, her little eyes widening at the thought of life in the big city.

"Can I come up and see you?" she had asked,

Her mother's face was already rigid at the thought,

"No one's going to Belfast" she snapped, "no one in their right mind anyway" she levelled directly at Gabrielle,

In response Gabrielle could only laugh and knew she had her moment,

"Well actually you may all be going to Belfast" she started,

Her mother shrewd as she was, raised her eyebrow and asked about this "Max fella". Gabrielle braced herself for the inevitable questions. How much time she was spending with him? Did he know Belfast well? What did he do? The list went on and on. It was now or never, time for her announcement.

Gabrielle took a deep breath and tried to suppress her grin before blurting,

"We got engaged!!"

Her mother and fathers immediate reaction was why this Max hadn't asked for their permission. Good grief they were so old fashioned Gabrielle had thought. She forced a deep sigh and reminded them that times were changing; it was almost 1973 for heaven's sake!

"Well he's not marrying you" she barked in her fiancés defence,

Her little sisters sniggered whilst her parents ignored her comments preferring to begin the art of extracting information from her. Gabrielle felt like an orange being juiced, they already knew about Max, that she had met him in Derry; that he lived in Belfast and that he was an accountant. Gabrielle had told them everything, so much so that she had nothing but pulp left to give them. It was as if they were determined to ask her each question over and over, an inquisition. She was sure the army would have vacancies for them; their interrogation skills were impeccable, second to none.

Her parents knew he was kind, financially stable and most importantly; all that they really needed to know was that she had never been happier.

Yet they continued to quiz her, she answered all their questions and waited for her father's inevitable question.

"Is he Catholic this Max?"

Gabrielle bristled, as Max wasn't a Catholic and she knew that this would not be taken well. All the positive things she had told them about Max would evaporate when they were given the answer,

"No Dad, he's Protestant, but it doesn't bother me"

Her father's reaction was not as bad as she had expected,

"I suppose he could convert, if he's keen enough; I'd rather you married in the Catholic Church"

Gabrielle was slightly taken aback by her father's acceptance of this fact and nodded. Yet she knew that it was highly unlikely that Max would convert. It was even more unlikely that she would ask him. What a thing to ask someone to do! For now though she guessed that her father could content himself with thinking that this may be the case.

"So when can we meet this Max?" her father asked

"Well I'm working next weekend, but perhaps I could swap Sunday with someone…. would that suit?" she gushed

"Grand" her father said.

Her mother was already preparing for the visit, talking about what she would serve, what she would wear, what her father would wear. Would dinner or a buffet be better? Who would she invite, just close family or a wider circle of friends? What would the little ones wear, and could Father Converey make it? Would it be acceptable for Father Converey to be there at all since this man hadn't converted yet? Maybe she would discuss this with Father Converey first before she decided.

Her mother was then to pipe up with another question,

"So Gabrielle, what will your new surname be?"

"Olorunda" she casually informed her,

Her mother looked confused and turned to her father who was nodding knowledgably,

"Aye, that would be a Western name hails from around Donegal and Sligo, a lot of the planters brought that with them" he said, clearly self-satisfied with his display of Irish genealogy.

"Not quite", she said laughing, "Unless you mean Western African?"

Silence.

Gabrielle recalls hearing the remnants of her laugh echo around in her head.

Her mother mouthed words for some time before any emerged, hand over her heart she whispered,

"*Is he black?*"

Gabrielle nodded. "Well you don't get many white Nigerians!"

As Gabrielle looked from her father to her mother she saw nothing, no reaction, none at all. Seconds later her mother left the room. Her father followed.

Not knowing how to react Gabrielle got up and went out to the garden.

Her parents were obviously deliberating her situation. She was concerned but not overly so. It would be a shock to them, but they would get used to the idea. Her father was a good man and her mother although they had their moments, was a lot of things but she was not a bigot. She could never be consumed with such hatred.

She was certain her father would call her in soon, both her parents were simply getting used to the idea. Once they had they could go on discussing the plans for next weekend. Sure enough her father came out and she waited for him to tell her to bring Max home as planned.

She smiled at him but it wasn't reciprocated,

"Your mother thinks it's time you went back to Belfast, Gabrielle" he said and without looking at her he continued "you need time to come to your senses"

Gabrielle stared back stunned

"You see Gabrielle you need to think of the children such a, such a, am ……… a marriage would produce. What would they be? Where would they fit in? You have to think long term, now I'm sure this Max is a grand chap but maybe it's best you stick to your own eh?"

Not once had her father's eyes met hers which was just as well, as she no longer could look at him.

"And what do you think Daddy?" she had asked, fed up with this brow beaten man who never articulated his own feelings "be a man Daddy, I know you don't think that"

He still did not look at his daughter only a slight tremor in his hand belayed that she was right. Never before had she felt so angry with her once kindly father. Never before had his obedience to his wife irked her so much.

"Your mother is concerned about would the neighbours think"

By this stage his hands trembled as much as his voice. And rightly so Gabrielle thought these words came from the so called 'good Catholics' who had raised her. She was certain that unless things had changed drastically in her time away they weren't taught such attitudes in any mass she had attended. Gabrielle's estimation of her mother and father diminished there and then. She now saw one of them as a racist and the other a wimp. She went back indoors and blindly packed her things, she couldn't see through the tears. She hugged her little sisters, closed the door and left. On the bus back to Belfast she wept throughout the entire journey.

That was the day that she truly left home.

Chapter Fourteen

Although Gabrielle was deeply hurt by her parent's reaction she was annoyed with her father in particular. She knew without doubt that he did not share her mother's provincial opinions. She remembered him reading the 'Irish Times' world report (which he considered the oracle) and condemning Ian Smith as a tyrant. He derided him at every available opportunity and championed the plight of the indigenous South Africans to all and sundry. Once he even had asked her to say a special novena to St Jude the Patron Saint of Hopeless Causes, asking him to solve South Africa's problems, after Ireland's of course. Yet he was prepared to acquiesce with her mother's attitude, rather than brave contention in their cautiously harmonious home.

Regardless of the growing resentment she felt towards her parents her life seemed to trundle on as normal. For a while she held out the hope that they would be filled with remorse. She imagined them contacting her overcome with the error of their ways. Yet as the months passed she knew this was not to be. Reason told Gabrielle that she would be planning this wedding alone.

The definitive humiliation for her was telling Max her parents did not approve of him or of their engagement. He was visibly upset but seemed resigned to their feelings. By all accounts Max had learnt never to expect acceptance when encountering the unknown so he was perhaps disappointed but not surprised when Gabrielle reiterated her parent's words to him. Gabrielle knew that this was not the first blind rejection he'd faced; in her short time with him she had witnessed many. She also knew that he had looked forward to meeting her family; she talked of home a lot and had unwittingly built his expectations.

Max clearly felt that he was tearing her away from her family. Yet the family she thought she had, the family she used to be so certain off, no longer existed. Instead one hundred miles down the road, in the town she grew up in dwelled a family she didn't know. Their outward façade cunningly concealed their true nature. A nature she never wanted to encounter again. It was with confidence that she could tell Max that her family were no longer important, because right now, that was how she felt.

To prove Gabrielle's assertions further, she insisted that they set a date sooner rather than later. She wanted them to marry; Max would become her new family. They had friends, good jobs and happiness. She would let no one spoil that, especially not her parents.

With that in mind they set a date for June of that year, only six months away and began making arrangements. Max was put in charge of finding a home and Gabrielle would look after the preparations for the big day.

They decided to have a small civic wedding and secured a booking in Belfast city hall. As her family wouldn't attend they no longer needed to consider any religious perspective; that suited her. She wanted the day to be simple. Big weddings were designed for families and guests rather than the couple. Gabrielle decided that they would invite no one; they would quietly get married and slip away on honeymoon. Max was still not completely at ease with Gabrielle forging ahead with plans and her blasé attitude. He continually insisted that she would regret it later. Gabrielle on the other hand knew she wouldn't.

Max was aware that Gabrielle came from a staunch Catholic background and only agreed to progress with her plans if she at least had the wedding blessed. He claimed that if her parents eventually did assent, that they could at least prove they had done everything properly. To keep Max quiet, Gabrielle reluctantly spoke to a priest and arranged a blessing for the weeks after the wedding. Her parent's approval no longer mattered to her; they and everything that ever hurt her were boxed and placed them on her shelf.

Once again in the weeks approaching the wedding Max began nagging her, this time to try once more to involve her family. And just as with the church blessing his gentle but persistent goading won out. Gabrielle knew that the only way to quell his demands was to offer the white flag and invite them. The very act went against every fibre of her body, yet maybe just maybe Max was right and this situation, this deadlock could be rectified.

For Gabrielle the idea of being the one to initiate contact made her bristle, as far as she was concerned her parents knew that they were in the wrong. Why should she get in touch when they should be contacting her? Eventually she got used to the idea and began to think that perhaps they were waiting for contact from her. It was perfectly conceivable that Max's idea wasn't entirely outlandish. They were her parents and she at least owed them the courtesy of an invitation.

On my Max's part his family weren't much better but he had long since severed any ties with them.

Max had grown up in Lagos and came from a much superior background than Gabrielle's. His father was a senior figure in the Nigerian civil service. He was a strict disciplinarian and had expected greatness from his children. Max and his brothers and sisters were pushed into education, hobbies were quelled and fun was frowned upon. All focus was put on their studies. Each of them was encouraged to enter the medical profession. They were offered incentives such as having their university fees paid, all expenses taken care of whilst studying and a handsome reward on completion.Any career other than medicine was not considered acceptable.

Max's family was large he and two of his brothers were products of their father's first marriage. He did not talk much of his other siblings, they were his half brothers and sisters and from his demeanour when he spoke of them it was clear that strife of one form or another existed within the family. Since he never volunteered any information Gabrielle never probed him. He would tell her all about them when he was ready and she was willing to wait.

It seemed that with one notable exception, the wishes of his father were adhered to. One by one each sibling full and half had entered into and embraced medicine. All but Max had succeeded and were now either on their way to, or had already been crowned with the lofty title of doctor. Max was unique in his choice of accountancy, something his father strongly disapproved of. Gabrielle found the situation entirely nonsensical and used to joke with me when I enquired about it. After all if that was how his father reacted to an accountant imagine his reaction to a pimp!

Max's father had a plan for his children, their interests or autonomy were irrelevant. If they did not meet their father's expectations they became something to be ashamed of. Max possibly as a result of stubbornness and sheer obstinacy ignored his father's wishes and pursued his career in accountancy. He went to England and took an accountancy degree, after which he found a graduate position in one of the of the big five accountancy firms. He was transferred to Belfast and within the year fate brought him to Gabrielle.

For Max his alternative choice of career meant a struggle. He had not obeyed his father's instructions and was forced to pay his own way through university. So it was with a great sense of pride when he graduated unaided and embarked on his chosen career. His ultimate dream was to have his name on a plaque outside his office and one day to have his own chartered accountancy firm. So far he was heading in the right direction.

Gabrielle had never met any of Max's siblings, but she had seen pictures of them all, pictures taken in a place that was so alien and far away, that it could have been another world. The entire family were captured in a photograph outside Max's family home, a large imposing white house. They stood together dressed impeccably and smiled happily at the camera. I still have that album and looking at it, it is difficult to believe that this family was so fractured; the pictures showed such a joyous group.

In the back of Max's photo album was a picture of a lady of unrivalled beauty. Gabrielle assumed she was a relative and asked him who she was. She was aghast when he replied,

"This Gabrielle, is the most beautiful woman in the world" his chest swelled with pomposity as he continued "one of our many Nigerian, beauties, this is *Miss Nigeria*"

Gabrielle fumed, how he dare imply that Nigeria was swarming with beauties!

"If your Nigerian women are so bloody beautiful then why don't you go and get one?" she sulked.

A few days later they began to speak again. Never again was the beauty of the women from his homeland ever mentioned. The picture was never seen again, its place in the album was now filled as it should have been, with an Irish beauty, Gabrielle!

Max had had a happy childhood. He spent his free time playing under the Nigerian sun and holidaying in exotic Nigerian locations. Free time as a boy was not plentiful; leisure was a rare commodity, so he made the most of it when he got it. His childhood involved more schooling than most children, but even this he enjoyed. Gabrielle doubted that his boyhood self knew any different.

Max's childhood died with his mother, his father swiftly took on a new wife and started to build a new family. By all accounts this family was one that Max and his brothers were not a part of. They were not permitted to dine with his step brothers and sisters, weren't even allowed to play with them and only allowed to speak to them when they absolutely had to. His father so taken with his new wife never defended his hitherto precious sons. Instead he encouraged them to go and study medicine; to leave.

Max in choosing to study accountancy left home alone and unfunded. Moving so far away, to a strange land, didn't daunt him, he was simply relieved to leave his by then miserable home and callous step mother and never look back. In fairy tales the wicked step mother always gets her comeuppance, but Max's stepmother flourished in Max and his brothers' absence. She grew stronger and stronger, her tentacles reaching into every aspect of Olorunda life. Like Gabrielle's family Max's family were God loving and strict church goers. Church was paramount in all their lives, with the exception of his stepmother. Max's stepmother, the new Mrs Olorunda came from an utterly different world than the family were familiar with.

Nigeria was a country of many contrasts modern versus the traditional being one of them. Nigeria held a tradition of witchcraft and many people openly practised it. Max's father knew that his new wife came from the traditional Nigeria, but he was blinded by her beauty and was said to disregard her unchristian practises. He turned a blind eye to what was described as her pagan rituals, often finding them amusing and quaint. His only request was that their children be brought up in his church and she had honoured that.

Max always maintained that his father had been bewitched, that his new wife was more powerful than his father would ever know. Before leaving home Max had been privy to rumours, hushed whispers and frenzied warnings from concerned family and friends and sometimes even from strangers. They said that her magic was not a benign kind. Max had warned his father, but his words were futile. For Max the further he went from her and her strange rituals the better. Funding a place at university, thousands of miles away, was a small sacrifice for such an escape.

Max had a brother in Edinburgh who had promised to visit, but as the wedding date coincided with his exams, he committed to visiting later in the year. Max seemed happy enough with this and therefore so was Gabrielle. If only her family would have a change of heart they could have compensated for Max's lack of relations on the big day. Gabrielle knew that she was delving into the realms of fantasy when she dared to think of her family, but perhaps if reconciliation occurred, they would accept her fiancé as their own. He could have a new family. So for Max's sake, Gabrielle bought an expensive invitation and posted it to her parents, inside she inserted a letter.

For hours she had agonised over what to say, but in the end kept it simple. She asked them to come to her wedding, to meet her new husband. She listed the virtues that Max possessed, told them about his promising career and their plans to buy a house. She told them that they would marry in the City Hall and that they would be getting a church blessing. She told them of how much she loved her fiancé, and that she knew that they would too. If only they would give him a chance. Before Gabrielle could have any second thoughts she posted the letter.

Gabrielle spent the next few days waiting for a response. The very act of posting the invite, of writing the letter planted a little seed of hope in her soul and as the days passed the seed grew and grew and she visualised her family proudly welcoming Max into their lives.

Two weeks on, Gabrielle's hopes for her parent's attendance and desired blessing withered. They had received the invite by now. They had chosen to ignore it. Her parents were racist; she could not make excuses for them.

One week to the day of her wedding Gabrielle received a letter in a familiar hand, it was from her mother. At last they had a change of heart. She felt a mammoth weight being lifted off her shoulders, the little sealed box marked 'home' had its lid removed, and it was coming off her shelf.

She lit a cigarette and tore open the letter, eager to digest its contents. Excitement fluttered in her stomach, her parents had accepted her relationship,

**Dear Gabrielle,

We had hoped that since our last talk that you would have reconsidered your plans. It seems that this has not been the case and that you are intent on destroying your life and shaming your family.

We received your invitation and would like to inform you, that we will be unable to attend your wedding.

Regards

Mr and Mrs Caulfield

(**As described by Gabrielle)

Gabrielle reread her mother's caustic words and tossed them aside. The rest of that afternoon passed in a blur of tears. Why would they send that? Could they not have ignored the invitation? Instead they had to have the last word. They had to reinforce that they did not agree with her choice, that they thought that her fiancé was inferior. The impression that she had of her parents that day was one that would linger for a long time; they were simply old, dated bastards.

Gabrielle's sadness turned to anger; she ripped their letter up and threw it in the bin. Max would never know about this. Back to the shelf went her parents and to commemorate the occasion she blasted Frank Sinatra's 'I did it my way' to full volume and two vodkas later went off to meet her girlfriends for a hen party that she was determined to enjoy!

Chapter Sixteen

Gabrielle had never been one of those desperately romantic females whose fantasies revolved around demure princesses and handsome princes. Before Max marriage had never been highly rated on her list of life's priorities. Marriage was something people did when they reached a certain age, like birth and death it was simply a rite of passage. How wrong she had been.

When the wedding day dawned; she didn't experience a single shred of uncertainty, the anticipated fears of being jilted never materialised. She had slept soundly the night before and awoke refreshed and relaxed. In the hours leading to the ceremony she felt blissfully tranquil, secure in the knowledge that she had made the right decision in her choice of husband, despite opinions to the contrary.

Their preparations had gone smoothly and she did not anticipate any obstacles. Even now the huge white dresses and elaborate flowers of other girls' fantasies meant nothing. This marriage would mean more than frills and flounces; Gabrielle had designed it to impress no one. Her marriage was about one uncomplicated but beautiful thing. It was about Max and her declaring their love for each other. They would show her family and all their many adversaries that they were together in the eyes of God. The vows that they would take would cement their relationship, they would promise to love and honour each other, and allowing nothing and no one on this earth separate them. At least until death.

Gabrielle didn't need a ball gown, tiered cakes or countless tiny flower girls. Max didn't need a best man or ushers. They needed nothing but each other and their minimalistic ceremony would demonstrate that.

It took several painstaking, onerous weeks scouring what seemed like every shop in Belfast for Gabrielle to find her perfect outfit.

However her meticulous searches were not in vain and she was rewarded with an outfit that could not have been more perfect. It may as well have been handmade just for her. It was precisely what she had in mind; it consisted of a little cream dress and matching jacket. Its tailored cut and detailed finish exuded luxury, any onlooker would know that this was not a standard off the rail affair; even though it was! She was delighted with her choice. She had somehow managed to select an outfit that fitted many categories, for it was classy yet fashionable, and informal yet formal. Its versatility meant that Gabrielle could dress it up or down and that it would last her for years she knew such a classic piece would never date. As she had grown older, her taste in clothes had veered away from high fashion and evolved into neat lines and good cuts. Flares and maxi dresses were not for her. The pure simplicity of her wedding choice reflected this.

Like her dress she styled her hair in a chic fashion, she pulled it loosely off her face and wrapped it in a chignon. Everything about her entire look was intentionally plain and understated. To offset this she planned to accentuate her face. With the careful application of makeup Gabrielle would emphasise her eyes and her cheekbones. Her dark hair without regular trips to the hairdresser had a tendency to hang limp and straight. To prevent this, she had visited her regular hairdresser the day before, where he injected his usual magic. Her hair was now infused with volume and shining like never before.

Gabrielle's build was slim; she had good teeth, and large pretty eyes. Yet when put together her features never quite loaned themselves to the description of beauty. Her mother had once told her she had *'a big face'* insisting that she kept a fringe at all times to 'lesson' the impact. Her mother's flattery and adulation served to ensure that Gabrielle was never over confident. She had to work hard to look good, careful grooming was part of her daily routine. With the injection of what at times constituted a mammoth effort, she knew she looked attractive. Sometimes, just sometimes, on days like her wedding day when she injected a hefty overdose of effort she was transformed. Her conventional attractiveness was replaced by beauty. She had aimed for a Jackie Onassis look and with a final glimpse in the mirror she felt secure in the knowledge that she had achieved just that.

The ceremony would include Gabrielle, Max and two witnesses. One witness was Gabrielle's friend and colleague Ann the other was Max's friend James. They hadn't even planned a reception; instead they would take their witnesses to dinner and have a few celebratory drinks before embarking on their honeymoon. That night they would take the train to Dublin, where they would spend four days before returning home as man and wife.

Gabrielle and Ann met outside Belfast City Hall on the big day. They were delayed entering when Ann gushing at Gabrielle's 'beauty' insisted on taking copious amounts of photos. Gabrielle smiled for the camera and willingly let Ann photograph her from every angle she requested. Unexpectedly a small rumble rose in the far reaches of her mind and shook her shelf. The box marked *'family'* threatened to break open. Evidently even now, a tiny part of Gabrielle hoped for reunion, that her mother and father would see sense and be waiting at the City Hall alongside Ann. Of course this was not the case. Gabrielle quickly sealed the box and pushed it to the most distant corner of the shelf that she could find. Just to ensure it stayed put she gave it a firm hard kick. She had the rest of her life to think about her family and now was not the time.

Gabrielle and Ann made their way into the City Hall giggling childishly,

"Oh it's like Romeo and Juliet" Ann sighed, she was a romantic through and through,

"Not quite…. besides didn't they die?" Gabrielle said deadpan.

"Well, you know what I mean" Ann huffed "you two eloping and all, it's just sooooooo romantic."

"I wouldn't call it elop…." there was no point in correcting her; she knew Gabrielle's situation and the problems she and Max had faced. Rather than allow Ann to continue Gabrielle changed the subject,

"Ann, thanks so much for coming along, what would I do without you" she said and hugged her.

They were escorted to the registry office soon after. Austere heavy brown doors were now the only thing that stood between Gabrielle and Max. Their escort pushed them open with a flourish and removed the final barrier. The opened doors revealed an empty room with rows of empty chairs. On seeing the chairs once again the stark realisation that she was doing this alone struck her. Yet when she looked towards her groom, she saw nothing else. The elegant yet empty room, the registrar, Ann and James all became invisible. Max turned when the door opened and as far as Gabrielle was concerned he looked more handsome than ever before. Even now she can still see him smiling, warm and open, except then unlike now, any loneliness she had felt evaporated. Gabrielle met his eyes and walked through the empty room towards him.

One hour later, James and Ann were raising their glasses in a toast to the new, confetti strewn, Mr and Mrs Olorunda. The drink was flowing and merry chatter filled the tiny restaurant. It was a small gathering, yet Gabrielle couldn't have wished for a better one. Holding Max's hand they thanked the owner who on realising they were newlyweds surprised them all and gave them two free bottles of wine.

They stayed in the restaurant for two hours, to them it was like two minutes, before they knew it, it was time to say their goodbyes. They had a train to catch and a honeymoon to begin. It was time for them to make their way to the train station.

It was a first visit to Dublin for them both and it seemed like another world. Gone were the oppressing security checks of Belfast's shops, gone were nasty stares, the people were friendly and the city seemed somehow brighter. They spent their days laughing and revelling so much so that the holiday passed in a whirl.

Chapter Sixteen

Gabrielle must have really trusted Max as she had given him the task of securing their first home. Despite this anxiety surfaced every now and then as she wondered what kind of home she would be met with. She began to fear that perhaps Max was a typical man after all and he might truly surprise her, surprise her in the wrong way!

She reassured herself that she shouldn't be too apprehensive though, after all she had prepared Max as best she could. Long before Max had begun searching for a flat; Gabrielle had given him a list of the areas where he was permitted to flat hunt. She had spent countless days quizzing him on the said list, making him recite *her* choices over and over. To Gabrielle's shame she had even insisted that he memorised it. By the time he went house hunting he knew the list so well that it would be impossible for him to choose the wrong area. If nothing else Gabrielle knew the location would be okay, yet that was all she could be sure off!

This house or flat would be a rental and chosen by men, Max had enlisted the aid of his accountancy friends who had a good knowledge of the city. Gabrielle fretted that those he had enlisted, wouldn't have the gumption be concerned with whether or not their new home would be aesthetically pleasing. She knew they would simply be concerned with areas. Another niggle of trepidation struck her as she imagined outside toilets, electric fires and damp walls.

They planned to rent for six months whilst they arranged their first step onto the property ladder. The engagement and wedding had occurred so quickly that they didn't have time to look for something permanent. But they were young and had no ties and a rental meant that they would have six months to find something they really loved.

Frustratingly as their return train approached Belfast Max had still given nothing away. He didn't offer a solitary clue as to where they would be living; he just kept smirking and saying 'nearly there'. Never one for surprises Gabrielle was getting increasingly infuriated.

In the taxi from central station she paid close attention to the road they took, scrutinising the drivers every turn. As they went through the city centre relief flooded through her, the route the driver was taking confirmed that they were going in the direction of South Belfast. Evidently Max had been a good student, he had memorised her list well. By choosing South Belfast he had proved that he knew the theory behind her location test. Where they would stop would prove that he knew how to put this theory into practice. Slowly but surely they reached Bradbury place, the junction at the top would dictate the location of the world's best keep secret more accurately. If the taxi veered right, then they would be living somewhere in and around the Lisburn road, if it turned left they would be living in the Stranmillis or Malone area. She hoped it would go left, her mind screamed at the driver, *left, left, left.*

As if the driver had heard her, he indicated and went left. Now the location was easier to deduce. She knew that they would either be living in Stranmillis or Malone. Gabrielle would have been happy with either location, but her preference was undoubtedly Malone. She began a further chant in her head, *Malone, Malone, Malone.*

The Malone road was one of South Belfast's jewels, glittering bright against the granite drabness of the cities grey terraced streets. In Malone, the avenues were wide and lined with row upon row of leafy trees, the houses were sprawling and grand. If Max had even secured an outhouse on the Malone Road Gabrielle would be ecstatic.

She sat up a bit straighter, her alertness at epic levels, as the taxi came to University Road, straight ahead was the Malone road and she was now sure that was where they were going. She quivered with excitement. She was already planning boasting to her friends about their new house and its grand location. Internally she was rehearsing saying "I live in the Malone area", "that would be just off Malone, dear" in an affected voice.

"Thanks so much Max!" Gabrielle exclaimed rather prematurely yet her new knowledge was making it too difficult to remain silent.

He looked at her questioningly, Gabrielle assumed that look meant he was peeved that she had guessed his great surprise; well the best part of the surprise at any rate.

After a while he responded, "I worried that you wouldn't like it" he was visibly relieved

"Not like it? Well it was on the list" she reassured him, "Malone was actually the place I wanted most, there was a reason why I put it at number one!" she smiled, positively glowing with delight.

Before she could say anymore the taxi stopped, confused she looked to Max then out the window. They hadn't quite reached the Malone road. Certainly they had travelled in the right direction but for reasons unbeknownst to her, they had stopped on the University road. The driver turned to them to ask further directions she assumed he was lost (there could be no other reason for him to stop here). Yet it wasn't a question he asked it was more of a statement,

"That'll be £1, mate" he said to Max.

Max reached into his jacket, fished out his wallet and paid the driver. As the driver went on to help offload their bags Gabrielle struggled to pick her jaw up from the ground. She failed and her mouth hung open gormlessly.

She looked at the scene that confronted her; a grim row of dark terraces, all three stories high and dark, so very dark. Paint peeled off the windows and the doors. Each door held rows of letter boxes, suggesting multiple occupants. The only description her mind conjured up for this grimy row of houses was dingy.

The houses on the University road, whilst in a perfectly good area, had been subdivided many years ago to provide flats and bedsits to the students of the university opposite. These houses weren't reputed to have been in even adequate conditions, tolerable would be the best one could hope for here. The flats that this road offered were aimed at students, students who wanted cheap and functional accommodation close to their studies. She was not a student nor did she want cheap and functional. Someday she wouldn't have a choice.

The taxi pulled off and Max grinned at her. *He won't be grinning much longer* she thought, wait until I get him indoors. On gauging her reaction, the daggers her eyes were shooting at him, his stupid grin withered, he even had the audacity to look surprised!

"You said five minutes ago that this was where you wanted" he attempted, "five minutes ago"

"Malone Max, I said Malone" she sulked,

"Just wait until we get inside" he said noticing that they were attracting attention;

Not to be perturbed she continued,

"I am a married woman Max, I am NOT a student and I am NOT setting foot in any of these, these hesitating she searched for a word to portray her disgust, on finding it she shouted "Slums!"

Before she could protest any further Max grabbed her and slung her over his shoulder, she thumped and thumped at his back yelling,

"Put me down, put me down,"

He disregarded all her screams and assaults on his poor back and continued towards one of the houses. He fumbled in his pocket with his free hand and extracted a key. All the while Gabrielle was still kicking and thumping, now with even more might.

He ignored her protests and carried her up a flight of stairs, opened a flat door, deposited her in and left.

"I'm just going to get our bags" he said from outside the door and his footsteps retreated. She could visualise his broad shoulders slumped and his head hung in defeat. She was glad.

Now that she was on solid ground and alone, she took the opportunity to appraise her surroundings.

The small hallway she had been deposited in had three doors, she tried the one directly opposite her and found that it led to a large living room styled in browns and creams and furnished impeccably. A door leading off the living room led to a small compact kitchen, it was gleaming, so much so, that her mother would have been proud. Again it was styled in a contemporary pattern; the brown and cream theme continued, only here it was interjected with a splash of vibrant orange. She was ashamed to say it was beautiful. Had she been looking for a flat she would have chosen this too.

She could hear Max making his way up the stairs, so she didn't get to continue her inspection instead she sat on the sofa and pretended to still be annoyed. Yes the place was beautiful and yes she was impressed by his choice, but ultimately he had not complied with her list. He may have selected a rental in South Belfast, but he had strayed from her choices. For that reason she would let him stew. She obviously didn't let him stew for too long though, as two weeks later she discovered she was pregnant.

Chapter Eighteen

Max was overjoyed with the news that Gabrielle was expecting. Fatherhood was something he had always dreamed off, he loved children and wanted a large family. He clearly imagined a Walton style home filled with children, noise and oozing with family values. Within just one day of discovering that Gabrielle was pregnant, he was already planning how this child would be raised, even going so far as researching schools. Gabrielle considered his jubilation as ridiculous, it was wasted on her.

She just could not comprehend how she had been foolish enough to fall pregnant. She hadn't got a single maternal bone in her body. She had hoped that one day this would change, but for now aged twenty four, the thought of having a child was repugnant.

Every time she thought of her predicament, she was assailed with flashbacks of the traumatic day during training, when she witnessed the horror of childbirth first hand. That scene was just as grotesque to her now as it was at the time. She hated the very thought of being transformed into an uncouth, sweaty and bloated mess, displaying her bits to an army of staff.

She had never left Max under any illusions. He knew she had grown up surrounded by children, he knew all about her 'ordeal' during training. He had found the tales of her experiences hilarious, telling her that as she got older her feelings would change. Max only had to look at a child to be reduced to gloop. However as far as Gabrielle was concerned, unless he was completely dense, (which watching him float around ecstatically, she wondered if he was) he should have known that children were unlikely to be part of the deal.

With a nervous disquiet, she watched his growing excitement at his impending fatherhood. She genuinely feared he would explode. She became increasingly suspicious that this was what he had hoped for all along. Evidently, he had thought that someday she would awaken and her fictional biological clock would begin to tick, and she would suddenly declare that she wanted a family.

When Gabrielle's doctor confirmed that she was indeed pregnant, to say she was not amused would be an understatement.

Many of the girls she knew when faced with similar quandaries, had taken it upon themselves to rectify their mistake. They had travelled across to England and aborted their children. Gabrielle may have been a modern girl, but abortion was not an avenue she would ever contemplate exploring. They had just had their marriage blessed by the Catholic Church, and the combination of the morals she had been brought up with, and a sprinkling of Catholic guilt prevented her from even considering abortion. Life was precious and if she was forced to give it, then she would. She would just have to adjust to her pregnancy and prepare for it. On the plus side, at least she was married, they were financially secure and going by Max's reaction she would have a supportive husband.

Gabrielle began reading up on pregnancy and wishing she had paid more attention to the countless lectures on gestation during training. She researched every aspect of pregnancy she could and along the way something very peculiar occurred. She began to look forward to having her baby. She would watch other mothers wheeling their prams, loiter at the baby sections in shops and mull names over in her mind. A mere two months into the pregnancy she had already selected her favourite names for baby boys and girls.

Work posed a dilemma as the pregnancy progressed. In the seventies not many women worked when they had children and she hoped by raising the issue of her pregnancy that they would allow her to continue. She had worked hard to qualify and loved her job, she had planned a career and times were changing. She could see no reason why having a child should interrupt anyone's career.

Max wanted Gabrielle to give up work, yet she stalwartly refused. She had a profession and would not see it end because of a child.

She would certainly reduce her hours but she would not stop nursing. Anyway she would only ever have the one child; Max's 'Waltonesque' dream would stay just that, as in future Gabrielle would be even more meticulous with contraception.

The pregnancy flew in and before she knew it her slim figure was obscured by her bulging stomach. None of her usual clothes fitted and for anyone she hadn't yet told it wouldn't be hard for them to guess her predicament.

When she was seven months gone, she was finishing up a shift after a long day on the ward, preparing her report for the handover. Pregnancy was taking its toll and weariness was sweeping through her bones. She rubbed her face and concentrated on staying awake. The cleaner who came daily at this time, emptied the bin and as usual ignored her. This cleaner had once been an affable, chatty woman but over the course of time she became more and more distant. She would slam Gabrielle's bin on the ground after emptying it and bang the door on her way out of the office. Gabrielle only saw her at the end of her shifts so she wasn't overly concerned with the woman's obvious dislike. This particular day rather than make her customary hasty retreat, the cleaner seemed to hover in the office. Gabrielle looked up, curious as to what the woman was doing. She was staring at her. Smiling at her unsurely, Gabrielle put her head back down and continued with her report,

"How dare you" the cleaner hissed,

"Pardon?" Gabrielle asked, utterly bemused

"How dare you bring another black bastard into the world" she sneered.

Obviously feeling she had made her point, she lifted her bin bag and made to leave. This time she achieved the impossible and slammed the door with even more aplomb than ever before.

Gabrielle was shaken to the core. Revolted, she ran from the office and made it just in time to the bathroom, where she wretched and wretched. The cause of the cleaners growing dislike was now clear.

A colleague found her and between tears Gabrielle recounted the incident to her. She repeated over and over,

"It's just a baby……….a baby, how can people hate it?"

In the hours immediately after, Gabrielle was shaken by a growing sense of unease, what kind of a world was she bringing her child into? Fear for her unborn child permeated her terrified mind; she would have to be more than a mother. She would have to become a protector too, shielding this child from the hatred that this world was obviously infested with.

When Max returned home from work, she had composed herself. She didn't mention the incident, deciding that he did not need be hurt too. There was nothing to be gained by letting that woman's spiteful remarks upset him as well. In a sense Gabrielle became not only the protector of her child, but also her husband. If this was to be her new role then she would step up to the mark, for it was a small price to pay for the privilege of having her beloved family.

When Gabrielle returned to work the following day, the cleaner was not there. It didn't matter though, the damage was done. Yet the woman had instigated the realisation, acceptance even of her new role for that at least she was grateful.

Chapter Nineteen

After months of searching Gabrielle and Max found their first home. It wasn't quite on the Malone Road, but it was situated in a pleasant residential area not far off it. It was in a development of handsome semi-detached houses with gardens front and rear and lots of young families. It was perfect and exactly what they had envisaged. When the last stick of furniture was delivered to the house, they said goodbye to their University road flat and made the move.

Fortunately Max had promised to decorate, he had often boasted of his handyman skills, his talent with a paintbrush and all things DIY. After the expense of the move and acquiring furniture, at least they would save on hiring a decorator. Gabrielle selected the paint and paper and Max took a few days off to begin work.

By day two Max's efforts contradicted his talk of his great talents. If his talent was painting floors, windows and brand new furniture, then certainly he was an expert. If his talent was turning wallpaper to bubbling shreds, then he was a genius. Yet none of his talents were what Gabrielle had in mind. Before he painted anymore furniture, or destroyed another roll of her expensive wall paper, she advised him that unless he wanted a divorce he was banned from attempting a single piece of work in the house again. Max was swiftly despatched back to work and his handyman skills thoroughly discredited. Gabrielle resorted to seeking the services of a professional decorator. It was tight but he managed to get the house finished within two weeks of the due date.

The new neighbours were lovely. They consisted of mainly young couples like themselves either starting a family or planning to. Within two weeks of moving in, they had made a wealth of new friends all thoroughly welcoming and hospitable. Gabrielle was confident that in the remainder of her maternity leave she certainly wouldn't feel alone.

They had decorated the baby's room in lemon. Gabrielle was superstitious and didn't want to know the sex; nor make too many preparations before the birth. The room was simply painted and carpeted. Anything else needed would be bought after the child's arrival.

The only thing that Gabrielle felt she could do at this stage without tempting fate was to hang the curtains. She made her way to the babies little room and began adding curtain hooks to the edge of the curtain, carefully counting in the pleats. Just as she was about to hang them, a knock came to the front door. She shuffled down the stairs making slow progress as her mobility was constrained by her enormous bump. A whole two minutes later she reached the door. Fearing that the caller would have left she didn't peak through the safety hole that Max insisted on and instead she quickly opened it. There on the door step stood her mother and father. She was astonished she didn't have any words or thoughts she just stood there wide eyed and regarded them.

"Hello Gabrielle" her mother said "May we come in?"

Gabrielle opened the door wider, stood back and let them pass.

"Well you certainly have a lovely home" her mother said, visibly impressed

"Thanks",

Confused now, she asked "how did you know where I live?" she hadn't been in touch with her parents since the letter she had received prior to the wedding.

"Max" her father said "he wrote us a letter" he continued "He told us that you were married and that you were pregnant"

Her mother interrupted, "We couldn't ignore the letter and we certainly couldn't ignore our first grandchild" she said

"Oh", Gabrielle was touched that Max had contacted her parents, even more touched that he had kept it to himself.

She cried, she can't say that they were tears of joy (more shock) but her parents took this as some sort of a sign because before she knew it she was inundated with hugs,

"John go and put the kettle on" her mother demanded dismissing her father to an unfamiliar kitchen, in an unfamiliar house. Some things never change.

"It's ok, I'll do it"

"You will not, not in your condition," her mother demanded and ushered her to sit down.

Before long in her mother's infamous interrogation style, she had caught up on the marriage, the Catholic blessing and her pregnancy. She seemed satisfied with her findings.

Her father returned with the tea and they all talked about the impending arrival. No apologies were made. Gabrielle doubted that any would be offered. She would instead assume that the gesture of travelling all the way to Belfast was apology enough, so she let it slip.

One question still hung in the air, Max. They had not met him yet and he was due home from work soon.

"Mum, Dad, Max will be home soon" she said,

They looked at each other but didn't make to leave,

"Grand" her father said affecting false casualness.

Sure enough ten minutes later, the sound of Max's key in the door alerted them to his arrival.

Gabrielle held her breath as he entered the living room, her parents eyed the door

"Well the bus was……….." Max stopped mid-sentence and looked at the arrivals

"Max, meet my parents" Gabrielle said

"You actually came" Max said eyes wide in surprise, "thank you" he added humbly.

Her father was immediately on his feet shaking Max's hand, and her mother was behind him. It was a surreal scene, something she had never expected.

"Pleased to meet you Max" her father said

"Hello" her mother said,

An awkward silence ensured so Gabrielle went to the kitchen and put on more tea. She thought she would leave them alone for a while to either get acquainted or knowing her luck *and her mother* unacquainted. She started to make up some sandwiches and took her time about it.

When she estimated that at least twenty minutes had passed and that the front door hadn't been touched Gabrielle re entered the room. She didn't know what to expect but certainly not what she found.

She stood in the doorway and surveyed the unlikely scene. Her mother was on the edge of her seat in deep conversation with Max and her father was nodding along knowledgably. Gabrielle released a little cough and walked into the room. She sat the tray on the coffee table and busied herself serving teas; it was as if she was invisible. It seemed her mother had found a fellow conversationalist in Max, they were talking about the boring issues that Gabrielle tended to glaze over at. Yet the pair was engrossed. She looked at her father baffled and he winked at her.

Two hours later her parents left.

Gabrielle may have once found her parents racist, but when she looked at the events that occurred that day she knows they never were. Mixed race relationships have always been a contentious issue, couples this very day face difficulties and lack of acceptance. It was 1974, her parents were from the country a place where they had encountered very few, if any people of colour in their daily lives. Yet when they met Max, when they got over their previous reservations, their concern for their daughter and potential grandchildren, they bonded firmly and quickly. Her parents were never racist they were simply protective and before meeting Max filled with protective trepidation.

Two days after their reunion, Gabrielle's labour began and they were reunited once again. Gabrielle was engulfed with so much pain, that she was filled with empathy and respect for that brave, brave woman on the maternity ward in Derry!

That day Alison was born.

Chapter Twenty

Alison soon became completely and utterly spoiled and enjoyed by her granny, her great granny, her grandfather her many aunts and of course her doting father. Everyone loved baby Alison; she was a regular VIP in her grandmother's house and amongst Gabrielle and Max's circle of friends. Wherever she went she was indulged with toys, sweets, games and hours of undivided attention.

Any concerns about Alison becoming too spoilt were short lived. In the Christmas of 1975, just when order was restored to the house, Gabrielle was given a little surprise; she was pregnant again. Just when Alison was sleeping full nights in her own bed and more importantly going to bed at reasonable hour, Gabrielle was faced with reliving the whole experience again.

This time though the realisation that she was pregnant was no ordeal. She basked in the notion of carrying a little baby again. The feelings of doom and dread she had experienced just two years ago were replaced with sheer exhilaration. She was utterly thrilled at the prospect of becoming a mother again. Having Alison had shown her that she loved motherhood; that she was maternal after all. Maybe there was indeed such a thing as a biological clock because everything had changed for Gabrielle, an unmistakable something ticked inside her. The mere knowledge of having a second baby had set it off, and now it was ticking rhythmically through her very being. With each individual tick of the clock she was prodded with another little jolt of joy. A countdown had begun.

If Gabrielle was excited then Max was ecstatic. Even more promising was the fact that they were settled in a home of their own, one that had ample room to cater for another tiny person. Yes, this time around they were prepared in every sense.

Young Alison was a different story, like her mother before her; she loathed the idea of a sibling. After months of explaining the benefits of sisterhood, and not just any sister hood but *big* sister hood, they achieved success and converted Alison from a reluctant to eager big sister. Alison became more engrossed in this pregnancy than anyone else. By the time Gabrielle was due, Alison had become expectant big sister extraordinaire. She drew a new picture every day for her little brother or sisters nursery. Her parents ignored the fact that in each picture Alison was portrayed as a huge figure dominating the tiny dot that with closer inspection was to be her new sibling!

With this pregnancy Gabrielle's family were with her every step of the way, her grandmother on hearing the news had begun knitting tiny cardigans and booties. Both her mother and grandmother fed her with 'castor oil sandwiches' before the birth and stocked up on cabbage leaves for after.

The baby was due in November; once again a lemon room was prepared. This time Gabrielle was more primed as to what to expect. The labour went as smoothly as any labour can and when she was handed the little white bundle she didn't hand it back. On birth Alison had looked every bit as white as this little girl did. Gabrielle knew to expect the pigmentation to creep into her skin over the next few weeks and for her straight downy baby hair to be replaced by a network of tight wiry curls.

Max was once again over excited about the prospect of his second daughter, so much so, that it now exceeded the excitement he had displayed on the news of his first daughter. He was so high that Gabrielle honestly believed he could have flown! His reaction was so great that this was little girl was named after him; converting Max to its female equivalent Maxine. Max was so engaged with this new arrival that it was only right that she should be named after him.

Maxine by all accounts was a lovely child; she had a gentle nature and seldom cried or caused any fuss. She was adored by all and like Alison was spoiled beyond belief. She had huge brown eyes and as she grew, her hair settled into loose brown curls. She effortlessly progressed from a good natured baby into an easy going child.

Max's parenting skills propelled him into the status of a 'modern man', he loved his girls, his family were his world. He devoted his free time to tutor the three year old Alison. He insisted that she would read, write and count before school; his theory was that she needed to start ahead to stay ahead. Alison to put it mildly was not as laid back as her baby sister. She was a highly strung, bad tempered child and utilised her new found voice to its full. She constantly screamed to get her own way. This personality did not combine well with her father's attempts to teach her to read and write. The pair of them would sit at the table night after night. Max would take her through the alphabet and Alison would take him through her litany of ear splitting hysterics. He availed of many different methods to entice her to learn, colourful books, art sets and even nature walks. He would take her to the park and point out flowers and trees and try to phonically coax her into grasping the alphabet. By the summer of that year Alison had only managed to recite the letters a – e and Gabrielle swore her husband's hair had grown thinner. Gabrielle found the whole situation hilarious, rather than admit defeat Max continued trying, yet it was clear to all but him that his efforts were in vain. Even so Gabrielle was impressed; such actions showed a dedication that not many fathers possessed.

Once a bee flew in the open kitchen window, little Alison immediately began to swipe at the bee and her father stopped her angrily. He knelt down and caught the bee and as it landed on the table,

"This is a little life Alison, you cannot hurt any living thing" he said

"If you treat God's creatures nicely, they'll be nice to you" both of them regarded the bee walking around his palm.

"Now watch and I'll set if free" he got up and walked towards the window "oooooouch!" he screamed jumping nearly to the ceiling,

"The buggers stung me!" he exclaimed

"Well if you're nice to God's creatures they'll be nice to you eh Max?" Gabrielle said through fits of laughter. As for Alison one lesson and perhaps the only one she absorbed from Dad's months of tuition was that bee's sting; don't hold them in your hand!

Unfortunately, Max's love of God's creatures had not been perturbed by his sting. He had been talking about getting my sisters a dog since Alison was born, and so far Gabrielle had rebuked his pleas. She had enough to contend with two young children and work, without taking on a dog as well. Her husband worked full time so it didn't take a genius to know that Gabrielle would be left with the dog.

Gabrielle still remembered little Patch, she remembered being devastated when he died. Animals had ways of getting themselves killed from road accidents, to illness; she had no intention of inflicting death on her children. Northern Ireland had other ideas.

One day she arrived home after a late shift to see no sign of Max or her daughters. Aside from Rod Stewarts husky tones filling the empty kitchen, the house was quiet. It was then she heard gleeful little giggles coming from the garden. She went out smiling; wondering what could have filled the children with such delight. Her smile soon faded, for there was Max and her daughters with a huge dog. It was Alison, who saw her Mum first,

"Mummy, Mummy come and see, Daddies got us a dog"

"I can see that" she said, her voice was deadpan,

Sheepishly Max said "Gabrielle meet Lucky"

Hmm. *Lucky* evidently wasn't *lucky* by nature getting chosen by this fool she thought.

"Max, I need a word now" she said and beckoned him into the kitchen

"I know, I know" he said, "but I knew when you saw how much the girls loved him you would come around".

"Did you now?"

He smiled that big stupid childish grin again, she had enough,

"Max, what are you playing at" Gabrielle demanded "did you not think to discuss this with me first?"

He looked shamefaced,

"No because you would never have agreed".

"Exactly, Max. There's good reason for that, just who do you will be looking after this dog?"

"Gabrielle *I will*, you know that"

"When will you be doing this Max, between your teaching the girls? When you're studying or how about when you're working all day every day!"

"I'll make time"

"Yes Max, you will indeed make time, you'll make time right now and tell those children that the doggy has to go home" infuriated she continued "I have two children Max and a job and a house to look after and you think we need a dog,"

She gave him his orders storming from the room in a rage, before adding "I'm going to the shops, I want that dog gone, by the time I get home". She banged the door behind her.

On leaving in such a rush she realised she had forgotten her purse, she slipped back in quietly, careful not to alert anyone of her presence. She shouldn't have worried because Max was so deep in conversation he wouldn't have heard her had she entered with a brass band,

"Mum, what am I to do?" he was pleading,

One thing that annoyed Gabrielle most about Max was that he aired all their dirty laundry to her mother! Gabrielle completely enraged crept to the landing where he was sat by the phone. She snatched the phone from his hand and slammed it down. "Since when was she *you're* Mum" she snipped and as planned went to the shops.

When she got home that night, three pairs of pitiful eyes fixed on her morosely. As usual she was the villain, this time the one who had forced Lucky to go home.

Tensions remained high between she and Max over the next few days, but a new surprise was soon to dissolve them. This news put the argument over Lucky's demise and the general subject of canines to the back burner for quite a while.

Gabrielle was pregnant once again and by now she was so familiar with Max's jubilance that she let it wash over her. She was excited about this pregnancy too but for other reasons. Now that they had two girls she wanted a boy and she felt in her bones that this child was male. She had decided that her little boy would be named Christopher and as the pregnancy progressed she would talk to her bump referring to him by name.

It was during this pregnancy that she admitted a certain defeat. In a few months she would have three children, all aged under five. She would have to give up her career and focus on her children. The notion of no longer working didn't appal her as it once did. She had had four years' experience of motherhood and work, and already struggled to balance twelve hour shifts with two children. She knew that with three children this struggle would soon become insurmountable.

When she was six months pregnant she donned her nurse's uniform for the last time. She was struck by a little reluctance, as memories of her struggles to become a nurse surfaced, her training, the hours of studying and her parents finding the financial support she needed in tough times. Yet she had enjoyed her career, however short it was. She was sure that fragments of it could be put to good use, especially in motherhood. Perhaps when the children were at least of secondary school age and a bit more independent she could reconsider. Who knew what life would hold? Maybe she would enjoy being a mother and a home maker and never return to work; when the children were older she could be a lady of leisure!

All that she was certain of at this point was that nursing had to go. Motherhood came first for her now and that would be her focus for the considerable future. Little did Gabrielle know that she had no need to worry about giving up her career, she was fortunate in those days to have had a choice.

Chapter Twenty One

With the family rapidly growing, Gabrielle and Max contacted Max's brother in Edinburgh again, he had finished his studies so should be more flexible with his time. They sent him an open invite to come and meet his nieces and of course his sister in law. Unfortunately Femi was unavailable; he was working round the clock shifts and would find it difficult to get enough leave for a trip away. Gabrielle was fuming a two hour boat trip and even a night's stay wouldn't take much out of his busy schedule but she kept her thoughts to herself fearful of offending her husband.

Anyway they had little time to dwell on Femi being unable to visit as the house was always filed with Gabrielle's family. Her mother and father, brothers and sisters, grandmother and aunts and uncles were regular visitors. Gabrielle and Max loved having them around and the children adored the attention they were showered with. Many a great family gathering was held in that home, Gabrielle's grandmother and Max played card games, old stories were told and during those nights laughter and craic was guaranteed!

They did their best to make the journey to Strabane as often as possible. They loved going to Strabane as during the time they spent there they didn't have to lift a finger with the children. There was always a doting auntie or cousin keen and eager to take them off their hands. They could always be assured of a well-earned break when they visited.

A gang of them, Gabrielle and Max, aunts and those sisters who were now grown enough and even on the verge of marriage themselves, would spend Saturday nights at the local cricket club. Drinking many a drink and enjoying the banter. Gabrielle's father unfortunately could never join them, he was a pioneer, whether this was by his own choice or not was always difficult to ascertain! On many occasions Gabrielle would see him keenly eyeing a bottle of Guinness or gazing at their bottles of whiskey. All she could be sure of was that her mother viewed alcohol as the devils brew. With this in mind for an easy life her father's choice to be a pioneer - enforced or not was the safest option!

Her grandmother was fast becoming one of Max's greatest fans, she could be found talking to him in the side-lines of any gathering. Her eyes sparkling fondly and she never tired of telling Gabrielle;

"I think you have married a true gem. If it wasn't for his *obvious* deficiencies, I would think you had made the best choice out of any of them yet".

Gabrielle's Grandmother was a Catholic through and through, so devout was she that she was known far and wide for her powerful novenas. When she spoke of Max's obvious deficiencies she would never have even considered his colour, no he had much bigger deficiencies than mere colour. He was a heathen, a Protestant! If she had her way, this would change and sooner rather than later. Most of their conversations at some point involved her trying to arrange a visit from the priest, who would talk Max into the merits of belonging to the great Catholic Church. From Max's response to her persistence, Gabrielle believed her grandmother was beginning to wear him down. He began to openly ask questions about Catholicism, expressing genuine interest. Whether this was simply to appease her or genuine we will never know. Yet Gabrielle couldn't help but be amazed at how her little grandmother had brought about such a change of heart. If she kept this up she would be a very happy woman for Gabrielle was sure her perseverance was paying off and that Max, if only to keep his new grandmother happy, may actually consider the idea of conversion.

Max's relationship with his mother in law was one that bemused Gabrielle more than any other. Max had progressed from referring to her as Mrs Caulfield, to Irene to Mum. He would phone her more than Gabrielle would and discuss his slightest concern; usually his wife! The relationship was fully reciprocated as her mother in turn would introduce him to all and sundry as her son, Max.

The old saying be careful what you wish for, rang in Gabrielle's ears when she saw the two together. The pair shared a bond that she could never have predicted; they had become such friends that often she felt that the pair was ganging up on her. It got to the point that any arguments the couple had, any suggestion Gabrielle broached or plan she made her mother knew. Max told her everything, so much so that before they ever spoke, Gabrielle had to consider that every morsel of the information she imparted would be given to her mother. She had to be extremely careful with her words!

Her father from his regular reading of the world report in the 'Irish News', considered himself a man of the world. He was always interested in hearing Max's experiences of Nigeria. He would ask him all about his home land, the climate, the local wildlife, the food and the people. He was mesmerised and would wistfully return his questions with talk of Ireland, its legends and its history.

Her mother was also convinced that her third pregnancy would be a boy and was looking forward to the arrival of her first grandson. If Gabrielle had ever considered herself large with her first two pregnancies then this one could only be described as mammoth. This little fellow was obviously a strapping young man; for the bump he created was the biggest she or any of her family or friends had ever seen. He became known as the elephant in a running joke amongst them.

The due date was in October and coincidently fell on her mother's birthday; this made this particular pregnancy all the more special for her. A grandson would be a magnificent birthday surprise. Yet her mother's birthday came and went, and still Christopher hadn't arrived. They began to speculate that he was indeed an elephant. They were known to carry their young for years and by the looks of it, Gabrielle would too!

When the birth was deemed by the obstetrician to have been prolonged enough, Gabrielle was called in to be induced. Even with all the medication to speed up labour, Christopher still refused to venture out. It appeared her little boy did not want to face the world. Nature had to take his course at some time though and very soon it did.

My entrance into the world was not the joyous entrance that I deserved; on the contrary it seemed I was met by a very angry and confused mother. As I was presented to her the midwife said,

"Here she is, she's as fit as a fiddle"

"You mean *he*, don't you?" Mum asked concerned,

"No Mrs. Olorunda, it's definitely a she."

Thrilled as she was she couldn't shake the tiny fragment of disappointment that lingered, as she had had her heart set on a boy.

My Dad and grandparents arrived soon after to see the new arrival.

Apparently Mum's first words were "It looks like we'll have to try again Max, I want a boy"

"Let me get used to this one first" he laughed and lifted me for the first time; his brown eyes alight with pride.

Due to my being born the wrong sex I could no longer be called Christopher, so my parents quickly set about finding me a name.

They settled on calling me after both my grandmothers; Jayne-Irene.

Chapter Twenty Two

I take after my Dad in that I am a born worrier. Apparently he spent his days planning and budgeting, his budget didn't allow for another child just yet, but his wife wanted her little boy and his budget would just have to be compromised. Mum never had any time for people who penny pinched. Inevitably it wasn't long before she had persuaded him that a having a little boy was a good idea.

Outwardly he seemed happy enough and went along with the idea, he loved his children and Gabrielle was sure he would enjoy a little more balance between the sexes in the family. It would also mean that his Walton style family dream may come to fruition. Yet he began to stop sleeping at night, Mum ignored this at first but eventually she broached the issue, the answer she received was not what he had expected,

"Every time I close my eyes I see the same thing" his voice actually sounded afraid,

"What Max," she asked, anxious herself now "what do you see?"

It took him a while to reply, but when he did his words were to chill her to the core,

"I see a coffin and I don't know who it's for"

……………………………………………………………………

……………………………………………………………………

……

Alison was now five and attending her father's chosen school, an exclusive prep school that for a man on a budget Gabrielle viewed as a little ostentatious. She didn't remark though, for she was simply relieved to have just two rather than three infants at home with her full time. Maxine and I in keeping with our older sister seemingly preferred our Dad to our Mum. Mum took great umbrage at the fact, considering that she was the one who stayed at home with us all day, nursed us through colds and flu's and catered to our every whim. Despite her efforts each day at six o'clock, when Dad walked through the door, her three little girls deserted her and from that moment on only had eyes for him. Gabrielle often wondered what she was doing wrong or more to the point what was he doing so right!

Gabrielle still loved to shop and buying children's clothes became a favourite pastime. She says she wanted us to be the best dressed children in Belfast. To achieve this took great effort. She dressed us all the same and wherever we went she was sure to get a compliment on our presentation. She spared no expense on our little outfits, with the result that our wardrobes were brimming with unique and expensive little clothes for every occasion.

My Dad on the other hand disagreed. He constantly chastised Mum, backed up by her mother of course, about how much money she would spend on the children's clothes. As usual though, when Max went into his financial droning, Mum switched off. He had wanted children not her, so he would just have to accept the cost they incurred. Granted she could have bought cheaper clothes, but she felt if she was going to buy clothes at all, then she may as well do it right. Besides she felt that expensive children's clothes from the many little boutiques were so much more durable than those found on the general high street.

The one thing about the three of us that Mum couldn't come to terms with was our hair. As babies we all had has soft wavy curls, but as we grew the curls tightened and tightened and tightened some more. Each of us sported a tight little afro that for the life of Mum she just couldn't work with. She styled our little afros every which way; she used a hot brush and bought a multitude of products, but still our little afros refused to relax or take any shape.

Mum often talks about how she grumbled to Dad about our hair he just laughed telling her that the only solution was to grow it down. The longer the hair got, the looser it would become. Mum was mystified, thinking how the hell she could grow our hairs down? Surely at some point in the mid stages of growth she would need to be able to tie it back? If she couldn't tie it back, then she would have three little girls with hair so big that they would be constantly stuck in doorways! Our strange hair grew out not down and in a rage one evening Gabrielle decided to take matters into her own hands.

Watched by an aghast husband, she became what she believed to be a world class hairdresser.

One by one she sat each of us sat on her knee and chopped off the offending afro's.

"You've scalped them!" Dad said appalled,

"No Max I've made them sophisticated" she retorted "besides it'll grow back better, you'll see"

When each of us had been carefully coiffured by Mum's expert hand, she gathered up all the hair and tossed it into the open fire.

She thought nothing of it until Dad started coughing and choking

"For God's sake you big girls blouse, what's wrong now?" She demanded

"The smell Gabrielle, how can that not get to you?"

Certainly she could smell burning hair, but they had an open fire and any strong odour was swept up the chimney, only the slightest smell remained.

"Max you'd barely notice it"

"Well I can, it's making me gag, I can't stand it" coughing and spluttering he left the room.

Dad just could not handle the smell of burning. Then without the benefit of hindsight his protests would have appeared slightly strange.

The following night Ann, who had stayed close to my parents since their wedding was to call around. Gabrielle really looked forward to catching up on the shenanigans at the hospital but most of all to having some adult company. She told my Dad that he was to be home from work early and to keep the girls out of the way. She wanted some grown up time; she had bought a bottle of wine and planned to spend a few blissful hours relaxing.

Ann arrived promptly and discussed the hospital gossip, her recent affairs and her newly discovered 'gift'. Ann was the seventh of daughter of the seventh daughter. Irish superstition had it that being born in such a unique position brought with it some special gifts; one of them was the ability to see the future. Ann had been practising her newly discovered talents on all her friends and colleagues and had surprised herself at the strength of her predictions and their uncanny accuracy. Tonight before they even had a sip of wine Ann decided to demonstrate her skill. Mum was a sceptic, but rather than upset Ann's kind nature, she acquiesced.

Ann took herself off to the kitchen and prepared some tea. She was going to read Mums tea leaves. They would then discuss the findings over a bottle of wine.

She placed a cup of tea in front of Mum and made her drink as much as she could. Gabrielle worried about swallowing the tea leaves that swirled through it, but Ann insisted that they would settle at the bottom. Quickly she finished all but a small drop, the sooner she did, the sooner they could crack open the wine.

"Ok Gaby, let's see what the future holds for you" she said taking her cup.

"A boy and hopefully one very soon, oh and a house actually on the Malone road!" Mum laughed.

Ann examined her cup, then examined it again,

"Well?" she asked intrigued, Ann still hadn't lifted her head from the tea leaves.

When Ann did respond Mum wished she hadn't. Her eyes were wide with terror, her rosy cheeks had lost all their hue and her mouth hung wide open.

"Ann, that's enough" Mum laughed, "good joke" she said "but seriously enough is enough"

Ann left the table and collected her coat faster moving faster than Mum had ever seen her move before. As she made her way to the door Ann muttered, "I have to go. I've forgotten I had something…"

She didn't even finish her sentence she was out the door so quickly.

"Ah well all the more wine for me" Mum mused. She turned on the TV, watched a few episodes of *'Some Mothers do have them'* and completely relaxed, who needs company she thought.

Chapter Twenty Three

The incident with the tea leaves was soon forgotten as it seemed that my baby self was developing some sort of colic. At almost a year old, I had difficulty keeping down anything. Soon I was throwing up every morsel I swallowed. Doctors believed Mum was neurotic and she began to think so too until I began to show worrying symptoms. I lost weight, cried with sheer hunger and became alarmingly lethargic. It was only when Mum took me to the City Hospital that she was taken seriously. Having worked there before and having such a distinctive name had the benefit that she was recognised. Mum was told that her baby needed a barium meal. This thick, gooey liquid once swallowed would show exactly what was going on inside.

Dad arrived home from work the night before my barium meal and to Mum was uncharacteristically calm at the news that his baby was due to go into hospital the following day,

"Max, I don't think she's going to do" Gabrielle said utterly despondent, "she can't continue like this, all that retching wears the heart down"

His answer was strange and so much so that it stayed with Mum over the years.

"Oh she'll be fine, this child will be the best you'll have" he was so confident in his words that for a moment Mum let her fears vanish.

At the hospital Mum and my grandmother were met by the paediatrician who would be investigating my case. They told him all my symptoms, that I was keeping nothing down and therefore making me drink a barium meal would be a wasted effort. Yet he insisted,

"On your own head be it" Gabrielle told him "We'll just leave you too it"

To her mother she said "let's stand back".

Sure enough within fifteen minutes of swallowing the lumpy mixture, I apparently managed to project it all over the doctor, all over his office and over anything else within two foot vicinity. Even though my escorts were worried sick they couldn't help but laugh. The paediatrician was disgusted.

Fortunately there was enough of the solution left clinging to my stomach, that they were able to get a picture of what was going on inside. The news was not good. As I had developed my trachea hadn't, meaning that food could not make it to the stomach. On the positive side I would grow, as would my trachea. But for now if I was to receive any nutrients my oesophagus would have to be widened. To make matters worse baby me would require a tracheotomy whilst it healed.

Gabrielle was horrified; this was no solution, a child so young would pull a tracheotomy out. As for an operation to widen the oesophagus she had no objections, but without the tracheotomy the paediatrician and she were at logger heads. She resolved that this operation was not an option and hoped that she could keep my nutrient levels high enough until I grew. Yet her mind couldn't silence her husband's voice only a few weeks earlier when he stated, "*I see a coffin and I don't know who it's for.*"

In the middle of all this Dad came home slightly perplexed, not only was his child sick but he had met his friend from home, in Belfast of all places. He had been leaving his office in the city centre, when he heard someone call his name. It was no normal voice; it had the distinct inflection that could only be found in a Nigerian accent. On hearing the familiar tones of his home country he was intrigued. It was the first time he had heard them uttered by anyone in Northern Ireland and was momentarily transported to the dry sandy streets of Nigeria. He was taken aback yet thrilled to see an old friend from Lagos standing there in front of him! They hugged and talked for a while and Dad insisted that Kayode came home to meet his family and catch up. Kayode was appreciative of the offer, but would reluctantly have to pass; he was in a rush and couldn't be delayed. He reassured Dad that he would see him very soon and embraced him once again.

Dad came home and after checking on me regaled Mum on the news of his friend's arrival in Belfast. Although he hadn't ascertained why his friend was here, he was sure that when Kayode visited the house he would reveal all. The following morning Dad received a letter from Nigeria.

Kayode had been killed in a road accident just two days earlier.

Chapter Twenty Four

Christmas came and went and for Gabrielle it was the loveliest Christmas she had ever experienced. Santa came and our childish dreams came true. Boxing Day through to New Years was spent in our Grandmothers. Here any possible dream that Santa could have neglected was catered for.

I had just turned two and seemed to be improving. In the space of three months, I had progressed from a skeletal baby into a chubby little pudding. My prognosis was looking better by the day.

January soon arrived, bleak, drab and cold. It had always been Mum's least favourite time of year, the winter focus of Christmas gone and nothing left but gloom. However she did have some light on the horizon. As usual my Dad had given her money for her Christmas box. After their first Christmas together when he bought her a sewing machine and bore the brunt of her subsequent reaction, he had never dared buy her a present again; instead he took the safe option and let her choose her own.

The Christmas money soon felt like it was burning a hole in her pocket, because for over two weeks she had been unable to get an opportunity to spend it. If she didn't get one soon she would miss the best of the bargains that the January sales had to offer. She didn't want to lumber the neighbours with three children so sought a reliable babysitter. Eventually she secured one, a kindly lady who would be available for the entire afternoon. She seized the opportunity and acquired the babysitter's services, asking her to take the girls for few hours. At last she could go shopping!

The girls needed new shoes, and she wouldn't mind a new coat. Leaving the girls, she set off and began the process of bargain hunting. The city centre was thronged with shoppers who, like Mum, were availing of the sales; frantically grabbing the bargains which the town was filled with. Some shops offered a massive fifty percent off; Gabrielle was in her element.

She shopped and shopped until she had spent every penny of her Christmas box, the icy weather had slowed her down and she was surprised that it was now quarter to six. By this stage, she was opposite the Europa train station and thought rather than slip and slide all the way back to the main city centre to grab a bus, that she would take a train instead. It would be a little more expensive, but ultimately it would save a walk - or a slide! She'd had enough slips and slides for one day.

She was fantasising about going home, getting us bathed and hopefully settled for bed early. Battling through the crowds had tired her out more than she had expected. Judging by the weary faces around her, she was not alone in this sensation. Perhaps it was the time of year, the dark mornings and dark evenings were taking their toll on everyone.

Date: 15th January 1980

Time: 18.06.

Location: Europa Station Belfast.

The train station was full as shoppers and workers converged all trying to get home. Mum went to the ticket desk and purchased her one way ticket, shuffling her bags to find a free hand to pay. She wished she had researched her timings for going home, had she done she could have avoided all this. She would have to get on the train early if she stood any chance of getting a seat. She took her ticket from the cashier and looked around for the quickest way to the platform.

Her first indication that something wasn't right was when she suddenly became aware of being stared at. She instinctively looked in the direction of where the stare seemed to come from. In the distance, stood a woman that Mum describes as being dressed from head to toe in green. When I heard this I imagined a cloud of dark green surrounding the woman. Mum's initial thoughts were that the lighting in the station needs serious attention; either that or her eyes were playing tricks on her.

The woman was clad in elegant clothes, not the kind that could be bought anywhere Mum frequented and she was looking, no coming in Mum's direction. Mum looked behind her in case she was mistaken and she was obscuring the woman's intended target. Yet there was no one behind her. When she looked up again the woman was inches from her face. She couldn't fathom how the woman had reached her so quickly, somehow the woman had made her way across the long expanse of the station and weaved her way through the crowds at a speed Mum just couldn't comprehend. The scenario seemed odd to Mum, whatever could this woman want? Mum was certain she did not know her.

As Mum's eyes met the woman's she was assailed with such coldness that she thought she would never be warm again. She tried to peel her eyes away from the woman's penetrating stare, it was then that Mum realised that the woman wasn't a she; this woman wasn't anything Mum's humble mind had words for. She was faced with a creature - an IT.

Feebly Mum recited every prayer she could remember and when her memory failed her, she beseeched the heavens to take this thing away. Her pleas went unanswered and she stood there powerless.

She tried to scream, but no words came. She contemplated running but her limbs remained motionless. Even the simple gesture of averting her eyes from IT's penetrating gaze, became impossible. Mum was paralysed, her defenceless body forcing her to remain on the spot.

IT opened IT's mouth and words, lots of words tumbled out. IT spoke in a language that Mum had never heard before or hoped to hear again. IT's menacing tones were infused with vast hatred and malice. Only IT's finale was spoken in a human tongue, six words that shook my Mum to the core, "I curse you and I curse your family". (Exact words)

Instinct told Mum that she had encountered a being that represented all things evil. She had just been exposed to something that was not of this world.

In a green cloud IT was gone, back to the nowhere IT had appeared from. Mum remembers dropping to her knees so relieved was she at IT's departure. She stayed on her knees as she waited for the waves of terror to leave her. Her moment in darkness had seemed a lifetime. Yet it was 18.06, so no time had passed. Had she imagined the episode?

She glanced at the ground where IT had stood. Sure enough IT had left an ominous souvenir, some sort of green pendant. Then this thing *had* happened. Reassured that her sanity was still intact, she looked to the commuters, the people all around her, they would be shaken too. What had they made of this thing? Yet their faces registered no shock, they were simply the ordinary faces of ordinary commuters in a busy train station.

Everything around her went on as normal; no one looked at all shaken. It seemed only Mum had been witness to this incident. She tentatively reached for the pendant; it was ice cold to the touch. She didn't want it, felt filthy for even touching it but a sensible part of her felt that if she were to recount this story again, she would need proof. With the tips of her shaking forefinger and thumb she dropped the icy object into her pocket. Her relief was replaced by a great wave of sadness as IT's words echoed over and over her mind. Thoughts whirled in her head, faster and faster, they became jumbled and nonsensical, her head began to throb, the pressure too much. Then everything around her became grey then black, the pressure became too much to bear, and then there was nothing.

Chapter Twenty Five

"Thank you so much," Dad was saying as he closed the front door Mum came to at that point and looked around disorientated. She was uncertain of where she was and for one horrible moment she thought she was still at the station.

Dad came into the living room his brow furrowed in concern.

"You're awake" he said,

"How are you feeling?"

The events of the afternoon came back to her and she could feel the blood draining from her face,

"Max, something awful has happened" she whispered,

"Shush, Gabrielle, you need to rest, we can talk about it later"

She sat up and felt dizziness take her again, so reluctantly she lay down,

"How did I get home, I don't remember?"

"You passed out, some passers-by's got you a taxi, I've just seen them off."

The worry returned to his face again "you look really bad Gabrielle; I think I'll call a doctor."

"No, Max I'll be fine, just give me a moment" she sighed. Until she gathered her thoughts and made sense of today, the last thing she needed was a doctor.

"I've called Mum, she says you are to call her a soon as you're fit"

She nodded.

"I'll just get you a drink" he turned to towards the kitchen,

Suddenly remembering her daughters, panic clutched her heart,

"Max, where are the girls?"

"Alison and Maxine are next door and Jayne's in bed."

They were safe that was the main thing, but she needed to be sure.

"Max I need to see them, now" she insisted,

"Gabrielle you will, I just want to make sure you feel better, I'll get you that drink eh? Get some colour back in your cheeks, you're so pale"

Later that evening Alison and Maxine came home. Mum hugged them and held them to her with more enthusiasm than they expected, for she reports that they looked at her like an alien had replaced their mother. They played a few games before Dad took them upstairs for bed.

When they were settled Max sat down in the living room,

"Max something happened" clearing her throat to prevent her voice from faltering she continued,

"I didn't just faint."

He tried to put her off the topic, concerned that she wasn't yet well enough. This time she was adamant, he was going to listen to her recount the day's events.

When she had finished, Dad sat there stunned, but he didn't dismiss her account, instead he said,

"Gabrielle how many times have I told you never to make eye contact with strangers?"

Thank heavens, he believed her, or so she thought when he said, "you've just seen someone that looked a bit different, that's all."

"Max go to my coat," she said "look in my pocket - maybe then you'll know I wasn't just seeing something strange"

He put his hand in her pocket and pulled the green object out; he looked horrified, and dropped it as if it was dynamite.

"Where did you get this?" he demanded, raising his voice to a level Mum had never heard him reach before. Dad was a gentle man, would do anything rather than fight or raise his voice, his reaction was completely out of character and it scared Mum.

"Max I told you, IT left it behind"

"I want it out, out of this house now" he shouted, storming out the door.

It was at least fifteen minutes before he came home, and when he did he hugged Mum and said,

"Gabrielle it's gone, don't worry anymore and I'm sorry for shouting"

"Its okay" relieved that his anger had dispersed.

"Gabrielle if you could do just one thing for me?"

"Of course" she nodded,

"Pray". He said grimly.

My Dad wasn't usually a religious man, he tended to veer on the side of reason but by the look on his face Mum knew not to question him, instead she simply nodded.

Chapter Twenty Six

January 17th 1980

A few years ago I became very ill. I remember sitting in the living room struggling so hard to breathe that I passed out. In the moments before consciousness evaded me, I will never forget the despair and panic that I felt. No matter how hard I tried I just couldn't get back to me. I felt completely detached from my body as I watched my family frantically waiting for the ambulance. I was utterly sure that I was going to die and all I could think of was how I would never see these people, people that I loved so much again. I wouldn't get a chance to say goodbye. Although in the end I pulled through it was nevertheless a horrendous experience. I felt so alone.

On the 17th of January 1980, my Dad was to make his final journey, he made this journey alone. Often I torture myself by trying to see it through his eyes. I know that he was dressed in a heavy winter coat that day. I know that he hated the cold so much so, that he was known to grumble that even the bulkiest of coats offered him little protection from the elements. I know that he had wanted to bring my sister Maxine on his journey with him; he tried to involve his daughters in his life as much as possible. If he ever worked away from the office he always tried to bring one of his girls along. On this particular day my sister was recovering from a chest infection and my Mum, ever the nurse refused to let her accompany him. Disappointed though my sister was, Mum's refusal saved her life.

Dad boarded the Ballymena train; he arrived early and felt that he was making great progress on his audit. So much so, that he felt he could complete the entire audit that day. He called my Mum and told her that he would be home late, that he hoped to be back in time to say good night to his children. Mum's last words to him were

"I'll keep your dinner warm".

He boarded the train that evening for the return journey to Belfast; I imagine he was relieved, as he just made the train and no more, boarding with only seconds to spare. When he sat down he would have read his paper from cover to cover, he always read a paper on his journeys.

Perhaps he even turned his mind to Nigeria, something he always spoke of when the winter was in full force. Dad had grown up bathed in sunshine and had flourished under the acrid Nigerian sun. He wanted us, his girls to experience this too. He passionately wanted us to feel the heat of the ground beneath our feet and the sun caressing our faces. The cold, the winter was no life for anyone and certainly not his precious daughters.

My parents had discussed relocating; they had spent many evenings deciding on where they would live and where the girls would fulfil their childhoods. Dad had mentioned Nigeria and Mum had agreed that maybe the girls would be better off based there. It would be difficult for them growing up here. They would always stand out, be the different ones. Dad frequently maintained that he had chosen this life, he came here fully aware that he would not easily blend in with the crowds. His daughters hadn't been given a choice and he wanted them to have one. If we wanted to move further afield when we were older, then that was up to us, but while we were little he wanted us to escape the stares and the remarks. He wanted us to have a full childhood, where we would be normal and where we could be ourselves.

My Dad had never planned on staying in this strange land, but life doesn't always go to plan and he had met my Mum. In meeting her she had given him three wonderful children and just when he thought that this cold dreary place would never accept him, she had given him a new family. Mum's family had extended their arms to welcome him into their fold. In meeting him, these people had ventured into the unknown, hesitantly at first but had gone on to extend their arms and let him into their lives. The thought of his new family and how loved he felt never ceased to amaze him.

Mum and Dad planned to trial Nigeria for a year; they would let out their Belfast home, so that if all else failed they would have somewhere to return to. Dad had told Mum that Nigeria was so very different, that she may not adjust to life there and its ways, but Mum shrugged it off saying, if she could adjust to Belfast and its bombs and bullets she could adjust to anywhere.

....
....

Dad was seen rubbing the steam off the window and peering out. All he would have seen was darkness as it was pitch black outside. No landmarks to advise him of his location would have been visible. Even though two men had just boarded and sat beside him for some reason he didn't ask them for his location. Perhaps they were caught up, distracted by their own affairs, maybe he didn't want to interrupt them. Instead Dad spotted a passing conductor and stopped him,

"Excuse Me sir"

The man appraised my Dad and smiled,

"How can I help?"

"Will we reach Belfast soon?"

"Hmm" he looked at his watch, "aye, we will indeed, I'd say in approximately ten – fifteen minutes"

"Is that all? Great, thank you" Dad returned his smile

"No probs mate" the conductor said and made his way out of the carriage.

As Dad started to prepare himself for the hitting the dreaded ice wall he would face when he left the warm carriage, a deafening bang shook everything around him. He would have been immersed in blinding light and searing heat.

His ears would have been ringing; if he looked around to find the source he would have seen nothing but smoke and flames. By this stage the momentum of the train had stopped as the emergency brakes were pressed.

He was said to have flailed around trying to breathe but the pungent, smoky air would have served no purpose but to scorch his lungs. If he peered through the smoke he would have seen the chair opposite him in flames. He would have seen his legs engulfed in flames, flames that were reported to be white, then blue. "Please God, help me" he had screamed, his voice rasping against the white hot smoke. Those who had managed to get off the train heard his screams; they were the last sounds my Dad made.

....

....

Meanwhile at home Mum was just about to watch the TV, cup of tea in hand when a loud bang caused the house to shake. She immediately deduced that another bomb had gone off. This one must have been nearby; very rarely did the house actually shake. Moments later sirens blared followed by the distinctive rumbles of helicopters, going by their vibrations they right overhead. Curious Mum opened the back door to see if she could see them. She remembers never having seen helicopters fly so low before; they illuminated the dark sky, turning it an eerie blue as their huge search lights swept back and forth across the area.

Retreating back indoors, she started to think of what was nearby, what could have been destroyed this time? Nothing occurred to her. Five minutes later it did; the train line.

She turned up the news and awaited the customary newsflash that followed every loud noise in Belfast. Sure enough an announcement came through.

"News just in" the newscaster Gloria Hunniford read, "a bomb has exploded in a Belfast bound train on the Dunmurray line" Mum's tea dropped and spread all over the carpet, luckily it just missed the girls.

She looked at the time, it was now seven.

Max should be home.

She rang her mother, "Hi Gabrielle, I was just chatting about you…."

"Mum, a bomb was on a train, Max was on a train and he's not home, there was a bomb, Max isn't here" she frantically, incoherently tried to rely what she knew.

"Gabrielle, he said he would be late didn't he?"' slightly reassured Mum agreed, "We'll be up now" her mother said.

Mum took out the ironing board and began to iron, more news came in as she did so, casualties, fatalities, IRA, she heard it all, but kept on ironing.

She must have ironed for a long time, because her mother and father, grandmother and sisters were suddenly in the house. They lived two hours away.

Chapter Twenty Seven

In theory I was there but in practice I was too young to remember and I thank God for that. However, I did not escape from the events of that night in January 1980. The accounts of that night have been retold so many times that they are like the stuff of fable in mine and my sisters histories. Every year from Christmas to the 17th of January, Mum walks us through the chronicle of events leading to and the aftermath of my Dad's death using her illustrious flair. She needed to tell someone I suppose and in the absence of any form of therapy who better to tell than the only people she was left with? Her daughters.

That night has become a tangible part of Mum, the events relived so many times that they are as solid and real as I am. It is a night she will never forget; she will take it with her to her grave. For my sisters and me, it is likely that we will too.

That night as recounted to me:

Very quickly the house became full. Someone led the girls upstairs. Despite the news and despite her packed house all Mum could do was iron. Her father was glued to the TV and radio news. Cups clattered in the kitchen, the smell of stewed tea permeated the air, hushed chatter encircled her yet she continued to iron; she ironed for hours.

A loud knock silenced the room momentarily. Everyone was eager for news, for some clarification or better still for Max to return. Two men came in they identified themselves as CID. They needed to speak to Mum. Her parents stayed by her side and the room emptied. The men were hostile and standoffish their stern faces emitting waves of distrust.

"We have reason to believe that your husband Mr Olorunda, was travelling on a Belfast bound train this evening? As you are no doubt aware there was an explosion on a train, which we believe to have been a bomb."

"Passengers have identified your husband as having been in the carriage where the bomb is suspected to have detonated from"

The other man interjected,

"Why was your husband travelling on the train?"

They continued questioning and as they did they outlined the reasons for their suspicions,

"Somehow, someone who we believe to be the bomber escaped. It is imperative that you tell us why was your husband was on the train?"

Before Gabrielle could even reply her father was on his feet and threw the men out.

The night continued much like before, with countless people coming and going and all eyes on Mum. At 5.30 am the RUC broke the night's morbid routine, this time confirming that Max had indeed died on the train. Mum's eyes were drawn to her mother who was sitting on the couch. She was gently breaking the news to the utterly bewildered children...

"Daddy had to go to heaven" she heard her saying, her strong mother was struggling to hold back tears.

"God needed him really quickly and he had to go with him tonight. He told me to tell you that he didn't get time to say goodbye."

Three sets of mournful eyes searched her face; Alison's little face was a picture of absolute bleakness, for she understood her Grandmother's words and was slowly realising that her beloved Daddy was dead.

After that reality came and went for Mum, the only thing she is certain of was that the milk man called. By this stage she was no longer ironing so she answered the door to him. Bizarrely amidst all that was going on, she recalls telling him that her husband had just died and could he leave a full crate of milk. Apparently the milk man looked at her utterly perplexed.

Chapter Twenty Eight

In true Catholic tradition a wake was held. Over the next few days, people were reputed to have come from far and wide, politicians, journalists, colleagues, family, friends and neighbours; all keen to pay their condolences. Even Dad's brother finally managed to get some leave and made the journey across the water from Edinburgh to pay his respects.

When the full story of events emerged, it turned out that my Dad's train had been bombed by the IRA. Two bombers had sat down opposite him with a bomb, the bomb had gone off killing two innocents; my Dad and a teenage school boy. One of the bombers was also killed. It transpired that indeed someone had run from the train, the second bomber. They had of course found him and quickly established that he had carried the bomb with his cohort.

His accomplice had died at the scene.

Soon after his escape the surviving bomber collapsed, so severe were his injuries. He had been horrifically burnt in the bomb. He was sent to hospital and his recovery was doubtful.

The CID men, now clear on the sequence of events called to the wake and apologised to mum and her parents. The runaway bomber explained why they were so hostile when they first came and why searchlights had illuminated the sky immediately after the bomb.

As news of the bomb spread, tributes came from far and wide, the bombers were condemned. Conservative MP Winston Churchill appalled by the attack said,

"The fact is that innocent people are dead and the Provisional IRA is responsible, as they have been on hundreds of other occasions. Once again they stand condemned in the eyes of the civilized world."

Even the Catholic Church expressed its disapproval by refusing to allow the bombers remains to be placed in consecrated grounds.

The IRA released a long statement stating;

"The explosion occurred prematurely and the intended target was not the civilians travelling on the train. We always take the most stringent precautions to ensure the safety of all civilians in the vicinity of a military or commercial bombing operation. The bombing mission on Thursday night was not an exception to this principle. Unfortunately the unexpected is not something we can predict or prevent in the war situation this country is in, the consequences of the unexpected are often grave and distressing, as Thursday nights accident shows. Our sorrow at losing a young married man, Kevin Delaney is heightened by the additional deaths of Mr Olorunda and Mark Cochrane. To all their bereaved families we offer our dearest and heartfelt sympathy."

Despite their dearest and heartfelt sympathy, it was reported back to my family that in a pub, in the Markets area of Belfast (a known IRA enclave and coincidentally the then home to the bombers) that jubilant toasts were being raised. For not only had the bomb been a success, it had also been high profile and best of all, they had got a *'Niger'*.

Dad's coffin was sealed and later it would be revealed that the reason behind this was that so little of him remained. They had to identify him through his dental records. Mum sat with the coffin every second that it remained in the house. Now and again she would drift off and every time she woke she reached out to touch of remained of her husband and instead felt only lifeless hard wood. She did this so often that it became an automatic reflex, a reflex that stays with her today.

As she sat there she remembers hearing alien noises, agonised guttural moans. When she looked to find their source she was horrified to find that they were coming from her. Dad was buried in Mum's home town Strabane. Apparently there was a high presence of media and press covering the funeral yet she was not aware. The only residual memory she has of that day was that

Alison was by her side, repeating over and over through her tears, "I'll look after you mummy".

As they lowered Dad into his final resting place Mum collapsed, her life force ebbing away. Her guides no longer able to hold her weight such was the force of their own despair momentarily released her. Her day was to become the stuff of nightmares as she recounts falling forward into the dark wet place, down, down and down until she was laying on the coffin. She had fallen into the grave and she didn't have strength or inclination to even attempt to get out. She remembers thinking, "just bury me too."

Part Three

Tales from my childhood

Chapter Twenty Nine

When I was younger an old lady enquired about my Dad, when I told her that he had died she said "Sure what you don't have you'll never miss". That annoyed me. Does a starving child who doesn't have food not miss it? Does a draught ridden country not miss rain? Or even a bankrupt not miss having money? In losing Dad my family lost our link to Nigeria, half of our roots. My sisters and I became mixed race girls who were brought up in a world of only one race. Identity problems throughout childhood and into later damaged us all. The one person who could have helped us had been taken away.

The bomb meant that we didn't just loose a Dad and any identity we could have wished to have, but we also lost our Mum. Mum was still there in body but her mind was far, far away. Sometimes she came back to us, but when she did realisation of her situation hit her again and she retreated back into herself away from the here and now and away from us. So when someone tells me what I don't have I'll never miss I know they are wrong. I miss my Dad and what he could have taught me and most of all from an early age I missed my Mum. The implication of having no Dad and a shadow of a Mum blighted all our lives and perhaps affected the people we all became.

In the years immediately following Dad's death Mum never got a chance to quietly grieve. She was to go through the ordeal of a public court case which revealed all the gory details of the murder. It was in these early days that Mum was to realise that her life would never be the same again. For years after bombing different aspects of it regularly appeared in the papers and the news, constantly reinforcing to Mum that there could be no escape.

Mum doesn't remember much of the first year after Dad died, she describes these times as being simply blackness, a deep waking sleep in which events unfolded around her that she could only watch from a distant place in her mind. It was as if in that distant place she found a safe harbour somewhere she could frequent often when she felt the necessity.

I was very young, no more than preschool age when I first sensed something was very wrong in the house. I just knew that something was amiss; I could feel it in the air. On the days when I felt this, Mum would take to her bed where she could remain for weeks at a time. As I grew older I realised that the thing I sensed was very real, it was Mum's friend who I later dubbed 'Misery'.

In the early years Misery's arrival was triggered by the court case and details surrounding my Dad's death. In the future a bomb, a shooting, even a bomb scare dragged Misery back to our home and initiated Mum's confinement again.

I always felt it was easier for the prisoners, the murderers. They had a release date they could serve their time and move on. The victims could not. Each event, each death and subsequent televised funeral, right through to the emergence of the Historical Enquires Team and the Peace Process was to send Mum back to her own ordeal, to open the door and allow Misery in again. Now we know that many of the victims suffered from the condition of post-traumatic stress, but it was only in recent years that Northern Ireland's victims and survivors were deemed worthy of the disorder. Had this been addressed and treated early maybe things could have been different for my family and so many others.

I don't remember the court case but I have listened to my Mum's accounts of it and researched what I could find in the press archives. I do however remember Mum smashing cups and plates against the gable wall. I'm not an expert on grief but between spending days in bed and smashing plates surely someone must have noticed that this behaviour, especially after three or four years wasn't normal.

No one ever did.

When the court case was over and compensation dished out Northern Ireland washed its hands of my Mum and by doing so us. Nowadays when someone is murdered it is about more than compensation, grief therapy is offered to family members and they are counselled through it. Back then however Mum was left to rot; "You are a young woman with a profession" the judge had said. In other words get back to work and get on with it.

If only things were that easy.

Chapter Thirty

During the next year my family saw many changes. We were moved to Mum's home town of Strabane immediately after the death. Mum's parents had sold and packed up the Belfast home and moved her back to theirs. This was a time when she couldn't be alone, she would need their support. Alison was enrolled in the local school and the bedrooms doubled up to accommodate us. Only now Mum wasn't a child, this time she had three small children in tow. This time she was a mother, she was twenty eight years of age and she was widowed. She had unwittingly, through no fault of her own, become a single parent.

By this stage Mum had become well and truly acquainted with Misery; they were inseparable. Misery's friendship was all consuming. They spent all their time together and performed every task together even when it came to us. Mum performed her duties in a perfunctory manner her eyes blank and lifeless, she was always somewhere else. She had surrendered her body and spirit and let Misery take her away, away from the coffin, away from the grave and away from the pain. Misery was a clingy friend constantly clutching and grasping at Mum, she liked to keep her close and away from us. Yet now and again they became separated and Mum was granted tiny moments of reprieve. During these moments, when Misery loosened her grasp ever so slightly, Mum would wonder where Dad was, for she knew he would never leave her. Mum believed love didn't die, that it was eternal. Dad had been so alive, full of ideas and plans for his wife and his girls that he couldn't just vanish; he had to be somewhere. But when she looked for him, when she futilely tried to find him, Misery reached out her hand and Mum grasped. Misery was her friend now, she understood.

I'm told that Mum's friend Ann travelled from Belfast to see her once. She hugged Mum and they both cried. The last time they had hugged was on her wedding day. Misery joined them both that day making a grasp at Ann too, for as she cried she talked of her sorrows, about her fears for Mum and how would she cope.

Ann's sobbing was uncontrollable; Mum couldn't discern a word she was saying until she composed herself controlling her tears.

"Gabrielle, I saw this you know, that night when I read your tealeaves, I saw that something bad, something really bad was going to happen"

Sobbing again she wondered aloud,

"If only I had of said something rather than running off. Oh Gabrielle, please forgive me, I'm so sorry."

Mum stopped her as she was reminded of the woman in green that she had met the day before Dad's death. She knew that many would not believe the incident, too many people were sceptics, but Ann was open minded, she would at least believe. Mum recounted every detail she could remember to a silent Ann.

Before they could say anymore or try and analysis the visit her mother came in and all conversation ended. Yet a seed of doubt had been planted and in Mum's more lucid moments and indeed until this day she often thought that it was too coincidental to have seen that thing, to have been told those words and then have her husband murdered. Mum still maintains that Dad shouldn't have been on that train, what if IT had made him finish his audit in one day; witnesses say he had just made the train before it took off. A matter of mere seconds had sealed my Dad's fate. What if those few seconds, seconds that delayed the trains' departure, had been caused by a more powerful force? Had IT somehow engineered for Dad to be on that train.

Mum was assailed by anguish. Her thoughts turned to us girls, by losing our father, we too had been cursed. That creature had certainly achieved its goals, IT had been teasing her choosing it's location well, for IT knew Dad would die on a train.

Chapter Thirty One

As always when a murderer is found he or she is brought to some sort of justice, usually by trial. The surviving bomber was no exception. Mum the innocent party was put through the ordeal of a trial and facing the man who was responsible for her husband's death.

The man had proudly admitted his crime and was now to face trial. Over the next year Mum would be dragged to Belfast over and over again; they always insisted she came. It would bring closure they told her.

For Mum no trial would change the facts. Her husband was gone; nothing would bring him back. In the meantime she had no home of her own, three small children and to all intents and purpose was dead inside. To prove she was alive that she hadn't joined a league of the living dead, Mum began a process that would last throughout my childhood, the smashing of plates (and every piece of china she could see). She hurled each one into her parents' garden, letting it smash to smithereens. I imagine that she found something therapeutic in this, for her life resembled those broken shards of china. Her life was shattered and beyond repair and like the china it would never be put together again.

On the day of the court case Mum didn't anticipate that it would actually be held. The surviving bomber, the escapee had been severely burned. He was too ill to stand trial, which meant that so far each date that was set had been cancelled. Mum was made to prepare for court; they would drive all the way to Belfast, only to find that the bomber was still too ill. She didn't expect this particular day to be any different. Yet her father as always insisted that they drove to Belfast anyway, as it may just be the day that justice would be served. On this occasion he was right.

On this day the court case was not postponed, she would now see the man who blown her husband up and destroyed our family. She recalls not being prepared for this; it was something she could never have been prepared for. She made her way into the court room accompanied by family, friends and press and waited for Mr Flynn to be placed in the dock.

I don't like to think that I'm opinionated but when it comes to some of the verdicts administered in Northern Ireland for terrorist cases I am ashamed to find that I am. I have always found it difficult to reconcile the outcome of my Dad's court case with my sense of right and wrong. The bomber was not armed for any other reason but to take life, the bomb was meant for someone should it have been my Dad or someone else. I am no judge nor do I have any right to judge any other human being. Yet I do not understand how anyone found guilty of any terrorist atrocity or any activity that steals life for that matter, can be given such light sentences and even worse serve so little of them. Northern Ireland's justice over the years had caused great controversy with many terrorists serving sentences that do not reflect the gravity of their deeds, even worse in the post Good Friday Agreement those who were still incarcerated simply walked free. I am sure my family weren't the first to suffer from our judicial system it is something that all the victims simply had to accept. No one listened to them.

Mum's description of the trial never fails to upset me. She tells me that her little gathering seemed pathetic when compared to the bombers huge gathering of support. She remembers feeling afraid and intimidated when she realised that so many of his friends and family had come to support him. To them he was a hero. Incidents like this did not help my Mum's future prognosis and I can easily see how Misery took her hold. It must have been difficult for her to understand why people seemed to be celebrating her husband's death, could they not see that by murdering my Dad and a teenage boy that they had achieved nothing?

Mum remembers Mr Flynn's entrance being announced, the old doors of the now derelict Crumlin Road court house rumbling and groaning as they spat him out accompanied by two guards. His appearance was to send an audible gasp around the court room; low murmurs from spectators filled the air until the judge silenced them all with one swoop of his gavel.

Mr Flynn was small, shrunken and every visible piece of flesh was distorted. His body was wrinkled and gnarled, proving his burns had been severe. Mum knew his appearance would illicit sympathy, and became angry. He was alive, no matter what he looked like, he was alive. He had taken life yet he kept his. I believe that Mum was joined by a new friend that day, a louder more forceful friend than Misery. That day she was introduced to Anger.

Anger was aggressive and intent on destruction, Anger knew Mum was faced with the man who had destroyed her friend's life, the man who had left three little girls lives changed forever. Anger like any loyal friend not only stood by Mum, she did more than that, and she positively exceeded herself. She took control of the whole situation and possessed Mum's body, telling her that this man took innocence he preyed on all that was pure. Anger told her that this man had marks on his face that matched his soul. He was a murderer and all could see. Forever anyone who enquired about his appearance would learn what he had done and Mum was glad.

Anger now in total control of Mum's movements and thoughts, steered her and even spoke through her so that together they could attack. Anger wanted this man dead, wanted this man in the ground where he belonged and Anger would stop at nothing until she had succeeded.

Mum's family tried and failed to restrain her, it took two policemen to hold her now seven stone frame back and prevent her and Anger from achieving their goal. When they finally restrained and captured Mum she was led out. As she was escorted from the courthouse, Anger left her and her friend Misery was to return. They clung to each other and they shook and cried. A kindly policewoman sat with them in a small bleak room, until justice had been served.

Back them Mum wanted him locked away, shut away from humanity forever. I am thankful that Britain no longer sanctioned corporal punishment because I know Mum would have wanted to the kick the box beneath the gallows. Luckily her father did not share her opinion. Whilst she waited in the little waiting room; her father had taken to the stand and was pleading for leniency. He felt that this man, this murderer had suffered enough. He did not see how a tough sentence would bring his son in law back. Mum had always loved that her father was a man of peace, yet on this day for the first time in her life she took exception to those feelings.

Whether her father's pleas were heard or not remains unclear yet the judge Mr Justice Kelly obviously had similar thoughts as he awarded Mr Flynn's sentence, he was given just ten years for each manslaughter and seven years for the use of explosive devises to be served concurrently, the judge stating,

"I am satisfied beyond reasonable doubt you were one of the bombers. I am satisfied you and your associates did not intend to kill. Nevertheless, the explosion and fire caused the death of three people in most horrific circumstances. In sentencing you I am conscious you have suffered severe burns and scars, for the rest of your life which will be a grim reminder to you of the events of that day"

Misery was heaved aside by Anger, ten years for each life it didn't seem fair. In ten years from now the children would still be in school and wouldn't have their Dad. What about their secondary school days, their university days and their marriages; they would have no Dad for these days. To add insult to injury Mum knew that most prisoners never served their full sentences; back then Northern Ireland's jails were so full that most served just under half.

From that day on Mum had two friends fighting for her attention Anger and Misery; Anger had the loudest voice so in the main she won out. Little did Mum know that half a sentence was optimistic as a mere six years later Mr Flynn was released. Three years for each life he had taken.

Chapter Thirty Two

I am like Mum in the sense that I like to know the full story, to always glean the entire picture, regardless of what it entails. After the court case Mum met with her solicitor on many occasions and on each one demanded access to the unabridged details of the case. She had not been privy to these during the trial. The judge had deemed that the graphic details of Dad's death would be too upsetting, so she was removed from the courtroom when talks of the blast itself, witness accounts and identification began. Mum felt that she needed to know, she incessantly probed her father as it was he who had identified Dad's body on the ill-fated night. Yet he never released any information, not even to his wife. Many years later when Mum's father passed away he brought what he saw on that night, the 17th of January 1980 with him.

In her father's refusal to administer any information Mum had to press her solicitor for it. He warned her that it was graphic. The full extent of the bomb and its damage were held in a file that he was reluctant to release. Mum ignored his warning and eagerly took the file. She had to know what became of her husband; she had to know how he spent the last moments of his life.

Soon she did know, the transcripts held all the gory details. Two men had boarded the train carrying a bomb. They had sat opposite Dad and had intended to take the bomb to central station Belfast. No one could explain what had gone wrong, but something clearly had, so much so that thirty one years later the Historical Enquiries Team requested to reopen the case. The bomb had denoted prematurely, killing one of the bombers and almost fatally wounding the other. My Dad, a man from another land and a little boy returning home from school were simply their innocent victims. The little boy was a promising student with his whole life ahead of him.

As Mum read further she found the post mortem details. It was then that she ascertained exactly how her husband and my Dad had spent his final moments. She already knew that Dad had died alone, no loved ones surrounding him; not even a word from a kind stranger. In his last moments my Dad had been plunged into a living hell. After asking the conductor about his location, the conductor had closed the carriage door and almost immediately the bomb had detonated. A ball of flames engulfed the carriage and of course those in it. Those in the surrounding carriages managed to run, to gain safety in the grass verges on either side.

Dad and his fellow travellers had not been so lucky, for the blaze had come with such force that it caught each of them instantaneously, burning was unavoidable. Eye witnesses could hear someone screaming and tried as they may to get close to the carriage to help, the immense heat held them all back. Instead they listened as one man called out "Dear God Help me," they listened and listened until his cries melted with him into the train, into the night.

Firemen who approached the carriage were unable to help for they too could not tackle the flames, they were so ferocious. One of them attempted to climb aboard to answer the man's cries. He described what he had seen, *a man matching Dad's description, literally burning alive.* His legs were gone by now, yet consciousness remained. When the heat began to disperse the fire-fighters were able to board the carriage. All that remained where Dad had been was a heap of ashes. The brave fire-fighter who had tried in vain to help left the service shortly after.

Mum never willingly told me these details; I had to probe her just like she had to probe her father for them. I was always told that all I needed to know was that my Dad's coffin was empty; visiting the grave was a waste of time. It was not until three years ago when the 'Belfast Telegraph' opened its archives up that I was able to request all the details of my Dad's death, once I had gotten them I was able to ask Mum to confirm if this was what she knew. All she said was that her husband had suffered a death worse than any she could ever imagine.

From my own investigation I know he died a hellish death, it was as if he had encountered the fires of hell right here on earth. My Dad had hated the smell of burning I wonder if his fleeing the room when Mum had cut our hair was an unconscious premonition, either way he must have been so afraid. The 'Belfast Telegraph' reports made it clear to me why dental records were required in the identification process, why the CID called that night. They had no evidence; the two innocents in the carriage were reduced to nothing, it was impossible to tell one heap from the other. The bomber too had been obliterated. All they had known was that someone had run from the carriage but they had no way of telling who.

It dawned on me why the coffin was sealed, why Mum maintained the grave was empty; for she had buried nothing, nothing remained to bury. We never visit the grave instead we simply pray for his soul.

Understandably Mum could not process the details she found held in that solicitors file; not consciously anyway. Instead her dreams processed every intricate detail, dissecting and putting together her husband's last moments in that flaming carriage. In her waking hours she knew that if she dwelled on these details she would throw herself into a trap that she would never come out of. She had to put them out of her daily thoughts so she ripped up the transcripts, smashed some more cups and put the details of the death of the kindest man she had ever known in a box and stacked it on her shelf.

Chapter Thirty Three

Unbeknownst to my younger self my Dad's life was valued by the courts. They sought to put a price on the worth of a Dad and how much his widow and children should receive. The absence of my Dad's involvement in my sisters and my childhood was valued at £2000, which we would each receive when we were eighteen. For my Mum a life as a single mother was valued at five years of my Dad's salary. Maybe it was naivety on the Northern Ireland's office part that made them believe that someone could recover from such an event in five years; however I think it was a gross oversight.

It seemed to me that despite losing our Dad, Northern Ireland felt it was right that we should lose our Mum too; for from as early as I could remember my Mum worked and worked and then worked some more. Christmases' came and went, birthdays came and went and throughout it all Mum worked. She had hoped to spend our formative years with us, she had hoped to return to nursing when we were of secondary school age; instead she was sent back prematurely and I believe before she had a chance to fully recover. By the courts reckoning when I was aged just six, my sisters eight and eleven Mum should be able to support us on her own and worse that my Dad's influence was no longer valid.

One of my earliest memories is crying when Mum went out the door to work, begging her to stay at home, I couldn't fathom for the life of me why my Mum worked when everyone else's Mum was at home. My sisters would panic, Mum reports that the mention of work terrified them; their Dad had gone to work and not come back, what if this happened to their Mum too? It took years before they were completely reassured. Mum worked seven twelve hour day shifts, followed by seven twelve hour night shifts. These were broken with two or three days off. I remember her crying too, as she explained to me she didn't want to go, she had no choice. Mum had thought she had said goodbye to her nursing career for the foreseeable future but instead she had said goodbye to her husband and hello to feeding and clothing us alone; to single parenthood.

Unfortunately, my parent's reasonably new mortgage on the Belfast house meant that there was no collateral to speak of; just enough to cover the funeral and our move. My grandparent's house with us in it was full to overflowing, they couldn't afford four more mouths to feed and besides this they needed their crockery; they hadn't realised that when they brought their Irish daughter home that she would have developed Greek tendencies and smash every plate in their house!

The result was that whether she felt prepared or not Mum would have to start regaining some semblance of normality. She says she often mused whether God had taken the right parent, she did not think she was capable of raising three young children alone. She didn't want to let them down. Yet she did her best to rise to the challenge, beginning with buying a house.

Buying the little bungalow meant that my family were now firmly ensconced in Strabane. Mum had reluctantly laid roots there, roots that gave her some sense of attachment and somewhere to call home. She used the courts allocation of five years of Dad's salary against the house and retained some for its furnishing and decoration. This time though Mum took no pleasure in making the house a home, she did it mechanically; simply because it needed to be done.

Mum felt that her mother and father also deserved compensation; they had lived through the whole ordeal with her and I imagine without them she would never have coped. She gave them a little money, not nearly enough for all they had done but something to recognise their support. She bought a car that I remember even now; a little red mini. By Mum's calculations we should be okay for a year, maybe a year and a half if she was sensible with what little remained.

Mum should have known that things don't always go to plan, for as is customary in life when people have money they are sought after. It is shameful to think that even a new widow is a target. Some acquaintances needed a deposit for their first marital home, a friend was in debt and needed help, and on and on it went until we were left with nothing. Of course Mum had been reassured that she would be paid back but as life goes this was not the case. Promises of repayment never were honoured and she was too proud to ask for it back.

Chapter Thirty Four

In those bleak days the main things that fuelled Mum carry on, to sustain her empty shell with nutrition and breath, her children and the need for answers. The physical debris of the bomb that had taken my Dad may have been cleared away. The scene was made neat and sanitised, but the debris that remained of Mum's shattered life could not be cleared so quickly.

Mum was compelled to find answers; she needed to know what drove one man to kill another, why something as precious as life became meaningless and why they felt the need to take it. To discover the answers she would have to meet the murderer. I know now that Mum's pleading to allow such a meeting fell on deaf ears for a reason, she was not ready to meet the bomber; she wouldn't be for years.

Mum wrote weekly to the Maze prison, pleading with the governor to let her meet the man who had unflinchingly ruined her life. Each letter had the same response, the governor writing to her personally, sympathising with her plight but dissuading her from any sort of visit. It would be a waste he would say, for the culprit, the man who killed my Dad felt no remorse. I am grateful to that governor, I am grateful that he refused access to Mum. In later years she would meet the man who caused her nightmares but by then I would be old enough to intervene.

In the aftermath of Dad's death the priest would call to Mum's home frequently. He could never answer the only question she ever asked him; "Why?" Instead he would pray with her and utter clichés about God's master plan. Mum would interrupt his prayers and ask him to help her to arrange to meet the man they had held for the crime; he always said no. Mum lost any fragile religious beliefs she had felt until that point. If it wasn't for my grandparents influence my Catholic upbringing would never have come to fruition. Mum remembers what she viewed as the priests 'platitudes' being so pathetic that she chased him and his banality away.

Instead of religion, family or friends Mum was to rely on her one true confidante for the proceeding years; Misery, she was the only one Mum needed. I would never say that Mum neglected us for she was a good Mum, we became her life. Nothing outside her three daughters mattered, except Misery. I believe that the events of Dad's death and their aftermath changed my Mum, changed her very being, so much so that a depression set in and in the absence of any treatment it festered within her. It made her mistrustful of others, bitter and eventually many years later very ill.

My sister and I in adulthood have often discussed why no one helped, why no support was offered and we were left alone. We will never get our answers but had someone, anyone helped, they could have saved us from so much. Instead every so often Misery visited our house. When she did it became a dark, quiet place where we were afraid to move, we became self-sufficient during Misery's visits and looked after ourselves and our Mum. But Northern Ireland had done all it was going to do for us. As far as it was concerned the quandary of the fragmented Olorunda family was resolved.

Chapter Thirty Five

I don't remember much of my childhood, portions of it comes to me in flashes, in little snippets. It was as if our Mum's sadness eclipsed everything, yet the happy times we had enabled me to bury the difficult. Sometimes when I recall certain details I chastise myself, why didn't I see that something wasn't right? How did I miss such obvious symptoms? My only answer, the only thing that can pacify me is the fact that I was a child; I thought these things were normal.

The crockery smashing was one thing that continued in my early years. I remember her standing at the door and throwing plates at the gable wall swearing and muttering under her breath. I remember throughout my childhood being woken up in the middle of the night by the sound of furniture moving. We had an open staircase in that first house and I used to lie across the top stair and peer through to the living room. I would see Mum pushing chairs, cabinets and rearranging ornaments. When we would come down in the morning Mum would be either in bed or work and the rooms would be changed around. Usually she changed them back again the following night. Most of all I remember the tears; Mum didn't know we could hear but we could, she used to cry and cry, looking back now it is no wonder.

I remember that our cupboards tended to be bare. Mum would get cross at us if we wasted even the smallest morsel of food. One day she made stew, my least favourite meal as a child. I refused point blank to finish it or even eat a mouth full for that matter. I was told that I couldn't leave the table until my plate was cleared. I sat at the table until the small hand on the clock reached eleven and the big hand reached twelve. I woke up in bed; Mum must have let me escape that time. After that eating what was on offer became a battle of wills, for I freely admit I was not an easy child!

When Mum was at work I would go out and wreak havoc, I roamed the streets looking for trouble. On one occasion I remember throwing crab apples at a nasty old ladies window. I thought she deserved it because she had called me a 'black bastard'. I knew she didn't deserve it when the following day she burst into our kitchen and began to shout at Mum who had assumed I was doing my homework at the time of the incident.

A few weeks later I pushed a child in my class and knocked her front teeth out, again I thought she deserved it until my Mum was given a solicitors letter. My next incident involved shouting obscenities at a work man putting up a neighbour's wall; he had seen a black soldier and pointed him out to me as my cousin. I was incandescent and through the choice language I levelled at him I let him know. That night he came to our door.

I was eight years old, a tomboy and considered myself fearless that was until my Mum was to one day explode at my antics. She had had enough. I came home from school expecting her to be in her bed to find her waiting for me at the kitchen table with 'the stick'. After the stick and I had bonded I was sent to bed.

The following day when Mum returned home from work she sat me down and explained to me that things were hard and I was making them harder. She asked me why I did these things and I told her I was sick of being, as a classmate had described me 'an alien'. I even accused her of not being my real Mum. She was white after all and I was black. My sisters and I were the only black people for miles around. Mum seemed to mellow a bit and she showed me pictures of my Dad and spent the afternoon telling me all about him, how he had sometimes felt sad at what people said to him but he had risen above it. He had been brave and proud and I should be too.

From that point on I did my best to make my Dad proud, I knew he valued academic success so I applied myself at school. I knew he valued family so I worked hard at being nicer to mine. Best of all from seeing my Mum and Dad in the photograph I knew I wasn't adopted. Instead I knew that my Dad just wasn't there. Didn't he want me? Was the fact that I was so bad the reason he stayed away? If I was good maybe he would come back. I had been told that he was dead, but death was such an abstract notion that I never fully understood what it meant.

That weekend my Mum brought us to his grave, she sat me down and explained the bomb, really explained what had happened. Before all I had known was that bad men had taken my Dad away, now I was to be told all. From that day on I questioned my Mum, probed her for every detail I could get about this man, my Dad. Each memory she told me seemed to take a little bit out of her, for she would go quiet or retreat to bed after she had spoken of him. In those days it was as if even remembering sucked her lifeblood away. I didn't know then that she had put the worst memories, those that caused her pain away on her little shelf. Yet in those days I was annoying, I must have been, for I constantly questioned. I was relentless always grasping for any little nugget of information about this man I didn't know, the man who was half of me.

The more information I secured about my Dad the more I wanted to be the daughter I thought he would have wanted. I became competitive always trying to be the best, I became bookish and most of all I became proud. Proud that this man had been my Dad, and proud of my colour. I wanted to know more about my Nigerian side but Mum knew little, she had relied on my Dad to impart his culture to us; as he would have relied on her to impart hers. Without knowing anything about my Nigerian side alongside a stark awareness that I was different from taunts and comments rapidly made my pride turn to shame.

Chapter Thirty Six

When I was eight or nine, I became acutely aware that money was scarce. Mum worked hard but it seemed her overheads outweighed any surplus that she made. I can honestly say that Mum rarely treated herself, she had nothing; she lived for us. At the end of each month she would drive us all to Derry where we would stock up the cupboards and she would buy us whatever we needed. She wanted to ensure we never did without so no expense was spared, so much so that her entire pay check was often squandered in a day.

Yet she rarely got herself anything. On her days off she would wear her uniform for going out, insisting that she had so few days off that she didn't need a wardrobe. She spent so many days in bed through tiredness and depression that I'm sure she didn't require much. Mum always ensured through thick and thin that we had enough; any surplus money (and quite often non surplus money) went straight to us. Before the days of tax credits and the nanny state as it has come to be, surplus money on a nurse's salary was a rarity. Inevitably we often ran out.

That winter was especially cold the snow was thick on the ground and temperatures rarely left zero. That was the year of the brown coat and woolly gloves. As I was the youngest my sister's clothes were passed down to me. But by the time they got to me their condition left a lot to be desired. I begged my Mum that year for a new coat and she said she would see what she could do. I was so excited, my counterparts in school had lovely coats in shades of blue and pink and I had my eye on one just like theirs. I remember sneakily cutting out pictures from magazines or pointing to children on the TV or in the streets who had coats just like what I had in mind. I wanted to make sure that Mum knew exactly what to get. To ensure I didn't get hand me downs I waited until Mum was in bed and threw out all the old coats that were destined for me, that way I knew Mum would have to get me a nice new one. I was so excited and imagined myself being the envy of my friends as I walked into school in my fabulous new coat.

A few days later I walked into school coatless. I was furious and utterly humiliated, how dare my Mum expect me to wear such a thing! After all my hard work and weeks of pointing out exactly what I was looking for Mum had the audacity to come home from work looking as pleased as punch as she presented me with my new coat. It was in a big yellow bag and as she handed it to me she was telling me how smart I would look, I positively quivered with anticipation as I peeked into the big bag. The first thing that struck me was the smell; a musty sour note assailed my nostrils.

"Take it out" Mum was saying, as I lifted the coat out I swore I had never seen anything as ugly in my entire life. It was a woollen tweed creation the fabric a deep manure colour with threads I can only describe as curry colour weaved through it. I was appalled, horrified, "try it on" was Mum's next line. I looked at her dumbfounded as I could hear Alison and Maxine's sniggers in the background.

I dropped the repulsive garment and fled to my room, the tears were tripping me. So much for being the envy of my class, if I wore that they would be starting a collection for me never mind the black babies!

I stayed in my room for a long time that day, I was seething with fury. I vowed never to put that thing across my back. I decided that if this was what my family thought of me I would just have to leave, these people simply had no respect. I stomped downstairs and told my Mum that I needed a lift immediately; I needed to get to the Nazareth House, our local orphanage. Mum looked faintly amused and didn't say no as I expected her to, instead she shrugged her shoulders and said "if that's what you want". Ten minutes later we had stepped out into the freezing fog and got into the car, Mum switched on the engine and began to drive. Good, I thought at least the nuns won't expect me to wear a brown tatty brown coat! I buckled my seatbelt, folded my arms and settled back for the journey, going to Derry meant that we should head down the road yet it seemed Mum was heading up the road. Not understanding her detour I looked at her questionably, "where are you going, I thought you were taking me to the Nazareth house?"

"Yes we'll be going there in a minute, but first I think it would only be polite to say goodbye to your granny and granddad"

My tummy lurched as my best laid plans had been foiled,

"Do we have to?"

"Yes Jayne" Mum nodded,

That was it. The threat of facing my grandparents was enough to tell my Mum to take me home,

I could see her laughing even though she tried to hide it, yet rather than give in I said

"I need a day or two to come up with a good goodbye."

That was the end of my protest over the brown coat. I never did make it to the Nazareth house but I did make Mum laugh.

Later that evening, I peered down the stairs and saw my Mum sitting on the living room chair with jumpers which were strewn across the living room floor. Curiosity got the better of me and I ventured down and asked Mum what on earth she was doing.

She looked at me her face slightly drawn and said,

"Jayne, it's freezing outside and I have two weeks to pay day"

I looked closer at her work and saw six sleeves lying on the arm of the chair. Each one was stitched at the top.

"What are they?" I asked

"Gloves, yours are the cream pair, they'll match your wee coat".

Shame raced through me, I believe that was the first time that I realised that things were tough, that Mum was doing her best and that my selfishness was not helping. Demanding a new coat so close to Christmas when I suspected she had already bought our presents, (using her entire salary no doubt) had been a cruel thing to do.

"Thanks Mum, they're lovely" I said and retreated back up stairs.

The next day I donned my 'new' coat and gloves made from old jumpers and made my way to school. Despite feeling embarrassed the overwhelming feeling that prevailed was warmth for I had been fortunate enough to have my Mum who did her very best to ensure that we had what we needed.

Despite that as I got within one hundred yards of the school I took off my brown coat and my make shift gloves, rolled them in a ball and tossed them in my schoolbag. Warmth or not I had my pride!

The brown coat was a wakeup call to me; it made me notice how poor we actually were. Granted the end of each month Mum would stock up the cupboards but by mid-month they would grow bare and usually contained bread milk and beans. When those ran out we relied on Mum's little yellow book to feed us.

Every Monday without fail I remember Mum would sign the yellow book and leave it on the mantelpiece, one of us would take the little book to the post office and queue. When we reached the top of the queue the lady would stamp it and give us a few pounds. We used this to buy precious supplies. Occasionally I snuck a bag of sweets or two! It later became clear that this little book was a family allowance and in the absence of Dad this book was the only help my Mum got.

The other person we relied on was Mum's grandmother or 'nanny' as I called her. She would call at our house often and was a great support to Mum. She too had been widowed young and understood what Mum was dealing with. She used to come with a fresh loaf of bread and milk and all sorts of supplies for the cupboards. As early as when I was a toddler she would bath us and buy little necessities like vests and pyjamas. I used to find her gifts boring and would have preferred a toy or sweets but now I see that these little purchases were essential for a young family. Mum knew her Gran had used her limited funds to buy these and her kindness always touched her.

Chapter Thirty Seven

I liken Mum to a poem I used to hear when I was little it went, 'when she was good she was very, very good but when she was bad she was horrid'. When Mum was with us she was the best Mum in the world, yet when Misery snatched her from us as she frequently did Mum became horrid. She became silent and reclusive, her eyes became blank and she cared about nothing or no one. It was during these times that Mum gave up and we catered for ourselves. My sisters remember calling my grandparents and my nanny to come and help telling them that we were scared and that Mum was quiet again. I suppose they were petrified and in the end out of desperation Mums family brought the doctor out to see her. Mum was completely unresponsive yet she heard them utter, "Changed person", from her bed she let their words pass her by. When Misery was with Mum she walked and talked occasionally but was no more than a puppet imitating life, the strings that moved her were gone and she was lifeless.

Mum was diagnosed with a deep depression and was started on a strong course of anti-depressants; she was given sleeping tablets as well as she hadn't been sleeping. She had sitting up each night staring at nothing. Well that was what they thought, because Mum wasn't staring at nothing she was looking at Misery and Misery was holding her attention.

Looking back, drugs were the worst courses of treatment that my Mum could have been given. I wish they could have addressed the root of her problem, I wish they had offered her some therapy some help to cope. Drugs were never the answer, they were the easy option. I firmly believe that by introducing Mum to such drugs that set her on a path of no return. The more depressed my Mum became the more she remembered my Dad and thought of how things could be; the more drugs she was given. A dependency was created that had ramifications so strong that they would obliterate her later life.

My parents were stalked by racism in their time together. Admittedly they found it unsettling but they hadn't dwelled on it; they refused to let it defeat them. They had each other and they had their plans. When my Dad had fulfilled his contract to his firm they had intended to leave Northern Ireland and bring us girls up in a more tolerant society. The bomb that took my Dad's life had temporarily put a halt to these plans, yet in the back of Mum's mind she longed to someday fulfil them. This was reinforced all the more when the vile monster of racism reared its ugly head again. This time though it didn't level itself at adults, instead it targeted three innocent children.

Living as a mixed race family in Strabane or indeed any small town had its downsides, none of which made our lives any easier. Initially after Dad died, Mum refused to let us out the door. Every bang, bullet or bomb she heard seemed to alert her to the danger on the streets. She thought if she kept us all in and with her at all times that we would be ok. The barricading us in lasted for a few years until Mum reluctantly had to let us out to face the world.

Rather than terrorist threats the first thing that threatened us was something she hadn't expected. On the mornings when she could leave us to school she would watch us making our way in. We stood out so much from the other children; our little brown faces a stark contrast to the sea of white faces that surrounded us. Her heart reached out to us as she knew deep down that our differences would soon result in trouble.

Yet considering the circumstances Alison and I seemed to be settling into school. Maxine was the exception she had grown into an introverted child, her teacher had told Mum that she wasn't progressing academically and alarmingly was painting only black. Now it is clear that a depression had fallen on her. Once again no help, no counselling existed to help bereaved children of the troubles. Instead Mum resolved that watching and monitoring her was all she could do.

Mum had always kept she and my Dad's plans in the back of her mind before he had been murdered they had resolved to move us somewhere else, somewhere more mixed. Yet the events of the last few years had left Mum insecure and afraid of all things new. So much so that she began to question whether uprooting us to a far of place would be the best solution. However her doubts were to be conquered very quickly. Immediately after Dad's death she had turned a blind eye to the remarks, stares and questions about her daughters but as time passed they were to become more and more difficult to ignore.

One day she came home from work to find Alison in convulsions; she was sobbing her heart out and was vehemently refusing to go back to school. On further examination the events of her day were unfolded. The children in Alison's class had been given an exercise to draw themselves. Alison, who believed she was quite the little artist, drew a picture of herself skipping. When the teacher had collected all the children's samples, she had stopped at Alison's and became outraged. She shouted at her the rest of her class the audience,

"That is not *you!*" she proceeded to draw an alternative picture on the board "*this* is you"

On the board the teacher had scrawled a child with big lips, fuzzy hair and bad posture, she pointed to the board telling Alison, "*You* are a negro and negro's look like this!"

Furious, Mum arranged cover for the following mornings work and with Alison in tow, reported to the school at nine am the next morning. She demanded to see the head mistress and found a voice she never knew she had. She described to the head the events of the previous day and informed her that her complaint would be taken to the education board if she didn't receive an immediate apology from the culprit. Mum was told this would not be possible, the teacher involved was busy. Yet Mum would not be brushed aside she was determined to receive her apology, *their* apology. So she continued her battle.

"Not be possible? But it is possible for your staff to humiliate a child in front of her contemporaries?" She had said, continuing "if she is busy I will wait whilst you arrange someone to cover her. I warn you though if she is not here in ten minutes I will begin instigating her dismissal." Mum looked at her watch, taking note of the time and sat down, making it clear she was going nowhere.

The head mistress clearly defeated left her office and Mum and Alison sat waiting. The standoff was successful and precisely ten minute later Alison's shamefaced, mortified teacher along with the headmistress entered the office.

Mum and Alison were given an apology and reassured that such an event would never happen again. Seizing her moment Mum assured them that she would take this no further if they honoured one more request. That the teacher involved would have no further contact with any of her children again. Alison was removed from her class that very day and Maxine and I were never taught or spoken to by that teacher in the future.

Mum left the school feeling a lot stronger, she had done Max proud. But seeing her child so upset had a profound effect on her. This time she had been resilient and had coped with the situation, but what about the next and the inevitable next? Single motherhood was gruelling at the best of times, but being a single mother to three mixed raced children in an all white town added even more complications.

The incident in the school was not the only incident, in only a few years in Strabane Mum had encountered more bigotry than she had thought possible. Even her mother had not been immune, she had once taken us to Mass and an old friend approached her at the end of the service and commended her on her charity work. By virtue of having little money her mother was never a big donator, she gave what she could, when she could, but she could never afford to give enough to have her generosity highlighted. Needless to say she was puzzled and asked the woman what she meant.

The woman explained saying that by taking in those African children and feeding and clothing them, she was highly admired and deserved a medal. In fact they all thought so. She had looked up to see the woman's cronies oohing and ahhing in agreement. Always known for her diplomacy she had quickly corrected them, but had been deeply upset at the incident.

I remember after that day in the church, it took Mum quite a while to convince Maxine and I that we weren't adopted and shipped in from some far away African country! Not for the first time I would look at myself and then at Mum, weigh up the older ladies comments and conclude that the ladies and their friends were right. Somehow Mum had gone all the way over to Africa and picked us to bring back to Strabane. Despite being told about my Dad I didn't remember him, adoption was a much more logical explanation.

One afternoon Mum had left us in the little red mini on the main street whilst she ran to the bank to cash her salary cheque. The three of us were excited as Mum had promised us a trip to 'Wellworths' were we could each select a small toy. As it was the end of the month the queue for the bank was long and Mum seemed to take an age. I remember we were singing silly songs and laughing when all of a sudden someone peered in the window, very soon we were surrounded by spectators, all mystified by the strange but cute creatures that inhabited the car. I felt like an animal in a zoo. To our audience the sight of us three children in that little mini was as if an alien spacecraft had descended right there on the main street. Thankfully Mum returned and quickly dispersed the crowds using a few choice words! When she climbed back into the car she turned to us and tried to make a joke at how they were admiring our nice hair yet she quickly saw that we were all in tears. Mum says it took her a long time to compose us. We never got our toy that day instead she took us home and closed the blinds.

Those days became littered with battles; Mum must have felt like the towns very own Martin Luther King championing race relations on an almost every day basis. She grew sick of telling them over and over again that we were all the same until eventually she gave up.

That was the day when Mum decided that she would cast her fears aside and take us to Nigeria. She would never expose us to such experiences again. She was not foolish enough to believe that she could escape racism there but she knew such experiences would be lesser if her girls blended in a bit more.

Chapter Thirty Eight

Whilst Mum was planning our relocation the political situation in Northern Ireland was as dire as ever. Mum had thought that our part in Northern Ireland's history was over however in some ways it had only just begun. A few years earlier Mum had outed herself as anti IRA when the train bomb had made headlines again. This time the bomb it was to make the headlines for different reasons. A priest who saw himself as a crusader for victims of British incarceration regardless of what they were guilty of, had decided to take up the bomber Patrick Flynn's case for release. He launched a ferocious press campaign throughout Northern Ireland to free my Dad's murderer. Father Faul would stop at nothing until he secured freedom for the man responsible for killing two innocents. He had an army of supporters who felt that the bomber who lost his best friend in the blast and had been injured so terribly meant that he deserved released from the terrors of the Maze.

On hearing and reading the priest's campaign Mum was devastated. What kind of man of God disregards the devaluation of human life and advocates murder? Mum wrote an open letter to the 'Belfast Telegraph' voicing her disgust but it was never printed. Instead people from far and wide right across Northern Ireland condemned Father Faul's actions and in some respect reassured Mum that decency existed. Regardless of the weight of support against Father Faul's intervention in the judicial system, he was still successful. He secured the release of my Dad's murderer after having served just a few years of his already light sentence. Mum was once again joined by Misery and thoroughly distraught. As was customary in bleak circumstances she took to her bed and her drugs were increased.

The increase in her prescription allowed her to function and got her through the early release and allowed her to concentrate on us. That was until one day when we ran out of milk. I remember that day like it was yesterday, it all started so well. Mum was off and feeling well and that morning she announced that we needed to get ready as we had to get milk and since she was off, we may as well go for a drive as well. As children we loved getting out for a drive and as Mum's days off and 'well' days were scarce we excitedly seized the opportunity. I remember my sisters and I playing paper, scissor and stone to decide who would get the privileged position of sitting in the front. Of course I choose stone so I was outwitted and relegated to the back beside Maxine. Alison was the winner that day so she would sit in the front. It didn't really matter though as Mum had promised us a long run and said we could listen to whatever tape we wanted on the journey. As Alison had won the race for the front seat Maxine and I could choose the tape. We choose Michael Jackson because he was cool.

For the most part Mum had taught us to ignore the town and its people. It was a staunchly republican town and IRA victims, catholic or not would never have been popular, not to mention black IRA victims. As such in those years we did most of our shopping in Derry, we only bought the very basic essentials in the town.

As I remember we certainly went for a run that day, but not the kind of run my sisters and I had in mind.

We got to the shop only to find that it was closed, the next shop and the next shop were too. Twenty four hour petrol stations didn't exist back then. But as this was a normal day there was no apparent reason why the shops would be closed. Mum and

Alison double checked the time and according to them the shops should definitely be open. After all it was eleven o' clock. Baffled we moved on to the last shop we could think off, it too was closed. Mum made us all laugh when she suggested that we would have to drive out of the town altogether and find a cow. If we kept driving we would be in the country soon all we needed was a bucket and we could fill up. I remember giggling and giggling as if it was the funniest thing I had ever heard. I was quite looking forward to milking a cow! We were still squealing with laughter five minutes later as each of us proffered our parts in the milking process. We were a happy little bunch as we continued our drive around the town looking for a shop.

It didn't take long before Mum spotted a familiar face from the town walking his dogs. She pulled over beside him and asked him why all the shop were closed,

"What's going on" she enquired genuinely curious,

"It's the commemoration of the Easter rising" he replied perhaps a little too proudly.

It was then I noticed Mum staring ahead, I think we all did as soon we were all following her line of sight. Up ahead stood a gathering of people, no, more of a procession. A big man dressed from head to toe in black and wearing a mask raised his hand at Mum to stop the car until the procession had passed on.

The men in the march all had their faces covered and were all dressed in black. They carried a huge tricolour. I thought they looked like zombies because they walked so slowly. In response to the dog walker Mum said;

"IRA, you mean?"

"Yes the new commemorating the old" he proudly nodded.

I knew then that this was worse than walking into a zombie horde for the word IRA was a word that to my sisters and I was synonymous with death, bombs, bullets and of course tears. Our jovial little family outing was instantly transformed into one of utter fear. As Michael Jacksons 'Thriller' filled the car terror filled us. Mum became unrecognisable, she paled, she tensed and she swore. Mum's rage was palpable. When I remind her of that day she says that those 'bastards' holding up the road were murderers, and she was supposed to just sit there and idly let them pass by. There they were alive and breathing, walking and talking whilst the innocent rotted in their graves. She said she thought of my Dad at that moment his death was all the more reinforced by looking at his daughters sat in the back seat fatherless. She was reminded of my Dad's smiling face, she saw her mother telling us that our Daddy had gone and Anger took over her completely and utterly.

For once I was fortunate that I had not won the competition to sit in the front seat for all of a sudden my Mum pressed her foot to the accelerator and drove faster and harder than I had seen her or anyone else do before. As Michael Jackson sang I remember thinking of how all these men in balaclava's danced just like him. From my backseat vantage point it seemed their footwork was just as intricate as they dived for the pavement. They couldn't hear the music but they certainly must have heard Mums car because I could see them running and scattering in all directions. Yet that wasn't enough for Mum, she was adamant; she was on a mission to annihilate each and every one of them. Faster and faster she went not stopping until our car made contact with bodies, lots of them. I remember the thuds as one by one, they bounced of the boot, even those who sought refuge in the pavement could not escape Mum's little red mini.

As I peered behind me I could see men were scattered in various positions on the road behind. Even more alarming Mum had started to make the car go backwards; she was going to run over all the men strewn on the road. Luckily she decided against the idea and quickly made the cars go forward again; maybe she decided that hitting as many as she could, would be easier and more effective. I screamed, Maxine and Alison screamed, we had never seen anything as frightening before. It was as if the sound of our hysterics shook Mum back to reality for as she looked at us and her face changed, it started to register normality again, she was beginning to look like our Mum once more. Calm was restored as Mum appraised the situation around her; I think she saw what we saw. Our Mum, feral and dazed, wildly knocking down hordes of balaclava wearing men.

Mum simply turned the radio off, turned the now silent car around and drove us back home. She went straight to bed; I could have sworn I saw tears glisten in her eyes.

We didn't get the milk that day.

Over the next few weeks Mum worried about the repercussions as she had knocked down at least six men. The extent of their injuries was unknown. Yet for now with Misery by side I believe she hoped they were dead.

In Northern Ireland it was a well known fact that the IRA meted their own justice. From what my Mum had been told it was only a matter of time before they exercised it. We were once again barricaded in.

Chapter Thirty Nine

One thing the road rage incident did was spur Mum on to make concrete plans for the move to Nigeria. Our local priest Father Mulvey was instrumental in helping her make contacts. He had known a friend of a friend as Irish people generally do, who was working in Nigeria and slowly but surely she began to make arrangements. Mum saved as much she could. This would not be a cheap move, yet life in Nigeria seemed cheaper in comparison to here so we would save when we were there. The main thing for Mum was getting there and finding a job. She contacted some hospitals in and around the Lagos area and enquired if they had vacancies for nurses.

Slowly but surely the Nigerian plans began to take shape, in the meantime we continued to *exist* in the town. Mum had no friends a fact that I found so sad, if she had had friends perhaps her life would have been easier, they may have brought out the lively person she once was. Instead she simply had us, her work and Misery. Mum continued to have good days and bad days. The bad days tended to be the result of news of yet another terrorist atrocity or yet another bereaved family. Each new death compounded her own experiences.

To escape Misery befriended her and together in the darkness of her bedroom they shut out the world. She was a good friend to Mum and her friendship overtook everything else, us, work and her plans. We always prayed that the bad days would end and the good days would return. For it was on these good days that we caught a glimpse of what our mother could have been.

At this stage Mum worked in the towns health centre as a district nurse. The staff there got to know her well and had an understanding of her shattered life. Many of them were sympathetic. One of the doctors that Mum worked with was prompt to guess what was happening; that Mum was suffering from a deep depression. During one bout he called to our house and assessed Mum. Again Mum's drugs were increased and Misery not wanted to leave Mum completely released her hold enough to let Mum function.

It seemed that every time Mum got depressed, when she succumbed to Misery she was given more drugs. They succeeded in pushing Misery a little further away each time so she could work and focus her mind on us and the move. Mum admits that if she kept focused on something, anything at all, that she felt stronger.

Yet Mum didn't know then that the commemoration events that our little drive had interrupted, were only a prelude to the main parade. That year's main parade unbeknownst to Mum was the talk of the town. One day when she was calling at a patient's house to undertake the glamorous task of dressing yet another rotten bedsore, she became privy to the towns anticipation. The patient informed her that the parade would "honour the town's fallen heroes." She told Mum of how they had lost their lives at the hands of the "Brits". She delighted in informing her of how they had so bravely fought and thrown their own lives down for Ireland.

Mum didn't reply to the patient, but remembers thinking *'murderers you mean?... IRA bastards'*

The patient lost in her own romantic visions of Ireland's patriots went on to make the mistake of telling Mum that this year's day would be even more special than ever. The town could expect a special guest that day, one of the most heroic men of them all; Martin Mc Guinness. Mr Mc Guinness would even enjoy a short ceremony in the grave yard where he would fly the glorious tricolour high above all the graves as a mark of respect to all the heroes.

As soon as Mum had finished the patients dressing she drove straight to the parochial house. Mr Mc Guinness in those days was a known as an IRA commander. Mum was sure he would be made very welcome in Strabane, she was also sure that she would not let him fly his despicable flag in the grave yard. At the parochial house Mum met with Father Mulvey.

Father Mulvey was a nationalist priest but he was not a republican, he became famous during the troubles for condemning the IRA and their actions. As a child he was one of the few people who got across our front door. He and Mum got on well, mainly due to their shared political beliefs. He was a stern man, but a sensible man. He believed in right and wrong and had little time for the troubles. Father Mulvey spoke his mind and his beliefs were not always popular.

When Mum told him what she'd heard he confirmed that he also had heard the same. However, as far as he was concerned no one had sought his permission to fly any flag over the graveyard. He assured Mum that even if someone did ask for such permission it would never be permitted.

Chapter Forty

Soon the day of the parade was upon the town, a day I don't remember but I certainly remember the aftermath. Excited chatter hung in the air. As far as the townsfolk were concerned something *very* special was happening, someone *very* special was coming. Mr Mc Guinness would be gracing their streets. Their attention was so focussed on the VIP arrival that they came out in force. Unlike the procession of a few days ago this parade was on the town's main road, its length lined with supporters. The procession weaved its way through the town and stopped outside the grave yard. There the men said a few words and all heads bowed. They then were on the move again, this time preparing themselves to turn through the grave yards gates.

Martin Mc Guinness snaked through the road followed by legions of fans. Armed with a huge tricolour they were surprised encounter a priest standing in their path. They asked permission to fly the flag in the grave yard as a mark of respect to the town's heroes. Father Mulvey denied it. He knew of what had happened to Mum and many, many others as such he was not a supporter of their cause. Jesus said turn the other cheek, not to fight as they did. That was his philosophy and his reasons for refusing their entry.

Mum recalls his commanding voice booming through the crowd,

"You might want to honour your victims, but I have to bear in mind *their* victims, so I am sorry I do not and can not give you permission to fly anything political on consecrated ground."

He folded his arms and continued to block their path. Mum had never been a lover of the church, but today she found herself adoring it. A catholic priest standing up to the IRA was unheard of and a sense of justice pervaded her.

Jeers from protesters pelted Father Mulvey from every angle; he was heckled from far and wide. In the absence of any supporters for this brave man, Anger seized Mum and together stood beside him. Father Mulvey called for others to join them, unsurprisingly no one did. Some stood in silence; others hung their heads, all were afraid to be seen confronting the public face of the IRA.

So it happened that there outside that little graveyard something utterly unheard of took place. A small but significant battle was unfolding, a tiny peace protest, where two stalwart campaigners faced an army that few dared to tackle. Side by side, a small town priest and a country victim stood together and openly against the IRA. I am so proud of my Mum for standing there that day; it must have taken every ounce of her courage.

"Murders" she remembers shouting as she made her way directly to Mr Mc Guinness. She doesn't remember the full content of the conversation but she knows that that was the day that she added a little Northern Irish French to her vocabulary! From that day on swear words became an integral part of her every day speech. Yet on that day she had a small victory, because Mr Mc Guinness and his hordes marched on by waving their flag behind them.

The following day my sisters and I greeted Mum after school with forlorn faces,

"What's wrong?" She had asked

"Mummy are you ill?" Alison replied.

"No, why?" Mum answered,

"Because everyone says you're sick"

That was how anyone who went against the consensus of this republican little town was viewed. As sick.

For a few months Mum heard nothing more about the event but inside she became worried, had she put her daughters at risk? These men were cold blooded killers; she doubted very much that killing a child would even tickle their conscience.

The plans for Nigeria soon became crucial and all consuming. Mum took to calling the hospitals and unlike before this time she spoke to staff about available jobs not possible jobs. Her plans were so advanced that she even put our house on the market. If a job or a sale came through then we would go, Mum would take us girls and run.

Chapter Forty One

Mum's actions boycotting the tricolour in the grave yard, confronting Martin McGuiness and knocking over a few IRA men meant that our family not only stood out because of our colour but also for being anti IRA. Mum in her bravado had made us potential targets. Which brings me to days I remember well; the days of the army raids which became a part and parcel of daily life in the town. On a regular basis the homes of many if not most of the town's residents were 'raided'. It became a common talking point amongst the locals usually concerning who was raided and what had been successfully hidden from the army glare. The raids involved the British army searching houses for weapons, explosives or any clues pertaining to terrorist connections. It seemed that at least one time or another, every house in the town had had a raid. All but ours.

Often we would arrive home to find every front door in the street wide open, many having been kicked down; personal effects would be strewn across hallways that were on open view to all.

All of this was evidence that frantic searching had went on; that another no warning raid had taken place.

The people we lived next to would eye us with distrust; suspicions were high in those days. They must have wondered why we were being excluded, if we watching them or worse if we were we were some sort of informers. At this stage Mum was already running scared due to her previous stunts. She didn't need any more reasons to be targeted.

Soon the other children began making comments, calling us 'Brits' or what they took to be the ultimate insult 'Protestants'. It got so bad that in the end Mum went to the police and explained our predicament, how she was quite possibly the only non-sympathiser in the town. They swiftly informed her that they knew exactly who she was. They too had heard of her one woman mission to rid the country of IRA! An officer brought her into an interview room and told her that she had every reason to fear, these people were unscrupulous.

That day the police arranged for our house to be 'included' in any further raids. This simply meant that when the army raided our street that they would also come into our house. In practice it meant that whilst everyone else had their front doors kicked down, their possessions scattered and often destroyed we had our front door carefully opened, never would we find an item out of place. Sometimes a little note was left stating they walked through as requested!

I wondered now why no one noticed that our door was never damaged, that the contents of our house were never rummaged or destroyed. Yet the cunning rouse was successful and before long the natives believed that we too was subject to searches and enemy suspicion. We had successfully assimilated as far as the natives were concerned.

That day the police officer also gave Mum something which she found very valuable but which terrified me. She was furnished with a little mirror which she was instructed to use every morning before she left the house. The mirror was a means of scanning under the car before attempting to move it. It would alert Mum to any tampering and show up any devices that may have been planted. Mum was also given a quick vigilance brief in which she imparted to us, it told us what to look out for and contact numbers if anything, anything at all bothered us.

Even with the new devices Mum never felt entirely safe and our Nigerian plans became more and more real. When she found a buyer for the house, she knew it was time to make the move. I recall her sitting us three down and telling us the plans. She told us that she would always be there for us and we would be much happier there. Once again she told us about the bad man who killed our Dad and explained that the men that she had knocked down were his friends. She told us that the town was full of his friends.

I was so excited at the prospect of moving to the other side of the world, it would be such fun, never ending holiday. My sisters and I were happy to leave as we were young and adventure appealed to any child. Mum told us that we would be able to buy a new house there and that she would find a job. I was the most excited of all as apparently I was beginning to pick up some of my Dad's traits. I the one who never knew him was beginning to walk like him and worry like him. Yet one trait dominated above all the others; I loved animals like him.

Mum had described Nigeria as the land of milk and honey where dreams came true, so in my little mind I would have a dog or even better my very own pack of dogs. She agreed that when we got there I could have a pet; this was most likely to pacify me. I think I would have gladly moved to the moon if the promise of having a pet was fulfilled. Over the next few weeks, whilst my family were concentrating on Nigeria, I was naming my dog, pretending to walk it along with pointing out every waif and stray I saw. Mum really hoped this was a passing trait, she had enough on her plate and a four legged friend was not an addition she would relish.

Mum had arranged the big move for that summer thanks to the help of Father Mulvey she had several properties to see when we got there and a recommendation of a good boarding house where we could stay until we acquired a home .

Chapter Forty Two

When I asked Mum especially in later years why our move hadn't come to fruition, why it *really* hadn't occurred, she furnished me with what I then deemed to be a ludicrous tale.

She described sitting with her mother one afternoon over tea discussing the finer points of the trip when a knock came to the door. They hadn't been expecting anyone and it was strange to have a caller so early in the afternoon. Her mother answered the door and when she returned to the living room she was accompanied by some sort of priest. He was dressed from head to toe in white, and wore robes, robes like they had never seen before. He was swarthy and although not classical good looking he boasted a striking appearance. He had deeply tanned skin, dark brown hair and when Mum's eyes met his he had the kindest eyes she had ever seen.

"Gabrielle?" he inquired,

She nodded, looking from him to her mother trying to find some sort of answer as to why this man was here, to ascertain who this strange visitor was. Behind his back her mother shrugged and then as was customary for anyone who entered the house offered him a tea or coffee.

He declined anything and instead sat down when invited.

His eyes never left Mum's face and when they discussed his appearance afterwards they both felt that he seemed to glow, to radiate some sort of light. Her mother put it down to the bright day and his chair being positioned in the brightest corner of the room. That day the sun was blazing in and concentrated precisely on where he sat. Mum said nothing but as far as she was concerned she was in the presence of an extremely holy man.

When Mum was very young her grandmother used to tell her that when a priest was saying Mass that she was to not to look at him as a man. When a priest stood on the altar and uttered his sacred words he became far greater than man. Mum was to look beyond the man and see Jesus. Despite her Grandmothers words any Mass that Mum had ever attended or priest she had ever encountered had always been a mere man to her. She could see Jesus in them as much as she could see Jesus in a horse. Her grandmother would chuckle when she told her this, always careful to disguise her laughter and tell her off for being disrespectful.

That day this exotic man's presence instantly reminded Mum of her grandmother's words and for the first time ever, she saw Jesus in that beautiful priest in the living room. When she paid him the reverence she had been brought up to show any priest, this time she didn't do it to appease her family, she did because she meant it.

"I have had to travel to see you today" he said, his soft voice had no discernible accent, all that she remembers extracting from it was gentleness.

"Oh" she said utterly dumbfounded,

Her mother seeing her lost for words, was quick to intervene,

"Father, Gabrielle has been through a lot and is grateful for your visit; she's just a little quiet today"

He laughed revealing a smile that was as beautiful as the rest if him,

"I know, I know Mrs Caulfield" he leaned forward and was now sitting directly opposite Mum,

"Gabrielle I cannot stay long, but I come with a very important message for you"

"Oh" she said again, she really couldn't get any words out the whole experience was just so strange,

Smiling still he continued,

"Dear child, I know all about your plans, I know every one of them. I am telling you to cancel them"

"Oh" she said again, blatantly aware that a pattern was emerging on her side of the conversation. This man was going to think she was a complete fool!

Luckily for her, her mother again intervened.

"What plans father? She has quite a few"

"Nigeria" he said

"You're here about Gabrielle's plans for Nigeria?" her mother inquired,

"Yes" he said flatly, his smile vanished and was replaced with a look of intent as he placed his hands over Mums and said

"Do not go to Nigeria, you have my word that you and your children will be safe here"

"Oh" again words continued to fail her she felt such an eejit,

"Father she has arrangements in place" her mother said,

"Un-arrange them Gabrielle" he said, "Can you do that for me?" his eyes reaching into her very soul,

This time she surpassed herself and uttered a word rather than oh,

"Yes" she muttered,

"Do I have your assurance?" he asked still focussed intently on her face

She nodded.

"Good, then it is done" and with that he thanked her mother shaking her hand, gave Mum another dazzling smile and left.

Her mother saw him out and sat down in his place. She simply looked at Mum and said nothing, Mum simply looked back. They regarded each other for a while, before they both lit a cigarette and went over the incident.

The worst thing was that neither of them had seen him arrive or depart. Her mother admitted that she was every bit as baffled and stunned as Mum, she had just hidden it better. They never did get his name nor did they ever find out where he was from.

For Mum though she went home that day feeling a great sense of peace, waves of calm flowed through her and she slept. She slept for a long time and for the first time since Dad had died she didn't visualise the train. Mum kept her word and abandoned our move to Nigeria. Instead Mum found us a home in the outskirts of the town, a little more expensive than she could afford, but at least it us away from the majority of people. I was disappointed when Mum told us that our Nigerian adventure was cancelled, but as all the planes had been stopped we had little choice but to stay. Mum had said the only other way there was if we could by magic carpet and she couldn't find one. We were all so disappointed but I resolved to keep my eyes peeled for such a carpet and in the meantime I would try and get Mum to commit to her promise of a dog.

In a moment of weakness Mum relented. She claimed that without a father I had one less thing to love than my counterparts; maybe a dog wouldn't be such a bad idea. She must have rued the day she relented, because very soon every waif and stray from far and wide was collected. I spent my childhood days administering to creatures, seeing beauty in even motlest of mutts and driving my family mad in the process!

Chapter Forty Three

It didn't take long for us to move to our new house and settle in. Mum had furnished it with such attention to detail that it felt more like a show house than a home but it was nice that she had something to focus on. Mum still had her bad days but my sisters and I had learnt to accept them. She was working extra shifts to allow for the increased mortgage costs so we rarely saw her anyway. The house had needed to be purchased quickly as we had sold our last home for the move to Africa. It meant that Mum had to inject almost all of our savings for Nigeria to secure it. Mum was right though in that I didn't notice her absence or wasn't as needy when I had my dogs. All my spare time was fully occupied especially when much to my amusement one delivered a new litter of pups! I wasn't amused however when she ate two of them.

I loved it when Mum had a day off I used to count the days until her shifts finished. Although she would be tired and sometimes down at least she would be there. We may have had a beautiful home but we never really saw Mum. Mum had said that my Dad was extremely cautious with money he would have to justify the spending of each and every penny and always ensuring that we always had a contingency fund in the form of savings. He would tell her that saving for a rainy day kept crisis away. I'm sure the lack of savings did niggle Mum I remember her planning to build up new savings over the next few years.

Mum's second encounter with the woman in green or IT as she refers to her was to occur almost two years after our move to Nigeria was cancelled. Mum was still constantly improving the house and updating the decor. Cushions, curtains, new bed linens and pictures were changed frequently to match the going colour schemes of the time. To keep up with changing interior fashions Mum enlisted her mother to accompany her on a trip to Derry to finalise her needs once and for all. She recounts the events of that day as if it were yesterday; I suppose if I experienced them I would too.

The day began like any other trip to Derry they drove across distinctive blue and white Craigavon Bridge towards the city centre. The traffic lights ahead had turned red so Mum slowed the car to a stop. As they were waiting on the lights to change she looked at the river Foyle below musing that it seemed extra high that day.

Her thoughts on the height of the river Foyle were interrupted when she heard her mother mutter "Jesus, Mary and Saint Joseph." She saw her mother rustle in her handbag and extract rosary beads. When Mum looked up to see what had unsettled her so much she saw a familiar face. A face she last saw before her husband died. The green monster 'IT', who Mum had encountered on the 16th of January 1980 in the Europa train station, was standing in front of the car. Once again IT had appeared from nowhere. This time it was to find Mum on the Craigavon Bridge in Derry. IT loomed over the bonnet and stared directly at her and like their previous encounter transfixed Mum to the point of paralysis. Her mother prayed and prayed. Mum now whiter than white clutched the steering wheel so tightly that her knuckles were transparent, her bones threatening to protrude through the flesh. Her mother shook her and said "Gabrielle drive".

Her words also shook Mum too, for she came out of trance and turned the car. She followed her mother's instructions and drove all the way back to the town and straight to the parochial house.

They recounted the incident to the new priest Father O' Kane and he left them for a moment. Father O'Kane ran a charismatic prayer group within the town and was known to be close to God. When he returned to the room he said he would pray over them. He spent a long time with Mum yet rather than take comfort in that it made her more afraid.

The last words Mum remembers him uttering to her that day send shivers down my spine,

"I believe Satan takes many forms, and I believe you encountered him today, you must pray Gabrielle, you must keep praying."

Shaken they thanked him and left. Her mother now remembering the previous encounter Mum had told her about before Max died looked utterly mystified. Yet her devotion to the church and faith in God was so strong that she kept believed whatever they had seen was no threat, she said that she would keep praying and reassured Mum that she would be okay.

In the weeks and months that followed the apparition Mum was extra vigilant keeping us close and taking extra precautions with the car and the house. She ensured that no bomb had been planted, that no gun man could break in and that every possible danger was removed. Yet nothing happened. I developed severe asthma a month later and Mum says that she convinced herself that this was the reason behind the appearance; that I was going to die. I always laugh as I remind her that this wouldn't have been possible, after all only good die young! I remember missing a lot of school but I was fine. Alison and Maxine were also fine. Mum just couldn't understand the reappearance of that thing.

Father O'Kane came and blessed our house scattering Holy Water in every nook and cranny of each room. He would sit and pray with Mum. Yet nothing untoward happened. Mum began to think that the visit that day was simply to serve as a reminder that she was cursed, to tell her that whatever vendetta IT had against her was still in force.

Chapter Forty Three

It was only when Maxine and I in particular started asking Mum about our Dad again when the mystery was solved. One cold evening we sat by the fire and Mum took out a sealed box, it contained Dad's personal effects. Things she had put away because she couldn't bear to look at them. Yet she kept them as she wanted to have some sort of memorial for us when we would be old enough to understand. I think on this night she decided that we were old enough. She took out a pair of scissors and cut the tape of the box, I remember it contained lots of newspapers articles, romantic letters he had written to Mum, sympathy cards and a photo album which I still retain today. We had seen pictures of our Dad in Northern Ireland before with Mum and his extended family; we used to pour over the pictures. Yet we had never seen the album from Nigeria, I remember its thick green leather cover and the fine paper between each page. I remember absorbing every minute detail.

The men wore funny clothes I had thought and laughed, I now know that they were wearing the Nigerian national costume. The women were so pretty. I was so taken with examining every detail of every picture, looking at these relatives that I didn't know. I was so engrossed that I didn't notice that Mum had stopped talking that she was silent and holding her breath. One of us asked her what was wrong for her reaction unsettled us, yet she shook her head and said she was fine. She picked up the album and put it back in the box.

A few years later I was to learn that in the back of the album Mum had seen a picture that at first looked like any other family gathering. It was only on closer inspection that she saw a familiar face smiling at the camera, a familiar set of eyes. It was the woman, the 'IT' the bearer of bad tidings, that had haunted Mum since 1980. When Mum looked at the names listed below the figures she confirmed what instinct was already telling her. That the strange sinister force she had been visited bore a striking resemblance to her mother in law. This was something she could never confirm but a suspicion she cannot shake. That day alongside the physical shelf where Dad's box was stored, Mum placed the conundrum of her mother in law, her possible uncanny ability to visit her on a metaphorical shelf in her head.

Whilst no one significant incident occurred to account for the visit, I do believe that many minor incidents were all somehow heralded by it. I remember Mum sending Alison initially to a Catholic secondary school, but when she came home talking in Irish she was removed and placed in the nearest Protestant School she could find. Her mother was furious and not for the first time they were at loggerheads. Under her mother's instruction priests were dragged to our door to enlighten Mum on the errors of her ways. Mum was absolutely raging; she would decide where her children would be educated. No one, not her mother, not the priests or even the pope himself would sway her.

Mum did not need to be dictated to again and to ensure this was the case her solitary disposition came to the fore and she retreated from her families fold.

Over the years Mum blew hot and cold with her parents. I remember not seeing them for years at a time. I think they grew used to Mums erratic behavioural patterns and left her to sulk. As far as they were concerned she knew where they were if she needed them. Mum's independent streak and her bond with misery made certain that she seldom came back.

Chapter Forty Four

It didn't take long, not more than a year after the visitation that Mum started to believe that the curse was alive and well. In stringent, merciless NHS cutbacks she lost her job. That job was all that kept us afloat; it was hard enough when Mum was working. I panicked; I just couldn't see how we would cope. I was now ten or eleven and was acutely aware that we still hadn't accumulated any savings, every penny that came in was needed, there simply wasn't enough left to put away. It took three months for Mum to succeed in finding a new post, as Mum was paid at the end of the month it would be four months before we hit the all important pay day. The other problem was that even though the hospital was geographically less than a mile away it was in the Republic of Ireland; to the tax man this was a different country. Strabane was a border town and considered a part of Northern Ireland whilst Lifford where Mum's new post was, was considered to be in Ireland. In reality all that physically separated Ireland and Northern Ireland for residents of border towns was a mere footstep. Yet each country, neighbouring or not had different systems and governments, which had the implication that Mum would be paid in punts and that her tax rates would be different than what she had been used to.

As it transpired when Mum received her pay slip it looked great, yet due to heavier tax in Ireland she would lose almost than half of her earnings and even more again in the exchange of currency. Even though Mum worked, in effect we weren't much better off. The result being that she had to take on more shifts just to keep us afloat, until she was working what seemed to be continuously.

As we grew older we grew more expensive, secondary school uniforms, keeping up with our peers and even feeding us all required bigger budgets. A budget Mum no matter how hard she worked could not fulfil. When she did it was to the detriment of something else. Now on Mum's days off I would come home from school and find her staring at nothing, rather than being in bed. She would have a pile of unopened letters in front of her and the phone would be off the hook. It was as if she was cutting herself from all communication, what she didn't know couldn't harm her. Sometimes she would cry, she would say that it's hard to believe she was married to a chartered accountant yet all alone in this. I knew she was scared but remember a cruel part of me thinking 'get over it' and worse 'get on with it'.

I was eleven by this stage and being so young my life span was my eternity, I couldn't imagine anything gone before. I knew my dad had died nine years earlier but to my young mind that may as well have been ninety years earlier. Now I know that such a time frame is a blink of an eye.

One day after Mum had left for work (I knew she would be away for twelve hours) I resolved to get to grips with the situation myself. My sisters were at secondary school and out more and more with their friends, the repercussion being that I had lots of time to myself. I may as well make myself useful I mused. I came home from school and as usual lit the fire, peeled the spuds and put the dinner on. This day though was different for rather than retreat to the table to do my homework I went to the drawer in the living room where Mum had stashed the letters from the last fortnight. I took the heap out and worked my through the pile. There were bank statements, final demands and numerous bills. Some emblazoned with capital red letters and marked urgent.

Even then and as young as I was I knew the situation was dire. In the four months between pay checks we had lost almost everything and with Mum's pay being lower I just didn't know how we could regain it. I sat up late that evening trying to work something out to create a new budget based on clearing overheads and somehow getting us out of debt. It was much later that I remember it being said that most people are never more than three months away from the streets, when I look back on those times I know how true that saying is.

I tried my best to work out a solution but it seemed unworkable to my young mind. Mum's bond with her parents had been severed by her own accord. She had no one to turn to for help, despite searching everywhere it seemed that no financial assistance was available and losing our home was unfortunately inevitable. Mum began to crumble. I would shout at her that we needed money; she would shout back that she couldn't do any more. It was a dreadful time and Mum became depressed again. She found her old friend Misery and retreated to bed. All the letters and phone calls in the world couldn't find her there.

One day I had had enough, I was so upset and afraid that I confronted Mum bearing a cup of coffee and begging her to get up.

Mum's new drugs induced a trance like state so for the most part my pleas were ignored. My sisters were now accustomed to Mum's unpredictable behaviour so tended to avoid being home where possible. Yet somehow Mum listened to me this time, she saw her GP who introduced her to a new drug to keep her nerves and anxiety at bay: Diazepam. Misery retreated back from Mum a little and only tried to gain entrance when she wasn't busy.

After a few weeks the Diazepam and other drugs had taken their effect. Gone was Mum's trance like state and at last we were able to sit down and look at the letters,

"Mum, I've used all the money there's nothing left"

"It's ok," she reassured me "I'll get something organised"

"I spoke to the bank" I said afraid of Mums reaction "they're taking the house" bawling now I wailed "I tried to pay them as much as I could, but we ran out, I'm so sorry," I think my distress shook Mum into action.

The gravity of the situation confronted her; there was no going back on the banks decision. As all the letters and communication attempts were ignored we now had just twenty eight days to leave. Our last day in the house would be Christmas Eve.

"Right young lady" Mum said "it looks like, we're homeless, I suppose we'll be needing boxes to live in, there's four of us so one each perhaps? Or would you like to share?"

Her joke was lost on me and I wailed even more by this stage my understanding of the predicament was too strong. I even reminded Mum that this was no laughing matter.

That was the day that my proud Mum threw herself at the mercy of the state. Since Dad's death she had struggled alone, she had sought help from no one until now. Hesitantly and dripping in shame, she claimed social security and put her name down on the councils housing list. The man in the council offices had said that the timeframe she had given him was tight and it would be unlikely that a home would arise at such short notice, especially with Christmas coming up. Mum says that she panicked inwardly, but came home and told us to pack up, that she had secured a home.

The next few weeks were a waiting game; we had packed up our belongings but had nowhere to go. Homelessness loomed. Then when least expected with only three days to Christmas Mum received a call from the council.

A house had become available, enormous relief washed through her and she had to sit down to continue the call. Lighting a cigarette she braced herself to take in the good news. It was a good thing that she had sat down, for it seemed the only house that the council could find us, the only way we could avoid homelessness was to accept a house in the town's largest and most republican estate.

The estate was notorious, a large brown and grey sprawling development that housed many known terrorists, it was the hiding place for IRA arms and the meeting place for IRA campaigns. It was flooded with army on a daily basis. It had such a name that when we heard that someone lived there it was assumed that they were *in it up to their eyeballs*.

Mum used to warn us against befriending the children from the estate, as she feared ever coming into contact with their parents. Now we would be *from* the estate. Mum's stomach plunged and she begged the council to find something else, anywhere else. Unfortunately they could not. And so it became that the woman who had made a stand against the IRA, one of the town's only victims was left with no alternative but to live amongst them. It was a very unhappy Christmas that year.

Chapter Forty Five

Reluctantly we moved into the unknown enclave, only this time we were stony broke. We needed to carpet the house from top to bottom, get curtains and paint throughout. Council houses weren't left decorated and pretty like houses on the private market. The house had all necessary safety fixtures and fittings but it hadn't seen a coat of paint in many years. How we were to get the money in the wake of our Christmas repossession was a conundrum but one I soon solved by looking in the local paper.

A local car garage was paying cash at 'best' rates for cars and since that was about the only thing we had managed to cling onto I asked Mum if she would be prepared to sell ours. Like me she thought that this was a great idea, however she didn't relish the idea of selling the car locally. Instead she instructed me to go and get the 'Belfast Telegraph' where we could scan the classifieds for a garage further away, one that offered similar promises. Low and behold we found one, Mum gave them a ring and they agreed to buy our car on inspection and even replace it with another cheaper model, thus providing us with cash in hand whilst still having a means of transport. How they were going to do this was beyond me as our current car was far from new and worth little. Yet miracles did happen so Mum and I arranged to go to Enniskillen to meet the amazing car dealer.

Alison was cynical and preferred to stay at home whilst Maxine going through the awkward teenage stage preferred to mope to romantic music in her room. It would be just Mum and I on this journey.

After what seemed like an endless drive we arrived in Enniskillen and found the garage easily enough. The man Mum had spoken to on the phone met us and looked over our car; he nodded all the while seemingly happy with what he saw. He brought us into his office and told Mum he would take the car of our hands; he would give her £500 cash and another cheaper car. I was delighted and although Mum sat poker faced I knew she was too.

When everything was signed and sealed the salesman brought Mum and I out to the back of the garage, a place not seen by his regular customers. There he presented us with our new car. It was gorgeous red and so shiny, a four door Nissan Sunny a model that was all the rage back then. This car was better than the car we had traded in! Mum nudged me excitedly and eagerly took the keys from the sales man and we made our way towards our new car.

"Where are you going?" The sales man asked bemused,

"To the car" Mum replied,

"Sorry love I know we pride ourselves with value but we're not magicians" he said shaking his head laughing,

"Your cars against the wall there" He pointed to the very back of the yard.

Eclipsed by the shinning Nissan was our car. It was parked tightly against the wall in the furthest most reaches of the garage; it was as if even they were ashamed to have it. I can honestly say it was a banger like no other. A brown fiesta so old it looked like if you touched it, even sneezed beside it, it would disintegrate. It was difficult to determine if its unique colour was rust or paint. It wasn't difficult to determine the colour of our faces however, for both our faces burned red with shame.

Ten minutes later still red faced we both clambered in, we couldn't get out of the yard quick enough; the cars slow pace did not help in our efforts. When we got round the corner Mum pulled over at a cafe and said we may as well get our tea. We entered the cafe and sat down laughing so hard that we didn't get a chance to look around us. When we did it was too late. The cafe was straight out of a time warp. It consisted of two tables with little blue and yellow (formerly white) checked table cloths, locals gossiping in the corner and 1950's decor. The waitress was upon us before we could escape or even comment,

"Just two teas" Mum said

"Auck is that all? We have good specials on today too" she said "two for the price of one"

Mum sighed and asked what they had; we were hungry after all,

"Stew or beef burgers" she said,

"Maybe the burgers, do you want one Jayne?" Mum asked.

The waitress looked at me with such pleading eyes that I was afraid I would offend her if I said no, so I reluctantly agreed to have a burger and nodded my answer to Mum.

"Two burgers then" Mum said

We anxiously awaited our burgers rather frightened at what we would presented with, all the while watching as the oldest lady I had ever seen tucked into a bowl of stew.

Eventually our burgers arrived delivered by the smiling and as we discovered to our horror, toothless waitress. A smile is always a pleasant sight but when one smiles with no teeth the overall picture is not at oil painting to put it mildly.

When she left us Mum looked at her burger then at me, in the middle of the baps was a meat ball it clearly hadn't been flattened or had undergone any attempt at being shaped like a burger. We dissolved into giggles much to the distaste of the clientele. Afraid for our lives we quickly composed ourselves and ate around the baps.

Just like in the garage half an hour earlier we couldn't get out quick enough and as Mum went to pay for our interesting dinner I watched as the stew eating old lady scraped her bowl clean, her spoon clattering against the dish as she scooped up every drop. Clearly not satisfied that every morsel was gone, she removed her false teeth and with her forefinger she scarped the remainders of her stew from the rim and sucked it. The image stayed with me for a long time.

Once we paid we readied ourselves for our journey home. We climbed into the car and began the trip back to Strabane, it was a long trip not helped by the fact that the car shuddered when it reached more than thirty miles per hour. Yet the journey gave us time to count the holes on the floor. In true Flintstone style we slowly made our way back laughing all the way. We decided that we would have been home quicker if we'd walked! I always remember that in the absence of a disguise I ducked as low as I could on entering Strabane. That was how I spent any journey I was ever forced to go on in that car.

Now we lived in a council estate and drove a banger, I wondered could we get any lower. On the plus side we had had a hilarious day and had secured enough to get the house decorated so I supposed it wasn't all bad.

Chapter Forty Six

Gradually we settled into the estate, our immediate neighbours were an elderly couple and we grew very fond of them. Directly behind our house was the back of another house. As this house was elevated slightly more than ours, it meant that its residents could see into our bedrooms with ease. As our house was lower than theirs we could only see into their kitchen and gardens. We tried not to look, the same way we tried to ignore the residents hiding guns in the manhole and the comings and goings of shady figures in the night.

This was going on right across the estate, right across the town right and right across the country. In light of the enormity of such dealings, Mum warned us all to ignore anything we had seen or heard. It was like living in a gold fish bowl and like goldfish we would have to have very short memories if we were to survive here. Yet I knew Mum was seething; if pride comes before a fall then she must have been the proudest of them all, for she had certainly fallen not just once but over and over again. Everything my Dad had aspired to, every dream he had, Mum was unwillingly doing the opposite.

To make matters worse, a thousand times worse Mum's kindly grandmother, Dad's main champion, began to take ill. She started to become confused and disorientated and no one needed to tell Mum that she was suffering from dementia. The symptoms grew and grew until she no longer recognised her family. Within two years of their onset she had died. I was young at the time so don't remember much about Nanny taking ill I just remember how upset Mum was and that she cried and cried.

Every month when Mum exchanged her month's punts into sterling, we would watch what looked like a decent salary fade to a pittance. We were still being pursued by the bank on what was left of the mortgage and found that many other bills were falling behind. This was when I remember Mums shifts really increasing. Now that we were all a little older Mum nursed around the clock. To access Mum these days it was easier to phone the hospital because when she was at home she was so tired she just slept. When I asked Mum about those days she says she was angry, angry that we were growing and just as in our early years she was missing out on us. She would watch other woman working normal hours if working at all and she grew bitter. She was working so much she barely had time to live; she worked to support us the irony being that in supporting us she never saw us.

It was in those early days that I remember having my first thoughts on my weight. I began to worry about my normal body shape and in some sort of dysmorphic mind-set I saw myself as obese. I started to skip the occasional meal; after all who no one was ever there so no one would notice. As long as I had the dinner ready and the house tidy no one was around to see if I ate. Besides which I had more important things to deal with than food, I had to make sure we kept afloat.

Mum used to allow me to go and cash her salary cheque, this was especially essential when she worked nights. When I cashed the cheque I dished out the money to the various creditors and would spend hours trying to work out how to make it elastic so it would stretch until the end of the month. It was a puzzle I never solved.

Maxine at the time was getting in with a bad a crowd, I remember Mum trying her best to dissuade her, but with the hours she worked she just wasn't there long enough to check up.

Alison now eighteen had shunned the academic route and travelled down the route of beauty. She entered beauty contests province wide and even made it into the finals in Miss Northern Ireland. She had started courting a young man from the country and when not posing for the camera, she spent all her free time with him.

It would have been hard on two parents having three teenage girls but for Mum she had to exercise the role of both mother and father and become a tight disciplinarian. That was when she got the time. I'm sure she needed support in these days more than ever, a husband, someone to help her with us. She says that she was painfully aware of our dad's absence during our teens. All we were painfully aware of was a presence rather than an absence; the stick! Mum had introduced her childhood nemeses to us in order to retain control.

Chapter Forty Seven

After years of working full time and then some, Mum grew tired of nursing she simply had nothing more to give. Once she had compassion and respect for each and every patient, but now she viewed them all as great big time consuming *lumps*. She began to resent her patients and feared that they resented her too. She did her best to plaster a smile on her face when she was treating them and for the most part it worked.

Mum often told me about the day when she finally had enough. She had been asked by a colleague to draw blood from a lady in the hospital. Mum had always been expert in finding veins, where none seemed available. If any of her colleagues had difficulty in extracting blood they would call her. After struggling to find a vein in the old ladies paper like skin, the young nurse whom Mum was on duty with called for her assistance. Mum tied the lady's arm and for the first time in almost twenty years of nursing failed to find a vein.

She apologised to the patient telling her that she would try her other arm. The woman was old and the situation could be seen as traumatic for her, so she was as gentle as she could be.

Just as she was tying her other arm, the woman said,

"I'm not surprised really,"

"Oh?" Mum said, not really listening to her, so intent she was on not hurting her,

"Sure you can do nothing right"

"Pardon?" Mum was all ears now.

"You couldn't even have children right; didn't you end up with three black bastards?"

Mum dropped everything and turned her back on the horrible woman. She didn't care if they had to enlist Count Dracula himself to take her blood. In fact she hoped they did! Her colleagues were also disgusted and the woman was despatched to a different ward where Mum wouldn't have to see her hideous face again.

Of course Mum had had racist jibes before, especially working in the small towns in and around Strabane, but never had they made her want to pack the whole thing in. If it wasn't for our dire financial mess, she would have turned her back on nursing there and then but unfortunately she couldn't. She was tied to the job, to big *lumps* forever, it seemed.

Even with all Mum's hours our cupboards were still bare, Mum still didn't have any friends it seemed her life revolved around work and rest. I felt sorry for her then as to me she was so pretty yet she never had any fun or even a fragment of a life; all she had was worry.

Alison helped as best she could but her low wage barely skimmed the edges of our debts. She was at secretarial training college and got paid a trainee wage enough to get her to and from work. Maxine was in her final year at school and I was only thirteen. We were useless to Mum. I used to tell her how useless I felt and she would say even if we were millionaires she would not expect anything from her children. All she expected from us was for us to be happy. If only she knew that with the situation as bleak as it was, we never could be. How could we be happy when she was so sad?

Maxine and I didn't have any clothes and shopping became a distant memory. Mum began wearing her uniform even on her day off. One of my saddest memories was Mum dividing one beef burger, all that remained in our freezer between four and serving it up for dinner. No one complained, this was just how it was. We all lived for the end of the month, when we could stock the cupboards again.

We fell into a feast or famine pattern, when Mum got paid she would stock up the cupboards, heat the house and even get us small gifts. The result was that for three weeks out of four we had no food, no heat and often no electric. Things appeared so grim that I feared Misery returning. Mum pre-empted her though and went to the doctors who instantly increased her drugs

I was now fourteen and I remember Mum buying the 'Belfast Telegraph' more often than usual. I guess she was assessing our current predicament, she seen that she didn't have any friends or money, in fact the only thing that held her to the town was her job. She contemplated what she was doing there after all she hated it and we hated it. It was then she realised that nothing, absolutely nothing was holding us there. Mum made a decision then, a decision that pains me most of all because it shows me that Mum tried, she wanted happiness and she wanted a chance. There was still something in her then.

She had been happy once, she had been happy in Belfast. Mum would chase that happiness and put this gloomy town behind her, she would return to where she once had a life. We would all be happy; we would blend in more in a city. Mum reasoned that it was 1993, and the world had moved on from the 1970's, racism was generally condemned and we could make a fresh start. By now Belfast would have changed, Mum was sure that by now it would be home to more families from different ethnicities. Our family would no longer stand out; we would no longer be oddities.

All the horrible incidents of Mum's past were firmly placed on her shelf; she had a glimmer of hope on the horizon and we were all swayed by her enthusiasm. I was not so keen on moving to Belfast but Mum's optimism was contagious and at last for the first time in my life it seemed Misery was a friend Mum wanted to dump. To me Mum was filled with hope; her new plans may just make the disposal of Misery possible. It was therefore settled that we would all move back to Belfast.

Chapter Forty Eight

We moved to Belfast in March 1994, we began our time in the city full of hope and gullibility. For Mum the move heralded a new start, just what her family needed. Just as twenty years before the big city lights beaconed to her once again.

Mum didn't have any friends in Strabane she had resolutely stayed away from the townsfolk and once again was on bad terms with her family, so we had few goodbyes to say.

Mum's now thoroughly blackened credit rating ensured that buying a house was out of the question, the Housing Executive had nothing available on its transfer list so the only option we had was to find a rental. Every day we scoured the Telegraph for something within our measly price bracket. Mum was astounded to find that we were priced out of South Belfast area. The rents there were alarmingly high. Even if she worked twenty-four-seven, her wallet would just not be big enough.

This didn't discourage her though; instead she said we would have to consider new unknown parts of the city. We knew form the daily news bulletins that the West was predominately Catholic and the East predominately Protestant. Coming from a small town that was entirely Catholic Mum wanted to live in a mixed area. She said she couldn't cope with the thought of a religiously segregated area again. Where segregation existed bigotry was bred. So we took a risk and went with the only other part of Belfast that was left, the North.

It was a fun time as we searched for houses; we would scroll through the small print of the Telegraph's classified and put a big circle around the houses that we could afford. Then we would phone the landlords and ask questions about the smaller details, what type of heat it had, were pets allowed etc.

It didn't take long before we found a house that seemed ideal, it was a good price and the landlord claimed it was in a quiet family area. Google didn't exist in those days so Mum went on trust; he seemed a genuine man. Over the next year he would be working on a series of repairs, but for now it was clean and comfortable. When he assured her that the house would be a long-term let and that we could have it for as long as we wanted it she was sold. Rather than make the two hour journey to Belfast to view Mum took him at his word and signed all the relevant paperwork from home. She wrote a cheque for the deposit, a month in advance and the next month's rent. She paled at the amount of money it had cost but all the furniture was included and we had nothing to do but move in. We could sell our current furniture and gain some of the money back. In that respect it could be viewed it as a saving; she would just have to find a job as soon as we arrived to ensure further rent instalments were made. Within five days the keys arrived in the post and we were good to move.

Naivety was always one of Mum's strong points and on seeing the new home she knew her strong point had not let her down!

I will never forget it; it was the most dilapidated house I had ever seen. Before we even set foot in the door I knew that Mum had made a huge mistake. I think she did too I knew by her face which was clamped into a tight frown. I wanted to run back to the grim council estate but even then at fourteen I knew it was too late. Anywhere would be better than this ramshackle excuse for a house.

As the removal men moved what little furniture we had brought in I cringed, this was Mum's good clean furniture, furniture that I remember her struggling to buy. After a week in here it would surely be destroyed. The windows were paper thin, some were even cracked. If I had applied any pressure to them I knew they would shatter. The walls were decorated with little blue black splodges that could only be damp. On opening the kitchen cupboard I encountered an army of ants.

We were all horrified, but there was nothing for it we were here now, so we got stuck in and began to help Mum attempt to clean the place up. As soon as our phone was connected Mum called the landlord and told him of her concerns that his house was not as described. He reassured her that he knew there was work to be done and that it was his top priority. Mum called him every week at the start, soon she gave up.

The move meant that I had missed a considerable amount of school and I was keen to escape the damp house. I asked Mum if we could find a school over the next few weeks, she agreed and together we sat over a map of Belfast to find the nearest grammar. Low and behold it seemed that we were within a mile of a school, we called it and they were happy to see me. Within two weeks I was ensconced in Belfast Royal Academy (BRA).

There I had my eyes opened, I had come from a small country convent school and all of a sudden was faced with a school with over a thousand pupils and things I had never encountered; boys and Protestants. I can honestly say that prior to BRA I had spent my life surrounded solely by Catholics, Protestants were few and far between where I had grown up. The school meant that I mixed with people from all walks of life and religions and I found that this was a good life lesson, perhaps the only thing I can be thankful to the school for. In those first few years I hated it, I hated the uniform a long sweeping grey ankle length skirt, I hated the pretentiousness and I hated the city children with their mature ways. The school had a certain coldness to it and from my perspective seemed to value the more affluent children.

I knew I wanted to go to university, I knew to do so I would have to be at school. Reluctantly I spent four years in that school; most of which involved polishing up my maths skills as I counted down how many days I had left before I could leave!

Chapter Forty Nine

A month into life in Belfast we all had plans or knew what we were intending to do. I was now in school and Maxine and Alison were looking for work. Alison quickly found an office job and Maxine a place in the local technical college. Mum too found work, for it seemed the city was littered with nursing homes; it wasn't long before she was once again buried in rigorous twenty-four hour shifts alternating her weeks between day and night duty.

I could see little difference in our daily life in Belfast but Mum had wanted to move here so much I decided to give it more of a chance, I was sure that the city must have some merits. Very quickly it emerged that Belfast wasn't what Mum had thought it would be either. The people she encountered in Belfast were not what she had remembered. She didn't approach her old friends; she had lost touch with them when we had been moved back to Strabane. When I asked her why she wouldn't contact them she would say she couldn't let any of them see her living like this. Rather than give up though she tried to make contact with the locals, Mum wanted friends, she had lacked them for so long, yet no matter how friendly she was they clearly weren't interested in befriending her.

I feared she would reach out for her old friend Misery again but luckily enough Mum had found a new GP in Belfast. This doctor seemed more promising than Strabane's doctor when Mum explained her symptoms he had Mum assessed by a psychiatrist and even secured a diagnosis. Mum had severe depression a result of two factors; nursing carnage victims of the troubles and of course Dad's murder. Mum had been experiencing flashbacks for many years along with extreme depression and suicidal thoughts. She could never function normally with such a condition. Unfortunately, no treatment existed and the doctor believed that counselling at this stage twelve years after the bomb would be futile, instead based on the psychiatrists' recommendations Mum was started on a new course of drugs. These would help her; they would keep Misery away I thought.

When Mum received her first pay cheque, I was a little shocked to see how little the private nursing homes paid, I didn't voice my thoughts but I can remember panicking a little wondering how we would cope on it. I knew what had happened before in the absence of savings and I worried about a repeat performance. I worried so much that I began to become introverted as my mind ran over all the possible scenarios. I remember going to schools friends houses and being acutely aware of how differently they lived of how their Mum's were so *normal*, of how they stayed awake all day and of how they had fathers. My response was to stop eating. It gave me a chance to concentrate on something other than our current predicament, on my Mum who even then I knew was just not right.

My overwhelming memory of the time was being so unhappy. I had been swept up by Mum's enthusiasm to move, yet the city was now an unknown entity. We had gone for a walk around on our first weekend here and every street was scarred, the Antrim Road, the Limestone Road, Cliftonville Road and the Shore road. It didn't matter which for as we walked along them Mum listed the atrocities that had occurred on them. A shooting on this one, a bombing on the other, the streets of this city she had said are like little memorials, each one had its own part to play in the troubles.

That was the day when she asked me,

"How could any place be good when all this bloodshed has occurred?"

My stomach plunged as I knew Mum hadn't moved any further forward. In fact Belfast seemed to take her right back. The move hadn't made everything okay like I had thought, that was when I had a shiver of dread, of knowing. What if moving back to Belfast had make things worse? What if the move was an even bigger mistake than I had initially thought? I was slowly realising that by moving Mum had simply been chasing a past.

A past that like my Dad was dead.

I really looked forward to our first trip to the city centre Mum had said that we all deserved a day out and that she would give us a tour. In the absence of our fiesta, or the 'brown bomber' as I had dubbed it (it had fallen apart before the move) we got a taxi into the city centre rather than brave the buses. I sat quietly in the back seat looking around me, Belfast then seemed so huge, the buildings were taller and the streets wider than anything I had been used to. When we reached the back of Castlecourt we got out of the taxi. Alison and I rushed ahead eager to experience the thrill of the big shops that the 'Clothes Show' and 'Mizz' magazine ranted on about. It was a great day at first; everything was so new, glossy and modern. We were so busy taking in the sights that it was only when we were walking along the upstairs of the shopping centre that I noticed all eyes were on us,

"Mum look" I said feeling my face reddening under the harsh lights.

Mum looked around for what I saw and could clearly find nothing out of the ordinary. It was then she noticed that things were very ordinary, too ordinary. She saw what we always saw when we were out. People were staring, heads whirled around as we passed, eyes directed towards us, taking us up and down. It was horrendous, I stared back, hoping they would avert their eyes but they continued to gawp. It was then that I looked at the scene surrounding us and noted that yet again, my sisters and I were the solitary black faces in the whole centre.

I wanted to cry Mum had promised that things would be different here, that city life was perfect for us; instead my sisters and I were the subject of curiosity, oddities once again. People believed they could stare openly at us if because our skin was brown, as if it wouldn't hurt us. Our shopping trip ended quickly that day and I became resigned that in Northern Ireland, the place where I was born and bred, that my sisters and I would always stand out like sore thumbs.

Chapter Fifty

After three months, twelve long weeks in the damp miserable dwelling the landlord hadn't darkened the door. We were wasting our money even phoning him. I knew that the promised repairs were never going to be carried out. I could see Mum's eyes beginning to go vague, she was seeing but not seeing. I knew

Misery was approaching. My sisters and I managed to block her just in time before she sunk her claws into Mum. We had Mum seen by her friendly GP who topped up her medication again. It is only now that I am older that I can definitively say that Mum's condition was to worsen in my teens because she had more time to think about her past.

The treatment offered by any doctor Mum had ever seen was more drugs, she became like a walking pharmacy yet they kept prescribing more. I used to tell her that she would rattle if shook. A link with post-traumatic stress and victims of the troubles was an abstract tentative notion back then. Unfortunately it has only recently been discovered as a valid illness for people in Northern Ireland. The late link between the illness and victims meant destruction for Mum and the bulk of her adult life and as a direct result the lives of her children.

However at fifteen I found Mum's doctor a God send, I knew little about mental illness back then. All I knew was that Mum's doctors willingly dispensed her any drug she felt would be of use. It was easier for them, easier to ignore the root of her problems. For me it meant that the drugs kept Misery away or at least held her back a little, it meant I had my Mum back.

Having Mum's full attention was crucial in that house; with no success with the household repairs it was time for us to move again. We were fortunate in that we found a little home that was clean and fresh and in an area that was wonderfully friendly. We all liked the house and after living in such a hovel the basic little terrace felt palatial. We didn't get our deposit back from our old landlord but no one complained, not even Mum who had to work on her days off to build a new deposit, and instead we were just relieved to be on the move.

Not that I saw much of my sisters these days. Alison had become engaged to a man she had met in her beauty queen days. She was constantly accompanied by her new fiancée. Maxine had become even more withdrawn and independent than ever and took advantage of Mum's working patterns.

Much to my annoyance my abnormal eating patterns began to get noticed. I had thought I had hid my new slim-lined self well, obviously not well enough. My baggy tee-shirts and jeans failed to conceal the bones that now poked through my skin. I was skeletal. Soon my Mum and sisters were constantly ranting and wailing at me. One day they would be cross, the next sympathetic but on all days they tried to make me eat.

In the meantime I continued making the dinners, cleaning, cooking and looking after the household bills. It took my sudden collapse before the doctor who had tired of getting dragged to make a diagnosis. I had developed anorexia and bulimia. A lethal combination one that I would carry with me into early adulthood, any time the going got tough from that point on my eating patterns became peculiar.

Mt fifteenth and sixteenth years were spent avoiding everything to do with food. Mum had Misery and I had my eating disorder, everyone had their coping mechanisms I would reason, mine was just more noticeable than others.

Now Mum tells me that she was so desperate for me to get well that she began praying again, she would pray to my Dad imploring him to help. She knew she needed to spend time with me but she also needed to work if we were to have a roof over our heads.

She said she needed him for so many things, to give her the okay on Alison's fiancée and to bring Maxine back within the fold. Yet Mum faced the problems alone.

I was taken to the Mater hospitals A&E after a further collapse; they could do little but recommended some sort of counselling. Mum remembers leaving the hospital that day feeling totally useless. She blamed herself she spent what little free time she had monitoring me and gradually I gained weight, although even now I can say that I never fully recovered.

Meanwhile life went on as it tends to do and the public holidays were approaching. This particular holiday, was celebrated nowhere in the world but Northern Ireland. As the glorious twelfth of July loomed our friendly little street soon was a little less friendly. It became littered in red white and blue flags and sectarian connotations. The stones on the pavements were painted to match the flags. We never had to deal with this particular holiday in Strabane so watched the spectacle with interest.

On the night before the holiday, 'the eleventh' the festivities began. Revellers lit a huge bonfire and partied around it until the small hours. The bonfire was stacked high. I was ashamed to admit that Mum had contributed to it! In a bid to get rid of some pieces of old rickety furniture that had come with our house, we had given it to children who collected wood from the doors in the weeks before the twelfth. I remember how delighted Mum was; giving them the wardrobes saved us the hassle of getting rid of them ourselves.

On the top of the bonfire stood an effigy of a famous IRA politician, Mum laughed when she saw it and decided then and there that she was born into the wrong side of the fence. If only the effigy were real she thought! That night I listened to them condemn the IRA, show their strength by shooting bullets into the air. It was their final actions that sent a chill through my core, they condemned each and every Catholic, they tarred all Catholics with the terrorist brush. I think Mum was taken aback by the levels of hatred they showed as well and she told me to come away from the window and go to bed.

The bitterness emanating from their words presented Mum with another side to Northern Ireland, a side just as bitter as the side she hated. This place was poisoned she would say, one sides as bad as the other, there will never be peace here. I understand her reasoning because the parents of the entrenched on both sides would infect their children and on and on it would go. Hatred and suspicion would always remain and with it other families would be shattered like mine.

It didn't take long for the locals to discover that they had Catholics in their midst, I really believe they smelt us! Little threats came through the letter box and once again we were on the move.

This time we choose a Catholic area, again in North Belfast. Yet soon IRA supporters discovered; they always had their ways, exactly who we were. A few years later we were to try living in North Belfast again, we got a reasonably priced rental on Alliance Avenue. We didn't stay there long.

Chapter Fifty One

I began to notice that Mum was growing tired, more tired than I had ever seen weariness was etched on her face. We had been in Belfast now for three years and moved five times. In the background the peace process had began. The news that peace had been delivered was broken to Mum and I by a jubilant crowds in a chemist shop. She was collecting her prescription when the hugging and celebrating began. We asked them what the occasion was? We were told we had peace; Northern Ireland was at peace at last.

"Well it's come too late for us" Mum said, but her voice was drowned out by their cries of jubilation.

We had moved back to South Belfast, the rents were higher but at least the areas were mixed. None of us could stand living in one sided areas. More to the point the last few years proved that these areas couldn't stand us either! So to cope with the rents Mum took on even more hours and now worked seventy two hour weeks. She was paying a high price to live in this area so much that ironically she never saw our house.

I was doing my A- Levels at the time, I remember the days passing in a whirl of essays and exams. The only real thing that stands out for me during those years was meeting Mum on her way home from work one day. She had left me a fiver to get some provisions after school, which I had done so I took my little dog to the park. The dog became over excited and ran off and then I noticed that he was running in the direction of someone in the distance, as I got closer I saw it was Mum. She looked all done in but I remember she smiled pleased to see me and my crazy dog. I remember remarking what she was doing walking; she normally caught the bus or got a lift. She muttered something about it being a dry day. We began to walk home together when I noticed that Mum wasn't keeping up, she was a good six steps behind. I looked at her puzzled saying "get a move on" when my eyes were drawn down.

Mum's heels were bleeding, her red blood a stark contrast against her white nurses shoes.

"Mum what happened?" I asked

Then it occurred to me, before she could even answer I said,

"Please don't tell me you walked"

"Okay I won't" she laughed

Mum had given me her last that morning, she had known she couldn't make it home from work yet she said nothing. Instead she walked all the way from the Sanddown Road to the Lisburn Road.

I was lost for words and she and I made our way home in silence.

Luckily Mum soon found another nursing home nearby, it was during her time working there that she once again came home worse for wear. It transpired that a colleague approached her and told her that a younger nurse working there was also from Strabane. Apparently she had been talking about Mum.

It took a while for me to extract the full story but it seemed that the younger nurse took great delight in telling all Mum's colleagues that Gabrielle horror *of horrors* had three black daughters! She took great delight in running my sisters and I down it seemed. The nurse was snobbish and spoke of her background as if she stemmed directly from royalty. Mum just couldn't work out who she was. The country girl in Mum came out, as her small town habits came to the fore. Hailing from a small town everyone knew everyone or they knew someone who knew someone! Yet Mum could not place her.

It was only when she discovered that she was married, that things began to click. Mum had been trying to establish exactly who she was using her married name, no wonder all her leads ended nowhere. As soon as she discovered her maiden name she established exactly who she was. Mum also learned exactly what she had been saying about our family. She looked down on us and Mum in particular all because we were black. Now that Mum knew who she was however, it wasn't long until she turned the tables. This nurse, this snobbish creature had been the offspring of one of the town's most working class families; in fact working class was too high a title, rather than coming from great things Mum claimed that this girl had come from the gutter.

When Mum revealed the younger girls true background and her surprise at her newly acquired plumy tones, the rumours soon stopped. Yet Mum was horrified that someone at the bottom, the very bottom of the social heap, felt that because she had black daughters that she was someone to be looked down upon. The staff were supportive and told her to take it with a pinch of salt. Even though Mum had felt she had brought an end to the situation and that it wouldn't happen again I remember feeling awful, I was so upset that someone could talk about my Mum like that.

All because of us.

After hearing Mum's experience it was reinforced to me that racism was everywhere and I think Mum realised that it was something she would always have to cope with. Just because my Mum had married the man that she loved and had his children she would forever be tarred. Mum had done nothing but follow her heart I still fail to understand how that was so wrong. Even years later, people still believed that Mum was guilty of a heinous crime. My Mum would always be punished for falling in love.

I think that incident where Mum was made to feel bad about meeting and marrying my Dad was when his box that she had tucked far away in her mind, began to rumble. She would voice more often that she wanted him here so much. If he were here she wouldn't be in this mean place, she wouldn't have to listen to such remarks, to be judged. My parents could have faced these people together. If my Dad were here, my sisters and I wouldn't have needed our incessant questions. If Dad were here Misery and Mum would never have been acquainted.

Chapter Fifty Two

One night after a few drinks Alison's boyfriend picked up his car keys to prepare for his journey home. He was drunk so Mum promptly snatched the car keys from him and demanded that he slept on the sofa. His reaction came from nowhere. He pushed Mum with such force that he slammed her into a wall; he even kicked one of my dogs, so hard that he broke her tiny rib. Inside Mum says she screamed for Dad as she knew she couldn't take this man on alone. She didn't have to. Maxine and I were screaming at him to leave her alone, we pulled at him and eventually restrained him. Alison just sat there, she was in shock.

Alison ran out after him and the pair drove off into the night. That night he had a car crash. Alison who didn't drive was said to have been behind the wheel. Yet eye witness accounts claimed otherwise. Mum banned my sister then in her early twenties from seeing that man ever again. If a man could show that type of violence to his mother in law then what could she expect. Alison ignored Mums warnings and within a year they were married. We did not attend the ceremony.

Maxine was the next to fly the nest; she had been in the city centre one day when someone asked her the question that my sisters and I were often asked,

"Where are you from?"

"Belfast, then Strabane, and then Belfast again!" She had replied

"But where were you from before that?"

"The only other place I've lived in was Strabane "she had said

"Aye, but where were you born?"

"Belfast" she replied,

The woman had laughed asking her what age she was, when Maxine told her she was twenty, the woman had responded,

"People like you aren't born here; there was no one like you here twenty years ago."

That week she had a few more racist jibes and came home in tears.

"Mum I can't listen to these people anymore; they won't allow me to say I'm from here"

She had no answer for her.

Two months later my sister and my best friend moved to London. She said she would never be back. To date bar one special occasion she has kept her promise.

Mum was growing more and more tired and once again falling behind on the bills, I did my best to pay them but A–Levels took priority. Then a rent increase left us in severe trouble. Our cupboards held half a bag of sugar and a tin of beans. After my previous bout with eating disorders I wasn't a big eater, nor was Mum but we were so hungry a tin of beans would barely take the edge of it.

Mum was working so hard that on the face of it we should have been surviving, holding things together but all the moving took its toll, each new house we got required some sort of furniture, some sort of improvement whether it was furnished or not. Each house required a removal van for our personal effects we had no car, and most expensive of all each house required a month's rent in advance and a deposit. We never saw our deposits again there was always an excuse for not fulfilling them. We grew tired of filling other peoples oil tanks, carpeting their floors, painting their walls and carrying out repairs that were not our duty to do. Eventually we were spent out; we were left with the choice pay the rent or eat.

For the first month after the rent increase, we choose to pay the rent. That month I remember being poorer than ever before and knowing no solution. I would tell Mum I would leave school get a job but she always steadfastly refused. My Dad wanted us to have an education, she would never force one on us like his parents did, but when one of us was interested she would never and could never take that option from us. If she made me give up on my university dream she would have failed me and more importantly my Dad's wishes. We made a loaf of bread last for a week and raised £1, which we used to buy a bag of potatoes.

When I peeled the first potato I discovered it was off; I had inkling when a rancid odour wafted my way when I opened the bag. I bundled the bag up, receipt in hand and went to the shop keeper who I had just bought them from. He had told me he hadn't sold me those. I pointed out to him that he had, showing him the pile I had gotten them from and he chased me away, saying,

"You blacks are always trying to take the hand". We did without our potatoes that week and had thrown away our precious pound.

Chapter Fifty Three

I had always aspired to go off to university and would turn eighteen soon. It would nearly be time for my compensation payment awarded to me by the state on Dad's death. Mum and I were in a mess so I promised her that whatever funds the state had awarded would be used to help us out. Our spirits were lifted as we knew we only had to endure this situation for a few more months.

It was during this time that Mum received a call from home, her father had become unwell. He would be treated in Belvior hospital in Belfast. She was able to see him every day as he was being treated in the city. The nurse in Mum had seen his diagnosis many times before and therefore knew his prognosis was not good. Her father had lung cancer. He deteriorated quickly, it was so, so sad. Her father loved a yarn, he would talk to whoever would listen yet he was left with a disease that took away his breath, it had rendered him speechless.

It wasn't long before we received another call; her father who had returned back to his home town in a break from treatment, had taken a turn for the worst. Mum had to get to the hospital in Derry that night. Yet we had no funds. We had nothing and no one to ask. Mum called the hospital in Derry and asked them to phone her with any news, if he got worse or if he became stable. That night my Mum received a call from her sibling.

"Your fathers dead" she said and disconnected the call. I watched as Mum sunk to the floor, she remained there for many hours.

Alison was informed and with her fiancée we made the trip to his wake and his funeral. We were ignored by most and lambasted by others. No one cared why my Mum couldn't make it that night; she wasn't there, that was all that mattered.

Yet she carried her father, the other great man in her life with her and thought of him daily.

Chapter Fifty Four

Mum must have gone to work and listened to her colleagues' talk of holidays, socialising and nights out as I do now. Even if they spoke of something as basic as shopping, she must have felt about an inch high. She had an empty cupboard, empty wardrobe and empty stomach. For the pleasure of living in South Belfast, the only place we were *allowed* to live, the rent was strangling us. At the end of that month she asked me not to pay the rent. Instead she said we would phone the landlord and tell him we were struggling, he seemed an affable man. Maybe we could arrange some sort of repayment plan with him. We would buy some food, even get an outfit each and have a nice day out. That's what we did and again on the next month and the next.

Therefore our eviction came as no surprise; once again we began a search for another house. This time we were back at the mercy of the council. They found us a house on Belfast's Ormeau road, and we tried our best to make a home of it. Unfortunately we faced the usual dilemma; we had no money and no furniture. Privately renting didn't allow us to accumulate furniture as the landlords used their own. The house had recently been renovated, bare walls and cement floors were its main features. For the first few months we slept on bundles of the few clothes we had.

Then at last my money came through and like my sisters before me Mum expressed her disappointment. In her grief stricken state 16 years earlier she had trusted the state to invest the money awarded on the death of our Dad with care. Since mine had been held the longest, Mum assumed that I would attain a good sum. Instead I received £150 more than Maxine, who received £150 more than Alison. My sisters and I began 16 years ago with £2000 each and we all finished with just under £5000.

Yet neither Mum nor I were in a position to complain, how we needed that money. To me it seemed liked millions! I had hoped to attend Trinity University to study Law if my A level results were good enough and intended this money to fund my studies. I had second thoughts when I compared what I received with the price of a degree in Dublin. Instead I decided that I would spend her university years here in Belfast and stay at home to save funds.

Mum admits now that inside she seethed. My Dad had considered education his top priority. Mum couldn't help she could barely support us as it was. Had my Dad been alive I knew I could have attended ten universities fully funded if it meant I was pursuing an education. The box marked Max in Mum's head had begun to rumble again and she could feel her old friend Misery approach. This time I believe she struggled to push her aside.

Chapter Fifty Five

The TV was now full of news about the victims of the troubles; I watched keenly and thought that maybe we would be okay after all. There were over three thousand victims and something was to be put in place to help them. Maybe these new incentives could help Mum? I thanked the heavens, Mum had shouldered too much alone. The new Labour government with the bright young Tony Blair at the Helm was forward thinking and committed to devolving the country. It seemed we would get some sort of recognition for those who had been lost.

Mum and I didn't get time to dwell on the news as yet again we had another house to furnish and fix. Mum had to do this between her long shifts and me between A–Level revision. I wondered where we would get the time. With my money we did what we could with the house and created a comfortable home.

By some miracle I got the grades in my A- Levels I needed to attend the Law course in Trinity, Mum was so proud, she said Dad would have been too. Mum cried that day, although she was elated she was saddened too because my Dad wasn't there. In the end the Trinity course was too expensive and that was before we had even looked into Dublin accommodation. Mum and I agreed that Queen's was a good choice and that a university was a university (within reason).

I started Queen's in September 1997, as I hadn't applied there for law I couldn't study law that year and would have to wait for the following year's intake. One year seemed so long to my eighteen year old self, so I got a place reading my next favourite subject; History. Mum was still working away and a routine was gradually taking shape. Until late one night we had a visitor.

Alison who we hadn't seen in over a year came to the door. My sister was a married woman now and had coincidentally moved around the corner. Mum was so glad to see her that she immediately reached out and embraced her. She may not have agreed with her choice of husband, but it was her bed so she could lie on it. In the meantime she appeared happy. We were just so glad to see her.

It felt like our family was reunited and I would even say happy for a while. Mum even tried again with Alison's husband, if he was going to be a part of her daughter's life, then she may as well get used to him.

Alison and her husband became regular fixtures at our house and Mum and I went to theirs each week. In between all that I squeezed in my university career in which I loved. I had started a part time job in Mum's nursing home and was enjoying a social life, frequenting the 'Bot' and the 'Egg' like my parents many years before. I was enjoying my freedom, alcohol and men and more than anything being open about my smoking hobby which I had managed to conceal for years! An announcement over a family dinner one evening made things even better. Alison declared she had something to say and hushed us all before she said,

"Mum I'm pregnant"

It was like music to Mum's ears; she loved children and was excited already. She must have been like my Dad on hearing the news of his daughter's conception all those years ago. It wasn't until a day or so later that realisation struck Mum. It is a true to say that for Mum every silver lining has a cloud, and this new sure had a cloud; for she would be a granny!

"Surely I'm too young for that?" she exclaimed!

On a sadder note she said she had not imagined facing the news of her first grandchild alone and thought wistfully of how my Dad would have reacted to his daughter's announcement. She only hoped he was looking down on Alison and making sure that everything to do with this little one was as it should be.

Nine months later I sat (admittedly slightly hung-over) in the Royal Hospital in Belfast and waited as Mum's first granddaughter and my niece came into the world. Maxine had come over from London especially for the occasion. I remember the combination of the previous night's drink and the idea of childbirth made me feel positively green, I was disgusted by the whole thing. Yet Mum was overjoyed.

On the 6th of September 1998, my niece Sarah-Jayne was born. She was a beautiful baby; if you liked that sort of thing that was! Mum said she reminded her so much of her little ones when we were at that stage.

To me Sarah-Jayne was a strange little thing, she was white and on checking her little fingers as Mum had told us to do with all mixed race children, no pigmentation existed. It seemed she would stay white. Sarah-Jayne had a head full of black hair and a little African nose. She reminded Mum of Alison and of course her grandfather. It was then that it really struck Mum that this child would never know her grandfather. Mum's shelf began to shake a little more furiously than usual. Yet she ignored the tremors and told her doctor of them. Once again her drugs were upped and her shelf was stabilised. Now Mum had a new reason for living; her little granddaughter.

Mum spent all her free time at Alison and her husband's home. She really could not get enough of this little girl. Mum loved her as much as she loved her own and discovered that a grandchild was just another child to worry about. For me it was great that Mum had something more in her life, she deserved some joy and Sarah-Jayne brought it to her by the bucketful.

That winter was a lovely one, the new baby injecting some sparkle into our dull world. She brought so much laughter into our house that we spent that Christmas smiling and for once filled with hope.

Yet in the February of that year the sparkle turned to ash, when once again our door knocked late in the night. Just like the year before Alison was on the doorstep, this time with a baby.

"Mum I've left him" she said,

Mum brought them in as it was so cold outside and through her tears Alison explained how unhappy she had been.

This was no place for *'I told you so's'*, instead Alison was taken in and once again under Mum's roof. In the months that followed Alison and her husband fought a bitter, acrimonious battle. Dragging their marriage through the courts as both of them fought for custody of the baby.

Mum wanted no part in the battle and ignored it where possible; with the exception of Dad's trial no one in her family had ever been to court. "What on earth would Max have thought?" she asked me on one occasion. Even though Mum felt she should have supported my sister more she said she was empty, she had nothing left to give.

Instead we concentrated on immediate concerns such as the need for a bigger home. If Alison and Sarah-Jayne were to remain with us we would need at least one extra bedroom. So when the courts decided that Sarah-Jayne would stay with her mother, we were once again searching for another home.

As Sarah-Jayne grew she took to calling Mum granny Bumba, she couldn't pronounce Olorunda no matter how hard she tired. I couldn't really blame her as most adults I met couldn't! The name stuck and for a while Mum became known to us all as Granny Bumba.

If Sarah-Jayne needed anything or if Mum was mentioned in a conversation with Sarah-Jayne she was referred to as Granny Bumba. I would hear her ask for Granny Bumba every day and found amusement in how such a little child could change the name that my Mum had been known by for fifty years.

It didn't take long to find a house to hold us all and one that we could afford. This house was again in North Belfast but had a nice layout. It didn't need much more than a few coats of paint. We moved in and made it our home. We seemed to settle in well, that was until that summer when riots broke out. I had never seen riots before and it seemed that all hell had been unleashed! The world's media descended at the top of our street. They watched crowds of men, women and in many cases children fighting bitter battles. Every night, Catholics faced Protestants and fought across a peace wall. Our side of the wall was on the Catholic side. It was just our luck that the wall that divided the two communities was right behind our house.

Each night fell petrol bombs were launched over our house; we crammed into a room in the middle to avoid being struck and to drown out the voices of the angry mob.

One night they needed to get through our row of houses to the other side,

"Go through the Niger's house" they cried.

We were terrified not to mention shocked, when we first moved there the community boasted of its anti-racist attitude, the poor Catholics faced similar plights and claimed to empathise with the many black communities around the world. I lost count of how many taxi drivers and locals told us we would be perfectly safe here. That was until their true opinions emerged, as my Mum always maintained scratch the surface and you'll find a bigot. In times of tension in Northern Ireland this surface was well and truly scratched. For once Mum had nothing to say instead of taking her usual stance and defending us she passed out. I think her shelf rumbled more than ever before shaking her to the core.

We moved from that house within a week, loosing another deposit in the process and I believe a large chunk of Mum. I graduated during these years gaining a 2:1, Mum was proud but she cried on the news because Dad wouldn't be there to hear. We made a decision then that due to his absence we would miss the graduation and have a quiet family dinner instead.

Chapter Fifty Six

Belfast was changing with more and more black faces; who as far as many locals were concerned, were blotting the landscape. Yet Mum said these faces weren't like our Dad, these new people on the whole were not professionals they weren't middle class. They were refugees and asylum seekers. They had come here out of sheer distress; many had nowhere to go. Within a few months they filled out the many rentals in Belfast. Some of the houses housed so many that they were full to overflowing.

I would hear remarks of the locals, "they're everywhere", or "they're coming here to steal our jobs, our benefits and our houses". Suddenly Alison and I found ourselves labelled; what little individualism we had was gone, we were simply immigrants. So far we had been asked if our cousin or brother or sister lived down the road, had been in the same shop as us or had been on our bus. It seemed that to the Northern Irish all black people were related, regardless if they resembled each other or spoke in the same tongue or even came from the same country! I was once asked if a lady from Thailand was my sister, despite the fact that our ancestors hail from different parts of the Globe. Mum would tell us if they were to ask again, to point out a random white person and ask the person enquiring, what their relation to them was.

Even though Mum began to depend on me more and more she still had her mothering instinct and Mum grew scared for us. Her fears didn't go unfounded. They materialised one day when I was walking my dog in the local park.

I was attacked. I remember that a black man had jogged past me; he was simply out for a run harming no one. After he had passed a white man approached me. It was all too much for his little mind to have a black man passing him followed in quick succession by a black girl. He exploded and took his disgust out on me. He had grabbed my shoulders his fingers digging roughly into my bones and shook me. He spat at me to go back home and "Get the fuck out of his country". His explosion finished with a punch.

I returned home shaken and bruised and told Mum of my ordeal. We didn't go to the police, instead Mum meted out her own justice. She dragged me to the park every day at the same time until we finally ran into the attacker. I identified a large man in his late fifties as the culprit. Mum approached him and he continued his rant to her. She gave him an opportunity to apologise, but when she saw that none was forthcoming, she did what I least expected. She called on her old friend Anger, and together they attacked him. Mum says she didn't know where her strength came from that day; perhaps he received every blow that every racist she had encountered deserved. It wasn't long before he screamed for mercy. He apologised frantically and I believe sincerely to me. He reassured me that he would never, ever utter another racist word again. When I looked at how he groped his neither regions after Mum's kicks, something told me to believe him!

Dealing with the attacker unfortunately did not put an end to the racial tensions that were unfolding all over Belfast. The locals were none too happy at having something new in their midst and being Northern Irish weren't afraid to express themselves. Their opinions didn't surprise me; these people couldn't live with each other, so it was no revelation when they struggled to live with anyone else!

One day I went out to our back yard to find it splashed with a swastika, the following morning the tires on my little banger, my pride and joy were slashed. A brash warning was thrown in our letter box. We packed our belongings and fled.

Chapter Fifty Seven

Our fourteenth house was just outside Belfast in the village of Holywood, and Mum loved it. She said in an alternative world had she and Dad decided to settle in Northern Ireland this was where she would have chosen. It was in this house that Mum's tiredness reached epic proportions and I pleaded with her to give up work. I was beginning a Master's degree but was also working part time, Alison was working full time. My sisters and I weren't high earners but we combined my part time income with her wage from temping and decided we would cope. Mum was worn out she needed a break and this new house in this pretty village was the perfect place for her to recuperate, to allow her to regain strength.

Recently Mum just had no strength; she was tiny and began to look so frail. Her hands shook and her conversation became fragmented. There was some benefits for Mum though because whilst Alison was working Sarah-Jayne and her Granny Bumba spent their days together. They would go to the local beach, the park and make all manner of buns and cakes. Mum would say that she was doing what she missed out on with us.

We spent a year in that house until our rent fell behind. Alison's contract came to an end and my job had to go, the final stages of my masters were becoming intensive. Once again we were faced with pay the rent or eat.

We ate, we were evicted and we were faced with moving to house number fifteen.

We moved into house number fifteen on a Tuesday and we were evicted on the Friday. Things were worse than ever, this time we really had struck rock bottom, we were homeless. I couldn't take any more yet alone Mum. She was collapsing more and more I can only liken it to a powerful blow hitting her head, I imagine her skull reverberating in pain, as she felt the hinges that supported her shelf being ripped one by one from the wall. Dust and debris filled her consciousness and the wall shook. Painful remnants of her past, shelved neatly away until now assaulted her, striking her from every direction. Her childhood, nursing during the troubles, my Dad, racism, endless moves and poverty all came back to her. I believe Mum's shelf collapsed.

2005 -2010

Chapter Fifty Eight

From a very early age I remember suffering from a recurring dream. I used to wake at night shivering and terrified. Some dreams are forgotten when consciousness returns yet the frequency of this one meant that it always stayed fresh. I used to dream that I was standing outside Melmount Church in Strabane, and looking for Mum amongst the crowds leaving the Mass. I would see her standing near the doors and make my way towards her. When I would get near the crowds would disappear and I would look up to find three people who all looked like my Mum. I knew that only one was the real her and that the other two were bad. Yet I had no way of telling them apart, they were all identical.

Each one would be beckoning me and I never knew who to go to. I would eventually make up my mind and approach the one that I felt was Mum. Then I would wake just knowing that I had made the wrong decision. Now I look at my dream with an uneducated interpretation, I think I was always seeking the good Mum, the one who I saw now and again, the one who wasn't depressed, angry or tired.

After our eviction and Mum's complete breakdown I was on my own. I couldn't fathom why our landlady had suddenly asked us to leave and could only assume Mum had said something wrong, pushed her too far. I was furious my only thoughts at the time were 'what *has she done now?'* or *'that's another fine mess she's got us into'*. I had used every last penny of my final wages and then some to secure this house and Mum had just bloody told me that the landlady wants us out.

The mortification of it all! How would I ever begin to explain this one? The few friends that I had clearly assumed I was from a travelling background, as no sooner had we moved into one house were we packing up for another.

Recently Mum had become a law onto herself. She had been acting so strangely. She would forget her phone number, her date of birth and even more scarily her name. I worried about her all the time.

For the most part though, Mum made me laugh. She had begun to say the most terrible and inappropriate things, she would comment on strangers' right to their faces, telling them they were fat or worse point out features like big noses or their general ugliness (as she perceived it). I spent my days silencing her; she really was going to get herself into trouble.

I began to take her everywhere over those years, she was behaving so oddly I feared she might get lost. Or worse and more likely, that she would say the wrong thing to the wrong person. I had taken her to the doctors one week and two ladies were talking amongst themselves in the waiting room. Mum began to show signs of irritation and eventually looked at me and asked,

"Are they ever going to shut up?"

I invariably shushed her, looking over my shoulder to ensure they hadn't heard. They hadn't and went on with their talking. This was unfortunate; for them. As they continued talking Mum turned to them and bellowed,

"Would you fucking shut up" they looked at her aghast, as did I, "this is a doctor's I have a headache and your droning is making it worse, now if you want a social gathering why don't you go elsewhere? Instead of sitting here making the sick sicker" she had tutted.

I put my head in my hands and chastised myself; *I should have seen this coming.* Mum had been getting agitated. This was my fault.

The doctor must have heard the commotion, and realised what its source was because within seconds, Mum was ushered into the office. If nothing else Mum certainly knew how to beat the queue!

When the door closed, I looked at the two stunned ladies and apologised, they smiled and nodded. I assumed my apology had been accepted, yet they never regained their conversation. Well

I mused inwardly if they hadn't needed a doctor before, they certainly needed one now, so at least they were in the right place.

It transpired that Mum had asked the Landlady to fix the electric cable that connected the cooker to the mains and for new flooring in the living room, these demands were too much. Within ten minutes of Mum's request, we had been blamed for tampering with her oil boiler; 'something we often did as a family pastime', and an eviction statement rather than notice was administered.

I was so angry, the thought of another move and one so soon made me feel sick. How could I have been so silly and not predicted this? It's not as though we hadn't experienced landlords before. Good grief I had known more landlords in this town than I had hot dinners and I meant that literally. I should be able to see a scoundrel by now. I had done most of the dealings with this one, Mum was loose cannon these days and Alison was out and about with her new boyfriend. This eviction was therefore all down to me.

With some regret I let myself wallow for a while, if only we could have some permanency, just some time to plant roots. I wished we could just stay in one place long enough, if we could save something, have something behind us so we could be prepared for crisis. We could be proactive for once. In all my years it seemed that Mum had done her best, but circumstances had driven her to be reactive.

Hearing that we had set a new family record, perhaps even a world record in having the shortest tenancy in history, I became enraged. The house had once been a student house and looked like one. At least three slovenly young lads had lived in it. Not only had we just moved back to bloody Belfast, we were stuck with yet another hovel. The coastal town that Mum adored had few private rentals at our asking price. I had scoured the papers and shop windows searching for something, anything that could keep her there, nothing had been available. As we were once again behind on the rent we had little time to find this house, as usual we had no time to plan.

We had packed up all our things and moved in; for the umpteenth time I arranged the transfer of electric and phones and re-directed the post. Alison arranged for Sarah-Jayne to attend yet another unfamiliar school.

Chapter Fifty Nine

We were expert at this moving business, I couldn't do a lot of things but hand me a tenancy and a new set of keys and I excelled. Mum and I with the help of Sarah-Jayne, in reality the hindrance of Sarah-Jayne had spent three days cleaning before we could unpack.

Many houses can be described as bursting with life, this was one was positively exploding with it. The kitchen looked like it could walk away all by itself, and the bathroom nurtured its very own species.

For the umpteenth time since our move to this city, we started to clean the kitchen first and then worked our way through the house. We scrubbed the house and it's furnishings down from top to bottom, our hands were red raw and blistered. At least the place now smelt clean and fresh and we could begin to unpack.

We had no furniture of our own anymore, over the years anything we had accumulated we had lost in our many moves. Sometimes we hadn't lost anything at all, but it was easier to think that we did. The reality was we had had to sell even the chairs we had sat on, money was tight it had always been, but these moves were taking it out of us.

As usual each house needed a deposit, a month's advance rent and removal vans. They all needed a cash injection. To raise funds we borrowed and when that option was exhausted we sold something. The loan repayments grew so high that we were working for nothing, at the end of each month when everyone was paid back there was barely enough to buy a few food items. A trip to the pawn merchant became a part of the monthly cycle.

This time though we were spent out and had nothing left to sell. For the previous move, Mum had parted with the remains of her jewellery. The last item left in a once impressive collection was her wedding ring, to my shame this too had to be pawned. I was glad she had pawned it rather than sell it; I wanted so much to buy it back for her and was until now making good progress towards that goal.

Our new landlady had other ideas; she was intent on throwing us out. I knew then that I could forget the promise I had made of retrieving the ring, it was like everything else we ever had of value, a thing of the past. On the positive side I had just received the news that I had achieved my Master's degree, I was elated. It also meant that I was no longer a student; I could now look for proper work. I could support Mum. This next move although unplanned would be easier I would secure a job and I would ensure that the rent was paid. Mum was even cheered by the news of my Masters; she seemed to liven up a little and even promised to attend my graduation. I had missed my first graduation so was looking forward to attending this one. First though I had to secure a house.

Chapter Sixty

Mum briefly displayed signs of life on hearing I had gained my Masters, yet ten minutes later she was sitting on the armchair absorbing the news that we would be moving again,

"How long have we got here four or five days Mum?" I asked her, I needed to know what time frame I was working on.

She didn't answer. I asked her again and still no answer was forthcoming. She was upset I supposed, so I left her and went to our newly installed phone and called the landlady. She was nasty and angry and when pressed for the reasons behind our eviction she told me that she couldn't cope with a tenant who was so demanding. I tried to persuade her to let us stay but she was having none of it. No contracts had been signed, our low budget rentals rarely came with any contracts and she would like us out in a week.

There wasn't any point in wallowing; the cow obviously wasn't going to change her mind, there was no persuading her. With great difficulty I swallowed my pride and asked about our deposit. The cow went on to confirm that if the house was in good condition we could have our deposit back on the day we left. I bit my tongue, wondering if she was talking about a different house than the one we had got. The house had never been in good condition! Due to our hard work and back breaking labour she should be paying us. We would be debt free if she refunded us for the price of cleaning products alone. She had had the place intensively cleaned for free. We had lifted the used condoms from under the filthy beds, cleaned the strange smelling items of the kitchen floor and scrubbed her bathroom that was sprouting glorious green algae.

Putting down the phone I turned to Mum again. I called her but she was just sitting there, a cigarette in her hand staring into the distance. I followed her gaze to see what she was looking at. The wall held nothing of interest to me.

She looked so pitiful, her little hands shaking, as they had started to do recently. My heart went out to her and I gave her a little hug,

"You sit tight, and I'll get a paper, don't worry we'll find something and when we do we'll have a lovely day at Queen's for my graduation". I grabbed my coat and went to the shop. On the way there it occurred to me that Mum hadn't answered me, in fact, she hadn't responded at all. That was the day that I really noticed that my Mum's had taken a turn for the worst.

I couldn't dwell on Mums' predicament though; I had four days to find us a new house. Plenty of rentals were available but not many were available the following week.

In the end I found one. A dark ugly terrace, in the heart of an area that left a lot to be desired. Yet for now it had a roof, so it fulfilled the basic function of any home; shelter. I would clean it up as best I could before Mum saw it and hope for the best.

One week later we had moved into our seventeenth home. My knowledge of Belfast was extensive at this stage, not a wonder I supposed considering we had lived all over it. I laughed to myself thinking that if all else fails I could always become a taxi driver.

This new house was the same as most of the others, smelly and damp. When I asked the electric board to come and connect us, the electrician told me that the little box that housed the electric meter was filled with woodworm. If there was woodworm there, then I could expect the place to be riddled with it he'd said. I cringed inwardly slightly embarrassed but thanked him for his observations.

In the meantime I had a deposit to collect, so returned to the old house to meet the landlady. I was so angry I would have done anything to avoid her, but if we wanted to retain our new roof I needed the money. The cow knew we had paid royally to arrange the move and had arranged all our affairs around this address. Yet to her she felt giving a family one weeks' notice to pack up their belongings was reasonable. That being the case I dreaded confronting her.

I knocked the door of the house that had been our home for one week and she greeted me, coolly. I knew that we had left it cleaner than we had found it. We had even made a few alterations, hanging a new shower curtain to replace the old mouldy one and to lesson our removal costs left a solid mahogany fire place in the living room. We had even left a little vase of flowers on the top.

The cow trotted through the house ensuring I was following behind her. I could see she was looking for a reason, any reason to refuse repaying the deposit. So far she had found none. Then we got to the living room. She appraised the room, then me from head to toe. I don't know what was stronger her disgust at the fireplace we had left, or her disgust at me. As she chewed her cud and took in all seven stone of me, I knew something was coming that I wouldn't like.

I was right, for the cow went on to swallow her cud and say,

"I want that gone" and pointed at the fireplace "then we can discuss deposits"

A cough came from the door behind us and I looked around to see a man standing, he smiled and informed me that he was this barnyard creature's husband.

"Hello" I said to him, then to her "okay I'll have that arranged"

"No dear" she moooed, "you will move it now, I'm going today so won't be back and I want this house cleared"

"Okay" I said gulping as I looked at the girth of the fireplace; it took two men to carry it in. I just wondered how I was going to carry it out.

I looked at her looking at me and saw she wanted action immediately. Well I thought, we needed the money so by hook or crook I would have to remove this bloody fireplace. She stood back and watched me push and push, her only remark was "mind my floor dear".

I continued pulling, pushing and tugging and managed to move the beast out of the living room and down the front steps. I was exhausted already and decided if I could get the heavy piece of furniture just to the back-lane a stone's throw away I could arrange for it to be moved later.

Tears pricked my eyes as I assessed my strength; even to get this moved around the corner right now seemed an epic task. I could hear talking from inside and glanced up in time to see her restraining her husband, who was coming to help,

That's when the tears really came. How was I going to move this thing another inch? The cow noticed my intent seeing the direction I was angling the piece.

"I hope you're not taking that to the back-lane"

"Yes" I panted "just until I can get it lifted. I can call the council and they can collect it"

"Well in the meantime, you're not leaving that outside my back, take it to the other side of the lane"

I looked up the long terraced street at least one hundred houses in length and knew what she wanted. She wanted me to drag this deadweight of a fireplace all the way down there. On my own, I had no choice; I ignored the glances of those walking and driving by and began dragging the lead like piece of furniture down the street. When I was halfway down, her husband must have been granted permission to assist and he helped me. He struggled himself even with my assistance, to drag and push the fireplace to the other side of the back lane.

I walked back to the house, the cow was now satisfied that I had been thoroughly humiliated and her tramps palace was now in order. She gave me back my deposit.

I looked at the envelope in my hand and thought, I may have lost any sense of pride I ever had and completely mortified myself in the process, but at least we would eat this week. To that end it had been worth it.

Chapter Sixty One

The day of my graduation dawned and I was so excited, Alison and little Sarah- Jayne and most importantly Mum would be attending. We made our way to Queens' University and I donned my black graduation gown. Mum had a little tear in her eye but didn't say much. Sarah-Jayne on the other hand said lots! She laughed at all the people dressed like ghosts and was shushed too many times to remember during the ceremony.

It was only after the ceremony that Alison told me that Mum had bawled, she had said that someone was missing. We didn't go for a meal that night but we did have an Iceland party! Alison had bought lots of little party treats and we all sat together and had a lovely night. Mum talked of Dad a few times and of how proud he would have been but other than that she didn't say much.

I knew Mum was not improving; she was spending more days than usual in her bed. It was often just she and I in the house so conversation was scarce.

I coaxed her awake one day and dragged her with me to approach the Housing Executive. She hated doing anything like that, but by this stage she was so far gone I didn't believe she was aware of what she was doing. Together we sat in their offices and applied for a house. We joined the housing waiting list in 2007.

Sarah-Jayne was growing up fast, our succession of moves ensured that by the age of seven she had attending four different schools. I often wondered how this would affect her, but she was such a bubbly child she seemed she seemed to take everything on the nose.

As luck would have it I found a job and as my luck had it I swiftly lost it. Mum needed more and more care, concentrating on work and home became too much and something had to go. I let the job go. Alison was always out with her new boyfriend so she was rarely around. I didn't blame her, I knew that happiness was a scarcity and believed that it should be clung to when found.

Mum and I were once again plunged deeper into debt. I laughed when people admired my slim figure, for it was not through choice my dieting days had long gone. Instead I was slim because I existed on the few basics we could afford. We could no longer heat the home and had long ago made the choice that we would eat rather than heat.

I had my Mum and two little dogs and they became the focus of my shrinking world. As long as they were fed and watered it didn't matter about me. As a child Mum routinely gave up her meals for us, I had vivid memories of counting out what scraps we had, when I would cut them between four and Mum would say,

"Split it three ways. I'm not hungry"

Well now it was my turn, I was now splitting the food between them and if I was fortunate I even managed some myself.

Yet I held true to what I had been taught, Mum always said hold your head high. No one ever has to know what you live like, we may not be have much but we have our pride. Our father didn't plan for this life for us. He came here and faced his adversaries with his head in the air; he never let them see that they hurt him. Mum would say, "Never let this place see its beaten us Jayne, hold your head in the air too and remember this was not how things were meant to be".

Chapter Sixty Two

Race relations in Belfast had gotten worse; many families from different ethnicities were being burnt out of their homes. I got scared; really sacred. In that that year I was spat on, called some horrendous names and accustomed to being greeted with "Go back home". Some really funny people showed more creative uses for their jibes, one day in a crowded bus stop, two sober men approached and sang me a little song,

"Consider yourself at home; consider yourself one of the family".

I didn't get the bus that day instead I walked home and hung my head in shame. Their serenade rang in my ears even hours later.

I *was* at home yet these people would never see it that way. Despite the fact that I had been born here, educated here, worked here, paid taxes here and spoke in an accent from here, my skin was brown. That meant to them that I would never be truly from here.

I broke down a little that day and cried, I wanted out and for the first time ever I began to hate them as much as they hated me.

Mum who was in bed got up that day to ask me what was wrong, I told her and she just nodded. I didn't leave the house much after that. Instead I focussed my attention on Mum, who in between her increasing prescriptions was acting strangely. She claimed she couldn't sleep yet spent her days in a darkened room, only really becoming animated when little Sarah-Jayne would come up saying in her sing-songy voice "Granny Bumba".

Mum would sit with Sarah-Jayne and tell her all sorts of stories and for those moments our house was happy.

"Why is Granny Bumba so sad?" Sarah Jayne would ask and I would reply with the only answer that came to me, "because the world made her that way."

Mum went steadily downhill. She refused to get out of bed and started to talk in a strange gibberish, I lost count of the many times I took her to the doctors in despair. Eventually after a few years we found ourselves at the Royal Hospital where Mum was to see a psychiatrist.

I waited a long time for her whilst she seen by him, I was worried sick but she came out bright and breezy. She had entered his office removed and remote and I wondered what had brought about this sudden change. This man must have been a miracle worker; I began to think I would like an appointment too! Whatever medicine he had administered had worked because Mum was looking more like her former self than she had done in years.

It was the thought of medicine that triggered a little alarm bell in my head. It stopped me in my tracks. I looked at Mum's hand to see if she had a prescription; sure enough she did. Mum hadn't been cured; no problem had been solved. As always when Mum got depressed they solved the problem by giving her yet more drugs.

Chapter Sixty Three

We left the hospital and crossed onto Belfast's busy Falls road. We needed to get a taxi home and with no taxi's in sight I called into a local shop and asked for directions to the nearest taxi depot. As luck would have it there was one just around the corner.

We followed the directions the helpful shopkeeper had given us and quickly found the taxi depot. It was a dark office in a residential terraced street. We walked from the light into the gloom and I approached the grid in the wall. It served as a divider between the waiting room and the office. I ordered our taxi and looked up. At a games machine in the corner was a man who was badly scarred. He was staring at me like I was a ghost. I was used to be stared at so shot him a filthy look, yet something in this man's demeanour made me take another look.

He looked like he *knew* me. I racked my mind trying to pull something or some point from my past where this man familiar. No, nothing came to the fore. Mum on noticing my reaction followed my stare, she instantly tensed.

The growing silence in the room was interrupted when Mum spoke,

"Jayne meet the man who killed your father"

That was it. That was why this man was staring at me. He may not have been familiar to me, but I was certainly familiar to him.

I was a bit flummoxed and thought what am I supposed to say to this one?

As always when in doubt I remembered my manners. I stepped forward, held out my hand and said "Hello"

The man was surprised, yet he took my hand and shook it.

"I've followed you girls" he said "I know you went to Queens', did you finish your degree?"

"Yes" I replied and "and my Masters"

"What about the other two? I know one had a baby"

I told him about both my sisters. Mum stood there, she just stood there.

We had discussed what we would do if ever this situation arose and I knew that Mum would not be thinking along the lines that I was. I knew that if this man valued his life he should flee, but he remained.

Okay, it was over to me. I did my best Archbishop Tutu impersonation and decided there was nothing else for it but to become mediator.

"Mr Flynn, how do you feel about it all now?" I asked

"I was a soldier" he said,

Mum was coiled so tight that on hearing his reply I was waited for her to unravel and pounce. I had to act fast,

"Yes" I said, "I don't agree with that or with any war, but funnily enough I studied Irish history, so I can see your cause" I said full of fake bravado, "but do you regret, my Dad?"

Everything hung on his answer and part of me expected the worst. World War III was about to break out in this tiny west Belfast taxi office. I braced myself to duck from the inevitable carnage.

He didn't reply, instead he did something I least expected, he cried. His answer was there in those tears running down his scarred cheek.

I turned to look at my Mum and found that she was crying too. The pair embraced, him expressing his regret and my Mum saying one poignant line which will always remain with me,

"I will never forget what you did, but I forgive you. I forgive you"

We all stood there for a while in that dark taxi office in West Belfast. Time became irrelevant, because a miniature ceasefire had taken place. The victim and the terrorist united in pain, the pain that this Godforsaken land produced.

That day I realised that we were all victims, victim of our past, victims of evil circumstances and misfortune. The carnage, the bloodshed and the tears destroyed not only the innocent's lives, but also the lives of those who were unfortunate enough to carry life threatening weapons. Not all involved in Northern Ireland's struggle have souls; many of the murderers still do not repent. Those who repented, those who stood up and regretted their actions proved they possessed souls and that their souls felt hurt and suffering like everyone else's. They were victims too, their lives were also destroyed.

Chapter Sixty Four

After the encounter in the taxi depot Mum released a lot of her bitterness. I could never say she loved the IRA, but she had reached some sort of acceptance within herself. She had reconciled her differences with the man of her nightmares and clearly felt some relief. This relief opened new doors for her; she began to tell me all about my father. I would hear the same stories over and over until I felt that I knew him too. Stories would pour out of her, more than I had ever heard before. It was as if her meeting with Mr Flynn had opened the floodgates and nothing or no one could close them.

She still had trouble sleeping and I asked her why, she was on so many drugs that such a cocktail would literally knock a donkey out. Her reply was to tell me about the aftermath of the bomb all those years ago, of how she had reached out for the coffin, to make sure Max was still with her.

"Every time I go to sleep, Jayne I see the coffin, I still reach for it. I wake up and it's gone, he's gone. I go back to sleep again and wake up and go through the same process over and over."

My heart reached out to her like most people, I had known love before and I had lost it. Yet I had lost love naturally, none of my relationships had been serious so they had simply faded and died. The relationships that I had experienced had died a metaphorical death, no lives were lost and no one was hurt. Mum had known such a greater love, her one true love, this had been taken from her and her life had been spent trying to ascertain why and of course putting the pieces back together. She cried again that day,

"I loved him Jayne…… I still do"

I cried too, it was hard to conceive that someone could know such pain and loss and carry this around every waking day. The years had not diminished my parents love, instead they had simply created questions, another world of what ifs. She would never see this other world; she would never see how her love would progress.

Chapter Sixty Five

We spent those years freezing and for the most part hungry. I could see no solutions. Then one night the First Minister filled our TV screen as his party gave its party political message. He informed the nation that Northern Ireland had reconciled with its past. Its victims had been taken care off. The country could move on in the security that it had done right by all.

I thought of Mum's tears and wondered how she had been taken care off. She had been waiting three years for a council house. I had told the Housing Executive of her situation, of how she had suffered from Post-Traumatic stress and why, yet they had no policies in place to help victims. She had watched the wives of my Dad's colleagues grow into very wealthy ladies, as their husbands became partners or opened their own firms. Yet here she was husbandless and in a ghetto.

Since my Dad's death she had never had a permanent home or stability. The 17th of January 1980 had ruined her life and it had never been repaired.

I rarely grew angry, but on seeing the First Minister broadcasting his delight to the nation I saw red. All my mother had asked for was a council house. She had not moved an inch on the waiting list in the three years since she had went on it. From all accounts Northern Ireland's intuitions were now recognising its victims; I could see no proof of this.

That was when my campaign began. I tried to speak to the first minister but he was too busy. Even his PA had little time for me. I spoke to every victims group that the millions of pounds allocated to help the victims had been ploughed into. They could offer Mum some acupuncture or even some art lessons, but they couldn't help with housing or her mental illness. Surely these issues were the real issues? Why plough millions of pounds into victims, create numerous jobs yet leave the victims with useless help. One victims group headed by Willie Frazer was the only group that bothered to help my Mum. I wondered was it because its founder however militant, was a victim that he actually understood. A stark contrast from the numerous civil servants and third sector employees, who knew as much about being a victim as they did about nuclear physics. Unfortunately for us Mr Frazer's group were unable to help in the end, but at least they provided some support. With no one left to turn to I went to the newly installed victim's commissioners.

Now they held promise. We no longer had an interim victim's commissioner, who had used Mum's story in her report, Mum being covered under a pseudo name of Anne. We now had four commissioners, they had been appointed by the government tasked to work on behalf of the counties victims. I was so excited at last Mum would be saved; she wouldn't be ignored any more. I ran up to Mums room and told her of their establishment. I jotted down the address and left it on the mantel piece. We would go to them, they would help.

Over the next months we had spoken to them on the phone, but never formally met them. I had started a new job in the city centre and was based close to their offices. I planned on booking an appointment right away.

Mums condition continued to deteriorate. Once a woman who had once taken such pride in her appearance, she now thought nothing about stepping out with her night dress under her coat. Her shaky hands meant that the buttons were never matched right, always some were missed or in the wrong place, the result was that her nightdress was visible to all. I did not worry about this too much, as Mum rarely went out. She would panic when I left her in the house alone.

Every day when I left for work I would leave her a little note listing some tasks, some things she could do with the day. The tasks were always basic, wash the dishes, read a magazine or watch a certain programme on TV. Sometimes she even rang the commissioner's office asking for help with housing, my entrance to teacher training, whatever she could think of at the time. I knew if Mum had something to do, no matter how minor she would panic less.

Most of the time my lists were never read, instead Mum would retreat to her room. There I would hear her engaged in conversation, so deep and fluid that sometimes I believed that someone was actually there with her. She would talk to and answer her invisible friends with such accuracy that it was difficult to imagine she was alone.

One day, like Lazarus my Mum rose and decided to come down the stairs. I had left for work already and left her a list, but she had other ideas. She ignored my list and instead found the details of the Victims Commissioners I had left out. She had something to focus on a grain of hope. Somehow she made it to the city centre and to their offices. I received a call in work from my Mum, she was in the city centre and she was stuck. Could I come and get her?

I left my desk immediately and rushed out to meet her. She was in tears, she had called to their office, a huge glossy building, had even passed a commissioner on his way out of the office wearing an exquisite linen suit and carrying a bunch of flowers. She had made her way to the opulent reception and asked to speak to a commissioner. She was told to take a seat and she had waited. After a while she was told that no one could see her. She begged and pleaded with the staff and dissolved into tears. Still no one could see her. She left the office and a kind lady had enquired if she was okay, she had extracted my work place from Mum and called it to reach me. I took her home and she went back to her bed. Not even Sarah Jayne could rouse her from this depression.

Shortly after, maybe on having enough Alison and Sarah Jayne moved out, leaving me alone with my Mum.

The incident in the victim's commissioner's office roused anger in me. I had exhausted every avenue I could to try and get my Mum some help, and even those who were put in place because of people like my Mum could not help. I called them and arranged a proper appointment for Mum and I this time to meet with a commissioner. I secured an appointment with Bertha Mac Dougal and remember cringing as Mum and I sat in her office on the day. Mum was pouring her heart out, all the while the office door remained open, everyone could hear.

I had had enough and decided I would take matters into my own hands. I began a campaign bombarding every politician in the country. I started with telephoning Stormont in 2008. Speaking to them first, then emailing. What follows is one of my first emails to the First Ministers office;

Friday, 7 November 2008, 13:42
Hi David,

My Mum has asked me to email you I only hope that she has taken your address down correctly.

I don't know where exactly to start but I'll try to summarise her case.
My Dad was murdered by the IRA in 1980 and ever since then she has never been settled. We honestly have never had a permanent home. After Dad who was a chartered accountant died my Mum was unable to maintain the mortgage (though

working full time as a nurse her salary was just not enough) and unfortunately had the home repossessed.

We then moved in with my grandparents and had lived there until 14 years ago when my Mum decided to move to Belfast. As a mixed race, mixed religion family it was difficult to find affordable rents in 'mixed' areas and as a result rents were always beyond our means. We have never had a permanent home something my Mum lost on Dad's death and never regained. Since moving to Belfast we have lived in 18 homes 2 off which we were forced to leave on the basis of my colour. When a few years ago victims issued hit the headlines I think we felt so hopeful and my Mum thought that now at last she could get a permanent home. Talk then was of Northern Ireland's institutions addressing victims and their issues so we naively thought that the Housing Executive would be one of them and sought the help of the then victim's commissioner to help us. Mrs McDougall was then full of hope and stated that as soon as she was instated properly we would be her top priority. She even used us in her interim commissioner's draft - my Mum under a pseudo name as Anne.
So when the victims commissioners were appointed this year my Mum contacted Bertha right away and in my opinion was more or less told she was no longer top priority and that the commissioners had no remit to deal with the Housing Executive. My Mum broke down in their offices, something which as her daughter I am accustomed too but find it hard to bare.
Bertha wrote my Mum a letter and rather than address her as a victim to the executive simply went through to the executive using the same procedure as one would use for any applicant - a request for an appeal. Her letter implied that we should seek another landlord and didn't state that she was a victim and that she should have some kind of concession for that (which was what she had previously stated).
My mother has also been banned from the NI memorial fund. She got a grant from them 4 years ago to furnish yet another house. Because she did not supply receipts they have banned her permanently. On appealing to Bertha to help her with this once again it wasn't in her remit. Unless my mother could get receipts then she would not be helped by the memorial fund. My mother suffers from post traumatic stress a common illness suffered by victims, effecting memory, nerves etc how on earth

is she to even remember what she purchased or even where. After 18 homes things become a blur even for me! So as for the last 3 years my Mum has not been allowed to apply even for the hardship grant a grant to help victims and not shame them and once again the commissioners could not assist with this. In a way that's £3000 that the state has set aside for victims that she is not entitled to, to me that is unfair especially for a system set up to help, not to make her feel like
a beggar. Again the commissioners were unsympathetic and could not help.

In the meantime my Mum, my niece and I live in a house without Central heating, mould growing on the kitchen ceiling and walls slick with damp. On seeing Mr Robinson's Party political broadcast he mentioned human rights for victims, and I would ask why hasn't my Mum been helped? She is no longer coping and I fear that I will lose my Mum as well and am quite frankly sick when I see or hear people mention victims' rights, because as a victim myself, growing up and now looking after my Mum I feel we have been stripped of any dignity we once had, and if our Dad were to see how we now live he would turn in his grave. Why can no one seem to help and is my Mum to be left living like this because it is not in the commissioners remit? after 5 years on the waiting list for a 3 bed house, it is clear that NI cares no more about its victims then it does about its rubbish.

Jayne Olorunda Bssc, Msc

I waited and waited for a response and finally I approached them for one.

Hi David,

My Mum contacted the office of the first minister early November and was told someone would look into her case. Unfortunately no one has gotten back to her. I'm assuming the matter was investigated by now?

Regards

Jayne Olorunda

--- On Mon, 10/11/08,

The response they sent looked promising;

> To: jayneolorunda
> Date: Monday, 10 November, 2008, 3:21 PM
> Jayne,
>
> Confirmation that I received your email, at long last! The
> First Minister has instructed officials within his
> Department to investigate your Mum's case with a view to
> getting back to you as soon as possible.
>
> Kind regards,
>
> David.

Nothing ever came of these 'investigations' and I would phone regularly to find out what had happened.

No one was ever available to take my calls. It looked like I was being ignored by the First Minister.

With no other option I bypassed him and went to the then Prime Minister Gordon Brown, from him I went to the secretary of state for Northern Ireland. Victim's issues were on the news every day, to the stranger to Northern Ireland it would appear that our First Minister had been right, the victims were dealt with. Their presence in the headlines every night confirmed this. Yet upstairs in our pitiful accommodation lay one victim who was completely ignored. It seemed that Gordon Brown and the secretary of state were busy as well, but at least they bothered to respond. So I went to BBCNI and then re-approached.

The emails between the secretary of state and I are documented below,

---Original Message-----
From: jayne olorunda
Sent: 25 February 2009 17:58
To: SOS
Subject: Urgent help required! BBC E-mail: Victims' 15 year search for home

Dear Mr Woodward,

As you are the secretary of state for Northern Ireland I have decided to ask you for assistance. I have tried various victims groups, the victim's commissioners and the First minister, all to no avail.
My problem is summarised in the BBC link below, however since that date our situation has escalated. By bringing the BBC team into our house we have now been evicted and are to leave here in approx 12 days. All the Housing Executive could offer is temporary accommodation in the form of a hostel.
My mother has severe post traumatic stress and my sister and her daughter are vulnerable. We cannot live in a hostel. We have been on the Housing Executive list for 5 years and still no permanent home has been found.
Essentially on our imminent eviction we will go into temporary accommodation, until such times when a permanent home can be found. This will mean another two moves bringing out total houses moves to 17 in 15 years. I know this will kill my mother, this country has taken my Dad and I don't want to to take my

Mum too.
I dislike having to do write to you as I'm sure you have more pressing matters to deal with, but let me assure you my family and I never aspired to an executive house. Yet this is what we have been reduced to and now after 5 years on the list are having to beg.
We are victims of the troubles, my reasoning for putting my Mum on the Housing Executive list was that Northern Ireland had pledged to look after it's victims. The victims commissioners in their draft report even claimed to have the remit to intervene in government bodies when it could make the lives of victims easier (Bertha Mac Dougall even used my Mum's case in her interim commissioners draft proposals, Mum under a pseudo name as Anne. She promised her that when she was instated properly we would be top of her list and that wheels would be set into motion to make the housing executive make concessions for victims in its point allocation system). Instead when my Mum sought their help she was left so feeling so insignificant that she was reduced to tears in their office. They suddenly did not have the 'remit' to help her. No one showed her any sympathy, they just sent her home for me to pick up the pieces.

The first minister also pledged to help, his PA alluding (I have copies of the emails)that the first minister was investigating matters to find the best possible solution for my Mum. It took him four months to tell us he could do nothing.
My second issue is the Northern Ireland Memorial fund, again I have approached the first minister and the commissioners for help with them. Four years ago my Mum got a discretionary grant from the Northern Ireland Memorial fund to furnish yet another house. Six months later she was asked to provide receipts, unfortunately due to racial abuse we had left that house and receipts were not provided. At which point due to Mum's condition Post Traumatic Stress she couldn't remember what she'd bought anyway! Memory loss is common with suffers of PTS, which surely even the memorial fund will appreciate. Or so I thought as it claims to help such sufferers.
When my Mum applied again last year (victims should be entitled to this grant on an annual basis) she was turned down again for the grant, something that all spouses of victims - especially those suffering from Post Traumatic Stress are entitled to, all because she didn't submit receipts.

Now we are homeless, well we will be in 10 days and in desperation I explained to the Memorial fund our plight. Again they could not help unless receipts were provided. Frankly I feel this is ridiculous and unjust, this money was set aside for victims in hardship, which is exactly what my poor Mum is facing now, yet she can't have it. Once again she has been sidelined.
What right do they have to deny her her basic entitlement, we have suffered enough over the years and all we have ever asked for is a home (something we lost when my Dad was murdered) and a discretionary grant. All the recent efforts to help victims are not working, they are surrounded by red tape and not getting to those who need them. They are not help and shouldn't be classed as such, they are more of a hindrance, essentially prolong the suffering which they were established to alleviate.
Again I am sorry Mr Woodward for such a rant, but I keep hitting brick walls. We are now in DESPERATE need (we have 10 days and it seems no one can/is prepared to assist) and I am hoping that you could find the time to intercede for us, something which the various institutions to help victims could not do.
My contact details are xxxxxxxxx or mobile xxxxxxxxxx, my email address is above.
I would also appreciate it if my message to you could be passed to Mr Brown, as I believe victims here, well the people who have not raised scenes are being ignored.

Please see report below for a brief description of our story.

The response I got reduced me to tears – we were being passed from pillar to post

FROM: <u>SOS</u>
TO:

- jayneolorunda@yahoo.co.uk

<u>Message flagged</u>
Friday, 27 February 2009, 13:52
Dear Jayne

Thank you for your e-mail addressed to the Secretary of State.

I note your concerns over housing and the NI Memorial Fund. In respect of the former, as you are probably aware, responsibility for the NI Housing Executive has been devolved to a local Minister, Margaret Ritchie MLA and you may wish to contact her office regarding any issues you have on your housing problems.

The Minister can be contacted by the following means:-

By post

email:

Telephone:

In relation to your issues with the Northern Ireland Memorial Fund, the Fund is an independent charity governed by a Board of Directors. In light of this I have passed your correspondence on to Mr Dennis Licence, Fund Chairman and have asked him to investigate the issues you have raised and respond to you directly.

I understand that this may not be the response that you were seeking but I hope that you will find the information contained in my e-mail to be of some assistance to you.

Assistant Private Secretary
Secretary of State's Private Office (Belfast)

In the end it was the BBC's coverage that secured us help, shortly after we got a house.

In February 2009, our story made headline news across Northern Ireland, Alison (who was now back home) and I took up most of the interview as Mums footage for the most part was incoherent. Our absent landlady evicted us the next day, concerned about the state of disrepair her home had fallen into. Not once in four years had she checked the house, she never fulfilled her promises of annual decoration, instead she sat back month after month and extracted the rent. The last time the electrics were safety tested was in 1990, after a succession of electric shocks and fungal infections from, the mould we had long ago had the house condemned as being unfit for human habitation. When my Mum and I went to the council offices almost four years earlier they had viewed our current dwelling and had on the spot registered us as homeless.

The day after our eviction notice a housing officer called and within a week Mum was given her first permanent home, one she could afford and even better one in an area that was neither Catholic nor Protestant. It was the first time she had had this since losing our Dad in 1980.

Of course we were given a home but no funds to furnish it and once again were faced with the prospect of moving house with no money and no furniture. I pulled together every penny I could selling every last non-essential we had and got us moved. We moved in with three new beds and sat on cushions in the living room.

Over the next few months I again did the rounds of the various victims groups for help. One of whom, the 'Northern Ireland Memorial fund' promised assistance to victims in need; perfect I thought, I called them and was dumbstruck to find that I was treated like a beggar. In fact that was exactly what I had become, their need for evidence of our poverty and sending someone out to the house to prove it, simply reinforced this. It was bad enough having to ask for help, but to have an organisation requesting proof was humiliating. The organisation in question had been set up to help victims not to strip them of what remained of their dignity. As far as I was concerned the only criteria they should have needed was central to their being; that those asking for help were victims.

Well I would take what they gave because we would need it. They awarded us £750 and I did my best to buy as many essentials as I could, they demanded receipts for every purchase which I sent to them but vowed never again.

It was a well-known fact that those who had been released from prison early during the peace process were given houses immediately and given finds to decorate and buy basics. Yet here I was trying to furnish my Mum's house and being made to beg for droplets of help. I remember thinking that this country really did have an upside down way of dealing with things, by rewarding its guilty and penalising its victims.

Chapter Sixty Six

On being given the home after years in the no-man's land Mum changed. Unlike in fairytales where happy endings are guaranteed in real life this was not the case. If only it was. If I thought Mum was bad before, her behaviour in this home showed me what deteriorating really meant. She became angry and confused. Everything angered her, she would sit scowling at the TV, swearing at whoever's poor face happened to grace the screen.

Her tablets once again were increased, but this time even they didn't help. Every time I would wander up the stairs I would find her talking. What was more alarmingly was the fact that she often invited me in to join her and her acquaintance. Or worse, she would be talking to me and I hadn't even opened my mouth yet; there she would lie responding to my every non-existent comment.

Often she would talk as if she lived in the 1970's, as if she were my age and talk about her three little girls. Once she ran downstairs and asked me why the police were in the living room, who had died?

I would laugh and ask her what she was talking about, sometimes she would even laugh back, quickly realising her error, reacting to the concern in my eyes.

She then turned nasty criticising Alison's every move, so much so that Alison fled the house with Sarah-Jayne in tow, seeking sanctuary in Women's Aid. When they left the strange behaviour continued and intensified.

Mum would talk to a little grey haired woman who appeared at the end of her bed. She loved her visits and the pair of them talked for hours. When I came in, the grey haired woman disappeared because she was 'shy'. Mum even watched TV in her room and would tell me all about the great film she had seen. She didn't have a TV in her room.

Then the suicide attempts began, I had started another job and wasn't at home with her as often as I should have been. Every job I started, I had to give up; Mum's condition whatever it was, demanded that she had someone with her constantly. It was difficult as I needed to work to support us but I couldn't work if I wanted to support her.

In one suicide attempt Mum had slashed her wrists. This was followed by a succession of overdoses and yet more strange behaviour. Most worryingly of all were the falls. I couldn't leave her unattended; she was so unsteady on her feet. She would get up from her chair and fall, overnight she would try to go down the stairs and fall, or she would simply pass out. I was at my wits end and had no one to turn to.

In the end it was on yet another trip to A&E, where she had worked many years before, that seen the doctors eventually recognise that something was amiss. They kept her in overnight, concerned about her falls but they quickly released her. I began to worry so much so that I began to wonder if I too would become ill. I would take strange headaches and wake to find that hours had passed that I wasn't aware off. I wondered what would become of us both. I prayed that God would bring my Mum back, but she got progressively worse.

Chapter Sixty Seven

One evening I had fed her and got her to bed, I was watching TV with my dogs when the smoke alarm erupted. The dogs went mad at the high pitched sound and I ran upstairs to investigate. Outside Mum's room a fire raged, it climbed up her door eating at the wood. I ran for a towel from the bathroom and frantically swotted it. When I checked if she was ok, I found her sitting in her bed waiting for the flames to take her.

She knew me that night and she cried sore, she wanted it to end; she had had enough of struggling, of being alone, of the poverty and she wanted Max. I didn't know what to do; at my wits end I called the doctor and went with Mum to the hospital.

That night Mum was taken to a secure mental health unit. Here she could no longer hurt herself or inadvertently hurt others. My mother had been driven insane and I couldn't help her.

The nurses interviewed me for a brief history and one question they asked saddened me,

"She claims to be a nurse where does that come from?"

I nodded sadly, "she is, or was" I said. My mother had been a nurse and whatever else they choose to believe about this new patient that fact remained. Mum had nursed until she could nurse no more; she had worked long and hard on the wards, so hard that just thinking of nursing sickened her. It was a career she had once loved, but fates intervention had made her a prisoner of the wards and turned this love into hate. Nevertheless her work had kept us sustained through childhood and beyond, it had kept a roof over our heads. It was one title that I would not let her lose.

Mum had always been a good storyteller; I had grown up fed on tales of her past, from voodoo curses delivered by a green woman all the way from Nigeria, to visitations from mysterious Christ like priests. Mum had loved nothing more than a good yarn and in me she found a captive audience. Now as she sat in this bleak hospital I wondered if I would ever hear her tales again, I wondered if they were true.

I left the hospital that night with an image of my Mum that would stay with me forever. A once strong and courageous woman who had stood up against racism and the IRA had been broken. She had admitted defeat. She had fought her hardest against poverty, she had loved us and she had loved Max. As she sat on her bed in a mental health ward; all that remained was a frail, scared, shrunken woman. Her empty eyes and twisting hands had become despair itself.

On my way out of the ward, the nurse gave me a bag of Mum's effects. So many everyday things were viewed as hazardous and removed from the patients. Even her nightgown strap was viewed as a danger. That night I would put them away for her, she would have them for when she came home.

As I drove home I passed a famous cemetery in Belfast. I had visited there once and curiosity drove me to the republican section. This section was the hero's part of the cemetery, a section of the cemetery devoted to Ireland's greatest fighters, to the heroes of the republican struggle. It has its own dedicated marble pathway and each grave in the section is elaborately finished. All the graves lay in the shadow of a patriotic speech inscribed on the wall. People come from far and wide to pay their respects and it remains on the tourist trail to this very day. In this section of the graveyard lies the man who killed my Dad, forever glorified for his brave actions furthered Ireland's cause.

As I passed, I wondered who was paying their respects to these hero's right now and in the back of my mind I was reminded of another grave one hundred miles away. A grave which marks the life of an innocent man; a family man, guilty of nothing but boarding a train. This grave is unmarked and unattended, as I have been told that this grave lies empty, that nothing of this man was left. All that remains of him lives on in his family, his granddaughter, his daughters and his wife, who incidentally now sits in a little mental health unit in Belfast. That night was one of the saddest of my life I felt so alone. I placed my feelings about the two very different graves and Mum's illness a little shelf I had created in my mind.

Epilogue

Now Mum is doing better, she is still being treated by drugs but at last it has been discovered that there is a definite link between victims of the troubles and post- traumatic stress. Many of those who worked in the emergency services during those years were severely affected. Mum's nursing combined with Dad's death dealt her a double blow. Now Mum has good days and I think for the most part they outweigh the bad and that is all I can hope for. Throughout it all Mum had her friend Misery.

Northern Ireland today is a partially changed place, unfortunately we still see the occasional terrorist murder and more grieving families, but not on the scale of many years ago. Yet Northern Ireland's future is a very delicate balance, now and again tensions simmering beneath the surface boil up and threaten to overflow. Luckily enough they are quickly cooled, before any additional bloodshed occurs. This little country although beautiful has an ugly side, a side that always runs parallel with progression.

As for Northern Ireland's victims I still see no evidence of any tangible help. No-one is out there to treat post-traumatic stress, no-one is there to prevent families falling into the abyss that mine fell into. Above all no one is there to help the children of the struggle. Certainly some groups do exist, the legacy of the troubles meant that a myriad of victims groups were set up. Each group, third sector or government has paid members of staff; each being paid and benefiting from others misfortune, hurt and loss. The millions of pounds set up for victims doesn't reach them all, instead it reaches only the very few, the rest is pumped into the pockets of too many people. To some extent Northern Ireland has benefited from its victims but who are the real winners? Those who need it? Or those who prey on innocents? To me countless victims are being exploited for the gain of a few.

Money allocated to victims would be better spent on training doctors, medical staff, government institutions and private institutions. These people would have been instrumental in preventing my Mum's suffering and countless others. Northern Ireland should ensure its institutions recognise its victims and provide them with some sort of dispensation for what they have suffered at the hands of their country, the place they call home. No-one should have suffered like my Mum and mechanisms should be put in place to ensure such suffering like the troubles is a thing of the past.

Mum still plays a song from her youth and often I listen to it and think how true it's lyrics are and I feel they sum up my Mum's life and how some things can never be changed. We can only move forward.

'For what's done is done

And what's won is won

And what's lost is lost forever'. (Phil Coulter)

THE END

Legacy

Jayne Olorunda

Dedicated to Mum, thanks for everything.

In memory of Abayomi Olorunda a.k.a 'Max'

Foreword.

Mum was once a strong, determined person or so I was told. Personally, I found her quite flighty, almost silly although she did make me laugh. Granted she had her moments when she was sensibility itself but these moments were glimpsed rarely, now they are so few and far between that I wonder if I imagined them. Mum always had some ridiculous stories and strange little ways; when it comes to the past Mum's accuracy is scrupulous, yet when she talks about the present she confuses names, numbers and even addresses. She often told me that we had been cursed, that made me laugh the most; until now.

In the winter of 2010, Mum was placed in a secure mental health unit where she could no longer harm others and more importantly herself. It was during this time that I began to wonder about Mum's tales. I began to question my scepticism, my persistent doubts, because surely no one could attract as much bad luck as Mum and my family.

Mum always loved to tell me about her youth, the fun she had had and the happiness that she experienced. She would tell me about my childhood and that of my sisters. Her stories were so vivid that I felt I was seeing what she saw and experiencing what she had experienced. She had a gift, a God given talent that allowed her to bring the spoken word to life. Anyone who listens to a true storyteller rely their craft becomes a captive listener and for a time I was in the front row, her main audience. As I grew older Mum's tales became more and more frequent and to my shame more and more irrelevant. I was constantly urging her to look forward and stop looking back, to say goodbye to yesterday.

I now care for Mum and try to maintain as stable a life as possible. It is ironic that I once a cynic, have come to see Mum's accounts of yesteryear as my way forward; necessary if I am to ever understand me, where I came from and who I am. Unexpectedly, Mum's story now holds the key to my present and the answers to why my family is such a strange little gathering. It explains the circumstances that led to us being unable to fit into any boxes.

Not fitting in has always been the route of our problems, for my family could be described as neither black nor white, not really Catholic, and not really Protestant, not really working class, yet not really middle class. Hence the dilemma; we fitted in nowhere, Mum raised us in a no man's land. She did her best to get us out, but she never managed to steer us away from that place. She tried with all her might to follow the signposts to stability, happiness and security, but fate always intervened and gave them a little twist. No matter what direction she turned was wrong, her best intentions steered us deeper and deeper into nowhere.

Often she would reach out to a passer-by, asking and even screaming at them for help, but they were busy. Times had moved on and every one of them turned their back on her, leaving her there in that no man's land with no-one but her three children for company. Her children found life in no man's land difficult; those that left could not be blamed. I would never leave; I would never leave Mum alone in that cold place.

In their teens most children are passed houses, cars, knowledge or the family dynasty. I was left with no dynasty only that of picking up the pieces from a soiled legacy. The legacy of a man I did not know, whose existence and death had set in motion a chain of events that had such momentum they had taken on a life their own.

Last year the British Queen, the figurehead of the UK met Martin McGuiness, the former commander of the IRA. Publically they shook hands to show how much Northern Ireland has moved on. To the outside world and those who went unscathed in the troubles, this historic handshake represented the current beliefs of the population. Yet what of the silent masses? The three thousand plus dead and countless injured? As foes became friends the widows, the widowers, the orphans, the brother less, the sister less and the maimed were pushed into Northern Irelands closet, the door was marked '**The Past'** and categorically closed. How did the occupants of the closet feel? Did the handshake reconcile their pain, did it bring back their dead, their lost limbs or minds, and did it heal their broken hearts? Or did they wonder as they watched the scene unfold, what was it all about? Countless lives wasted, seemingly atoned for with a simple shaking of hands.

For those like Mum who were left behind, there will never be peace; they carry their losses with them each and every living day. All the handshakes in the world cannot erase her memories nor undo the tattoo etched permanently yet invisibly across her psyche. All the victims have a story to tell; this is the story of just one victim and her unique family. A victim who fought against all to marry, who gave up on everyone and everything she knew to pursue her heart.

I will try to tell her tale as I see it, I will piece together stories she imparted to me and the stories from my memory to describe how it all unfolded. This is my account of Mum's story. What follows is my view of events.... (Some names have been changed only those of non-essential characters).

Prologue

Date: 15th January 1980

Time: 18.06

Location: Europa Station Belfast.

The station swarmed with rush hour crowds. Around her commuters rushed to and from their trains. Gabrielle was invisible to them, so was 'IT'. A few minutes earlier she had been just another face in the crowd. Now she was alone with the exception of one companion, *terror*.

'IT' had come out of nowhere and stood less than six inches from her, its darkness infiltrating her every pore. All light, all happiness, any joy she had ever been exposed to evaporated. 'IT' had captured her in its web, wrapping her in strand after strand of its sinister silk.

Feebly, Gabrielle recited every prayer that she could remember and when her memory failed her, she beseeched the heavens to take this thing away from her. Her pleas went unanswered and she stood there powerless.

Gabrielle tried to scream but no words came. She contemplated running but her limbs were motionless. Even the simple gesture of averting her eyes from IT's penetrating gaze, became impossible. She was paralysed, her defenceless body forcing her to remain on the spot.

'IT' opened its mouth and words, lots of words tumbled out. It spoke in a language that Gabrielle had never heard before or hoped to hear again.

Its menacing tones were infused with hatred and malice. Only its finale was spoken in a human tongue, six words that shook Gabrielle to the core, "I curse you and your family".

Instinct told her that she had encountered a being that represented all things evil. She had just been exposed to something that was not of this world.

In a green cloud 'IT' was gone back to the nowhere it had appeared from. Gabrielle dropped to her knees relieved at its departure and waited for the waves of terror to leave her. Her moment in darkness had seemed a lifetime. It was 18.06, no time had passed. *Had she imagined the episode?*

She glanced at the ground where 'IT' had stood. Sure enough 'IT' had left an ominous souvenir, some sort of green pendant. Then this thing *had* happened. Reassured that her sanity was still intact, she looked at the commuters the people all around her, they would be shaken too. What had they made of this thing? Yet their faces registered no shock, they were simply the ordinary faces of ordinary commuters in a busy train station.

Gabrielle's ordeal had been invisible to them and so had 'IT'.

Part One

Go placidly amid the noise and haste, and remember what peace there may be in silence.

As far as possible without surrender be on good terms with all persons.

Speak your truth quietly and clearly; and listen to others, even the dull and ignorant; they too have their story.

Avoid loud and aggressive persons, they are vexations to the spirit.

If you compare yourself with others, you may become vain and bitter;

for always there will be greater and lesser persons than yourself.

Enjoy your achievements as well as your plans.

Keep interested in your career, however humble; it is a real possession in the changing fortunes of time.

Exercise caution in your business affairs; for the world is full of trickery.

But let this not blind you to what virtue there is; many persons strive for high ideals;

and everywhere life is full of heroism.

Be yourself.

Especially, do not feign affection.

Neither be critical about love; for in the face of all aridity and disenchantment it is as perennial as the grass.

Take kindly the counsel of the years, gracefully surrendering the things of youth.

Nurture strength of spirit to shield you in sudden misfortune. But do not distress yourself with imaginings.

Many fears are born of fatigue and loneliness. Beyond a wholesome discipline, be gentle with yourself.

You are a child of the universe, no less than the trees and the stars;

you have a right to be here.

And whether or not it is clear to you, no doubt the universe is unfolding as it should.

Therefore be at peace with God, whatever you conceive Him to be,

and whatever your labors and aspirations, in the noisy confusion of life keep peace with your soul.

With all its sham, drudgery and broken dreams, it is still a beautiful world. Be careful. Strive to be happy.

© Max Ehrmann 1927

Chapter One

They say the grass is always greener on the other side and for Gabrielle's father never a truer phrase was uttered. Standing with him at the garden gate looking over the field beyond it, she would listen to him reminisce of when the country was one. He would pick her up on his broad shoulders and point just past the field to his beloved Ireland; for there and only there, was the grass truly green.

He loved to regale her with his family history of how they had come from Co. Mayo, bringing their 'Protestant' name with them. When probed about this as he often was, he would scratch his head and inform his audience that in Co. Mayo his name was not a Protestant name, in Mayo it was the most Catholic name of them all. A more inquisitive person would ask her father about his unique colouring, something she often pondered over, for it was certainly true that he did not have an Irish complexion. Her father's hair was dark as the night and his skin a rich mahogany even in the harshest of winters. Yet her father would convince anyone who enquired that in Co. Mayo, all the natives were as dark as him. Her father convinced not only himself, but everyone he met that he was an Irishman through and through and with a conviction as firm and deep set as his, he was rarely doubted.

Gabrielle entered the world in 1951, a time of hope and prosperity. Born and raised in the border town of Strabane, she had an idyllic, carefree childhood. As the eldest of a large family she was fortunate to relish in being the only child for six years.

Then, the only thing she hated was school. Every day she was encouraged out the door with a little aid from her mother's constant companion, 'the stick'. Unfortunately, 'the stick' was to cross the generational gap and became an integral part of my childhood too!

For Gabrielle everything about school unsettled her, the huge grey crumbling building, the dank dingy corridors and most of all the wrinkled, torturous gargoyles called 'nuns' who roamed them. The gargoyles were responsible for providing the then only cloud on her otherwise blue sky of a life. The gargoyles and their beloved dunce's cap, a great big red and blue striped hat emblazoned with 'I am a dunce' became the bane of her childhood. Gabrielle spent most of her school days facing the front of the class, shamefacedly modelling the gargoyles carefully crafted couture.

Gabrielle had many friends, however her very best friend was a little Jack Russell terrier called Patch. Wherever Gabrielle went Patch followed, they were a twosome adored by the adults around them. This situation changed when Gabrielle reached the age of six, when her cosy *only child* bubble was burst.

It happened on an ordinary summer's day, she and Patch were playing when her mother casually informed her that the stork would be coming soon. The stork would bring her a little brother or sister. Now she wonders if a childish remark from her may have had some part in the storks visit. She remembers her mother entertaining guests whilst she was happily drawing in the corner. She wasn't normally privy to adult conversations, so as all children do when given the chance she soaked up every enticing little morsel. The women were talking about their husbands and sharing their beds; apparently it was a necessity to do this when you were married. If you didn't undertake the arduous task of sharing a bed, then children would never be granted. Gabrielle was utterly perplexed by the conversation as for as long as she could remember, her mother shared a bed with her. Questions began to form in her little mind; how on earth was *she* made then? Her internal dilemma and no doubt external facial contortions were obviously visible to all, as very soon one of the ladies noticed her exertion and asked,

"Gabrielle what's wrong?"

Gabrielle pondered briefly and answered

"If Mummy and Daddy are married, why does Daddy sleep across the hall?" She further explained "When he thinks I'm asleep he gets all upset and calls for Mummy to join him, she calls him a dirty auld brute and tells him to get into his bed". Gabrielle's mother now a deep shade of scarlet bristled whilst the other ladies burst into raucous laughter; ever since her mother shared a bed with her father!

Unfortunately, for Gabrielle that summer's visit was not to be the first visit from the horrid stork, if she could have clutched that loathsome bird then and there she would have wrung its neck, plucked and stuffed it.

Instead in the absence of the elusive stork, she sought the gypsies. They were never far from the doors of the town, regularly peddling anything from mats, to books and if you were very lucky they even took goods off your hands. Gabrielle hoped she would be very lucky, as *she* was about to offer them a whole new market , *she* would offer them her baby brother or sister and she wouldn't even set a price; as far as she was concerned they could have this little irritation for free!

Not even the gypsies were interested.

She would just have to get the used to the idea of sharing her mother, father, grandmother, aunties, and uncles with this new little creature. She was not happy as like any only child who is '*blessed*' with a new sibling, she suspected that as soon as the new arrival came her life would change; no longer would her every whim be catered to, from now on she would have to share. This thought did not sit comfortably.

Sure enough the bloody stork came to her house delivering a little brother and a few years later delivering a sister. For the next twenty years it delivered another and yet another until her little house was full and she was well and truly dethroned. The storks delay between visits created an age gap, one that prevented Gabrielle from feeling close to her siblings. With the exception of her brother, she was in her teens when most of them were born. Perhaps this caused the fiercely independent streak that overshadowed her future and the future of those who would follow.

Chapter Two

The arrival of Gabrielle's siblings ushered in a period of austerity. With more and more mouths to feed and backs to clothe, family life settled into a routine of mundanity. Her mother took up dressmaking to cut down on the clothing bills and baking to maximise the food supplies. Her father worked longer and harder than ever before.

Gabrielle was usually put in charge of the children a task she hated, so much so that when the weather was dry she took the yard brush and brushed the screaming little horrors out to the garden! Life became a case of economising, nothing was ever wasted in their house and everything was shared. Even the meals took on a feeling of routine with each day being assigned a particular dinner. If you were to ask

Gabrielle now this very moment, she can still memorise her meal pattern; Monday remains of Sundays roast, Tuesday cabbage and bacon, Wednesday stew and so on until they reached Sunday (not to mention Friday when they enjoyed 'Fenian Steak'). This pattern continued throughout her years at home as did the most unbearable pattern of all; cleaning.

Every Saturday, Gabrielle was to wake up to not only to her daily dose of thick porridge but the prospect of an entire day of scrubbing, brushing, washing and polishing. In her childhood a clean home was revered and no stone was left unturned. This was a tradition she brought into adulthood and enforced on her own children. I remember Mum used to make us start at the top of the house and work our way down, when this was finished Mum just like her mother before her would check on our work; running her finger along surfaces, lifting our mattresses to check on the bed and opening doors to ensure that even the door seams were gleaming. If we neglected to clean even the tiniest particle we could rest assured Mum's keen eye would find it and as always we would be made to start again. Mum could not tolerate a dirty house, over the years she instilled the conviction that a person could be judged by their home into each of us. I wonder now if this belief was what plunged her into the state of mind that would attempt to destroy her later in life; she judged herself by her own standards.

During Gabrielle's teenage years Saturday night was just another night. While most young people were planning trips to the cinema, walks around town or even a stolen kiss Saturday night for her meant red raw fingers and an aching back. After cleaning all she was capable of doing was crawling into her bed. Her mother had teenage control down to a fine art. Until Gabrielle's late teenage years she didn't have time or the energy to even contemplate a social life.

Little Patch's demise came when she was just thirteen. Gabrielle was sent to the town's chemist to get baby supplies, when she was faced with her first glimpse of tragedy. Being sent to the chemist was a routine request, one she loved as she benefitted from half an hour's independence and a walk around the town. On this particular day she and Patch set off through the field and over the bridge, they didn't rush their journey instead they meandered at a leisurely pace taking in all the sights and sounds of their home town. They went to the chemist, made their purchases and began to make their journey home.

When they got to the bridge, they picked up their pace; they had already taken more than the half hour she was allowed, if she wasn't home soon her mother would come looking for her. When she got halfway over the bridge, a loud horn startled her and broke the tranquillity that had until then surrounded her. She turned quickly in its direction, seeing a car drive away. What she saw shattered her tiny world; little Patch lay in a bloody heap on the other side of the road. She could see that he had lost a lot of blood and remembers dropping the chemist bag, neither looking left nor right as she flew across the road to his side. Her speed made no difference as already her first friend was dead. He was so still and small, his little head crushed on the left side, she knew he would never, could never wake. She petted him and called him over and over until she couldn't see through her tears, but Patch was still. She watched horrified as the blood flowing from his lifeless body slowed and settled into a stagnant puddle around him, soaking into his once gleaming white coat, and drying on his face. That was the first time Gabrielle felt pain and to her it was the worst pain imaginable, she couldn't do a thing. Her insides grew heavy and her heart swelled in pain as she sat beside Patch and watched death take him away from her.

Gabrielle never forgot the death of little Patch for it shook the foundations of her world.

Sudden death would come back to her again one day, this time more shocking than she could ever imagine and once again she would be powerless to stop it. That day in Gabrielle's thirteenth year was one of the saddest days in her childhood but a minuscule taster of what was to come......

Chapter Three

The most dominant element of Gabrielle's early life was the influence of the Catholic Church. Her parents were staunch Catholics and like the rest of the small town spent each Sunday and any day of religious significance 'kissing the altar' rails. For Gabrielle the unfortunate part of their adherence to the Roman Catholic convictions was that she was made to join them. Every Sunday was Mass day, when the entire family donned their Sunday bests with the rest of the town and walked to Mass, never did they miss a day. No matter how sick anyone was, they were well enough to go to Mass. Gabrielle's compulsory and non- negotiable attendance at Mass felt like a prison sentence especially in her teens. Even if illness had taken her, she firmly believed that she would have been wheeled to Mass on her deathbed rather than be permitted to damage her mortal soul by missing one service. On top of the weekly Mass on Saturdays, they also had confession and during the week they usually had at least one visit from Father Converey.

To have a priest as a regular caller to one's home was a great honour, it was one thing that her parents did not take lightly. When Father Converey called it was like the Great Lord himself had graced them with his presence, the best china came out, the children were dismissed and the conversation became closed and serious. Even if they passed a priest on the street they were made to bless themselves and say "Hello Father" in such a respectful manner that they just stopped short of genuflecting. Nothing was more important to her parents than the church, the priest embodied this great organisation and what he said went. They lived their lives according to Roman Catholic dogma, something Gabrielle took for granted as they recited the nightly rosary and fasted for a saint's day. It was only as she grew older that she decided that such a strong and unquestioned devotion was not for her.

Strabane, which was once home to both Catholics and Protestants gradually became almost entirely Catholic. As news trickled through the grapevine of Protestant families being removed from Catholic towns and Catholic families being removed from Protestant towns, her neighbours began to doubt their safety. Protestant families and neighbours moved out one by one over the years. Their confidence was eroded and worn so thin that they left the town. They moved away and joined larger more Protestant towns and cities across the North. By Gabrielle's early teens all that remained in the once mixed town was an increasingly bitter Catholic enclave.

It was during her teenage years that Gabrielle began to question her upbringing, to doubt the preaching's of the church and to formulate her own opinions on Ireland North and South. She bravely began to question these teachings, to test her mother on her iron resolve that her take on life was correct. She began to assert her independence, to formulate her own viewpoints being careful to ensure that they were on opposing angles to her mother's and more importantly that they shunned the Church.

In her late teens Father Converey spent most of his Mass preaching on the evils of the mini skirt. In protest to his outburst she proudly flaunted her mini and paraded up and down the street. She ensured that all the neighbours witnessed her modern fashion sense and saw how little regard she had paid to

Father Converey. Arriving home that night, Gabrielle was met by the stick and was told to apologise to the Sacred Heart picture that permanently loomed above her mother's chair. She was dispatched to bed without so much as a 'God Bless'. Rather than be ashamed, on the contrary she stomped to bed; well shuffled as her skirt, all two inches of it did not allow for much movement!

In her room she went straight to her satchel, pulling out pen and paper and composed a letter to the 'Sunday Independent'. She stated the case for mini's, modernity whilst lambasting the church, its preaching's and it's dinosaur of a Pope. She posted her rant first class the very next morning.

Immediately after posting the letter she regretted it but she doubted her treachery would ever be discovered. A week later she was shocked to find that her rant had been published!

She talks of how it was father Converey who 'outed' her, so much for following the Lord's teachings! He called around that evening slamming the letter on the table, then instructed her mother to deal with her daughter and promptly left. Her mother was understandably incandescent with rage, 'the stick', the Sacred Heart and a few choice obscenities came out that night. For the next few years Gabrielle continued to test her mother with her elaborate antics; the stick would come out often. By way of avoidance she began to spend more and more time with her kindly grandmother, often staying overnight and generally avoiding home and 'the stick'.

Chapter Four

Gabrielle had always wanted to be a nurse. In the late sixties career choices for girls were limited and when faced with the alternatives nursing was definitely the best option. Nowadays girls can leave school and study for anything they like; choices are so vast that for many it is as difficult to decide on a career plan as it is to actually embark on a career! Yet back then by all accounts the choices for girls consisted of getting married on leaving school and not many would relish that idea, to become a teacher (for Gabrielle this would have been fine if children were removed from the equation!). The remaining options for her and most of her generation was to become a civil servant or a bank clerk neither prospect held much appeal.

Luckily for her a further option glimmered in the distance, to become a nurse. As far as she was concerned there was no choice, the other options were repugnant. She had been an avid follower of Doctor Kildare, read far too many hospital based Mills & Boons and even studied Florence Nightingale for her O-Levels! The culmination of these led her to believe that a more glamorous, worthy career for a young woman just didn't exist. She romantically pictured herself waltzing up and down the wards in a commanding yet feminine uniform, leaning over the bedsides of the infirm and whispering teams of endearment. She would be surrounded by movie star handsome doctors and work all over the world.

She focused on passing her exams and getting all the experience she could in order to gain a much coveted place in the local Derry hospital to begin her training. She spent two years volunteering with the St John's Ambulance Core and in her spare time read up on biology and anatomy so that by the time she was offered a place on the course she was brimming with confidence and well equipped.

Gabrielle's parents were pleased with her choice, her Fathers chest puffed out with pride at the very thought of his little girl entering into such a noble profession. Her mother who had herself aspired to become a nurse was also overjoyed. Her mother didn't tell her this but Gabrielle had heard her mention it at every available opportunity. Should the conversation be about autumn leaves or the price of butter, her mother somehow managed to manipulate the topic around to her daughter's acceptance into nursing.

To embark on her studies Gabrielle required what seemed like an impossible amount of supplies, the hospital had sent a long and expensive list. She would need everything from thick nursing textbooks, standard nursing shoes, a nursing coat, and even a fob watch. It was with great reluctance that Gabrielle presented this list to her parents she knew they could not afford even one of these items, yet alone the entire list.

On seeing their stunned faces as they read the list she was besieged with guilt. Rather than ask her struggling parents to pay for such a quantity of items she decided to be a martyr and tell them that nursing wasn't for her. She stoically told them about an office job she had seen advertised in Derry and how much it appealed to her. She laughs as she remembers conjuring up as much excitement as she could as she talked about learning to type and take important phone calls.

Only a few days later her mother was to ask her to go material shopping with her as she was making up some dresses for her little sisters and needed to choose an attractive yet hardwearing fabric. Gabrielle was still inwardly glum at having given up on her dream but she re-pasted her happy face on and agreed to accompany her. First they went to the material shop, where her mother selected the various materials and bits and bobs that she would require. Followed by a trip to the general store, when her mother surprised her and instead of walking their usual route to the food supplier, they went upstairs and in the direction of the shoe department. Her mother made small talk with the shopkeeper and then asked a question that took her breath away.

"Do you stock any suitable nurses' shoes?"

Gabrielle was speechless and looked at her mother wide eyed, where she quite casually replied,

"Well you're going to need them."

Gabrielle had never been as grateful to her parents as she was that summer when they somehow managed to buy all of her supplies. She will never forget their generosity.

She remembers being so overwhelmed that she had to blink back the tears as her mother patted her shoulder and said "make us proud". She doesn't know where her parents obtained the money from as it was never mentioned. All she knew was that by some miracle come September, she was fully kitted out and ready to embark on her training.

Gabrielle would go on to suffer three years of gruelling nursing training a time of laughs, horror, fun and tears. To a country girl the hospital was huge, an endless maze of corridors swamped with doctors, nurses and patients. She describes hospital life as a world within a world, an insular bustling environment that she yearned to be a part of. Yet one obstacle stood between Gabrielle and her full immersion into that world; three years of rigorous training.

The figurehead of that obstacle was the Matron who oversaw all the trainee nurses. Nothing got past her. She inspired terror in them all Gabrielle portrays her as an unkind, strict and demanding woman who ensured all of the trainees were put through their paces, constantly testing them and pushing them to their limits and beyond. Matron was to make each of them start at the bottom scrubbing floors and lockers with pungent disinfectant, serving food to patients and getting used to the reality of life on the wards. She loved to allocate them to 'slush room days' and reinforce to them every day that they were the lowest of the low. This was aided by the qualified nurses who delighted in barking as many orders at them as Matron.

Gabrielle's time was split between equally between the ward and the classroom. She dreamt of the serenity of the classroom and of being away from the constant wailing of "nurse, nurse" and Matrons perverse commands.

Chapter Five

The training was rigorous and at times Gabrielle felt that it was insurmountable but the good times outweighed the bad. During her training she lived in the nurse's home where life was more bearable. She enjoyed the camaraderie with the girls and despite the strict curfew of ten o'clock each night (unless on duty) they had fun. Twice a week, when Matron's watchful eyes finally closed and the lights went out, the girls would creep out of the nurse's home and escape into Derry.

They would tiptoe downstairs and climb out the kitchen window always ensuring that it was pulled down just enough so it appeared closed. If anyone was caught going in or out after this time they would be suspended or worse. The young nurses who had gone before them had kindly tipped the girls off about the kitchen window; so far everyone had managed to escape. The Matron did a final check of the corridors of the home around half ten locking all doors and windows and switching off the lights. The kitchen window with its loose handle was the exception to her search, in Gabrielle's three years in the nurses home the Matron never once checked beyond the kitchen door and of course the fridge lock.

The Matron's unusual lapse was to the girls gain; they were free to enjoy themselves dancing, drinking and following the infamous show bands until the wee small hours (often reporting to the wards having had no sleep at all!).

There comes a time when all girls grow up, even country girls and it was during these wild days that Gabrielle proudly admitted to discovering cigarettes, booze and men. She boasts at having made it her point to regularly sample all three! Gabrielle smoked twenty a day (still does), drinking and dating as often as she could. She was determined to enjoy her youth and freedom. The girls suspected that Matron, a small joyless woman had an inkling that the girls were going out after curfew yet she simply lacked the proof. Despite her vigilance and almost daily security checks she never discovered their exit route. Without proof there was little she could do with regards to her suspicions.

Hospital life meant that Gabrielle met people from all around the world, especially men! Many young doctors came to work and study at the hospital and by the time she was twenty she had dated Protestants, Indians, Spaniards, Italians and young men from as far afield as Egypt and India. She could even boast of having dated an officer from the British army and a policeman. Life in Derry immersed her into a world that was a million miles away from her strict upbringing; a world that would never have been possible had she stayed in her insular home town. She was never silly enough to mention her antics at home. Even then she was savvy enough to know that tolerance of anything other than a Catholic, a good Irish Catholic at that would never be granted.

Gabrielle's training involved a rotation where she worked in various different areas of the hospital from theatre, to A&E and paediatrics until she was competent in them all. Everything seemed to be going reasonably well until Gabrielle was faced with the challenge of the labour ward. She had an idea that she wouldn't enjoy this particular rotation, but knew that in order to pass she would have to endure it.

Gabrielle went with a hopeful and cautiously optimistic mind to begin her first day on the labour ward, where she was met with a woman who was in the final stages of labour. The woman's hair was wet with sweat and glued to her red and purple face. She appeared utterly inhuman as she frantically pushed the child out, puffing and panting, her legs akimbo with untold fluids dripping out of what seemed like every private orifice. The image disgusted Gabrielle, so much so that something strange happened, her stomach heaved and she threw up. If this was the miracle of life, then life didn't offer much! She had seen so much during her training, people's inners, vomit, burns, diarrhoea, pus and countless other horrors. Yet none had the same effect on her as watching that woman giving birth.

After being sick she took to her two size fives and ran, she never wanted to see such a display again. She was well and truly traumatised.

When she had gained a good distance from the hospital, she stopped running, smoked three cigarettes in a row and waited until the shaking subsided. Unsure of what to do she recalls racking her brain for a plan because she knew she would never darken the doors of that foul cesspit again. What seemed like eons passed until she decided that there was only one thing to do; *go back to her old rotation on the recovery ward and act like nothing happened!* If she kept her head down and went on with her usual work, she naively believed that no one would question her presence.

How wrong she was!

Within an hour of escape from the labour ward she sensed that she was being watched. She quickly clambered behind a locker and ducked her head down. It was too late. Gabrielle was caught. A voice that sent shivers down her spine boomed down the corridor,

"Nurse Caulfield!"

With those words her stomach lurched. "Oh God", she was in a living hell. She unfolded herself from her hiding place and forced an answer.

"Yes, Matron" she whimpered

"My office please" Matrons clipped tones replied.

Gabrielle was now sweating as profusely as the woman on the labour ward. Her legs felt like jelly as she manoeuvred them in the direction of Matron's office. She could barely tap the door her hands were shaking so much,

"Come in" barked Matron.

Gabrielle stepped in to the stuffy smoke filled office and approached the desk. Matron didn't even look up from her writing, her chubby fingers gripping the pen to the point of strangulation, the only indication that she was aware of Gabrielle's presence.

"Nurse Caulfield, why are you not on the maternity ward? Why am I faced with you this morning?" she demanded.

This was it after two years of hard slog it was over, the cretin would expel her. Gabrielle answered with the only excuse she had,

"Matron I didn't like it" she faltered, already aware of how feeble her words would sound.

"*You* didn't like it?"

Gabrielle nodded unable to meet her steely eyes.

"*YOU* didn't like it" she roared, in a mixture of bemusement and disgust.

"How dare you! How *dare* you! Since when can a nurse pick and choose her duties, this is not a holiday camp" (More a concentration camp, thought Gabrielle).

"That ward is a vital part of your training, it is not about *like*" Matron sneered.

Gabrielle, who always had an answer regardless of the situation, was for once gobsmacked. She was so caught up in her own world that she could barely listen to the Matron's rant. She could see Matrons brow furrowed and could hear key words, "disappointment, disgrace, and specimen"; she could see Matron's spittle but was too concerned with the ramifications of her actions. It was at the moment when Matron scraped her chair back and stood in front of her, her rotund body rigid with outrage as she muttered the word 'suspended' that Gabrielle woke up.

Gabrielle felt her blood run cold; the room began to spin.

"Collect your belongings and leave, I will be in touch when I have made my decision."

Still gobsmacked words still eluded her she simply turned and left the office. She was in trouble. She was suspended until further notice until Matron decided on what further course of action she would take.

This time it took four cigarettes to compose herself, there was nothing she could do now. She would either be allowed to finish her training or not. The only positive that came from that day's development was the fact that she would never have to set foot in the labour ward again. Or so she thought; as fate would have it she would have to endure the labour ward not as a nurse but as a patient three more times in all.

She called her father and told him she was given a week's leave; her hours were on a rota basis so he wasn't surprised at her having given no warning regarding her days off. It was a risky step for Gabrielle to take, as there would be no way of knowing if a week was long enough because Matron had given her no indication of how long the suspension would last. One thing she was sure of was that Matron would let her stew; she would not rush to put her out of her misery. She craftily omitted to mention to her father that she might never need returned back to the nurse's home. She would impart that information when she had heard definite confirmation, but for now she was going to try and enjoy her unexpected unearned break!

It was to be exactly a week to the day that she returned home when an ominous looking letter arrived. It was etched with the hospitals official stamp instantly Gabrielle knew its contents revealed her future. Of course in her home there was never any privacy, she grew up surrounded by an endless stream of visitors and family. This is a sharp contrast to my childhood where very few, if any, got past our door.

Aware of being watched by a full house Gabrielle managed to keep herself composed and casually tore the thick envelope open. She was aware of her mother watching her from the side of her eye; she had never had a letter from the hospital in her two years of training. So she knew that her spectator was wondering what she had done now. Well she wasn't going to enlighten her.

"What are you all gawping at" she raged.

She knew her mother would call her up on this rudeness later, but right now she didn't care. For now her outburst ensured everyone in the room had averted their eyes and went on with their tedious conversation.

Gabrielle scanned the contents of the letter quickly being careful not to re attract any attention to herself. It seemed that she had had a reprieve and was due back on the ward the following Monday! Better still she was due at A & E and the labour ward was not mentioned.

She was triumphant as her little protest had been successful!

The suspension had been the longest time Gabrielle had been separated from her work and it forced her to admit that she actually missed it. She would return to Derry and work harder than ever and she would be diligent, obedient and dedicated. She would prove to Matron that she was a worthy contender to her now ardently craved title of 'nurse'.

The journey back to the hospital would have followed the river Foyle it was a journey I was to take several times in my childhood. I'm sure her view was much the same as mine on approaching the city. She would have passed the Waterside's now familiar railway station, its row upon row of terraces, children playing out, neighbours on doorways gossiping and of course the steaming windows of the many pubs.

Back then Derry was an industrial, hardworking city but overall a happy one. A real sense of community prevailed. Looking over her shoulder she would have seen the river Foyle's waters parting the city in two, with the hills of Donegal looming in the background creating a picturesque scene. Unlike me, Gabrielle was glad to be there; she fitted in.

When the old gasworks wall would have scaled her vision she would have known that in less than a mile she would be back at the nurse's home. Now Gabrielle could get back to work and normality. The suspension only made her see what she had almost lost.

Chapter Six

Gabrielle arrived early because she remembers whiling the day away in the communal room. Although it was 1970, TV was still a real treat and the fact that the nurse's home had one was an attraction for all the girls. She greeted the few girls who were in the room with a nod and turned her attention to the TV.

Something about what was on attracted Gabrielle and meant that it wasn't long until she was completely engrossed. The English journalist was reporting all the way from America and was covering the plight of the African Americans. Equal rights had been granted in many states but prejudices were still commonplace. The TV switched to show a picture of the late Dr. Martin Luther King, and she listened intently to what he was saying. From Gabrielle's stance the Americans struggles seemed implausible, yet civil rights and the injustices faced by these people were never far from the news. She just couldn't comprehend why anyone would make such a distinction between human beings, why one race felt they had the right to demean another. She listened actively to see if any explanation was proffered, unsurprisingly there was none. There never would be.

When Gabrielle was growing up she remembers seeing a person of colour in Strabane, she can't recall much about them except for the fact that they were so attractive. She pleaded with her family in the months leading up to her fifth Christmas for a black baby doll. When that Christmas came, no black baby doll arrived. She was so disappointed that none of her other presents held any appeal. Santa was a bad man he had let her down and ruined her Christmas. However, one kindly aunt's efforts were to prove successful in pacifying her. Her aunt promised her that someday she would have a real black baby. It was as if her aunt had a crystal ball.

Gabrielle's work meant encountering people from all over the world; she couldn't imagine creating a distinction between people. She could never be an American. Her dislike for Americans and their hatred was the only real political conviction of her youth.

That day she discreetly studied one of her fellow students from the corner of her eye. Modupe was a pretty girl, stalwartly studious and excruciatingly quiet. The result was that Gabrielle didn't know her very well. She knew that Modupe was from Africa, and her parents had sent her here to complete her nursing training. She surveyed her for a while trying to ascertain these differences that the Americans claimed to see. Yet everything about her was exactly the same as her white counterparts. The only difference she could see was that her skin colour was darker. She marvelled at how so many people believed that having darker skin somehow made a person inferior and would have continued to do so had Modupe not noticed her appraisal and stared openly back.

Embarrassed she flushed, looked away and gave up on her train of thought. It wouldn't be long until such thoughts would keep her awake at night.......

Chapter seven

After the fiasco of the labour ward Gabrielle was placed in A&E and loved it. She loved not knowing who or what would come through the swinging doors; she loved the buzz. She describes her days as being adrenalin fuelled and hectic. To her this was what nursing was all about, not watching women debase themselves pushing out goo covered babies.

During training Gabrielle's home life remained constant, her mother asking about her studies and enquiring if she had met any young men. Luckily her mother was usually bent over the sewing machine so couldn't see Gabrielle's face as she lied and said she hadn't met any. Her siblings ran in and out from the back garden, the noise was piercing as they played whatever new game they had invented. Gabrielle was relieved to be living away from this madness, children babbling and shrieking incessantly gave her a headache. Every time she went home she vowed never to succumb to having children of her own. She always felt that that no one should ever be expected to put up with noisy children. Not to mention endure the miracle of life.

One evening an unannounced caller gave away her talk of never having had a boyfriend in Derry. She was almost ready to prepare for bed when a knock came to the door, assuming it was the gypsies or worse the priest she let her father answer it. This was a mistake because her father was to invite the caller in and it certainly wasn't the gypsies, or the priest. It was a boy she had been dating in Derry and had told no one at home about.

Her father had sent this boy to the sitting room. It was a room that they seldom used except when they had their best company. Whoever he was had obviously impressed.

Her father told her that her visitor was,

"A lovely chap, very posh, called Harry"

Gabrielle went puce at the very mention of his name; she hoped her parents didn't notice. Her mother rose and wiped away the threads from her sewing off her dress,

"Gabrielle go and greet your guest" she ordered.

As she walked into the living room she found Harry sitting awkwardly on the settee,

"Hello" she said feigning surprise "what brings you here?"

"I decided it was high time I met your family" said Harry making her cringe.

As if on cue her mother walked into the room.

"Hello" she said in her authoritative voice reserved for visitors or trouble, "I'm Gabrielle's mother, pleased to meet you"

Harry jumped to his feet and went over to shake her mother's hand.

Gabrielle was delighted with Harry's show of manners because she knew her mother would appreciate it.

"Harry Thornton, pleased to meet you Mrs Caulfied"

"Have a seat John's just preparing some tea"

"Thank you" he answered sitting back down on the settee.

"You have a beautiful home Mrs Caulfield" he remarked. Gabrielle wasn't convinced that her boyfriend's comments were genuine. After all he came from a family of Doctors and lived in one of the most affluent areas of Derry. Whilst Gabrielle's home was tastefully decorated, fashionable and clean she doubted it would impress Harry.

"Gabrielle didn't let us know she had plans so I can only apologise for not expecting you" her mother said.

"That's entirely my fault Mrs Caulfield we actually didn't have any plans. I just decided to call on the off chance that Gabrielle would be free. It's so rare to get a weekend off these days."

"Really Harry? May I ask what line of work you're in?" Her mother enquired.

"I'm a doctor; I work in Altnagelvin as well"

"I see" said her mother "so you're obviously very busy, well we're delighted you could take the time to call"

"Gabrielle, why don't you go and help your father, Harry would you rather tea or coffee?"

"Coffee please if it's not too much trouble".

Mum remembers hurrying to the kitchen to find her father rattling and banging plates,

"What's keeping you?"

"Just checking to see what biscuits we have"

"Do you need a hand?"

"No, no, you go up to your guest. I've found some shortbread"

"Grand thanks for your help"

"Gabrielle, one more thing he seems a nice lad, I just wondered if he's................"

She didn't let him finish, she already knew what her father was getting at,

"For God's sake, if you must know he's Protestant!" she said storming off.

Doctor or not now she knew now that her parents would not be impressed. She suppressed a fleeting thought that they didn't have any shortbread and made her way back into the living room.

"Aye that's what I thought" Mumbled her Dad.

She joined her mother and Harry in the living room where the conversation was flowing. Being the woman she was her mother had a keen interest in current affairs and she was glad to have someone to discuss them with.

"Gabrielle, we're just talking about the situation in Derry"

The British army were a considerable presence in the city but it wasn't anything Gabrielle was particularly interested in.

She was already bored and let them resume their conversation.

Finally her father came in carrying a tray with four cups and saucers, milk and sugar.

"Gabrielle will you do the honours?" he asked.

"I'm just going to get some biscuits, shortbread okay for you Harry?"

"It's my favourite Mr Caulfield' "Harry replied.

"Grand," her father eyes twinkling went to fetch the shortbread.

Two minutes later her father returned with the plate of shortbread.

He approached Harry first.

Harry's face registered shock but immediately recovered, thus drawing Gabrielle's attention to the plate.

To her absolute horror when she looked at it she didn't see any shortbread instead a plate filled with tiny chunks of roughly cut stale bread. If this wasn't bad enough, rather than use the plates they had reserved for guests or even their own everyday plates it was clear that her father had gotten this 'plate' from the local skip. It was a mass of cracks and chips with filthy brown marks clinging to its edges and to top it all off was sopping wet. Gabrielle was mortified and still cringes as she recounts the tale; even more so when Harry obviously not wanting to offend took a piece.

Her mother was silent. Clearly she was horrified too but quickly regained her composure.

All of a sudden Harry jumped up,

"I do apologise, Mr and Mrs Caulfield, Gabrielle, but I've just realised I have an appointment". Looking flustered he swiftly added "I really must go".

With that he got up and made towards the door.

"That's a shame" her father said feigning disappointment, "I'll see you out, maybe you'll come for a good Irish dinner the next time?"

That was the first and last time Dr Thornton ever called for Gabrielle (or within a five mile radius of her home!).

Boyfriends came and went over the years, if they were Protestant and met her father they usually went. Her father had his unique disposal methods and each poor young man was sent away red faced.

Gabrielle's father came from an idealistic world, he despised snobs to him no one person was better than another. A person was distinguished by how they conducted their life and how close to God they were (in a Catholic way). A person should always be judged on their decency, honesty and integrity. A sense of humour also helped, but if none existed then so long as the other three were in abundance it could be sacrificed.

Chapter Eight

Gabrielle had come from a cosseted world; the safe familiar walls of the hospital reinforced this. But even she couldn't help observing how much life was changing in Derry. The city was rapidly becoming awash with armed soldiers, navy and police. A cloud of tension hung in the air even on the calmest days. She was no longer comfortable using her free time to explore the city and tended to stay close to the nurses home.

It was in Gabrielle's final year of training that a civil rights movement had called a march on the streets of Derry. She didn't know it then but she was about to become involved in a historic day. The marchers came out to protest at the perceived inequalities experienced by the Catholic people of Derry. It was conducted in the fashion of civil rights marches that had gone before in America and would highlight the Catholic people's struggles.

The general consensus at the time was that Catholics in Northern Ireland did not get equal rights in housing, education and jobs. Gabrielle didn't doubt their argument but had never felt subject to any form of inequality; so unlike most of her contemporaries she would not be joining the March. From an early age it had been instilled in her that a good education would carry one anywhere. She saw that all her friends had gone on to university and all of them herself included were in the process of gaining entrance into one profession or another. She hadn't experienced any inequalities nor had anyone she knew.

Gabrielle had never stood back to examine the wider picture. Growing up in an almost solely Catholic area meant that schools and houses were good; they never had to share these with another community. Catholics in other areas that were not as segregated as hers perhaps felt differently. Gabrielle was solidly ambiguous towards the plight of these people and suspected that little would change that.

Almost twenty years after the Catholic civil rights movement Gabrielle spoke to a colleague from a Protestant background that had grown up in the Shankill area of Belfast. By all accounts her upbringing was similar to Gabrielle's except for the inequalities, not on Gabrielle's part however. It seemed her colleague had lived in inferior government housing, had limited prospects of work and had grown up in a situation of abject poverty and little aspiration. Inequalities were across the board, they were a matter for the working classes; a class that Gabrielle was determined never to be a part of. If only she knew.

Keen to witness the march Gabrielle's mother suggested they go for tea in the City Hotel. The hotel overlooked the marcher's route and would allow them to get a good view as it passed. Nothing on this scale had happened before in the North West and her mother wanted to say that she had seen it. So on that freezing Sunday; Gabrielle was accompanied by both her parents on her journey to Derry. That day was to become known as 'Bloody Sunday'.

Gabrielle remembers her father taking the familiar journey extra cautiously. All along the road little patches of ice danced in front of the car, on each sighting he would mutter, "black ice, it's the most dangerous thing drivers face". Her Mother as usual rolled her eyes and tutted. His slow driving was one of the many things she chastised him about. On this occasion she claimed that they would have been quicker walking!

When they eventually reached Derry anticipation radiated from the very pavements the air was charged with positivity. It seemed that thousands of people had taken to the streets to join the march. Gabrielle and her parents were simply there to observe. Strict instructions were given to her father to collect them from the hotel in precisely an hour and a half. This would allow plenty of time to watch the march unfold. No real consideration was given to what her father would do in that time, even now Gabrielle cannot remember. She can only assume that he went home.

They were fortunate to get a window seat at the hotel. They sipped their coffees ensconced in the comfort of the lavish lobby. From here they watched as the march passed.

Gabrielle saw the marchers carry huge banners emblazoned with slogans demanding equal rights. The street was lined with Saracens. To some it may have looked ominous but to the people of Derry it didn't; heavily armed streets were now familiar. They watched the passage of the March in silence as it made its way towards the Bogside.

It didn't seem long until the chants of the demonstrators were overtaken by gunfire and angry screams. Gabrielle immediately knew that something was wrong, the sirens began to blare as more and more military swarmed the streets. She had never seen anything equal to this before and shock surged through her. The voices around them in the hotel became raised and some people rushed out. Inside the hotel mirrored the streets outside; pure pandemonium.

Within minutes the news that shooting had broken out got through to them. Wails of a new siren different to that of the police siren, confirmed that people were injured. The noise was deafening as the screams of the ambulance competed against the Saracens making an eerie tune.

Even as a trainee Gabrielle knew protocol and she would be expected to report to the hospital. She gathered up her belongings and prepared to leave. Sure enough just as she was fastening her coat the radio began to call for any medical personal to make their way to the hospital.

Outside she saw ambulances, police and people race by. It was like a warzone, she did not dare imagine what would confront her when she made it to the hospital.

When her father came to collect them from the hotel, he looked shaken yet his face was alight with relief when he glimpsed them. He had obviously been worried, another indicator that something very wrong was unfolding outside. Her parents were clearly unsure whether she should offer her services but she convinced them that protocol meant that she had little choice.

On reaching the hospital Gabrielle was confronted with complete and utter carnage. That day they dealt with twelve gunshot victims. This was made all the worse as in addition to the gunshot victims one poor young man had been suffocated in the skirmish that ensued. It was Gabrielle's first experience of such wounds but over the next few years she would become as familiar with gunshot victims as she would be with fractures.

She soon became immersed in a new brand of nursing; one that her training had not prepared her for. She was to become accustomed to rubber bullets forcing eyes out of sockets, shootings, kneecappings, tarring and featherings and the ultimate carnage - bomb victims. Her patients would range from armed police, to innocent civilians and even IRA men all of whom she was expected to treat in a moment's notice. In work Gabrielle was no longer shockable as she had learned to expect anything and everything.

Being so young it didn't take long before Gabrielle began to wish for an easier post, even the labour ward would be an improvement on this. Yet she can proudly say that despite wanting an easier post, she did her level best for all the people she treated, those who were innocent and of course the instigators. When I ask her how she could do that she simply replies that she was a nurse, it was not for her to judge any individual. She was there simply to treat, God could do the rest. The smells, sights and sounds of those years were a far cry from the glamorous career she had envisaged and a premonition of her own glimpse into hell.

It was the bomb victims who stayed with her, they were so charred their bodies were unrecognisable; the percentage of burns so high that sometimes even pain relief was futile. She inwardly grieved with their families; no one should have had to endure such suffering. She can close her eyes even now and be transported to those dark days in A&E; the smells once again assailing her nostrils, the mutilation of innocence seizing her sight, the anguished wails of the bereaved assaulting her ears. She will forever carry a little piece of their torment with her alongside her own.

In those days she was determined not to let these atrocities remain in the foremost regions of her mind. Yet they stayed with her somewhere. In Mum's recent tales she can recount each and every experience, she never forgot them. I think she found a convenient little shelf in her brain and alongside Patch, Matron and anything else that could harm her she stored them there and continued with her day to day living. Unfortunately for Gabrielle someday all the horror would come to the forefront of her mind and the shelf it was placed on would collapse.

Chapter Nine

During this time Gabrielle met and became engaged to a nice, local Catholic boy. I often wonder how she would have fared if things had worked out. That I will never know. So far advanced were the wedding plans that the venue was booked, the flowers organised and invitations sent. She had even booked the honeymoon.

It transpired two weeks before her big day that this wedding was not meant to be. Gabrielle called at her fiancés home to discuss the seating arrangements at the hotel. She hadn't given any notice (as she normally would) because she was so intent on getting this wedding right.

Gabrielle walked into his house and was surprised that he didn't even enquire as to who was there. Flippantly she looked for him downstairs. Not finding him, she sought him upstairs. She barged into his bedroom about to make him work through her crucial seating plan when she instinctively knew that something was amiss. As her eyes adjusted to the darkness her seating plan was no longer relevant; she saw what she had never wanted to see. Her fiancé was not alone; she could see the outline of another body lying next to him, could smell a sweet cloying perfume and saw the discarded clothes strewn around the room. On seeing Gabrielle he was immediately on his feet, his nudity confronting her, yet he had the audacity to claim "It's not what you think". Gabrielle rarely gave anyone a second chance and her fiancé was not to be the exception. She turned on her heel and walked out of his room, his house and his life for good. To top it all off after several attempts to contact her the cretin even went on the honeymoon – courtesy of Gabrielle!

For the next few months Gabrielle was so devastated that she didn't set foot outside. She stayed at home and cried, wallowing in her betrayal. Her friends tried everything to rouse her, but nothing would work. She was heartbroken, humiliated and nothing would bring her round. In the aftermath of her failed engagement her life became a cycle of work, work and more work. Work allowed her to escape thinking about the cancelled wedding. It allowed her to escape the stares and the sympathy. A jilted bride was always a good gossip point.

Eventually though her maudlin had to end. She began tentatively taking steps out, even having nights out again, though always careful to avoid men. One of her friends at the time noticed Gabrielle's stalwart avoidance of the opposite sex and decided to set her up on a blind date. Her friend would not take no for an answer, so after much cajoling Gabrielle reluctantly agreed. She was to go to a party at her friend's house and was promised that her 'perfect man' would be there.

Not expecting much from this mystery man she arrived at the party that night yet she saw nothing outstanding; the same old clones. Northern Ireland never offered much to Gabrielle by way of its men folk, which was one of the reasons she had expected little from her 'date'. She took a few drinks and was about to chastise her friend for dragging her to this silly party, when the back door opened and in walked a tall dark handsome creature, of course accompanied by a typical Northern Irish man. Her friend nudged her as if she thought that the new addition to the room had escaped her. Gabrielle simply prayed that the pasty Northern Irish man who accompanied the tall dark stranger was not the man her friend had in mind for the blind date.

Unlike the other excuses for men present, this dark man exuded dapperness; he held himself so proudly and confidently that to her he was the essence of class. He wore a clearly expensive suit and a heavy cashmere overcoat, he was tall and lean and he was completely and utterly gorgeous. This man was by no means classically good looking, yet he was unique and so, so attractive. His skin was a dark brown, almost black and he wore his hair shaved close. On seeing his chocolate brown eyes, Gabrielle didn't know it then, but she was smitten. This man was obviously older than most of her counterparts too old for her. She imagined he must have been at least thirty!

As sure as she had noticed him he had noticed her and it wasn't long until he approached and began making conversation. Gabrielle doesn't remember what they spoke about but she does remember that his accent was strange, guttural, nothing like the sing song feminine accents of the men she was accustomed to. On further investigation she soon established that he came from Nigeria, and his name was Max. He lived in Belfast but had travelled to Derry tonight in order to meet his friend who had accompanied him. He had practically been forced to attend this party.

Despite finding Max attractive, Gabrielle was still refusing to entertain any man. Should Omar Sharif have thrown himself at her right then and there she would have refused him. So, even when Max asked her out her out she firmly refuted his offer. The party ended later that night and as far as Gabrielle was concerned that was the last she would see of the handsome stranger called Max.

As fate conspired this was not the case, it seemed Max was in love, he was also a man who rarely gave up on what he wanted. Max wanted Gabrielle. For the next few weeks and months Gabrielle received flowers, weekly letters and phone calls. This was a man who would not take no for an answer. She tried to put his stubborn refusal down to a cultural barrier, she even went so far as to learn how to say "no go away" in Nigerian, yet her efforts were wasted. The fact that she had made clear to him after each of his advances that she wasn't interested irritated her. Who did this eejit think he was? His self-assurance and denial of rejection grated on her and she began ignoring all of his offerings concluding that he would give up eventually.

Chapter Ten

By the summer of 1973, Gabrielle had spent five years in Altnagelvin; three as a trainee and two as a qualified nurse. She could never say she was bored, but like most young people she felt the urge to spread her wings and move to pastures new. She considered working in both Belfast and Dublin and was surprised when the first hospital she had applied to offered her an interview. Belfast City Hospital had vacancies and she became set on gaining one.

A major barrier stood in her way, the interview date fell in the middle of the month. This was not the ideal time for her, her salary was long gone. Gabrielle was notorious for spending every penny within a week of payday and living even less than frugally for the remaining days of the month. She barely had enough money to pay the bus fare for the two hour journey to Belfast. Yet she wanted the job, she wanted a change. Maybe it would be worth starving for two weeks until her next payday to travel to Belfast. Always conscious of her figure Gabrielle felt that two weeks on a meagre diet would do wonders! She resigned herself to a fortnight of bread and coffee and made her plans to attend the interview. Her main regret was that she couldn't have made a day of going to Belfast and enjoying a quick shop as well. Gabrielle supposed if she was successful in the interview she would shop in Belfast all the time, so one missed shopping opportunity wouldn't be the end of the world.

With that Gabrielle determined to get the bus and give the best interview she had ever given. Even though the bus journey was long, she wasn't bored for a second of it. She always loved to travel and this was further than she had ever gone. Gabrielle spent most of the journey peering out the window at the many small towns they passed through. Towns that were now littered with sectarian graffiti destroying their otherwise friendly facades.

She arrived in Belfast early as she had no idea where the city hospital was located, she would have to ask for directions and in a city this size, she would no doubt have to ask more than once. Luckily enough she found the hospital without too much difficulty and made it in ample time for her interview. Her youthful ego meant that she was confident and prepared and with the exception of her stomach rumbling, she left the hospital secure in the knowledge that she had done enough to be offered the post.

Gabrielle had been so concerned with preparing for the interview that she had forgotten to bring lunch with her; now that the interview was over she was painfully aware of her growing hunger. She knew she couldn't afford to stop off at any of the cafes and restaurants she passed to refuel, well without offering to wash the dishes! Nor could she pop into a shop and buy even a snack. It would take at least four hours to get home and she wallowed at the thought of not having a bite until then. She continued to walk down the Lisburn road towards the bus depot. By now she was so full of self-pity at her self imposed fast that when she heard her name called it took a while to register. Hunger had her every thought. She supposed meeting someone she knew so far from home was a good reason to distract her even momentarily from the hunger pangs. She stopped and turned around to see who would know her here in Belfast.

Standing in front of her, showing off his pearly whites was Max. Once again Gabrielle was taken aback by his attractiveness. He looked so very exotic standing there in his crisp white shirt, peaking out behind a summer suit. In her mind he belonged more on the streets of a chic city rather than on the streets of Belfast.

Impressed as she was she inwardly groaned, she was not in the mood for small talk especially when she was wasting away. Her hunger was making her feel light headed and her stomach ached. Her mood instantly changed when her ears and stomach extracted from his mundane small talk three magic words that would seal her fate and mine, "There's a nice little restaurant across the road, how about we catch up over lunch?"

Part Two 1973 – 1980

"Belfast Belfast wonderful town doesn't matter if your skin is brown", Boney M

Chapter Eleven

Gabrielle's prediction was right. As expected she had succeeded in gaining the post in Belfast. Within six weeks of her interview she was firmly installed in the recovery unit at the City Hospital. She enjoyed the challenges of the job and soaking up the sense of community that this huge hospital encouraged amongst its staff. The only thing she had not considered was where she was going to live. Finding a home was a time consuming pursuit at the best of times, but when working full time and coping with so many changes, the prospect was not one she was eager to embrace. Gabrielle decided against trawling this alien city for a suitable flat and took up residence in the nurse's home.

The nurse's home offered an opportunity to make friends, avail of cheaper accommodation and reside within walking distance from the hospital. Living in the home would give Gabrielle time to explore the city and gain her bearings. Gabrielle decided that when she was more sure of her surroundings she would begin searching for somewhere of her own. For now, the accommodation on offer was more than comfortable, the rooms were bright and airy and the shared facilities clean and modern. Gone were the curfews and rules of her training. As a qualified nurse the nurse's home was exactly as described; a home. She often looked at the pale and drawn faces of the trainees who lived in the student building next door and couldn't help but feel a little pity for them. She understood their plight. Yet at the same time a little voice inside wanted to gloat. In hospital hierarchy she was their superior and the thought filled her with a wily pride.

Gabrielle's initial excitement at moving to Belfast was blemished slightly by the warnings of her colleagues. Already they had cautioned her on the 'no go areas', volatile areas where trouble was guaranteed and incessant. She absorbed every shred of advice and began crossing out the areas deemed dangerous on her little map of the city. When she got the chance to explore she would make a point of avoiding every area that had been mentioned. After two or three conversations however; it seemed an altogether easier option to list the areas she could safely go!

Gabrielle could barely find an area on her map that wasn't crossed out. By the time she had heeded every warning her map resembled a distorted treasure map. Any pirate would have been devastated on finding it; for the multitude of crosses on the map did not mark plunder and riches, instead they signified danger. When she finally found areas clear of crosses she was left with two or three 'mixed' or quiet areas to explore.

Gabrielle was soon to discover that even these 'safe' places were not altogether immune from the violence, they too experienced shootings and bombings; on a less frequent level granted, but nevertheless the unrest had infiltrated the entire city. In the end she threw caution to the wind and vanquished her list. If she needed to go somewhere then she would. If an area regardless of having crosses had shops then she would venture there.

In those early days in Belfast it seemed that everywhere she looked there was an armed soldier either on patrol, kneeling between gateposts or fences or standing on street corners. Gabrielle really didn't have any opinion towards them. She was blissfully ambivalent, until one day she was rushing out the door and tripped over one. From that point onwards Gabrielle saw them as health hazards! The colossal bump on her shin that the encounter left her with ensured that she became as watchful of the soldiers as they were of her. Yet all things considered she could endure the bomb warnings, she could turn a blind eye to the intimidating sectarian graffiti and even the growing number of soldiers. For Gabrielle craved city life, if these things were the downside then she would just have to accept them.

On one of her days off a colleague offered to take her 'into town' luckily for her it was the end of the month so she had money to spend. She gladly availed of the offer. They travelled into town on the bus and were offloaded directly opposite the historical building that was the City Hall. Belfast city centre revolved around one main street that was intersected by a few small streets. With the exception of new shopping centres it still remains like this today. On Gabrielle's first outing to the city centre she wanted to see every little street. Purse at the ready she was almost as armed as the soldiers and police! She fully intended to stock up her wardrobe and couldn't wait to enter the large shops that at home she had only read about. Her friend led her in the direction of the main street, Royal Avenue. On approach Gabrielle was astounded at the sight that met her because before she could even enter the street she would have to go through security.

Barriers large and menacing blocked entry to the entire city centre, the only way in was to pass through an armoured hut. People lined up to gain entrance and one by one in single file they passed through security. Here bags were searched and pockets were emptied. Gabrielle wasn't in the least bit daunted, the only feelings she had were those of frustration. The security hut meant that her much anticipated shopping trip would be delayed; patience was never and never has been one of Gabrielle's virtues. She would have to stand and wait in line for God knows how long. As usual when she was flummoxed she said a quick aspiration to the Holy Virgin Mary. This time she beseeched her to ensure that no one in front of her presented a threat. If they did then her wait would be extended even more and she only had one day off! The Holy Virgin Mary must have heard her because before long they had cleared security and were able to make their way to the first shop.

Gabrielle viewed security as an irritating inconvenience which was to become a stark contrast to her attitude of a few years later.

The searching was repeated in the next shop and the next, until she grew accustomed to it. By shop number four Gabrielle automatically opened her bag on entrance. In future she would plan her shopping trips not by hours or even by her favourite shops, but by which shops had the least security. Her time off was precious and she could see this constant searching becoming an annoyance. She began to wonder if it was worth all this hassle simply to buy a few dresses. But when she looked down Royal Avenue and wondered through CornMarket, she saw shop upon shop lining the streets. Gabrielle determined there and then that a few little searches wouldn't come between her and all this!

In those days it became habit for Gabrielle and no doubt the bulk of women in Northern Ireland to ensure their handbags were tidy and pockets empty before going shopping, an untidy handbag or full pockets only served to cause delays.

Gabrielle never did tour the city as she had planned, she preferred to spend any free time whiling away her days in the relative safety of the Lisburn Road or in the Fort Knox that was the city centre. The minute amount of news she listened to or read reiterated the same pattern day after day bomb, riots or shootings. Remarkably some of the news which she routinely disregarded must have subliminally entered her head, for as time went on and the troubles worsened she gained a healthy apprehension and rarely ventured into the unknown. This combined with her dire sense of direction always kept her within close proximity to the hospital.

Staying close to the hospital was never a chore her instincts were right; a change of environment was exactly what she needed. Within walking distance from the hospital was an array of shops, restaurants and bars flourished. These were thronged with students from the local Queens' University who despite their surroundings, were keen to experience the seventies. Their colourful clothing, long hair and flares brightened the entire area and lightened the atmosphere in the otherwise guarded and forlorn city. Their proximity to the nurse's home kept the girls surrounded by a charged, vibrant ambience that pulsed with youthful energy, making the city a fun place to be.

Chapter Twelve

The move to Belfast stimulated a fresh burst of life in Gabrielle and she looked forward to each new day. Her colleagues were a sociable bunch of girls and it wasn't long before she felt right at home in the big city. Her days passed in a whirl of laughter, learning and contentment and she wished she had made the move to Belfast months earlier.

It would be fair to say that Gabrielle could not attribute all of her fervour to her wonderful new job and friends, a much stronger compulsion fuelled her exhilaration. Max.

Gabrielle was totally consumed with love for Max. Since he had bought her that lifesaving lunch two months earlier, she had really gotten to know him. No longer did she reject his advances on the contrary she positively sought them. Much to the confusion of the girls in Derry, she had suddenly become available to take his calls and reply to his letters. Luckily for her he never questioned how busy she had once claimed to be. If he had asked the only truthful answer Gabrielle could have furnished him with would have been that she was busy, very busy in fact. Busy avoiding him!

Since that lunch everything had changed, they even met up in Derry once or twice. Yet one hundred miles separated them and this was a distance that seemed futile. Max lived in Belfast and Gabrielle would have moved heaven and earth to have been near him. The fact that she chose to move to Belfast rather than Dublin was no coincidence. During that first lunch any initial reservations she had regarding his perceived arrogance and ego evaporated. He single handedly restored her confidence in the male species.

On talking with Max she found a genuine, sensitive, assured and proud man. His stunning appearance simply secured the deal. She was sold. For the first time ever she could identify with the multitude of love songs and films she had been exposed to. Now they had true meaning, she knew without a doubt what all the fuss was about. Gabrielle was in love and her gut told her that she had found her soul mate. Her mother had always said when you meet the right one you will know, she was right on this point, because when Gabrielle was with Max she just knew. All that had gone before was simply child's play and she thanked God for being jilted, for her Fathers shortbread and the effectiveness of his whole host of male disposal efforts!

Within months of meeting they were spending every second of their free time together, yet somehow for Gabrielle it never seemed enough. If she had one day off she wanted two, two days she wanted three, going so far as to wish that she could somehow cut herself in half so that she could be with him all the time. The rest of her could carry on with work, visit home and conduct the dreary necessities of life. It was perfect, they were perfect and right then her life was perfect.

Chapter Thirteen

As always where there is light and beauty there is darkness and ugliness. For a dark shadow stalked Gabrielle and Max, wherever they went it went. It introduced Gabrielle to bitterness and acrimony, to the repulsive side of humanity. The shadow's name was racism and it continues to stalk my family to this very day. The shadow manifested itself in many different guises, from the upper and middle class 'polite' insult, to casual remarks from colleagues, right through to loud insults from aggressive and blatant strangers. Regardless of its form and the different mouthpieces it exploited, its perpetrators all looked the same. Their indignant faces would be twisted with bitterness; their hatred consumed all their features. They became warped and grotesque, as they regarded Gabrielle and Max with eyes that exhibited the depths of contempt that lurked inside.

When they were dating Gabrielle made light of any causally thrown comments, stares and malevolent remarks. Hours were spent laughing them off or rolling her eyes mockingly. Sometimes Gabrielle even managed to make Max laugh, mocking their persecutors in secret whispers and sarcasm. Sometimes they even tried to pre-empt the comments, they could almost tell by the individual how their comments were going to form before they had even been uttered.

Despite this a pattern emerged that would continue for the rest of her life. When she would lie down at night in the restless hours waiting for sleep, her mind would revisit the incidents of that day. She would explore them over and over again, trying to make sense of them, she never succeeded. She would contemplate the nature of those who could do such things. She could never and would never consider these individuals as human. Were these creatures blind? Could they not see the beauty that she saw? The kindness? The generosity of spirit? Gabrielle was always a deep thinker and when unsavoury events occurred she became introverted and would linger on events far longer than any mind could cope with. Perhaps it was this aspect of her personality, the fact that she cared so much that led to her problems in later life.

It was at times when Gabrielle experienced blatant racism that she was ashamed to be white, ashamed to have even the smallest strand of DNA in common with these monstrosities. Thinking back to her youthful views on the American people, she realised that her own people were not any different.

On one occasion Gabrielle and Max had decided to go for a quiet meal and had chosen a popular Belfast eatery. When they walked through the door the hustle and bustle of the busy restaurant instantly stopped, all eyes were on them. The silence that ensued makes me think of a rowdy cowboy in an old western at the moment when he saunters into a saloon bar demanding a duel with the town's hero. Gabrielle and Max were the rowdy cowboys to these people; they perceived them, Max in particular as a stranger - a threat. It would not have surprised me from the description of that night if tumbleweed had blown along the restaurant floor in front of them!

Max surely must have felt the atmosphere yet acted like nothing was amiss and escorted them to their seats. It was only when couples came in after them that Gabrielle noticed a maître de clamouring to welcome the new arrivals. He boasted of the specials whilst selecting prime seating for them. Gabrielle and Max waited and waited for a menu which arrived with a kindly slam on the table, Max's slam was given with additional force.

No kindly maître de recited the specials to them.

After waiting a further forty minutes for their order to be taken, Gabrielle grew increasingly agitated and pleaded with Max to allow them to leave. Max refused stubbornly insisting that they waited. Gabrielle was in no doubt angry, not only with the restaurant but also with Max; it was a miracle that they didn't argue. By this stage all who arrived after them had been served, some were even ordering desert.

As the situation unfolded around them Gabrielle was learning that Max was a proud man; he did not easily align himself with defeat, so it was with a heavy heart that she suppressed her anger and waited with him. When almost an hour had passed and still no food arrived, Max made his way to the maître de while Gabrielle looked on discreetly. After he had spoken to the maitre de Max turned to return to the table.

It all happened so fast; the maître de extended his right foot and hooked it around Max's ankle. Max immediately fell to the floor with an agonising thud.

Gabrielle heard bone collide with the hard ground. The maître de and the kitchen staff laughed, the other diners simply looked on. Gabrielle ran to him and this time he needed no pleading on her part to leave the restaurant.

As they left Gabrielle saw the maître de wipe their unused table; a bottle of disinfectant in hand.

Many other deplorable incidents occurred in those months, too numerous to detail. It is suffice to say that Max's handling of these, never complaining yet never quite accepting, only made Gabrielle admire him more.

It wasn't all doom and gloom on the social scene however, as a couple they had good friends, friends who restored Gabrielle's faith in humanity and the people she lived amongst. Her friends were predominantly from the hospital background. They were surrounded by a multitude of different races in their everyday life so they didn't bat an eyelid at Max. Nor did they flinch at Gabrielle and Max's relationship. Max's friends came mainly from his work. Gabrielle thought they were boring accountants', bookish nerds but Max was clearly fond of them so by default she was too. They went to many parties and in an unspoken agreement between them only frequented familiar and safe places. They became regulars at the 'Egg' bar, where if even a derogatory stare was thrown in their direction the staff would immediately remove the offender (s).

Their friends were also to become protective of Max; they like Gabrielle were utterly perplexed by the attitudes emerging around them. To Max's accountancy friends he was a strong contender in the race for the coveted title of 'chartered' accountant. To Gabrielle's medical friends he was simply 'Gabrielle's Max'.

All of them saw beyond Max's skin colour, seeing him for what he was; a professional young man, fun, mannerly and a great conversationalist.

....

After only a year together the couple became engaged, it was no surprise to their friends and congratulatory cards and gifts were showered upon them. Gabrielle's parents knew that she was dating someone and she looked forward to greeting them with the news. Max was going away for a training session the following week so Gabrielle planned a trip home. She would use this visit to seize the opportunity to announce her good news.

In their regular telephone conversations her mother had told Gabrielle of the antics in her home town, she seemed thoroughly disheartened by it all. She spoke of the increase in IRA activity and of how she would not stand for such inexcusable behaviour. She was outraged, she claimed that no battle was ever won through bloodshed, talking was what was needed.

"What kind of an outfit preys on young men, with their whole lives in front of them" her mother would lament.

Her mother's account of the situation at home seemed so bleak that Gabrielle knew a spoonful of good news would be just the tonic. Her mother would then have something to take her mind of events and something new to concentrate on. Gabrielle cemented the arrangements for visiting that very weekend.

For once Gabrielle actually looked forward to going home; she wanted to see the delight of her mother and father. By now all the girls that she had grown up with were happily married. Some were even on child number three! Yet she was twenty three and still residing in the exclusively female nurse's home. Gabrielle was worried that her parents doubted her sexuality!

When the weekend finally arrived Gabrielle took the bus home ensuring that she had the previous night's mass sheet safely ensconced in her handbag. Her mother liked to question her on her church attendance. Gabrielle discovered that collecting a mass sheet from the chapel and memorising it was enough to convince her that she was continuing in the Catholic life she had been lumbered with. Having not attended one mass service since moving to Belfast she had no intentions of starting now, she even went so far as to time her arrival home to coincide with the end of Sunday mass. She would simply say she had attended the night before. Belfast was so busy that the sacred Sunday mass was also held on Saturdays to ensure that all the devout got a chance to bask in the joys of boredom! This tradition remains until this very day.

Gabrielle would stay at home until Wednesday so she could get a good break and catch up on all the news. She was quite sure though that the upcoming wedding would outshine any news that they could throw at her. She also had an ulterior motive for her extended stay at home. Max's training would last until Wednesday, so he wouldn't be back in Belfast until then. There was little point in her being there without him. Without him Belfast would be a lonely place. A lesson she would one day learn, it's a pity her older self didn't heed her younger self's opinions, instead Gabrielle would chase the source of her happiness and one day return.

As the bus chugged along the road to Strabane, she took the two hour opportunity to memorise the previous night's mass.

Chapter Fourteen

As usual when Gabrielle arrived home she found that home life continued as normal. Her siblings still managed to eradicate any promise of silence, her father was still working long shifts and her mother was still holding throne. Gabrielle liked the sense of normality that home gave her regardless of what was going on in the world outside, behind that little front door nothing ever changed. The routines of her childhood were still practised, the same visitors still called and the teapot was always on. There is comfort in familiarity and after a hectic week on the wards this was exactly what she sought.

As it was Sunday they were having their Sunday roast and would all dine together at the table. For the remaining six days of the week the children ate at the 'children's' table a small collapsible table reserved strictly for them and their spillages.

The formality of today's dinner was lost on Gabrielle. She was positively bursting with excitement, eager to broadcast the news of her up and coming nuptials. She had so far flaunted her engagement ring in more faces than enough. To her disappointment no one noticed. The children were so concerned with avoiding the dreaded 'stick' that they concentrated solely on being good. Her mother was too busy pontificating and of course dissecting every blessed word the priest had uttered in the earlier mass. Her father was holding court with anyone who would listen. The result was that her huge sparkling diamond and sapphire ring went unnoticed. Blind as bats the lot of them she thought. She knew that for now she was fighting a losing battle, so concentrated less on the ring and instead on finding the perfect moment to reveal her news.

Over dinner, talk inevitably lingered on the current political situation and the rise in sectarian activity. Her mother expressed her unhappiness with Gabrielle's choice of Belfast as a home, stating that safety should be everyone's prime consideration.

"Innocent people get caught out too you know, do you think they would care about anyone who stood in their way"' her mother demanded.

Her father on the other hand, at the mention of innocents shot or murdered, shook his head at the very thought,

"No lives worth a blade a grass," he said,

Gabrielle's father firmly believed that if Ireland was ever to be united it should be done peacefully.

As the mood at the table became more and more sombre, Gabrielle knew that it was time to interject with her good news. She waited until the subject of Belfast was raised again before seizing her opportunity.

It was one of her little sisters who opened the conversation asking about the shops, cinemas and restaurants, her little eyes widening at the thought of life in the big city.

"Can I come up and see you?" she had asked,

Her mother's face was already rigid at the thought,

"No one's going to Belfast" she snapped, "no one in their right mind anyway" she levelled directly at Gabrielle,

In response Gabrielle could only laugh and knew she had her moment,

"Well actually you may all be going to Belfast" she started,

Her mother shrewd as she was, raised her eyebrow and asked about this "Max fella". Gabrielle braced herself for the inevitable questions. How much time she was spending with him? Did he know Belfast well? What did he do? The list went on and on. It was now or never, time for her announcement.

Gabrielle took a deep breath and tried to suppress her grin before blurting,

"We got engaged!!"

Her mother and fathers immediate reaction was why this Max hadn't asked for their permission. Good grief they were so old fashioned Gabrielle had thought. She forced a deep sigh and reminded them that times were changing; it was almost 1973 for heaven's sake!

"Well he's not marrying you" she barked in her fiancés defence,

Her little sisters sniggered whilst her parents ignored her comments preferring to begin the art of extracting information from her. Gabrielle felt like an orange being juiced, they already knew about Max, that she had met him in Derry; that he lived in Belfast and that he was an accountant. Gabrielle had told them everything, so much so that she had nothing but pulp left to give them. It was as if they were determined to ask her each question over and over, an inquisition. She was sure the army would have vacancies for them; their interrogation skills were impeccable, second to none.

Her parents knew he was kind, financially stable and most importantly; all that they really needed to know was that she had never been happier.

Yet they continued to quiz her, she answered all their questions and waited for her father's inevitable question.

"Is he Catholic this Max?"

Gabrielle bristled, as Max wasn't a Catholic and she knew that this would not be taken well. All the positive things she had told them about Max would evaporate when they were given the answer,

"No Dad, he's Protestant, but it doesn't bother me"

Her father's reaction was not as bad as she had expected,

"I suppose he could convert, if he's keen enough; I'd rather you married in the Catholic Church"

Gabrielle was slightly taken aback by her father's acceptance of this fact and nodded. Yet she knew that it was highly unlikely that Max would convert. It was even more unlikely that she would ask him. What a thing to ask someone to do! For now though she guessed that her father could content himself with thinking that this may be the case.

"So when can we meet this Max?" her father asked

"Well I'm working next weekend, but perhaps I could swap Sunday with someone…. would that suit?" she gushed

"Grand" her father said.

Her mother was already preparing for the visit, talking about what she would serve, what she would wear, what her father would wear. Would dinner or a buffet be better? Who would she invite, just close family or a wider circle of friends? What would the little ones wear, and could Father Converey make it? Would it be acceptable for Father Converey to be there at all since this man hadn't converted yet? Maybe she would discuss this with Father Converey first before she decided.

Her mother was then to pipe up with another question,

"So Gabrielle, what will your new surname be?"

"Olorunda" she casually informed her,

Her mother looked confused and turned to her father who was nodding knowledgably,

"Aye, that would be a Western name hails from around Donegal and Sligo, a lot of the planters brought that with them" he said, clearly self-satisfied with his display of Irish genealogy.

"Not quite", she said laughing, "Unless you mean Western African?"

Silence.

Gabrielle recalls hearing the remnants of her laugh echo around in her head.

Her mother mouthed words for some time before any emerged, hand over her heart she whispered,

"*Is he black?*"

Gabrielle nodded. "Well you don't get many white Nigerians!"

As Gabrielle looked from her father to her mother she saw nothing, no reaction, none at all. Seconds later her mother left the room. Her father followed.

Not knowing how to react Gabrielle got up and went out to the garden.

Her parents were obviously deliberating her situation. She was concerned but not overly so. It would be a shock to them, but they would get used to the idea. Her father was a good man and her mother although they had their moments, was a lot of things but she was not a bigot. She could never be consumed with such hatred.

She was certain her father would call her in soon, both her parents were simply getting used to the idea. Once they had they could go on discussing the plans for next weekend. Sure enough her father came out and she waited for him to tell her to bring Max home as planned.

She smiled at him but it wasn't reciprocated,

"Your mother thinks it's time you went back to Belfast, Gabrielle" he said and without looking at her he continued "you need time to come to your senses"

Gabrielle stared back stunned

"You see Gabrielle you need to think of the children such a, such a, am .... a marriage would produce. What would they be? Where would they fit in? You have to think long term, now I'm sure this Max is a grand chap but maybe it's best you stick to your own eh?"

Not once had her father's eyes met hers which was just as well, as she no longer could look at him.

"And what do you think Daddy?" she had asked, fed up with this brow beaten man who never articulated his own feelings "be a man Daddy, I know you don't think that"

He still did not look at his daughter only a slight tremor in his hand belayed that she was right. Never before had she felt so angry with her once kindly father. Never before had his obedience to his wife irked her so much.

"Your mother is concerned about would the neighbours think"

By this stage his hands trembled as much as his voice. And rightly so Gabrielle thought these words came from the so called 'good Catholics' who had raised her. She was certain that unless things had changed drastically in her time away they weren't taught such attitudes in any mass she had attended. Gabrielle's estimation of her mother and father diminished there and then. She now saw one of them as a racist and the other a wimp. She went back indoors and blindly packed her things, she couldn't see through the tears. She hugged her little sisters, closed the door and left. On the bus back to Belfast she wept throughout the entire journey.

That was the day that she truly left home.

Chapter Fourteen

Although Gabrielle was deeply hurt by her parent's reaction she was annoyed with her father in particular. She knew without doubt that he did not share her mother's provincial opinions. She remembered him reading the 'Irish Times' world report (which he considered the oracle) and condemning Ian Smith as a tyrant. He derided him at every available opportunity and championed the plight of the indigenous South Africans to all and sundry. Once he even had asked her to say a special novena to St Jude the Patron Saint of Hopeless Causes, asking him to solve South Africa's problems, after Ireland's of course. Yet he was prepared to acquiesce with her mother's attitude, rather than brave contention in their cautiously harmonious home.

Regardless of the growing resentment she felt towards her parents her life seemed to trundle on as normal. For a while she held out the hope that they would be filled with remorse. She imagined them contacting her overcome with the error of their ways. Yet as the months passed she knew this was not to be. Reason told Gabrielle that she would be planning this wedding alone.

The definitive humiliation for her was telling Max her parents did not approve of him or of their engagement. He was visibly upset but seemed resigned to their feelings. By all accounts Max had learnt never to expect acceptance when encountering the unknown so he was perhaps disappointed but not surprised when Gabrielle reiterated her parent's words to him. Gabrielle knew that this was not the first blind rejection he'd faced; in her short time with him she had witnessed many. She also knew that he had looked forward to meeting her family; she talked of home a lot and had unwittingly built his expectations.

Max clearly felt that he was tearing her away from her family. Yet the family she thought she had, the family she used to be so certain off, no longer existed. Instead one hundred miles down the road, in the town she grew up in dwelled a family she didn't know. Their outward façade cunningly concealed their true nature. A nature she never wanted to encounter again. It was with confidence that she could tell Max that her family were no longer important, because right now, that was how she felt.

To prove Gabrielle's assertions further, she insisted that they set a date sooner rather than later. She wanted them to marry; Max would become her new family. They had friends, good jobs and happiness. She would let no one spoil that, especially not her parents.

With that in mind they set a date for June of that year, only six months away and began making arrangements. Max was put in charge of finding a home and Gabrielle would look after the preparations for the big day.

They decided to have a small civic wedding and secured a booking in Belfast city hall. As her family wouldn't attend they no longer needed to consider any religious perspective; that suited her. She wanted the day to be simple. Big weddings were designed for families and guests rather than the couple. Gabrielle decided that they would invite no one; they would quietly get married and slip away on honeymoon. Max was still not completely at ease with Gabrielle forging ahead with plans and her blasé attitude. He continually insisted that she would regret it later. Gabrielle on the other hand knew she wouldn't.

Max was aware that Gabrielle came from a staunch Catholic background and only agreed to progress with her plans if she at least had the wedding blessed. He claimed that if her parents eventually did assent, that they could at least prove they had done everything properly. To keep Max quiet, Gabrielle reluctantly spoke to a priest and arranged a blessing for the weeks after the wedding. Her parent's approval no longer mattered to her; they and everything that ever hurt her were boxed and placed them on her shelf.

Once again in the weeks approaching the wedding Max began nagging her, this time to try once more to involve her family. And just as with the church blessing his gentle but persistent goading won out. Gabrielle knew that the only way to quell his demands was to offer the white flag and invite them. The very act went against every fibre of her body, yet maybe just maybe Max was right and this situation, this deadlock could be rectified.

For Gabrielle the idea of being the one to initiate contact made her bristle, as far as she was concerned her parents knew that they were in the wrong. Why should she get in touch when they should be contacting her? Eventually she got used to the idea and began to think that perhaps they were waiting for contact from her. It was perfectly conceivable that Max's idea wasn't entirely outlandish. They were her parents and she at least owed them the courtesy of an invitation.

On my Max's part his family weren't much better but he had long since severed any ties with them.

Max had grown up in Lagos and came from a much superior background than Gabrielle's. His father was a senior figure in the Nigerian civil service. He was a strict disciplinarian and had expected greatness from his children. Max and his brothers and sisters were pushed into education, hobbies were quelled and fun was frowned upon. All focus was put on their studies. Each of them was encouraged to enter the medical profession. They were offered incentives such as having their university fees paid, all expenses taken care of whilst studying and a handsome reward on completion. Any career other than medicine was not considered acceptable.

Max's family was large he and two of his brothers were products of their father's first marriage. He did not talk much of his other siblings, they were his half brothers and sisters and from his demeanour when he spoke of them it was clear that strife of one form or another existed within the family. Since he never volunteered any information Gabrielle never probed him. He would tell her all about them when he was ready and she was willing to wait.

It seemed that with one notable exception, the wishes of his father were adhered to. One by one each sibling full and half had entered into and embraced medicine. All but Max had succeeded and were now either on their way to, or had already been crowned with the lofty title of doctor. Max was unique in his choice of accountancy, something his father strongly disapproved of. Gabrielle found the situation entirely nonsensical and used to joke with me when I enquired about it. After all if that was how his father reacted to an accountant imagine his reaction to a pimp!

Max's father had a plan for his children, their interests or autonomy were irrelevant. If they did not meet their father's expectations they became something to be ashamed of. Max possibly as a result of stubbornness and sheer obstinacy ignored his father's wishes and pursued his career in accountancy. He went to England and took an accountancy degree, after which he found a graduate position in one of the of the big five accountancy firms. He was transferred to Belfast and within the year fate brought him to Gabrielle.

For Max his alternative choice of career meant a struggle. He had not obeyed his father's instructions and was forced to pay his own way through university. So it was with a great sense of pride when he graduated unaided and embarked on his chosen career. His ultimate dream was to have his name on a plaque outside his office and one day to have his own chartered accountancy firm. So far he was heading in the right direction.

Gabrielle had never met any of Max's siblings, but she had seen pictures of them all, pictures taken in a place that was so alien and far away, that it could have been another world. The entire family were captured in a photograph outside Max's family home, a large imposing white house. They stood together dressed impeccably and smiled happily at the camera. I still have that album and looking at it, it is difficult to believe that this family was so fractured; the pictures showed such a joyous group.

In the back of Max's photo album was a picture of a lady of unrivalled beauty. Gabrielle assumed she was a relative and asked him who she was. She was aghast when he replied,

"This Gabrielle, is the most beautiful woman in the world" his chest swelled with pomposity as he continued "one of our many Nigerian, beauties, this is *Miss Nigeria*"

Gabrielle fumed, how he dare imply that Nigeria was swarming with beauties!

"If your Nigerian women are so bloody beautiful then why don't you go and get one?" she sulked.

A few days later they began to speak again. Never again was the beauty of the women from his homeland ever mentioned. The picture was never seen again, its place in the album was now filled as it should have been, with an Irish beauty, Gabrielle!

Max had had a happy childhood. He spent his free time playing under the Nigerian sun and holidaying in exotic Nigerian locations. Free time as a boy was not plentiful; leisure was a rare commodity, so he made the most of it when he got it. His childhood involved more schooling than most children, but even this he enjoyed. Gabrielle doubted that his boyhood self knew any different.

Max's childhood died with his mother, his father swiftly took on a new wife and started to build a new family. By all accounts this family was one that Max and his brothers were not a part of. They were not permitted to dine with his step brothers and sisters, weren't even allowed to play with them and only allowed to speak to them when they absolutely had to. His father so taken with his new wife never defended his hitherto precious sons. Instead he encouraged them to go and study medicine; to leave.

Max in choosing to study accountancy left home alone and unfunded. Moving so far away, to a strange land, didn't daunt him, he was simply relieved to leave his by then miserable home and callous step mother and never look back. In fairy tales the wicked step mother always gets her comeuppance, but Max's stepmother flourished in Max and his brothers' absence. She grew stronger and stronger, her tentacles reaching into every aspect of Olorunda life. Like Gabrielle's family Max's family were God loving and strict church goers. Church was paramount in all their lives, with the exception of his stepmother. Max's stepmother, the new Mrs Olorunda came from an utterly different world than the family were familiar with.

Nigeria was a country of many contrasts modern versus the traditional being one of them. Nigeria held a tradition of witchcraft and many people openly practised it. Max's father knew that his new wife came from the traditional Nigeria, but he was blinded by her beauty and was said to disregard her unchristian practises. He turned a blind eye to what was described as her pagan rituals, often finding them amusing and quaint. His only request was that their children be brought up in his church and she had honoured that.

Max always maintained that his father had been bewitched, that his new wife was more powerful than his father would ever know. Before leaving home Max had been privy to rumours, hushed whispers and frenzied warnings from concerned family and friends and sometimes even from strangers. They said that her magic was not a benign kind. Max had warned his father, but his words were futile. For Max the further he went from her and her strange rituals the better. Funding a place at university, thousands of miles away, was a small sacrifice for such an escape.

Max had a brother in Edinburgh who had promised to visit, but as the wedding date coincided with his exams, he committed to visiting later in the year. Max seemed happy enough with this and therefore so was Gabrielle. If only her family would have a change of heart they could have compensated for Max's lack of relations on the big day. Gabrielle knew that she was delving into the realms of fantasy when she dared to think of her family, but perhaps if reconciliation occurred, they would accept her fiancé as their own. He could have a new family. So for Max's sake, Gabrielle bought an expensive invitation and posted it to her parents, inside she inserted a letter.

For hours she had agonised over what to say, but in the end kept it simple. She asked them to come to her wedding, to meet her new husband. She listed the virtues that Max possessed, told them about his promising career and their plans to buy a house. She told them that they would marry in the City Hall and that they would be getting a church blessing. She told them of how much she loved her fiancé, and that she knew that they would too. If only they would give him a chance. Before Gabrielle could have any second thoughts she posted the letter.

Gabrielle spent the next few days waiting for a response. The very act of posting the invite, of writing the letter planted a little seed of hope in her soul and as the days passed the seed grew and grew and she visualised her family proudly welcoming Max into their lives.

Two weeks on, Gabrielle's hopes for her parent's attendance and desired blessing withered. They had received the invite by now. They had chosen to ignore it. Her parents were racist; she could not make excuses for them.

One week to the day of her wedding Gabrielle received a letter in a familiar hand, it was from her mother. At last they had a change of heart. She felt a mammoth weight being lifted off her shoulders, the little sealed box marked 'home' had its lid removed, and it was coming off her shelf.

She lit a cigarette and tore open the letter, eager to digest its contents. Excitement fluttered in her stomach, her parents had accepted her relationship,

**Dear Gabrielle,

We had hoped that since our last talk that you would have reconsidered your plans. It seems that this has not been the case and that you are intent on destroying your life and shaming your family.

We received your invitation and would like to inform you, that we will be unable to attend your wedding.

Regards

Mr and Mrs Caulfield

(**As described by Gabrielle)

Gabrielle reread her mother's caustic words and tossed them aside. The rest of that afternoon passed in a blur of tears. Why would they send that? Could they not have ignored the invitation? Instead they had to have the last word. They had to reinforce that they did not agree with her choice, that they thought that her fiancé was inferior. The impression that she had of her parents that day was one that would linger for a long time; they were simply old, dated bastards.

Gabrielle's sadness turned to anger; she ripped their letter up and threw it in the bin. Max would never know about this. Back to the shelf went her parents and to commemorate the occasion she blasted Frank Sinatra's 'I did it my way' to full volume and two vodkas later went off to meet her girlfriends for a hen party that she was determined to enjoy!

Chapter Sixteen

Gabrielle had never been one of those desperately romantic females whose fantasies revolved around demure princesses and handsome princes. Before Max marriage had never been highly rated on her list of life's priorities. Marriage was something people did when they reached a certain age, like birth and death it was simply a rite of passage. How wrong she had been.

When the wedding day dawned; she didn't experience a single shred of uncertainty, the anticipated fears of being jilted never materialised. She had slept soundly the night before and awoke refreshed and relaxed. In the hours leading to the ceremony she felt blissfully tranquil, secure in the knowledge that she had made the right decision in her choice of husband, despite opinions to the contrary.

Their preparations had gone smoothly and she did not anticipate any obstacles. Even now the huge white dresses and elaborate flowers of other girls' fantasies meant nothing. This marriage would mean more than frills and flounces; Gabrielle had designed it to impress no one. Her marriage was about one uncomplicated but beautiful thing. It was about Max and her declaring their love for each other. They would show her family and all their many adversaries that they were together in the eyes of God. The vows that they would take would cement their relationship, they would promise to love and honour each other, and allowing nothing and no one on this earth separate them. At least until death.

Gabrielle didn't need a ball gown, tiered cakes or countless tiny flower girls. Max didn't need a best man or ushers. They needed nothing but each other and their minimalistic ceremony would demonstrate that.

It took several painstaking, onerous weeks scouring what seemed like every shop in Belfast for Gabrielle to find her perfect outfit. However her meticulous searches were not in vain and she was rewarded with an outfit that could not have been more perfect. It may as well have been handmade just for her. It was precisely what she had in mind; it consisted of a little cream dress and matching jacket. Its tailored cut and detailed finish exuded luxury, any onlooker would know that this was not a standard off the rail affair; even though it was! She was delighted with her choice. She had somehow managed to select an outfit that fitted many categories, for it was classy yet fashionable, and informal yet formal. Its versatility meant that Gabrielle could dress it up or down and that it would last her for years she knew such a classic piece would never date. As she had grown older, her taste in clothes had veered away from high fashion and evolved into neat lines and good cuts. Flares and maxi dresses were not for her. The pure simplicity of her wedding choice reflected this.

Like her dress she styled her hair in a chic fashion, she pulled it loosely off her face and wrapped it in a chignon. Everything about her entire look was intentionally plain and understated. To offset this she planned to accentuate her face. With the careful application of makeup Gabrielle would emphasise her eyes and her cheekbones. Her dark hair without regular trips to the hairdresser had a tendency to hang limp and straight. To prevent this, she had visited her regular hairdresser the day before, where he injected his usual magic. Her hair was now infused with volume and shining like never before.

Gabrielle's build was slim; she had good teeth, and large pretty eyes. Yet when put together her features never quite loaned themselves to the description of beauty. Her mother had once told her she had *'a big face'* insisting that she kept a fringe at all times to 'lesson' the impact. Her mother's flattery and adulation served to ensure that Gabrielle was never over confident. She had to work hard to look good, careful grooming was part of her daily routine. With the injection of what at times constituted a mammoth effort, she knew she looked attractive. Sometimes, just sometimes, on days like her wedding day when she injected a hefty overdose of effort she was transformed. Her conventional attractiveness was replaced by beauty. She had aimed for a Jackie Onassis look and with a final glimpse in the mirror she felt secure in the knowledge that she had achieved just that.

The ceremony would include Gabrielle, Max and two witnesses. One witness was Gabrielle's friend and colleague Ann the other was Max's friend James. They hadn't even planned a reception; instead they would take their witnesses to dinner and have a few celebratory drinks before embarking on their honeymoon. That night they would take the train to Dublin, where they would spend four days before returning home as man and wife.

Gabrielle and Ann met outside Belfast City Hall on the big day. They were delayed entering when Ann gushing at Gabrielle's 'beauty' insisted on taking copious amounts of photos. Gabrielle smiled for the camera and willingly let Ann photograph her from every angle she requested. Unexpectedly a small rumble rose in the far reaches of her mind and shook her shelf. The box marked *'family'* threatened to break open. Evidently even now, a tiny part of Gabrielle hoped for reunion, that her mother and father would see sense and be waiting at the City Hall alongside Ann. Of course this was not the case. Gabrielle quickly sealed the box and pushed it to the most distant corner of the shelf that she could find.

Just to ensure it stayed put she gave it a firm hard kick. She had the rest of her life to think about her family and now was not the time.

Gabrielle and Ann made their way into the City Hall giggling childishly,

"Oh it's like Romeo and Juliet" Ann sighed, she was a romantic through and through,

"Not quite.... besides didn't they die?" Gabrielle said deadpan.

"Well, you know what I mean" Ann huffed "you two eloping and all, it's just sooooooo romantic."

"I wouldn't call it elop...." there was no point in correcting her; she knew Gabrielle's situation and the problems she and Max had faced. Rather than allow Ann to continue Gabrielle changed the subject,

"Ann, thanks so much for coming along, what would I do without you" she said and hugged her.

They were escorted to the registry office soon after. Austere heavy brown doors were now the only thing that stood between Gabrielle and Max. Their escort pushed them open with a flourish and removed the final barrier. The opened doors revealed an empty room with rows of empty chairs. On seeing the chairs once again the stark realisation that she was doing this alone struck her. Yet when she looked towards her groom, she saw nothing else. The elegant yet empty room, the registrar, Ann and James all became invisible. Max turned when the door opened and as far as Gabrielle was concerned he looked more handsome than ever before. Even now she can still see him smiling, warm and open, except then unlike now, any loneliness she had felt evaporated. Gabrielle met his eyes and walked through the empty room towards him.

One hour later, James and Ann were raising their glasses in a toast to the new, confetti strewn, Mr and Mrs Olorunda. The drink was flowing and merry chatter filled the tiny restaurant. It was a small gathering, yet Gabrielle couldn't have wished for a better one. Holding Max's hand they thanked the owner who on realising they were newlyweds surprised them all and gave them two free bottles of wine.

They stayed in the restaurant for two hours, to them it was like two minutes, before they knew it, it was time to say their goodbyes. They had a train to catch and a honeymoon to begin. It was time for them to make their way to the train station.

It was a first visit to Dublin for them both and it seemed like another world. Gone were the oppressing security checks of Belfast's shops, gone were nasty stares, the people were friendly and the city seemed somehow brighter. They spent their days laughing and revelling so much so that the holiday passed in a whirl.

Chapter Sixteen

Gabrielle must have really trusted Max as she had given him the task of securing their first home. Despite this anxiety surfaced every now and then as she wondered what kind of home she would be met with. She began to fear that perhaps Max was a typical man after all and he might truly surprise her, surprise her in the wrong way!

She reassured herself that she shouldn't be too apprehensive though, after all she had prepared Max as best she could. Long before Max had begun searching for a flat; Gabrielle had given him a list of the areas where he was permitted to flat hunt. She had spent countless days quizzing him on the said list, making him recite *her* choices over and over. To Gabrielle's shame she had even insisted that he memorised it. By the time he went house hunting he knew the list so well that it would be impossible for him to choose the wrong area. If nothing else Gabrielle knew the location would be okay, yet that was all she could be sure off!

This house or flat would be a rental and chosen by men, Max had enlisted the aid of his accountancy friends who had a good knowledge of the city. Gabrielle fretted that those he had enlisted, wouldn't have the gumption be concerned with whether or not their new home would be aesthetically pleasing. She knew they would simply be concerned with areas. Another niggle of trepidation struck her as she imagined outside toilets, electric fires and damp walls.

They planned to rent for six months whilst they arranged their first step onto the property ladder. The engagement and wedding had occurred so quickly that they didn't have time to look for something permanent. But they were young and had no ties and a rental meant that they would have six months to find something they really loved.

Frustratingly as their return train approached Belfast Max had still given nothing away. He didn't offer a solitary clue as to where they would be living; he just kept smirking and saying 'nearly there'. Never one for surprises Gabrielle was getting increasingly infuriated.

In the taxi from central station she paid close attention to the road they took, scrutinising the drivers every turn. As they went through the city centre relief flooded through her, the route the driver was taking confirmed that they were going in the direction of South Belfast. Evidently Max had been a good student, he had memorised her list well. By choosing South Belfast he had proved that he knew the theory behind her location test. Where they would stop would prove that he knew how to put this theory into practice. Slowly but surely they reached Bradbury place, the junction at the top would dictate the location of the world's best keep secret more accurately. If the taxi veered right, then they would be living somewhere in and around the Lisburn road, if it turned left they would be living in the Stranmillis or Malone area. She hoped it would go left, her mind screamed at the driver, *left, left, left*.

As if the driver had heard her, he indicated and went left. Now the location was easier to deduce. She knew that they would either be living in Stranmillis or Malone. Gabrielle would have been happy with either location, but her preference was undoubtedly Malone. She began a further chant in her head, *Malone, Malone, Malone.*

The Malone road was one of South Belfast's jewels, glittering bright against the granite drabness of the cities grey terraced streets. In Malone, the avenues were wide and lined with row upon row of leafy trees, the houses were sprawling and grand. If Max had even secured an outhouse on the Malone Road Gabrielle would be ecstatic.

She sat up a bit straighter, her alertness at epic levels, as the taxi came to University Road, straight ahead was the Malone road and she was now sure that was where they were going. She quivered with excitement. She was already planning boasting to her friends about their new house and its grand location. Internally she was rehearsing saying "I live in the Malone area", "that would be just off Malone, dear" in an affected voice.

"Thanks so much Max!" Gabrielle exclaimed rather prematurely yet her new knowledge was making it too difficult to remain silent.

He looked at her questioningly, Gabrielle assumed that look meant he was peeved that she had guessed his great surprise; well the best part of the surprise at any rate.

After a while he responded, "I worried that you wouldn't like it" he was visibly relieved

"Not like it? Well it was on the list" she reassured him, "Malone was actually the place I wanted most, there was a reason why I put it at number one!" she smiled, positively glowing with delight.

Before she could say anymore the taxi stopped, confused she looked to Max then out the window. They hadn't quite reached the Malone road. Certainly they had travelled in the right direction but for reasons unbeknownst to her, they had stopped on the University road. The driver turned to them to ask further directions she assumed he was lost (there could be no other reason for him to stop here). Yet it wasn't a question he asked it was more of a statement,

"That'll be £1, mate" he said to Max.

Max reached into his jacket, fished out his wallet and paid the driver. As the driver went on to help offload their bags Gabrielle struggled to pick her jaw up from the ground. She failed and her mouth hung open gormlessly.

She looked at the scene that confronted her; a grim row of dark terraces, all three stories high and dark, so very dark. Paint peeled off the windows and the doors. Each door held rows of letter boxes, suggesting multiple occupants. The only description her mind conjured up for this grimy row of houses was dingy.

The houses on the University road, whilst in a perfectly good area, had been subdivided many years ago to provide flats and bedsits to the students of the university opposite. These houses weren't reputed to have been in even adequate conditions, tolerable would be the best one could hope for here. The flats that this road offered were aimed at students, students who wanted cheap and functional accommodation close to their studies. She was not a student nor did she want cheap and functional. Someday she wouldn't have a choice.

The taxi pulled off and Max grinned at her. *He won't be grinning much longer* she thought, wait until I get him indoors. On gauging her reaction, the daggers her eyes were shooting at him, his stupid grin withered, he even had the audacity to look surprised!

"You said five minutes ago that this was where you wanted" he attempted, "five minutes ago"

"Malone Max, I said Malone" she sulked,

"Just wait until we get inside" he said noticing that they were attracting attention;

Not to be perturbed she continued,

"I am a married woman Max, I am NOT a student and I am NOT setting foot in any of these, these hesitating she searched for a word to portray her disgust, on finding it she shouted "Slums!"

Before she could protest any further Max grabbed her and slung her over his shoulder, she thumped and thumped at his back yelling,

"Put me down, put me down,"

He disregarded all her screams and assaults on his poor back and continued towards one of the houses. He fumbled in his pocket with his free hand and extracted a key. All the while Gabrielle was still kicking and thumping, now with even more might.

He ignored her protests and carried her up a flight of stairs, opened a flat door, deposited her in and left.

"I'm just going to get our bags" he said from outside the door and his footsteps retreated. She could visualise his broad shoulders slumped and his head hung in defeat. She was glad.

Now that she was on solid ground and alone, she took the opportunity to appraise her surroundings.

The small hallway she had been deposited in had three doors, she tried the one directly opposite her and found that it led to a large living room styled in browns and creams and furnished impeccably. A door leading off the living room led to a small compact kitchen, it was gleaming, so much so, that her mother would have been proud. Again it was styled in a contemporary pattern; the brown and cream theme continued, only here it was interjected with a splash of vibrant orange. She was ashamed to say it was beautiful. Had she been looking for a flat she would have chosen this too.

She could hear Max making his way up the stairs, so she didn't get to continue her inspection instead she sat on the sofa and pretended to still be annoyed. Yes the place was beautiful and yes she was impressed by his choice, but ultimately he had not complied with her list. He may have selected a rental in South Belfast, but he had strayed from her choices. For that reason she would let him stew. She obviously didn't let him stew for too long though, as two weeks later she discovered she was pregnant.

Chapter Eighteen

Max was overjoyed with the news that Gabrielle was expecting. Fatherhood was something he had always dreamed off, he loved children and wanted a large family. He clearly imagined a Walton style home filled with children, noise and oozing with family values. Within just one day of discovering that Gabrielle was pregnant, he was already planning how this child would be raised, even going so far as researching schools. Gabrielle considered his jubilation as ridiculous, it was wasted on her.

She just could not comprehend how she had been foolish enough to fall pregnant. She hadn't got a single maternal bone in her body. She had hoped that one day this would change, but for now aged twenty four, the thought of having a child was repugnant.

Every time she thought of her predicament, she was assailed with flashbacks of the traumatic day during training, when she witnessed the horror of childbirth first hand. That scene was just as grotesque to her now as it was at the time. She hated the very thought of being transformed into an uncouth, sweaty and bloated mess, displaying her bits to an army of staff.

She had never left Max under any illusions. He knew she had grown up surrounded by children, he knew all about her 'ordeal' during training. He had found the tales of her experiences hilarious, telling her that as she got older her feelings would change. Max only had to look at a child to be reduced to gloop. However as far as Gabrielle was concerned, unless he was completely dense, (which watching him float around ecstatically, she wondered if he was) he should have known that children were unlikely to be part of the deal.

With a nervous disquiet, she watched his growing excitement at his impending fatherhood. She genuinely feared he would explode. She became increasingly suspicious that this was what he had hoped for all along. Evidently, he had thought that someday she would awaken and her fictional biological clock would begin to tick, and she would suddenly declare that she wanted a family.

When Gabrielle's doctor confirmed that she was indeed pregnant, to say she was not amused would be an understatement.

Many of the girls she knew when faced with similar quandaries, had taken it upon themselves to rectify their mistake. They had travelled across to England and aborted their children. Gabrielle may have been a modern girl, but abortion was not an avenue she would ever contemplate exploring. They had just had their marriage blessed by the Catholic Church, and the combination of the morals she had been brought up with, and a sprinkling of Catholic guilt prevented her from even considering abortion. Life was precious and if she was forced to give it, then she would. She would just have to adjust to her pregnancy and prepare for it. On the plus side, at least she was married, they were financially secure and going by Max's reaction she would have a supportive husband.

Gabrielle began reading up on pregnancy and wishing she had paid more attention to the countless lectures on gestation during training. She researched every aspect of pregnancy she could and along the way something very peculiar occurred. She began to look forward to having her baby. She would watch other mothers wheeling their prams, loiter at the baby sections in shops and mull names over in her mind. A mere two months into the pregnancy she had already selected her favourite names for baby boys and girls.

Work posed a dilemma as the pregnancy progressed. In the seventies not many women worked when they had children and she hoped by raising the issue of her pregnancy that they would allow her to continue. She had worked hard to qualify and loved her job, she had planned a career and times were changing. She could see no reason why having a child should interrupt anyone's career.

Max wanted Gabrielle to give up work, yet she stalwartly refused. She had a profession and would not see it end because of a child. She would certainly reduce her hours but she would not stop nursing. Anyway she would only ever have the one child; Max's 'Waltonesque' dream would stay just that, as in future Gabrielle would be even more meticulous with contraception.

The pregnancy flew in and before she knew it her slim figure was obscured by her bulging stomach. None of her usual clothes fitted and for anyone she hadn't yet told it wouldn't be hard for them to guess her predicament.

When she was seven months gone, she was finishing up a shift after a long day on the ward, preparing her report for the handover. Pregnancy was taking its toll and weariness was sweeping through her bones. She rubbed her face and concentrated on staying awake. The cleaner who came daily at this time, emptied the bin and as usual ignored her. This cleaner had once been an affable, chatty woman but over the course of time she became more and more distant. She would slam Gabrielle's bin on the ground after emptying it and bang the door on her way out of the office. Gabrielle only saw her at the end of her shifts so she wasn't overly concerned with the woman's obvious dislike. This particular day rather than make her customary hasty retreat, the cleaner seemed to hover in the office. Gabrielle looked up, curious as to what the woman was doing. She was staring at her. Smiling at her unsurely, Gabrielle put her head back down and continued with her report,

"How dare you" the cleaner hissed,

"Pardon?" Gabrielle asked, utterly bemused

"How dare you bring another black bastard into the world" she sneered.

Obviously feeling she had made her point, she lifted her bin bag and made to leave. This time she achieved the impossible and slammed the door with even more aplomb than ever before.

Gabrielle was shaken to the core. Revolted, she ran from the office and made it just in time to the bathroom, where she wretched and wretched. The cause of the cleaners growing dislike was now clear.

A colleague found her and between tears Gabrielle recounted the incident to her. She repeated over and over,

"It's just a baby……….a baby, how can people hate it?"

In the hours immediately after, Gabrielle was shaken by a growing sense of unease, what kind of a world was she bringing her child into? Fear for her unborn child permeated her terrified mind; she would have to be more than a mother. She would have to become a protector too, shielding this child from the hatred that this world was obviously infested with.

When Max returned home from work, she had composed herself. She didn't mention the incident, deciding that he did not need be hurt too. There was nothing to be gained by letting that woman's spiteful remarks upset him as well. In a sense Gabrielle became not only the protector of her child, but also her husband. If this was to be her new role then she would step up to the mark, for it was a small price to pay for the privilege of having her beloved family.

When Gabrielle returned to work the following day, the cleaner was not there. It didn't matter though, the damage was done. Yet the woman had instigated the realisation, acceptance even of her new role for that at least she was grateful.

Chapter Nineteen

After months of searching Gabrielle and Max found their first home. It wasn't quite on the Malone Road, but it was situated in a pleasant residential area not far off it. It was in a development of handsome semi-detached houses with gardens front and rear and lots of young families. It was perfect and exactly what they had envisaged. When the last stick of furniture was delivered to the house, they said goodbye to their University road flat and made the move.

Fortunately Max had promised to decorate, he had often boasted of his handyman skills, his talent with a paintbrush and all things DIY. After the expense of the move and acquiring furniture, at least they would save on hiring a decorator. Gabrielle selected the paint and paper and Max took a few days off to begin work.

By day two Max's efforts contradicted his talk of his great talents. If his talent was painting floors, windows and brand new furniture, then certainly he was an expert. If his talent was turning wallpaper to bubbling shreds, then he was a genius. Yet none of his talents were what Gabrielle had in mind. Before he painted anymore furniture, or destroyed another roll of her expensive wall paper, she advised him that unless he wanted a divorce he was banned from attempting a single piece of work in the house again. Max was swiftly despatched back to work and his handyman skills thoroughly discredited. Gabrielle resorted to seeking the services of a professional decorator. It was tight but he managed to get the house finished within two weeks of the due date.

The new neighbours were lovely. They consisted of mainly young couples like themselves either starting a family or planning to. Within two weeks of moving in, they had made a wealth of new friends all thoroughly welcoming and hospitable. Gabrielle was confident that in the remainder of her maternity leave she certainly wouldn't feel alone.

They had decorated the baby's room in lemon. Gabrielle was superstitious and didn't want to know the sex; nor make too many preparations before the birth. The room was simply painted and carpeted. Anything else needed would be bought after the child's arrival.

The only thing that Gabrielle felt she could do at this stage without tempting fate was to hang the curtains. She made her way to the babies little room and began adding curtain hooks to the edge of the curtain, carefully counting in the pleats. Just as she was about to hang them, a knock came to the front door. She shuffled down the stairs making slow progress as her mobility was constrained by her enormous bump. A whole two minutes later she reached the door. Fearing that the caller would have left she didn't peak through the safety hole that Max insisted on and instead she quickly opened it. There on the door step stood her mother and father. She was astonished she didn't have any words or thoughts she just stood there wide eyed and regarded them.

"Hello Gabrielle" her mother said "May we come in?"

Gabrielle opened the door wider, stood back and let them pass.

"Well you certainly have a lovely home" her mother said, visibly impressed

"Thanks",

Confused now, she asked "how did you know where I live?" she hadn't been in touch with her parents since the letter she had received prior to the wedding.

"Max" her father said "he wrote us a letter" he continued "He told us that you were married and that you were pregnant"

Her mother interrupted, "We couldn't ignore the letter and we certainly couldn't ignore our first grandchild" she said

"Oh", Gabrielle was touched that Max had contacted her parents, even more touched that he had kept it to himself.

She cried, she can't say that they were tears of joy (more shock) but her parents took this as some sort of a sign because before she knew it she was inundated with hugs,

"John go and put the kettle on" her mother demanded dismissing her father to an unfamiliar kitchen, in an unfamiliar house. Some things never change.

"It's ok, I'll do it"

"You will not, not in your condition," her mother demanded and ushered her to sit down.

Before long in her mother's infamous interrogation style, she had caught up on the marriage, the Catholic blessing and her pregnancy. She seemed satisfied with her findings.

Her father returned with the tea and they all talked about the impending arrival. No apologies were made. Gabrielle doubted that any would be offered. She would instead assume that the gesture of travelling all the way to Belfast was apology enough, so she let it slip.

One question still hung in the air, Max. They had not met him yet and he was due home from work soon.

"Mum, Dad, Max will be home soon" she said,

They looked at each other but didn't make to leave,

"Grand" her father said affecting false casualness.

Sure enough ten minutes later, the sound of Max's key in the door alerted them to his arrival.

Gabrielle held her breath as he entered the living room, her parents eyed the door

"Well the bus was……….." Max stopped mid-sentence and looked at the arrivals

"Max, meet my parents" Gabrielle said

"You actually came" Max said eyes wide in surprise, "thank you" he added humbly.

Her father was immediately on his feet shaking Max's hand, and her mother was behind him. It was a surreal scene, something she had never expected.

"Pleased to meet you Max" her father said

"Hello" her mother said,

An awkward silence ensured so Gabrielle went to the kitchen and put on more tea. She thought she would leave them alone for a while to either get acquainted or knowing her luck *and her mother unacquainted*. She started to make up some sandwiches and took her time about it.

When she estimated that at least twenty minutes had passed and that the front door hadn't been touched Gabrielle re entered the room. She didn't know what to expect but certainly not what she found.

She stood in the doorway and surveyed the unlikely scene. Her mother was on the edge of her seat in deep conversation with Max and her father was nodding along knowledgably. Gabrielle released a little cough and walked into the room. She sat the tray on the coffee table and busied herself serving teas; it was as if she was invisible. It seemed her mother had found a fellow conversationalist in Max, they were talking about the boring issues that Gabrielle tended to glaze over at. Yet the pair was engrossed. She looked at her father baffled and he winked at her.

Two hours later her parents left.

Gabrielle may have once found her parents racist, but when she looked at the events that occurred that day she knows they never were. Mixed race relationships have always been a contentious issue, couples this very day face difficulties and lack of acceptance. It was 1974, her parents were from the country a place where they had encountered very few, if any people of colour in their daily lives. Yet when they met Max, when they got over their previous reservations, their concern for their daughter and potential grandchildren, they bonded firmly and quickly. Her parents were never racist they were simply protective and before meeting Max filled with protective trepidation.

Two days after their reunion, Gabrielle's labour began and they were reunited once again. Gabrielle was engulfed with so much pain, that she was filled with empathy and respect for that brave, brave woman on the maternity ward in Derry!

That day Alison was born.

Chapter Twenty

Alison soon became completely and utterly spoiled and enjoyed by her granny, her great granny, her grandfather her many aunts and of course her doting father. Everyone loved baby Alison; she was a regular VIP in her grandmother's house and amongst Gabrielle and Max's circle of friends. Wherever she went she was indulged with toys, sweets, games and hours of undivided attention.

Any concerns about Alison becoming too spoilt were short lived. In the Christmas of 1975, just when order was restored to the house, Gabrielle was given a little surprise; she was pregnant again. Just when Alison was sleeping full nights in her own bed and more importantly going to bed at reasonable hour, Gabrielle was faced with reliving the whole experience again.

This time though the realisation that she was pregnant was no ordeal. She basked in the notion of carrying a little baby again. The feelings of doom and dread she had experienced just two years ago were replaced with sheer exhilaration. She was utterly thrilled at the prospect of becoming a mother again. Having Alison had shown her that she loved motherhood; that she was maternal after all. Maybe there was indeed such a thing as a biological clock because everything had changed for Gabrielle, an unmistakable something ticked inside her. The mere knowledge of having a second baby had set it off, and now it was ticking rhythmically through her very being. With each individual tick of the clock she was prodded with another little jolt of joy. A countdown had begun.

If Gabrielle was excited then Max was ecstatic. Even more promising was the fact that they were settled in a home of their own, one that had ample room to cater for another tiny person. Yes, this time around they were prepared in every sense.

Young Alison was a different story, like her mother before her; she loathed the idea of a sibling. After months of explaining the benefits of sisterhood, and not just any sister hood but *big* sister hood, they achieved success and converted Alison from a reluctant to eager big sister. Alison became more engrossed in this pregnancy than anyone else. By the time Gabrielle was due, Alison had become expectant big sister extraordinaire. She drew a new picture every day for her little brother or sisters nursery. Her parents ignored the fact that in each picture Alison was portrayed as a huge figure dominating the tiny dot that with closer inspection was to be her new sibling!

With this pregnancy Gabrielle's family were with her every step of the way, her grandmother on hearing the news had begun knitting tiny cardigans and booties. Both her mother and grandmother fed her with 'castor oil sandwiches' before the birth and stocked up on cabbage leaves for after.

The baby was due in November; once again a lemon room was prepared. This time Gabrielle was more primed as to what to expect. The labour went as smoothly as any labour can and when she was handed the little white bundle she didn't hand it back. On birth Alison had looked every bit as white as this little girl did. Gabrielle knew to expect the pigmentation to creep into her skin over the next few weeks and for her straight downy baby hair to be replaced by a network of tight wiry curls.

Max was once again over excited about the prospect of his second daughter, so much so, that it now exceeded the excitement he had displayed on the news of his first daughter. He was so high that Gabrielle honestly believed he could have flown! His reaction was so great that this was little girl was named after him; converting Max to its female equivalent Maxine. Max was so engaged with this new arrival that it was only right that she should be named after him.

Maxine by all accounts was a lovely child; she had a gentle nature and seldom cried or caused any fuss. She was adored by all and like Alison was spoiled beyond belief. She had huge brown eyes and as she grew, her hair settled into loose brown curls. She effortlessly progressed from a good natured baby into an easy going child.

Max's parenting skills propelled him into the status of a 'modern man', he loved his girls, his family were his world. He devoted his free time to tutor the three year old Alison. He insisted that she would read, write and count before school; his theory was that she needed to start ahead to stay ahead. Alison to put it mildly was not as laid back as her baby sister. She was a highly strung, bad tempered child and utilised her new found voice to its full. She constantly screamed to get her own way. This personality did not combine well with her father's attempts to teach her to read and write. The pair of them would sit at the table night after night. Max would take her through the alphabet and Alison would take him through her litany of ear splitting hysterics. He availed of many different methods to entice her to learn, colourful books, art sets and even nature walks. He would take her to the park and point out flowers and trees and try to phonically coax her into grasping the alphabet. By the summer of that year Alison had only managed to recite the letters a – e and Gabrielle swore her husband's hair had grown thinner. Gabrielle found the whole situation hilarious, rather than admit defeat Max continued trying, yet it was clear to all but him that his efforts were in vain. Even so Gabrielle was impressed; such actions showed a dedication that not many fathers possessed.

Once a bee flew in the open kitchen window, little Alison immediately began to swipe at the bee and her father stopped her angrily. He knelt down and caught the bee and as it landed on the table,

"This is a little life Alison, you cannot hurt any living thing" he said

"If you treat God's creatures nicely, they'll be nice to you" both of them regarded the bee walking around his palm.

"Now watch and I'll set if free" he got up and walked towards the window "oooooouch!" he screamed jumping nearly to the ceiling,

"The buggers stung me!" he exclaimed

"Well if you're nice to God's creatures they'll be nice to you eh Max?" Gabrielle said through fits of laughter. As for Alison one lesson and perhaps the only one she absorbed from Dad's months of tuition was that bee's sting; don't hold them in your hand!

Unfortunately, Max's love of God's creatures had not been perturbed by his sting. He had been talking about getting my sisters a dog since Alison was born, and so far Gabrielle had rebuked his pleas. She had enough to contend with two young children and work, without taking on a dog as well. Her husband worked full time so it didn't take a genius to know that Gabrielle would be left with the dog.

Gabrielle still remembered little Patch, she remembered being devastated when he died. Animals had ways of getting themselves killed from road accidents, to illness; she had no intention of inflicting death on her children. Northern Ireland had other ideas.

One day she arrived home after a late shift to see no sign of Max or her daughters. Aside from Rod Stewarts husky tones filling the empty kitchen, the house was quiet. It was then she heard gleeful little giggles coming from the garden. She went out smiling; wondering what could have filled the children with such delight. Her smile soon faded, for there was Max and her daughters with a huge dog. It was Alison, who saw her Mum first,

"Mummy, Mummy come and see, Daddies got us a dog"

"I can see that" she said, her voice was deadpan,

Sheepishly Max said "Gabrielle meet Lucky"

Hmm. *Lucky* evidently wasn't *lucky* by nature getting chosen by this fool she thought.

"Max, I need a word now" she said and beckoned him into the kitchen

"I know, I know" he said, "but I knew when you saw how much the girls loved him you would come around".

"Did you now?"

He smiled that big stupid childish grin again, she had enough,

"Max, what are you playing at" Gabrielle demanded "did you not think to discuss this with me first?"

He looked shamefaced,

"No because you would never have agreed".

"Exactly, Max. There's good reason for that, just who do you will be looking after this dog?"

"Gabrielle *I will*, you know that"

"When will you be doing this Max, between your teaching the girls? When you're studying or how about when you're working all day every day!"

"I'll make time"

"Yes Max, you will indeed make time, you'll make time right now and tell those children that the doggy has to go home" infuriated she continued "I have two children Max and a job and a house to look after and you think we need a dog,"

She gave him his orders storming from the room in a rage, before adding "I'm going to the shops, I want that dog gone, by the time I get home". She banged the door behind her.

On leaving in such a rush she realised she had forgotten her purse, she slipped back in quietly, careful not to alert anyone of her presence. She shouldn't have worried because Max was so deep in conversation he wouldn't have heard her had she entered with a brass band,

"Mum, what am I to do?" he was pleading,

One thing that annoyed Gabrielle most about Max was that he aired all their dirty laundry to her mother! Gabrielle completely enraged crept to the landing where he was sat by the phone. She snatched the phone from his hand and slammed it down. "Since when was she *you're* Mum" she snipped and as planned went to the shops.

When she got home that night, three pairs of pitiful eyes fixed on her morosely. As usual she was the villain, this time the one who had forced Lucky to go home.

Tensions remained high between she and Max over the next few days, but a new surprise was soon to dissolve them. This news put the argument over Lucky's demise and the general subject of canines to the back burner for quite a while.

Gabrielle was pregnant once again and by now she was so familiar with Max's jubilance that she let it wash over her. She was excited about this pregnancy too but for other reasons. Now that they had two girls she wanted a boy and she felt in her bones that this child was male. She had decided that her little boy would be named Christopher and as the pregnancy progressed she would talk to her bump referring to him by name.

It was during this pregnancy that she admitted a certain defeat. In a few months she would have three children, all aged under five. She would have to give up her career and focus on her children. The notion of no longer working didn't appal her as it once did. She had had four years' experience of motherhood and work, and already struggled to balance twelve hour shifts with two children. She knew that with three children this struggle would soon become insurmountable.

When she was six months pregnant she donned her nurse's uniform for the last time. She was struck by a little reluctance, as memories of her struggles to become a nurse surfaced, her training, the hours of studying and her parents finding the financial support she needed in tough times. Yet she had enjoyed her career, however short it was. She was sure that fragments of it could be put to good use, especially in motherhood. Perhaps when the children were at least of secondary school age and a bit more independent she could reconsider. Who knew what life would hold? Maybe she would enjoy being a mother and a home maker and never return to work; when the children were older she could be a lady of leisure!

All that she was certain of at this point was that nursing had to go. Motherhood came first for her now and that would be her focus for the considerable future. Little did Gabrielle know that she had no need to worry about giving up her career, she was fortunate in those days to have had a choice.

Chapter Twenty One

With the family rapidly growing, Gabrielle and Max contacted Max's brother in Edinburgh again, he had finished his studies so should be more flexible with his time. They sent him an open invite to come and meet his nieces and of course his sister in law. Unfortunately Femi was unavailable; he was working round the clock shifts and would find it difficult to get enough leave for a trip away. Gabrielle was fuming a two hour boat trip and even a night's stay wouldn't take much out of his busy schedule but she kept her thoughts to herself fearful of offending her husband.

Anyway they had little time to dwell on Femi being unable to visit as the house was always filed with Gabrielle's family. Her mother and father, brothers and sisters, grandmother and aunts and uncles were regular visitors. Gabrielle and Max loved having them around and the children adored the attention they were showered with. Many a great family gathering was held in that home, Gabrielle's grandmother and Max played card games, old stories were told and during those nights laughter and craic was guaranteed!

They did their best to make the journey to Strabane as often as possible. They loved going to Strabane as during the time they spent there they didn't have to lift a finger with the children. There was always a doting auntie or cousin keen and eager to take them off their hands. They could always be assured of a well-earned break when they visited.

A gang of them, Gabrielle and Max, aunts and those sisters who were now grown enough and even on the verge of marriage themselves, would spend Saturday nights at the local cricket club. Drinking many a drink and enjoying the banter. Gabrielle's father unfortunately could never join them, he was a pioneer, whether this was by his own choice or not was always difficult to ascertain! On many occasions Gabrielle would see him keenly eyeing a bottle of Guinness or gazing at their bottles of whiskey. All she could be sure of was that her mother viewed alcohol as the devils brew. With this in mind for an easy life her father's choice to be a pioneer - enforced or not was the safest option!

Her grandmother was fast becoming one of Max's greatest fans, she could be found talking to him in the side-lines of any gathering. Her eyes sparkling fondly and she never tired of telling Gabrielle;

"I think you have married a true gem. If it wasn't for his *obvious* deficiencies, I would think you had made the best choice out of any of them yet".

Gabrielle's Grandmother was a Catholic through and through, so devout was she that she was known far and wide for her powerful novenas. When she spoke of Max's obvious deficiencies she would never have even considered his colour, no he had much bigger deficiencies than mere colour. He was a heathen, a Protestant! If she had her way, this would change and sooner rather than later. Most of their conversations at some point involved her trying to arrange a visit from the priest, who would talk Max into the merits of belonging to the great Catholic Church. From Max's response to her persistence, Gabrielle believed her grandmother was beginning to wear him down. He began to openly ask questions about Catholicism, expressing genuine interest. Whether this was simply to appease her or genuine we will never know. Yet Gabrielle couldn't help but be amazed at how her little grandmother had brought about such a change of heart. If she kept this up she would be a very happy woman for Gabrielle was sure her perseverance was paying off and that Max, if only to keep his new grandmother happy, may actually consider the idea of conversion.

Max's relationship with his mother in law was one that bemused Gabrielle more than any other. Max had progressed from referring to her as Mrs Caulfield, to Irene to Mum. He would phone her more than Gabrielle would and discuss his slightest concern; usually his wife! The relationship was fully reciprocated as her mother in turn would introduce him to all and sundry as her son, Max.

The old saying be careful what you wish for, rang in Gabrielle's ears when she saw the two together. The pair shared a bond that she could never have predicted; they had become such friends that often she felt that the pair was ganging up on her. It got to the point that any arguments the couple had, any suggestion Gabrielle broached or plan she made her mother knew. Max told her everything, so much so that before they ever spoke, Gabrielle had to consider that every morsel of the information she imparted would be given to her mother. She had to be extremely careful with her words!

Her father from his regular reading of the world report in the 'Irish News', considered himself a man of the world. He was always interested in hearing Max's experiences of Nigeria. He would ask him all about his home land, the climate, the local wildlife, the food and the people. He was mesmerised and would wistfully return his questions with talk of Ireland, its legends and its history.

Her mother was also convinced that her third pregnancy would be a boy and was looking forward to the arrival of her first grandson. If Gabrielle had ever considered herself large with her first two pregnancies then this one could only be described as mammoth. This little fellow was obviously a strapping young man; for the bump he created was the biggest she or any of her family or friends had ever seen. He became known as the elephant in a running joke amongst them.

The due date was in October and coincidently fell on her mother's birthday; this made this particular pregnancy all the more special for her. A grandson would be a magnificent birthday surprise. Yet her mother's birthday came and went, and still Christopher hadn't arrived. They began to speculate that he was indeed an elephant. They were known to carry their young for years and by the looks of it, Gabrielle would too!

When the birth was deemed by the obstetrician to have been prolonged enough, Gabrielle was called in to be induced. Even with all the medication to speed up labour, Christopher still refused to venture out. It appeared her little boy did not want to face the world. Nature had to take his course at some time though and very soon it did.

My entrance into the world was not the joyous entrance that I deserved; on the contrary it seemed I was met by a very angry and confused mother. As I was presented to her the midwife said,

"Here she is, she's as fit as a fiddle"

"You mean *he*, don't you?" Mum asked concerned,

"No Mrs. Olorunda, it's definitely a she."

Thrilled as she was she couldn't shake the tiny fragment of disappointment that lingered, as she had had her heart set on a boy.

My Dad and grandparents arrived soon after to see the new arrival.

Apparently Mum's first words were "It looks like we'll have to try again Max, I want a boy"

"Let me get used to this one first" he laughed and lifted me for the first time; his brown eyes alight with pride.

Due to my being born the wrong sex I could no longer be called Christopher, so my parents quickly set about finding me a name.

They settled on calling me after both my grandmothers; Jayne- Irene.

Chapter Twenty Two

I take after my Dad in that I am a born worrier. Apparently he spent his days planning and budgeting, his budget didn't allow for another child just yet, but his wife wanted her little boy and his budget would just have to be compromised. Mum never had any time for people who penny pinched. Inevitably it wasn't long before she had persuaded him that a having a little boy was a good idea.

Outwardly he seemed happy enough and went along with the idea, he loved his children and Gabrielle was sure he would enjoy a little more balance between the sexes in the family. It would also mean that his Walton style family dream may come to fruition. Yet he began to stop sleeping at night, Mum ignored this at first but eventually she broached the issue, the answer she received was not what he had expected,

"Every time I close my eyes I see the same thing" his voice actually sounded afraid,

"What Max," she asked, anxious herself now "what do you see?"

It took him a while to reply, but when he did his words were to chill her to the core,

"I see a coffin and I don't know who it's for"

....

....

Alison was now five and attending her father's chosen school, an exclusive prep school that for a man on a budget Gabrielle viewed as a little ostentatious. She didn't remark though, for she was simply relieved to have just two rather than three infants at home with her full time. Maxine and I in keeping with our older sister seemingly preferred our Dad to our Mum. Mum took great umbrage at the fact, considering that she was the one who stayed at home with us all day, nursed us through colds and flu's and catered to our every whim. Despite her efforts each day at six o'clock, when Dad walked through the door, her three little girls deserted her and from that moment on only had eyes for him. Gabrielle often wondered what she was doing wrong or more to the point what was he doing so right!

Gabrielle still loved to shop and buying children's clothes became a favourite pastime. She says she wanted us to be the best dressed children in Belfast. To achieve this took great effort. She dressed us all the same and wherever we went she was sure to get a compliment on our presentation. She spared no expense on our little outfits, with the result that our wardrobes were brimming with unique and expensive little clothes for every occasion.

My Dad on the other hand disagreed. He constantly chastised Mum, backed up by her mother of course, about how much money she would spend on the children's clothes. As usual though, when Max went into his financial droning, Mum switched off. He had wanted children not her, so he would just have to accept the cost they incurred. Granted she could have bought cheaper clothes, but she felt if she was going to buy clothes at all, then she may as well do it right. Besides she felt that expensive children's clothes from the many little boutiques were so much more durable than those found on the general high street.

The one thing about the three of us that Mum couldn't come to terms with was our hair. As babies we all had has soft wavy curls, but as we grew the curls tightened and tightened and tightened some more. Each of us sported a tight little afro that for the life of Mum she just couldn't work with. She styled our little afros every which way; she used a hot brush and bought a multitude of products, but still our little afros refused to relax or take any shape.

Mum often talks about how she grumbled to Dad about our hair he just laughed telling her that the only solution was to grow it down. The longer the hair got, the looser it would become. Mum was mystified, thinking how the hell she could grow our hairs down? Surely at some point in the mid stages of growth she would need to be able to tie it back? If she couldn't tie it back, then she would have three little girls with hair so big that they would be constantly stuck in doorways! Our strange hair grew out not down and in a rage one evening Gabrielle decided to take matters into her own hands.

Watched by an aghast husband, she became what she believed to be a world class hairdresser.

One by one she sat each of us sat on her knee and chopped off the offending afro's.

"You've scalped them!" Dad said appalled,

"No Max I've made them sophisticated" she retorted "besides it'll grow back better, you'll see"

When each of us had been carefully coiffured by Mum's expert hand, she gathered up all the hair and tossed it into the open fire.

She thought nothing of it until Dad started coughing and choking

"For God's sake you big girls blouse, what's wrong now?" She demanded

"The smell Gabrielle, how can that not get to you?"

Certainly she could smell burning hair, but they had an open fire and any strong odour was swept up the chimney, only the slightest smell remained.

"Max you'd barely notice it"

"Well I can, it's making me gag, I can't stand it" coughing and spluttering he left the room.

Dad just could not handle the smell of burning. Then without the benefit of hindsight his protests would have appeared slightly strange.

The following night Ann, who had stayed close to my parents since their wedding was to call around. Gabrielle really looked forward to catching up on the shenanigans at the hospital but most of all to having some adult company. She told my Dad that he was to be home from work early and to keep the girls out of the way. She wanted some grown up time; she had bought a bottle of wine and planned to spend a few blissful hours relaxing.

Ann arrived promptly and discussed the hospital gossip, her recent affairs and her newly discovered 'gift'. Ann was the seventh of daughter of the seventh daughter. Irish superstition had it that being born in such a unique position brought with it some special gifts; one of them was the ability to see the future. Ann had been practising her newly discovered talents on all her friends and colleagues and had surprised herself at the strength of her predictions and their uncanny accuracy. Tonight before they even had a sip of wine Ann decided to demonstrate her skill. Mum was a sceptic, but rather than upset Ann's kind nature, she acquiesced.

Ann took herself off to the kitchen and prepared some tea. She was going to read Mums tea leaves. They would then discuss the findings over a bottle of wine.

She placed a cup of tea in front of Mum and made her drink as much as she could. Gabrielle worried about swallowing the tea leaves that swirled through it, but Ann insisted that they would settle at the bottom. Quickly she finished all but a small drop, the sooner she did, the sooner they could crack open the wine.

"Ok Gaby, let's see what the future holds for you" she said taking her cup.

"A boy and hopefully one very soon, oh and a house actually on the Malone road!" Mum laughed.

Ann examined her cup, then examined it again,

"Well?" she asked intrigued, Ann still hadn't lifted her head from the tea leaves.

When Ann did respond Mum wished she hadn't. Her eyes were wide with terror, her rosy cheeks had lost all their hue and her mouth hung wide open.

"Ann, that's enough" Mum laughed, "good joke" she said "but seriously enough is enough"

Ann left the table and collected her coat faster moving faster than Mum had ever seen her move before. As she made her way to the door Ann muttered, "I have to go. I've forgotten I had something…"

She didn't even finish her sentence she was out the door so quickly.

"Ah well all the more wine for me" Mum mused. She turned on the TV, watched a few episodes of 'Some Mothers do have them' and completely relaxed, who needs company she thought.

Chapter Twenty Three

The incident with the tea leaves was soon forgotten as it seemed that my baby self was developing some sort of colic. At almost a year old, I had difficulty keeping down anything. Soon I was throwing up every morsel I swallowed. Doctors believed Mum was neurotic and she began to think so too until I began to show worrying symptoms. I lost weight, cried with sheer hunger and became alarmingly lethargic. It was only when Mum took me to the City Hospital that she was taken seriously. Having worked there before and having such a distinctive name had the benefit that she was recognised. Mum was told that her baby needed a barium meal. This thick, gooey liquid once swallowed would show exactly what was going on inside.

Dad arrived home from work the night before my barium meal and to Mum was uncharacteristically calm at the news that his baby was due to go into hospital the following day,

"Max, I don't think she's going to do" Gabrielle said utterly despondent, "she can't continue like this, all that retching wears the heart down"

His answer was strange and so much so that it stayed with Mum over the years.

"Oh she'll be fine, this child will be the best you'll have" he was so confident in his words that for a moment Mum let her fears vanish.

At the hospital Mum and my grandmother were met by the paediatrician who would be investigating my case. They told him all my symptoms, that I was keeping nothing down and therefore making me drink a barium meal would be a wasted effort. Yet he insisted,

"On your own head be it" Gabrielle told him "We'll just leave you too it"

To her mother she said "let's stand back".

Sure enough within fifteen minutes of swallowing the lumpy mixture, I apparently managed to project it all over the doctor, all over his office and over anything else within two foot vicinity. Even though my escorts were worried sick they couldn't help but laugh. The paediatrician was disgusted.

Fortunately there was enough of the solution left clinging to my stomach, that they were able to get a picture of what was going on inside. The news was not good. As I had developed my trachea hadn't, meaning that food could not make it to the stomach. On the positive side I would grow, as would my trachea. But for now if I was to receive any nutrients my oesophagus would have to be widened. To make matters worse baby me would require a tracheotomy whilst it healed.

Gabrielle was horrified; this was no solution, a child so young would pull a tracheotomy out. As for an operation to widen the oesophagus she had no objections, but without the tracheotomy the paediatrician and she were at logger heads. She resolved that this operation was not an option and hoped that she could keep my nutrient levels high enough until I grew. Yet her mind couldn't silence her husband's voice only a few weeks earlier when he stated, "*I see a coffin and I don't know who it's for.*"

In the middle of all this Dad came home slightly perplexed, not only was his child sick but he had met his friend from home, in Belfast of all places. He had been leaving his office in the city centre, when he heard someone call his name. It was no normal voice; it had the distinct inflection that could only be found in a Nigerian accent. On hearing the familiar tones of his home country he was intrigued. It was the first time he had heard them uttered by anyone in Northern Ireland and was momentarily transported to the dry sandy streets of Nigeria. He was taken aback yet thrilled to see an old friend from Lagos standing there in front of him! They hugged and talked for a while and Dad insisted that Kayode came home to meet his family and catch up. Kayode was appreciative of the offer, but would reluctantly have to pass; he was in a rush and couldn't be delayed. He reassured Dad that he would see him very soon and embraced him once again.

Dad came home and after checking on me regaled Mum on the news of his friend's arrival in Belfast. Although he hadn't ascertained why his friend was here, he was sure that when Kayode visited the house he would reveal all. The following morning Dad received a letter from Nigeria.

Kayode had been killed in a road accident just two days earlier.

Chapter Twenty Four

Christmas came and went and for Gabrielle it was the loveliest Christmas she had ever experienced. Santa came and our childish dreams came true. Boxing Day through to New Years was spent in our Grandmothers. Here any possible dream that Santa could have neglected was catered for.

I had just turned two and seemed to be improving. In the space of three months, I had progressed from a skeletal baby into a chubby little pudding. My prognosis was looking better by the day.

January soon arrived, bleak, drab and cold. It had always been Mum's least favourite time of year, the winter focus of Christmas gone and nothing left but gloom. However she did have some light on the horizon. As usual my Dad had given her money for her Christmas box. After their first Christmas together when he bought her a sewing machine and bore the brunt of her subsequent reaction, he had never dared buy her a present again; instead he took the safe option and let her choose her own.

The Christmas money soon felt like it was burning a hole in her pocket, because for over two weeks she had been unable to get an opportunity to spend it. If she didn't get one soon she would miss the best of the bargains that the January sales had to offer. She didn't want to lumber the neighbours with three children so sought a reliable babysitter. Eventually she secured one, a kindly lady who would be available for the entire afternoon. She seized the opportunity and acquired the babysitter's services, asking her to take the girls for few hours. At last she could go shopping!

The girls needed new shoes, and she wouldn't mind a new coat. Leaving the girls, she set off and began the process of bargain hunting. The city centre was thronged with shoppers who, like Mum, were availing of the sales; frantically grabbing the bargains which the town was filled with. Some shops offered a massive fifty percent off; Gabrielle was in her element.

She shopped and shopped until she had spent every penny of her Christmas box, the icy weather had slowed her down and she was surprised that it was now quarter to six. By this stage, she was opposite the Europa train station and thought rather than slip and slide all the way back to the main city centre to grab a bus, that she would take a train instead. It would be a little more expensive, but ultimately it would save a walk - or a slide! She'd had enough slips and slides for one day.

She was fantasising about going home, getting us bathed and hopefully settled for bed early. Battling through the crowds had tired her out more than she had expected. Judging by the weary faces around her, she was not alone in this sensation. Perhaps it was the time of year, the dark mornings and dark evenings were taking their toll on everyone.

Date: 15th January 1980

Time: 18.06.

Location: Europa Station Belfast.

The train station was full as shoppers and workers converged all trying to get home. Mum went to the ticket desk and purchased her one way ticket, shuffling her bags to find a free hand to pay. She wished she had researched her timings for going home, had she done she could have avoided all this. She would have to get on the train early if she stood any chance of getting a seat. She took her ticket from the cashier and looked around for the quickest way to the platform.

Her first indication that something wasn't right was when she suddenly became aware of being stared at. She instinctively looked in the direction of where the stare seemed to come from. In the distance, stood a woman that Mum describes as being dressed from head to toe in green. When I heard this I imagined a cloud of dark green surrounding the woman. Mum's initial thoughts were that the lighting in the station needs serious attention; either that or her eyes were playing tricks on her.

The woman was clad in elegant clothes, not the kind that could be bought anywhere Mum frequented and she was looking, no coming in Mum's direction. Mum looked behind her in case she was mistaken and she was obscuring the woman's intended target. Yet there was no one behind her. When she looked up again the woman was inches from her face. She couldn't fathom how the woman had reached her so quickly, somehow the woman had made her way across the long expanse of the station and weaved her way through the crowds at a speed Mum just couldn't comprehend. The scenario seemed odd to Mum, whatever could this woman want? Mum was certain she did not know her.

As Mum's eyes met the woman's she was assailed with such coldness that she thought she would never be warm again. She tried to peel her eyes away from the woman's penetrating stare, it was then that Mum realised that the woman wasn't a she; this woman wasn't anything Mum's humble mind had words for. She was faced with a creature - an IT.

Feebly Mum recited every prayer she could remember and when her memory failed her, she beseeched the heavens to take this thing away. Her pleas went unanswered and she stood there powerless.

She tried to scream, but no words came. She contemplated running but her limbs remained motionless. Even the simple gesture of averting her eyes from IT's penetrating gaze, became impossible. Mum was paralysed, her defenceless body forcing her to remain on the spot.

IT opened IT's mouth and words, lots of words tumbled out. IT spoke in a language that Mum had never heard before or hoped to hear again. IT's menacing tones were infused with vast hatred and malice. Only IT's finale was spoken in a human tongue, six words that shook my Mum to the core, "I curse you and I curse your family". (Exact words)

Instinct told Mum that she had encountered a being that represented all things evil. She had just been exposed to something that was not of this world.

In a green cloud IT was gone, back to the nowhere IT had appeared from. Mum remembers dropping to her knees so relieved was she at IT's departure. She stayed on her knees as she waited for the waves of terror to leave her. Her moment in darkness had seemed a lifetime. Yet it was 18.06, so no time had passed. Had she imagined the episode?

She glanced at the ground where IT had stood. Sure enough IT had left an ominous souvenir, some sort of green pendant. Then this thing *had* happened. Reassured that her sanity was still intact, she looked to the commuters, the people all around her, they would be shaken too. What had they made of this thing? Yet their faces registered no shock, they were simply the ordinary faces of ordinary commuters in a busy train station.

Everything around her went on as normal; no one looked at all shaken. It seemed only Mum had been witness to this incident. She tentatively reached for the pendant; it was ice cold to the touch. She didn't want it, felt filthy for even touching it but a sensible part of her felt that if she were to recount this story again, she would need proof. With the tips of her shaking forefinger and thumb she dropped the icy object into her pocket. Her relief was replaced by a great wave of sadness as IT's words echoed over and over her mind. Thoughts whirled in her head, faster and faster, they became jumbled and nonsensical, her head began to throb, the pressure too much. Then everything around her became grey then black, the pressure became too much to bear, and then there was nothing.

Chapter Twenty Five

"Thank you so much," Dad was saying as he closed the front door Mum came to at that point and looked around disorientated. She was uncertain of where she was and for one horrible moment she thought she was still at the station.

Dad came into the living room his brow furrowed in concern.

"You're awake" he said,

"How are you feeling?"

The events of the afternoon came back to her and she could feel the blood draining from her face,

"Max, something awful has happened" she whispered,

"Shush, Gabrielle, you need to rest, we can talk about it later"

She sat up and felt dizziness take her again, so reluctantly she lay down,

"How did I get home, I don't remember?"

"You passed out, some passers-by's got you a taxi, I've just seen them off."

The worry returned to his face again "you look really bad Gabrielle; I think I'll call a doctor."

"No, Max I'll be fine, just give me a moment" she sighed. Until she gathered her thoughts and made sense of today, the last thing she needed was a doctor.

"I've called Mum, she says you are to call her a soon as you're fit"

She nodded.

"I'll just get you a drink" he turned to towards the kitchen,

Suddenly remembering her daughters, panic clutched her heart,

"Max, where are the girls?"

"Alison and Maxine are next door and Jayne's in bed."

They were safe that was the main thing, but she needed to be sure.

"Max I need to see them, now" she insisted,

"Gabrielle you will, I just want to make sure you feel better, I'll get you that drink eh? Get some colour back in your cheeks, you're so pale"

Later that evening Alison and Maxine came home. Mum hugged them and held them to her with more enthusiasm than they expected, for she reports that they looked at her like an alien had replaced their mother. They played a few games before Dad took them upstairs for bed.

When they were settled Max sat down in the living room,

"Max something happened" clearing her throat to prevent her voice from faltering she continued,

"I didn't just faint."

He tried to put her off the topic, concerned that she wasn't yet well enough. This time she was adamant, he was going to listen to her recount the day's events.

When she had finished, Dad sat there stunned, but he didn't dismiss her account, instead he said,

"Gabrielle how many times have I told you never to make eye contact with strangers?"

Thank heavens, he believed her, or so she thought when he said, "you've just seen someone that looked a bit different, that's all."

"Max go to my coat," she said "look in my pocket - maybe then you'll know I wasn't just seeing something strange"

He put his hand in her pocket and pulled the green object out; he looked horrified, and dropped it as if it was dynamite.

"Where did you get this?" he demanded, raising his voice to a level Mum had never heard him reach before. Dad was a gentle man, would do anything rather than fight or raise his voice, his reaction was completely out of character and it scared Mum.

"Max I told you, IT left it behind"

"I want it out, out of this house now" he shouted, storming out the door.

It was at least fifteen minutes before he came home, and when he did he hugged Mum and said,

"Gabrielle it's gone, don't worry anymore and I'm sorry for shouting"

"Its okay" relieved that his anger had dispersed.

"Gabrielle if you could do just one thing for me?"

"Of course" she nodded,

"Pray". He said grimly.

My Dad wasn't usually a religious man, he tended to veer on the side of reason but by the look on his face Mum knew not to question him, instead she simply nodded.

Chapter Twenty Six

January 17th 1980

A few years ago I became very ill. I remember sitting in the living room struggling so hard to breathe that I passed out. In the moments before consciousness evaded me, I will never forget the despair and panic that I felt. No matter how hard I tried I just couldn't get back to me. I felt completely detached from my body as I watched my family frantically waiting for the ambulance. I was utterly sure that I was going to die and all I could think of was how I would never see these people, people that I loved so much again. I wouldn't get a chance to say goodbye. Although in the end I pulled through it was nevertheless a horrendous experience. I felt so alone.

On the 17th of January 1980, my Dad was to make his final journey, he made this journey alone. Often I torture myself by trying to see it through his eyes. I know that he was dressed in a heavy winter coat that day. I know that he hated the cold so much so, that he was known to grumble that even the bulkiest of coats offered him little protection from the elements. I know that he had wanted to bring my sister Maxine on his journey with him; he tried to involve his daughters in his life as much as possible. If he ever worked away from the office he always tried to bring one of his girls along. On this particular day my sister was recovering from a chest infection and my Mum, ever the nurse refused to let her accompany him. Disappointed though my sister was, Mum's refusal saved her life.

Dad boarded the Ballymena train; he arrived early and felt that he was making great progress on his audit. So much so, that he felt he could complete the entire audit that day. He called my Mum and told her that he would be home late, that he hoped to be back in time to say good night to his children. Mum's last words to him were

"I'll keep your dinner warm".

He boarded the train that evening for the return journey to Belfast; I imagine he was relieved, as he just made the train and no more, boarding with only seconds to spare. When he sat down he would have read his paper from cover to cover, he always read a paper on his journeys.

Perhaps he even turned his mind to Nigeria, something he always spoke of when the winter was in full force. Dad had grown up bathed in sunshine and had flourished under the acrid Nigerian sun. He wanted us, his girls to experience this too. He passionately wanted us to feel the heat of the ground beneath our feet and the sun caressing our faces. The cold, the winter was no life for anyone and certainly not his precious daughters.

My parents had discussed relocating; they had spent many evenings deciding on where they would live and where the girls would fulfil their childhoods. Dad had mentioned Nigeria and Mum had agreed that maybe the girls would be better off based there. It would be difficult for them growing up here. They would always stand out, be the different ones. Dad frequently maintained that he had chosen this life, he came here fully aware that he would not easily blend in with the crowds. His daughters hadn't been given a choice and he wanted them to have one. If we wanted to move further afield when we were older, then that was up to us, but while we were little he wanted us to escape the stares and the remarks. He wanted us to have a full childhood, where we would be normal and where we could be ourselves.

My Dad had never planned on staying in this strange land, but life doesn't always go to plan and he had met my Mum. In meeting her she had given him three wonderful children and just when he thought that this cold dreary place would never accept him, she had given him a new family. Mum's family had extended their arms to welcome him into their fold. In meeting him, these people had ventured into the unknown, hesitantly at first but had gone on to extend their arms and let him into their lives. The thought of his new family and how loved he felt never ceased to amaze him.

Mum and Dad planned to trial Nigeria for a year; they would let out their Belfast home, so that if all else failed they would have somewhere to return to. Dad had told Mum that Nigeria was so very different, that she may not adjust to life there and its ways, but Mum shrugged it off saying, if she could adjust to Belfast and its bombs and bullets she could adjust to anywhere.

....

 Dad was seen rubbing the steam off the window and peering out. All he would have seen was darkness as it was pitch black outside. No landmarks to advise him of his location would have been visible. Even though two men had just boarded and sat beside him for some reason he didn't ask them for his location. Perhaps they were caught up, distracted by their own affairs, maybe he didn't want to interrupt them. Instead Dad spotted a passing conductor and stopped him,

"Excuse Me sir"

The man appraised my Dad and smiled,

"How can I help?"

"Will we reach Belfast soon?"

"Hmm" he looked at his watch, "aye, we will indeed, I'd say in approximately ten – fifteen minutes"

"Is that all? Great, thank you" Dad returned his smile

"No probs mate" the conductor said and made his way out of the carriage.

As Dad started to prepare himself for the hitting the dreaded ice wall he would face when he left the warm carriage, a deafening bang shook everything around him. He would have been immersed in blinding light and searing heat.

His ears would have been ringing; if he looked around to find the source he would have seen nothing but smoke and flames. By this stage the momentum of the train had stopped as the emergency brakes were pressed.

He was said to have flailed around trying to breathe but the pungent, smoky air would have served no purpose but to scorch his lungs. If he peered through the smoke he would have seen the chair opposite him in flames. He would have seen his legs engulfed in flames, flames that were reported to be white, then blue. "Please God, help me" he had screamed, his voice rasping against the white hot smoke. Those who had managed to get off the train heard his screams; they were the last sounds my Dad made.

....

Meanwhile at home Mum was just about to watch the TV, cup of tea in hand when a loud bang caused the house to shake. She immediately deduced that another bomb had gone off. This one must have been nearby; very rarely did the house actually shake. Moments later sirens blared followed by the distinctive rumbles of helicopters, going by their vibrations they right overhead. Curious Mum opened the back door to see if she could see them. She remembers never having seen helicopters fly so low before; they illuminated the dark sky, turning it an eerie blue as their huge search lights swept back and forth across the area.

Retreating back indoors, she started to think of what was nearby, what could have been destroyed this time? Nothing occurred to her. Five minutes later it did; the train line.

She turned up the news and awaited the customary newsflash that followed every loud noise in Belfast. Sure enough an announcement came through.

"News just in" the newscaster Gloria Hunniford read, "a bomb has exploded in a Belfast bound train on the Dunmurray line" Mum's tea dropped and spread all over the carpet, luckily it just missed the girls.

She looked at the time, it was now seven.

Max should be home.

She rang her mother, "Hi Gabrielle, I was just chatting about you...."

"Mum, a bomb was on a train, Max was on a train and he's not home, there was a bomb, Max isn't here" she frantically, incoherently tried to rely what she knew.

"Gabrielle, he said he would be late didn't he?'" slightly reassured Mum agreed, "We'll be up now" her mother said.

Mum took out the ironing board and began to iron, more news came in as she did so, casualties, fatalities, IRA, she heard it all, but kept on ironing.

She must have ironed for a long time, because her mother and father, grandmother and sisters were suddenly in the house. They lived two hours away.

Chapter Twenty Seven

In theory I was there but in practice I was too young to remember and I thank God for that. However, I did not escape from the events of that night in January 1980. The accounts of that night have been retold so many times that they are like the stuff of fable in mine and my sisters histories. Every year from Christmas to the 17th of January, Mum walks us through the chronicle of events leading to and the aftermath of my Dad's death using her illustrious flair. She needed to tell someone I suppose and in the absence of any form of therapy who better to tell than the only people she was left with? Her daughters.

That night has become a tangible part of Mum, the events relived so many times that they are as solid and real as I am. It is a night she will never forget; she will take it with her to her grave. For my sisters and me, it is likely that we will too.

That night as recounted to me:

Very quickly the house became full. Someone led the girls upstairs. Despite the news and despite her packed house all Mum could do was iron. Her father was glued to the TV and radio news. Cups clattered in the kitchen, the smell of stewed tea permeated the air, hushed chatter encircled her yet she continued to iron; she ironed for hours.

A loud knock silenced the room momentarily. Everyone was eager for news, for some clarification or better still for Max to return. Two men came in they identified themselves as CID. They needed to speak to Mum. Her parents stayed by her side and the room emptied. The men were hostile and standoffish their stern faces emitting waves of distrust.

"We have reason to believe that your husband Mr Olorunda, was travelling on a Belfast bound train this evening? As you are no doubt aware there was an explosion on a train, which we believe to have been a bomb."

"Passengers have identified your husband as having been in the carriage where the bomb is suspected to have detonated from"

The other man interjected,

"Why was your husband travelling on the train?"

They continued questioning and as they did they outlined the reasons for their suspicions,

"Somehow, someone who we believe to be the bomber escaped. It is imperative that you tell us why was your husband was on the train?"

Before Gabrielle could even reply her father was on his feet and threw the men out.

The night continued much like before, with countless people coming and going and all eyes on Mum. At 5.30 am the RUC broke the night's morbid routine, this time confirming that Max had indeed died on the train. Mum's eyes were drawn to her mother who was sitting on the couch. She was gently breaking the news to the utterly bewildered children...

"Daddy had to go to heaven" she heard her saying, her strong mother was struggling to hold back tears.

"God needed him really quickly and he had to go with him tonight. He told me to tell you that he didn't get time to say goodbye."

Three sets of mournful eyes searched her face; Alison's little face was a picture of absolute bleakness, for she understood her Grandmother's words and was slowly realising that her beloved Daddy was dead.

After that reality came and went for Mum, the only thing she is certain of was that the milk man called. By this stage she was no longer ironing so she answered the door to him. Bizarrely amidst all that was going on, she recalls telling him that her husband had just died and could he leave a full crate of milk. Apparently the milk man looked at her utterly perplexed.

Chapter Twenty Eight

In true Catholic tradition a wake was held. Over the next few days, people were reputed to have come from far and wide, politicians, journalists, colleagues, family, friends and neighbours; all keen to pay their condolences. Even Dad's brother finally managed to get some leave and made the journey across the water from Edinburgh to pay his respects.

When the full story of events emerged, it turned out that my Dad's train had been bombed by the IRA. Two bombers had sat down opposite him with a bomb, the bomb had gone off killing two innocents; my Dad and a teenage school boy. One of the bombers was also killed. It transpired that indeed someone had run from the train, the second bomber. They had of course found him and quickly established that he had carried the bomb with his cohort.

His accomplice had died at the scene.

Soon after his escape the surviving bomber collapsed, so severe were his injuries. He had been horrifically burnt in the bomb. He was sent to hospital and his recovery was doubtful.

The CID men, now clear on the sequence of events called to the wake and apologised to mum and her parents. The runaway bomber explained why they were so hostile when they first came and why searchlights had illuminated the sky immediately after the bomb.

As news of the bomb spread, tributes came from far and wide, the bombers were condemned. Conservative MP Winston Churchill appalled by the attack said,

"The fact is that innocent people are dead and the Provisional IRA is responsible, as they have been on hundreds of other occasions. Once again they stand condemned in the eyes of the civilized world."

Even the Catholic Church expressed its disapproval by refusing to allow the bombers remains to be placed in consecrated grounds.

The IRA released a long statement stating;

"The explosion occurred prematurely and the intended target was not the civilians travelling on the train. We always take the most stringent precautions to ensure the safety of all civilians in the vicinity of a military or commercial bombing operation. The bombing mission on Thursday night was not an exception to this principle. Unfortunately the unexpected is not something we can predict or prevent in the war situation this country is in, the consequences of the unexpected are often grave and distressing, as Thursday nights accident shows. Our sorrow at losing a young married man, Kevin Delaney is heightened by the additional deaths of Mr Olorunda and Mark Cochrane. To all their bereaved families we offer our dearest and heartfelt sympathy."

Despite their dearest and heartfelt sympathy, it was reported back to my family that in a pub, in the Markets area of Belfast (a known IRA enclave and coincidentally the then home to the bombers) that jubilant toasts were being raised. For not only had the bomb been a success, it had also been high profile and best of all, they had got a *'Niger'*.

Dad's coffin was sealed and later it would be revealed that the reason behind this was that so little of him remained. They had to identify him through his dental records. Mum sat with the coffin every second that it remained in the house. Now and again she would drift off and every time she woke she reached out to touch of remained of her husband and instead felt only lifeless hard wood. She did this so often that it became an automatic reflex, a reflex that stays with her today.

As she sat there she remembers hearing alien noises, agonised guttural moans. When she looked to find their source she was horrified to find that they were coming from her. Dad was buried in Mum's home town Strabane. Apparently there was a high presence of media and press covering the funeral yet she was not aware. The only residual memory she has of that day was that Alison was by her side, repeating over and over through her tears, "I'll look after you mummy".

As they lowered Dad into his final resting place Mum collapsed, her life force ebbing away. Her guides no longer able to hold her weight such was the force of their own despair momentarily released her. Her day was to become the stuff of nightmares as she recounts falling forward into the dark wet place, down, down and down until she was laying on the coffin. She had fallen into the grave and she didn't have strength or inclination to even attempt to get out. She remembers thinking, "just bury me too."

Part Three

Tales from my childhood

Chapter Twenty Nine

When I was younger an old lady enquired about my Dad, when I told her that he had died she said "Sure what you don't have you'll never miss". That annoyed me. Does a starving child who doesn't have food not miss it? Does a draught ridden country not miss rain? Or even a bankrupt not miss having money? In losing Dad my family lost our link to Nigeria, half of our roots. My sisters and I became mixed race girls who were brought up in a world of only one race. Identity problems throughout childhood and into later damaged us all. The one person who could have helped us had been taken away.

The bomb meant that we didn't just loose a Dad and any identity we could have wished to have, but we also lost our Mum. Mum was still there in body but her mind was far, far away. Sometimes she came back to us, but when she did realisation of her situation hit her again and she retreated back into herself away from the here and now and away from us. So when someone tells me what I don't have I'll never miss I know they are wrong. I miss my Dad and what he could have taught me and most of all from an early age I missed my Mum. The implication of having no Dad and a shadow of a Mum blighted all our lives and perhaps affected the people we all became.

In the years immediately following Dad's death Mum never got a chance to quietly grieve. She was to go through the ordeal of a public court case which revealed all the gory details of the murder. It was in these early days that Mum was to realise that her life would never be the same again. For years after bombing different aspects of it regularly appeared in the papers and the news, constantly reinforcing to Mum that there could be no escape.

Mum doesn't remember much of the first year after Dad died, she describes these times as being simply blackness, a deep waking sleep in which events unfolded around her that she could only watch from a distant place in her mind. It was as if in that distant place she found a safe harbour somewhere she could frequent often when she felt the necessity.

I was very young, no more than preschool age when I first sensed something was very wrong in the house. I just knew that something was amiss; I could feel it in the air. On the days when I felt this, Mum would take to her bed where she could remain for weeks at a time. As I grew older I realised that the thing I sensed was very real, it was Mum's friend who I later dubbed 'Misery'.

In the early years Misery's arrival was triggered by the court case and details surrounding my Dad's death. In the future a bomb, a shooting, even a bomb scare dragged Misery back to our home and initiated Mum's confinement again.

I always felt it was easier for the prisoners, the murderers. They had a release date they could serve their time and move on. The victims could not. Each event, each death and subsequent televised funeral, right through to the emergence of the Historical Enquires Team and the Peace Process was to send Mum back to her own ordeal, to open the door and allow Misery in again. Now we know that many of the victims suffered from the condition of post-traumatic stress, but it was only in recent years that Northern Ireland's victims and survivors were deemed worthy of the disorder. Had this been addressed and treated early maybe things could have been different for my family and so many others.

I don't remember the court case but I have listened to my Mum's accounts of it and researched what I could find in the press archives. I do however remember Mum smashing cups and plates against the gable wall. I'm not an expert on grief but between spending days in bed and smashing plates surely someone must have noticed that this behaviour, especially after three or four years wasn't normal.

No one ever did.

When the court case was over and compensation dished out Northern Ireland washed its hands of my Mum and by doing so us. Nowadays when someone is murdered it is about more than compensation, grief therapy is offered to family members and they are counselled through it. Back then however Mum was left to rot; "You are a young woman with a profession" the judge had said. In other words get back to work and get on with it.

If only things were that easy.

Chapter Thirty

During the next year my family saw many changes. We were moved to Mum's home town of Strabane immediately after the death. Mum's parents had sold and packed up the Belfast home and moved her back to theirs. This was a time when she couldn't be alone, she would need their support. Alison was enrolled in the local school and the bedrooms doubled up to accommodate us. Only now Mum wasn't a child, this time she had three small children in tow. This time she was a mother, she was twenty eight years of age and she was widowed. She had unwittingly, through no fault of her own, become a single parent.

By this stage Mum had become well and truly acquainted with Misery; they were inseparable. Misery's friendship was all consuming. They spent all their time together and performed every task together even when it came to us. Mum performed her duties in a perfunctory manner her eyes blank and lifeless, she was always somewhere else. She had surrendered her body and spirit and let Misery take her away, away from the coffin, away from the grave and away from the pain. Misery was a clingy friend constantly clutching and grasping at Mum, she liked to keep her close and away from us. Yet now and again they became separated and Mum was granted tiny moments of reprieve. During these moments, when Misery loosened her grasp ever so slightly, Mum would wonder where Dad was, for she knew he would never leave her. Mum believed love didn't die, that it was eternal. Dad had been so alive, full of ideas and plans for his wife and his girls that he couldn't just vanish; he had to be somewhere. But when she looked for him, when she futilely tried to find him, Misery reached out her hand and Mum grasped. Misery was her friend now, she understood.

I'm told that Mum's friend Ann travelled from Belfast to see her once. She hugged Mum and they both cried. The last time they had hugged was on her wedding day. Misery joined them both that day making a grasp at Ann too, for as she cried she talked of her sorrows, about her fears for Mum and how would she cope.

Ann's sobbing was uncontrollable; Mum couldn't discern a word she was saying until she composed herself controlling her tears.

"Gabrielle, I saw this you know, that night when I read your tealeaves, I saw that something bad, something really bad was going to happen"

Sobbing again she wondered aloud,

"If only I had of said something rather than running off. Oh Gabrielle, please forgive me, I'm so sorry."

Mum stopped her as she was reminded of the woman in green that she had met the day before Dad's death. She knew that many would not believe the incident, too many people were sceptics, but Ann was open minded, she would at least believe. Mum recounted every detail she could remember to a silent Ann.

Before they could say anymore or try and analysis the visit her mother came in and all conversation ended. Yet a seed of doubt had been planted and in Mum's more lucid moments and indeed until this day she often thought that it was too coincidental to have seen that thing, to have been told those words and then have her husband murdered. Mum still maintains that Dad shouldn't have been on that train, what if IT had made him finish his audit in one day; witnesses say he had just made the train before it took off. A matter of mere seconds had sealed my Dad's fate. What if those few seconds, seconds that delayed the trains' departure, had been caused by a more powerful force? Had IT somehow engineered for Dad to be on that train.

Mum was assailed by anguish. Her thoughts turned to us girls, by losing our father, we too had been cursed. That creature had certainly achieved its goals, IT had been teasing her choosing it's location well, for IT knew Dad would die on a train.

Chapter Thirty One

As always when a murderer is found he or she is brought to some sort of justice, usually by trial. The surviving bomber was no exception. Mum the innocent party was put through the ordeal of a trial and facing the man who was responsible for her husband's death.

The man had proudly admitted his crime and was now to face trial. Over the next year Mum would be dragged to Belfast over and over again; they always insisted she came. It would bring closure they told her.

For Mum no trial would change the facts. Her husband was gone; nothing would bring him back. In the meantime she had no home of her own, three small children and to all intents and purpose was dead inside. To prove she was alive that she hadn't joined a league of the living dead, Mum began a process that would last throughout my childhood, the smashing of plates (and every piece of china she could see). She hurled each one into her parents' garden, letting it smash to smithereens. I imagine that she found something therapeutic in this, for her life resembled those broken shards of china. Her life was shattered and beyond repair and like the china it would never be put together again.

On the day of the court case Mum didn't anticipate that it would actually be held. The surviving bomber, the escapee had been severely burned. He was too ill to stand trial, which meant that so far each date that was set had been cancelled. Mum was made to prepare for court; they would drive all the way to Belfast, only to find that the bomber was still too ill. She didn't expect this particular day to be any different. Yet her father as always insisted that they drove to Belfast anyway, as it may just be the day that justice would be served. On this occasion he was right.

On this day the court case was not postponed, she would now see the man who blown her husband up and destroyed our family. She recalls not being prepared for this; it was something she could never have been prepared for. She made her way into the court room accompanied by family, friends and press and waited for Mr Flynn to be placed in the dock.

I don't like to think that I'm opinionated but when it comes to some of the verdicts administered in Northern Ireland for terrorist cases I am ashamed to find that I am. I have always found it difficult to reconcile the outcome of my Dad's court case with my sense of right and wrong. The bomber was not armed for any other reason but to take life, the bomb was meant for someone should it have been my Dad or someone else. I am no judge nor do I have any right to judge any other human being. Yet I do not understand how anyone found guilty of any terrorist atrocity or any activity that steals life for that matter, can be given such light sentences and even worse serve so little of them. Northern Ireland's justice over the years had caused great controversy with many terrorists serving sentences that do not reflect the gravity of their deeds, even worse in the post Good Friday Agreement those who were still incarcerated simply walked free. I am sure my family weren't the first to suffer from our judicial system it is something that all the victims simply had to accept. No one listened to them.

Mum's description of the trial never fails to upset me. She tells me that her little gathering seemed pathetic when compared to the bombers huge gathering of support. She remembers feeling afraid and intimidated when she realised that so many of his friends and family had come to support him. To them he was a hero. Incidents like this did not help my Mum's future prognosis and I can easily see how Misery took her hold. It must have been difficult for her to understand why people seemed to be celebrating her husband's death, could they not see that by murdering my Dad and a teenage boy that they had achieved nothing?

Mum remembers Mr Flynn's entrance being announced, the old doors of the now derelict Crumlin Road court house rumbling and groaning as they spat him out accompanied by two guards. His appearance was to send an audible gasp around the court room; low murmurs from spectators filled the air until the judge silenced them all with one swoop of his gavel.

Mr Flynn was small, shrunken and every visible piece of flesh was distorted. His body was wrinkled and gnarled, proving his burns had been severe. Mum knew his appearance would illicit sympathy, and became angry. He was alive, no matter what he looked like, he was alive. He had taken life yet he kept his. I believe that Mum was joined by a new friend that day, a louder more forceful friend than Misery. That day she was introduced to Anger.

Anger was aggressive and intent on destruction, Anger knew Mum was faced with the man who had destroyed her friend's life, the man who had left three little girls lives changed forever. Anger like any loyal friend not only stood by Mum, she did more than that, and she positively exceeded herself. She took control of the whole situation and possessed Mum's body, telling her that this man took innocence he preyed on all that was pure. Anger told her that this man had marks on his face that matched his soul. He was a murderer and all could see. Forever anyone who enquired about his appearance would learn what he had done and Mum was glad.

Anger now in total control of Mum's movements and thoughts, steered her and even spoke through her so that together they could attack. Anger wanted this man dead, wanted this man in the ground where he belonged and Anger would stop at nothing until she had succeeded.

Mum's family tried and failed to restrain her, it took two policemen to hold her now seven stone frame back and prevent her and Anger from achieving their goal. When they finally restrained and captured Mum she was led out. As she was escorted from the courthouse, Anger left her and her friend Misery was to return. They clung to each other and they shook and cried. A kindly policewoman sat with them in a small bleak room, until justice had been served.

Back them Mum wanted him locked away, shut away from humanity forever. I am thankful that Britain no longer sanctioned corporal punishment because I know Mum would have wanted to the kick the box beneath the gallows. Luckily her father did not share her opinion. Whilst she waited in the little waiting room; her father had taken to the stand and was pleading for leniency. He felt that this man, this murderer had suffered enough. He did not see how a tough sentence would bring his son in law back. Mum had always loved that her father was a man of peace, yet on this day for the first time in her life she took exception to those feelings.

Whether her father's pleas were heard or not remains unclear yet the judge Mr Justice Kelly obviously had similar thoughts as he awarded Mr Flynn's sentence, he was given just ten years for each manslaughter and seven years for the use of explosive devises to be served concurrently, the judge stating,

"I am satisfied beyond reasonable doubt you were one of the bombers. I am satisfied you and your associates did not intend to kill. Nevertheless, the explosion and fire caused the death of three people in most horrific circumstances. In sentencing you I am conscious you have suffered severe burns and scars, for the rest of your life which will be a grim reminder to you of the events of that day"

Misery was heaved aside by Anger, ten years for each life it didn't seem fair. In ten years from now the children would still be in school and wouldn't have their Dad. What about their secondary school days, their university days and their marriages; they would have no Dad for these days. To add insult to injury Mum knew that most prisoners never served their full sentences; back then Northern Ireland's jails were so full that most served just under half.

From that day on Mum had two friends fighting for her attention Anger and Misery; Anger had the loudest voice so in the main she won out. Little did Mum know that half a sentence was optimistic as a mere six years later Mr Flynn was released. Three years for each life he had taken.

Chapter Thirty Two

I am like Mum in the sense that I like to know the full story, to always glean the entire picture, regardless of what it entails. After the court case Mum met with her solicitor on many occasions and on each one demanded access to the unabridged details of the case. She had not been privy to these during the trial. The judge had deemed that the graphic details of Dad's death would be too upsetting, so she was removed from the courtroom when talks of the blast itself, witness accounts and identification began.

Mum felt that she needed to know, she incessantly probed her father as it was he who had identified Dad's body on the ill-fated night. Yet he never released any information, not even to his wife. Many years later when Mum's father passed away he brought what he saw on that night, the 17th of January 1980 with him.

In her father's refusal to administer any information Mum had to press her solicitor for it. He warned her that it was graphic. The full extent of the bomb and its damage were held in a file that he was reluctant to release. Mum ignored his warning and eagerly took the file. She had to know what became of her husband; she had to know how he spent the last moments of his life.

Soon she did know, the transcripts held all the gory details. Two men had boarded the train carrying a bomb. They had sat opposite Dad and had intended to take the bomb to central station Belfast. No one could explain what had gone wrong, but something clearly had, so much so that thirty one years later the Historical Enquiries Team requested to reopen the case. The bomb had denoted prematurely, killing one of the bombers and almost fatally wounding the other. My Dad, a man from another land and a little boy returning home from school were simply their innocent victims. The little boy was a promising student with his whole life ahead of him.

As Mum read further she found the post mortem details. It was then that she ascertained exactly how her husband and my Dad had spent his final moments. She already knew that Dad had died alone, no loved ones surrounding him; not even a word from a kind stranger. In his last moments my Dad had been plunged into a living hell. After asking the conductor about his location, the conductor had closed the carriage door and almost immediately the bomb had detonated. A ball of flames engulfed the carriage and of course those in it. Those in the surrounding carriages managed to run, to gain safety in the grass verges on either side.

Dad and his fellow travellers had not been so lucky, for the blaze had come with such force that it caught each of them instantaneously, burning was unavoidable. Eye witnesses could hear someone screaming and tried as they may to get close to the carriage to help, the immense heat held them all back. Instead they listened as one man called out "Dear God Help me," they listened and listened until his cries melted with him into the train, into the night.

Firemen who approached the carriage were unable to help for they too could not tackle the flames, they were so ferocious. One of them attempted to climb aboard to answer the man's cries. He described what he had seen, *a man matching Dad's description, literally burning alive*. His legs were gone by now, yet consciousness remained. When the heat began to disperse the fire-fighters were able to board the carriage. All that remained where Dad had been was a heap of ashes. The brave fire-fighter who had tried in vain to help left the service shortly after.

Mum never willingly told me these details; I had to probe her just like she had to probe her father for them. I was always told that all I needed to know was that my Dad's coffin was empty; visiting the grave was a waste of time. It was not until three years ago when the 'Belfast Telegraph' opened its archives up that I was able to request all the details of my Dad's death, once I had gotten them I was able to ask Mum to confirm if this was what she knew. All she said was that her husband had suffered a death worse than any she could ever imagine.

From my own investigation I know he died a hellish death, it was as if he had encountered the fires of hell right here on earth. My Dad had hated the smell of burning I wonder if his fleeing the room when Mum had cut our hair was an unconscious premonition, either way he must have been so afraid. The 'Belfast Telegraph' reports made it clear to me why dental records were required in the identification process, why the CID called that night. They had no evidence; the two innocents in the carriage were reduced to nothing, it was impossible to tell one heap from the other. The bomber too had been obliterated. All they had known was that someone had run from the carriage but they had no way of telling who.

It dawned on me why the coffin was sealed, why Mum maintained the grave was empty; for she had buried nothing, nothing remained to bury. We never visit the grave instead we simply pray for his soul.

Understandably Mum could not process the details she found held in that solicitors file; not consciously anyway. Instead her dreams processed every intricate detail, dissecting and putting together her husband's last moments in that flaming carriage. In her waking hours she knew that if she dwelled on these details she would throw herself into a trap that she would never come out of. She had to put them out of her daily thoughts so she ripped up the transcripts, smashed some more cups and put the details of the death of the kindest man she had ever known in a box and stacked it on her shelf.

Chapter Thirty Three

Unbeknownst to my younger self my Dad's life was valued by the courts. They sought to put a price on the worth of a Dad and how much his widow and children should receive. The absence of my Dad's involvement in my sisters and my childhood was valued at £2000, which we would each receive when we were eighteen. For my Mum a life as a single mother was valued at five years of my Dad's salary. Maybe it was naivety on the Northern Ireland's office part that made them believe that someone could recover from such an event in five years; however I think it was a gross oversight.

It seemed to me that despite losing our Dad, Northern Ireland felt it was right that we should lose our Mum too; for from as early as I could remember my Mum worked and worked and then worked some more. Christmases' came and went, birthdays came and went and throughout it all Mum worked. She had hoped to spend our formative years with us, she had hoped to return to nursing when we were of secondary school age; instead she was sent back prematurely and I believe before she had a chance to fully recover. By the courts reckoning when I was aged just six, my sisters eight and eleven Mum should be able to support us on her own and worse that my Dad's influence was no longer valid.

One of my earliest memories is crying when Mum went out the door to work, begging her to stay at home, I couldn't fathom for the life of me why my Mum worked when everyone else's Mum was at home. My sisters would panic, Mum reports that the mention of work terrified them; their Dad had gone to work and not come back, what if this happened to their Mum too? It took years before they were completely reassured. Mum worked seven twelve hour day shifts, followed by seven twelve hour night shifts. These were broken with two or three days off. I remember her crying too, as she explained to me she didn't want to go, she had no choice. Mum had thought she had said goodbye to her nursing career for the foreseeable future but instead she had said goodbye to her husband and hello to feeding and clothing us alone; to single parenthood.

Unfortunately, my parent's reasonably new mortgage on the Belfast house meant that there was no collateral to speak of; just enough to cover the funeral and our move. My grandparent's house with us in it was full to overflowing, they couldn't afford four more mouths to feed and besides this they needed their crockery; they hadn't realised that when they brought their Irish daughter home that she would have developed Greek tendencies and smash every plate in their house!

The result was that whether she felt prepared or not Mum would have to start regaining some semblance of normality. She says she often mused whether God had taken the right parent, she did not think she was capable of raising three young children alone. She didn't want to let them down. Yet she did her best to rise to the challenge, beginning with buying a house.

Buying the little bungalow meant that my family were now firmly ensconced in Strabane. Mum had reluctantly laid roots there, roots that gave her some sense of attachment and somewhere to call home. She used the courts allocation of five years of Dad's salary against the house and retained some for its furnishing and decoration. This time though Mum took no pleasure in making the house a home, she did it mechanically; simply because it needed to be done.

Mum felt that her mother and father also deserved compensation; they had lived through the whole ordeal with her and I imagine without them she would never have coped. She gave them a little money, not nearly enough for all they had done but something to recognise their support. She bought a car that I remember even now; a little red mini. By Mum's calculations we should be okay for a year, maybe a year and a half if she was sensible with what little remained.

Mum should have known that things don't always go to plan, for as is customary in life when people have money they are sought after. It is shameful to think that even a new widow is a target. Some acquaintances needed a deposit for their first marital home, a friend was in debt and needed help, and on and on it went until we were left with nothing. Of course Mum had been reassured that she would be paid back but as life goes this was not the case. Promises of repayment never were honoured and she was too proud to ask for it back.

Chapter Thirty Four

In those bleak days the main things that fuelled Mum carry on, to sustain her empty shell with nutrition and breath, her children and the need for answers. The physical debris of the bomb that had taken my Dad may have been cleared away. The scene was made neat and sanitised, but the debris that remained of Mum's shattered life could not be cleared so quickly.

Mum was compelled to find answers; she needed to know what drove one man to kill another, why something as precious as life became meaningless and why they felt the need to take it. To discover the answers she would have to meet the murderer. I know now that Mum's pleading to allow such a meeting fell on deaf ears for a reason, she was not ready to meet the bomber; she wouldn't be for years.

Mum wrote weekly to the Maze prison, pleading with the governor to let her meet the man who had unflinchingly ruined her life. Each letter had the same response, the governor writing to her personally, sympathising with her plight but dissuading her from any sort of visit. It would be a waste he would say, for the culprit, the man who killed my Dad felt no remorse. I am grateful to that governor, I am grateful that he refused access to Mum. In later years she would meet the man who caused her nightmares but by then I would be old enough to intervene.

In the aftermath of Dad's death the priest would call to Mum's home frequently. He could never answer the only question she ever asked him; "Why?" Instead he would pray with her and utter clichés about God's master plan. Mum would interrupt his prayers and ask him to help her to arrange to meet the man they had held for the crime; he always said no. Mum lost any fragile religious beliefs she had felt until that point. If it wasn't for my grandparents influence my Catholic upbringing would never have come to fruition. Mum remembers what she viewed as the priests 'platitudes' being so pathetic that she chased him and his banality away.

Instead of religion, family or friends Mum was to rely on her one true confidante for the proceeding years; Misery, she was the only one Mum needed. I would never say that Mum neglected us for she was a good Mum, we became her life. Nothing outside her three daughters mattered, except Misery. I believe that the events of Dad's death and their aftermath changed my Mum, changed her very being, so much so that a depression set in and in the absence of any treatment it festered within her. It made her mistrustful of others, bitter and eventually many years later very ill.

My sister and I in adulthood have often discussed why no one helped, why no support was offered and we were left alone. We will never get our answers but had someone, anyone helped, they could have saved us from so much. Instead every so often Misery visited our house. When she did it became a dark, quiet place where we were afraid to move, we became self-sufficient during Misery's visits and looked after ourselves and our Mum. But Northern Ireland had done all it was going to do for us. As far as it was concerned the quandary of the fragmented Olorunda family was resolved.

Chapter Thirty Five

I don't remember much of my childhood, portions of it comes to me in flashes, in little snippets. It was as if our Mum's sadness eclipsed everything, yet the happy times we had enabled me to bury the difficult. Sometimes when I recall certain details I chastise myself, why didn't I see that something wasn't right? How did I miss such obvious symptoms? My only answer, the only thing that can pacify me is the fact that I was a child; I thought these things were normal.

The crockery smashing was one thing that continued in my early years. I remember her standing at the door and throwing plates at the gable wall swearing and muttering under her breath. I remember throughout my childhood being woken up in the middle of the night by the sound of furniture moving. We had an open staircase in that first house and I used to lie across the top stair and peer through to the living room. I would see Mum pushing chairs, cabinets and rearranging ornaments. When we would come down in the morning Mum would be either in bed or work and the rooms would be changed around. Usually she changed them back again the following night. Most of all I remember the tears; Mum didn't know we could hear but we could, she used to cry and cry, looking back now it is no wonder.

I remember that our cupboards tended to be bare. Mum would get cross at us if we wasted even the smallest morsel of food. One day she made stew, my least favourite meal as a child. I refused point blank to finish it or even eat a mouth full for that matter. I was told that I couldn't leave the table until my plate was cleared. I sat at the table until the small hand on the clock reached eleven and the big hand reached twelve. I woke up in bed; Mum must have let me escape that time. After that eating what was on offer became a battle of wills, for I freely admit I was not an easy child!

When Mum was at work I would go out and wreak havoc, I roamed the streets looking for trouble. On one occasion I remember throwing crab apples at a nasty old ladies window. I thought she deserved it because she had called me a 'black bastard'. I knew she didn't deserve it when the following day she burst into our kitchen and began to shout at Mum who had assumed I was doing my homework at the time of the incident.

A few weeks later I pushed a child in my class and knocked her front teeth out, again I thought she deserved it until my Mum was given a solicitors letter. My next incident involved shouting obscenities at a work man putting up a neighbour's wall; he had seen a black soldier and pointed him out to me as my cousin. I was incandescent and through the choice language I levelled at him I let him know. That night he came to our door.

I was eight years old, a tomboy and considered myself fearless that was until my Mum was to one day explode at my antics. She had had enough. I came home from school expecting her to be in her bed to find her waiting for me at the kitchen table with 'the stick'. After the stick and I had bonded I was sent to bed.

The following day when Mum returned home from work she sat me down and explained to me that things were hard and I was making them harder. She asked me why I did these things and I told her I was sick of being, as a classmate had described me 'an alien'. I even accused her of not being my real Mum. She was white after all and I was black. My sisters and I were the only black people for miles around. Mum seemed to mellow a bit and she showed me pictures of my Dad and spent the afternoon telling me all about him, how he had sometimes felt sad at what people said to him but he had risen above it. He had been brave and proud and I should be too.

From that point on I did my best to make my Dad proud, I knew he valued academic success so I applied myself at school. I knew he valued family so I worked hard at being nicer to mine. Best of all from seeing my Mum and Dad in the photograph I knew I wasn't adopted. Instead I knew that my Dad just wasn't there. Didn't he want me? Was the fact that I was so bad the reason he stayed away? If I was good maybe he would come back. I had been told that he was dead, but death was such an abstract notion that I never fully understood what it meant.

That weekend my Mum brought us to his grave, she sat me down and explained the bomb, really explained what had happened. Before all I had known was that bad men had taken my Dad away, now I was to be told all. From that day on I questioned my Mum, probed her for every detail I could get about this man, my Dad. Each memory she told me seemed to take a little bit out of her, for she would go quiet or retreat to bed after she had spoken of him. In those days it was as if even remembering sucked her lifeblood away. I didn't know then that she had put the worst memories, those that caused her pain away on her little shelf. Yet in those days I was annoying, I must have been, for I constantly questioned. I was relentless always grasping for any little nugget of information about this man I didn't know, the man who was half of me.

The more information I secured about my Dad the more I wanted to be the daughter I thought he would have wanted. I became competitive always trying to be the best, I became bookish and most of all I became proud. Proud that this man had been my Dad, and proud of my colour. I wanted to know more about my Nigerian side but Mum knew little, she had relied on my Dad to impart his culture to us; as he would have relied on her to impart hers. Without knowing anything about my Nigerian side alongside a stark awareness that I was different from taunts and comments rapidly made my pride turn to shame.

Chapter Thirty Six

When I was eight or nine, I became acutely aware that money was scarce. Mum worked hard but it seemed her overheads outweighed any surplus that she made. I can honestly say that Mum rarely treated herself, she had nothing; she lived for us. At the end of each month she would drive us all to Derry where we would stock up the cupboards and she would buy us whatever we needed. She wanted to ensure we never did without so no expense was spared, so much so that her entire pay check was often squandered in a day.

Yet she rarely got herself anything. On her days off she would wear her uniform for going out, insisting that she had so few days off that she didn't need a wardrobe. She spent so many days in bed through tiredness and depression that I'm sure she didn't require much. Mum always ensured through thick and thin that we had enough; any surplus money (and quite often non surplus money) went straight to us. Before the days of tax credits and the nanny state as it has come to be, surplus money on a nurse's salary was a rarity. Inevitably we often ran out.

That winter was especially cold the snow was thick on the ground and temperatures rarely left zero. That was the year of the brown coat and woolly gloves. As I was the youngest my sister's clothes were passed down to me. But by the time they got to me their condition left a lot to be desired. I begged my Mum that year for a new coat and she said she would see what she could do. I was so excited, my counterparts in school had lovely coats in shades of blue and pink and I had my eye on one just like theirs. I remember sneakily cutting out pictures from magazines or pointing to children on the TV or in the streets who had coats just like what I had in mind. I wanted to make sure that Mum knew exactly what to get. To ensure I didn't get hand me downs I waited until Mum was in bed and threw out all the old coats that were destined for me, that way I knew Mum would have to get me a nice new one. I was so excited and imagined myself being the envy of my friends as I walked into school in my fabulous new coat.

A few days later I walked into school coatless. I was furious and utterly humiliated, how dare my Mum expect me to wear such a thing! After all my hard work and weeks of pointing out exactly what I was looking for Mum had the audacity to come home from work looking as pleased as punch as she presented me with my new coat. It was in a big yellow bag and as she handed it to me she was telling me how smart I would look, I positively quivered with anticipation as I peeked into the big bag. The first thing that struck me was the smell; a musty sour note assailed my nostrils.

"Take it out" Mum was saying, as I lifted the coat out I swore I had never seen anything as ugly in my entire life. It was a woollen tweed creation the fabric a deep manure colour with threads I can only describe as curry colour weaved through it. I was appalled, horrified, "try it on" was Mum's next line. I looked at her dumbfounded as I could hear Alison and Maxine's sniggers in the background.

I dropped the repulsive garment and fled to my room, the tears were tripping me. So much for being the envy of my class, if I wore that they would be starting a collection for me never mind the black babies!

I stayed in my room for a long time that day, I was seething with fury. I vowed never to put that thing across my back. I decided that if this was what my family thought of me I would just have to leave, these people simply had no respect. I stomped downstairs and told my Mum that I needed a lift immediately; I needed to get to the Nazareth House, our local orphanage. Mum looked faintly amused and didn't say no as I expected her to, instead she shrugged her shoulders and said "if that's what you want". Ten minutes later we had stepped out into the freezing fog and got into the car, Mum switched on the engine and began to drive. Good, I thought at least the nuns won't expect me to wear a brown tatty brown coat! I buckled my seatbelt, folded my arms and settled back for the journey, going to Derry meant that we should head down the road yet it seemed Mum was heading up the road. Not understanding her detour I looked at her questionably, "where are you going, I thought you were taking me to the Nazareth house?"

"Yes we'll be going there in a minute, but first I think it would only be polite to say goodbye to your granny and granddad"

My tummy lurched as my best laid plans had been foiled,

"Do we have to?"

"Yes Jayne" Mum nodded,

That was it. The threat of facing my grandparents was enough to tell my Mum to take me home,

I could see her laughing even though she tried to hide it, yet rather than give in I said

"I need a day or two to come up with a good goodbye."

That was the end of my protest over the brown coat. I never did make it to the Nazareth house but I did make Mum laugh.

Later that evening, I peered down the stairs and saw my Mum sitting on the living room chair with jumpers which were strewn across the living room floor. Curiosity got the better of me and I ventured down and asked Mum what on earth she was doing.

She looked at me her face slightly drawn and said,

"Jayne, it's freezing outside and I have two weeks to pay day"

I looked closer at her work and saw six sleeves lying on the arm of the chair. Each one was stitched at the top.

"What are they?" I asked

"Gloves, yours are the cream pair, they'll match your wee coat".

Shame raced through me, I believe that was the first time that I realised that things were tough, that Mum was doing her best and that my selfishness was not helping. Demanding a new coat so close to Christmas when I suspected she had already bought our presents, (using her entire salary no doubt) had been a cruel thing to do.

"Thanks Mum, they're lovely" I said and retreated back up stairs.

The next day I donned my 'new' coat and gloves made from old jumpers and made my way to school. Despite feeling embarrassed the overwhelming feeling that prevailed was warmth for I had been fortunate enough to have my Mum who did her very best to ensure that we had what we needed.

Despite that as I got within one hundred yards of the school I took off my brown coat and my make shift gloves, rolled them in a ball and tossed them in my schoolbag. Warmth or not I had my pride!

The brown coat was a wakeup call to me; it made me notice how poor we actually were. Granted the end of each month Mum would stock up the cupboards but by mid-month they would grow bare and usually contained bread milk and beans. When those ran out we relied on Mum's little yellow book to feed us.

Every Monday without fail I remember Mum would sign the yellow book and leave it on the mantelpiece, one of us would take the little book to the post office and queue. When we reached the top of the queue the lady would stamp it and give us a few pounds. We used this to buy precious supplies. Occasionally I snuck a bag of sweets or two! It later became clear that this little book was a family allowance and in the absence of Dad this book was the only help my Mum got.

The other person we relied on was Mum's grandmother or 'nanny' as I called her. She would call at our house often and was a great support to Mum. She too had been widowed young and understood what Mum was dealing with. She used to come with a fresh loaf of bread and milk and all sorts of supplies for the cupboards. As early as when I was a toddler she would bath us and buy little necessities like vests and pyjamas. I used to find her gifts boring and would have preferred a toy or sweets but now I see that these little purchases were essential for a young family. Mum knew her Gran had used her limited funds to buy these and her kindness always touched her.

Chapter Thirty Seven

I liken Mum to a poem I used to hear when I was little it went, 'when she was good she was very, very good but when she was bad she was horrid'. When Mum was with us she was the best Mum in the world, yet when Misery snatched her from us as she frequently did Mum became horrid. She became silent and reclusive, her eyes became blank and she cared about nothing or no one. It was during these times that Mum gave up and we catered for ourselves. My sisters remember calling my grandparents and my nanny to come and help telling them that we were scared and that Mum was quiet again. I suppose they were petrified and in the end out of desperation Mums family brought the doctor out to see her. Mum was completely unresponsive yet she heard them utter, "Changed person", from her bed she let their words pass her by. When Misery was with Mum she walked and talked occasionally but was no more than a puppet imitating life, the strings that moved her were gone and she was lifeless.

Mum was diagnosed with a deep depression and was started on a strong course of anti-depressants; she was given sleeping tablets as well as she hadn't been sleeping. She had sitting up each night staring at nothing. Well that was what they thought, because Mum wasn't staring at nothing she was looking at Misery and Misery was holding her attention.

Looking back, drugs were the worst courses of treatment that my Mum could have been given. I wish they could have addressed the root of her problem, I wish they had offered her some therapy some help to cope. Drugs were never the answer, they were the easy option. I firmly believe that by introducing Mum to such drugs that set her on a path of no return. The more depressed my Mum became the more she remembered my Dad and thought of how things could be; the more drugs she was given. A dependency was created that had ramifications so strong that they would obliterate her later life.

My parents were stalked by racism in their time together. Admittedly they found it unsettling but they hadn't dwelled on it; they refused to let it defeat them. They had each other and they had their plans. When my Dad had fulfilled his contract to his firm they had intended to leave Northern Ireland and bring us girls up in a more tolerant society. The bomb that took my Dad's life had temporarily put a halt to these plans, yet in the back of Mum's mind she longed to someday fulfil them. This was reinforced all the more when the vile monster of racism reared its ugly head again. This time though it didn't level itself at adults, instead it targeted three innocent children.

Living as a mixed race family in Strabane or indeed any small town had its downsides, none of which made our lives any easier. Initially after Dad died, Mum refused to let us out the door. Every bang, bullet or bomb she heard seemed to alert her to the danger on the streets. She thought if she kept us all in and with her at all times that we would be ok. The barricading us in lasted for a few years until Mum reluctantly had to let us out to face the world.

Rather than terrorist threats the first thing that threatened us was something she hadn't expected. On the mornings when she could leave us to school she would watch us making our way in. We stood out so much from the other children; our little brown faces a stark contrast to the sea of white faces that surrounded us. Her heart reached out to us as she knew deep down that our differences would soon result in trouble.

Yet considering the circumstances Alison and I seemed to be settling into school. Maxine was the exception she had grown into an introverted child, her teacher had told Mum that she wasn't progressing academically and alarmingly was painting only black. Now it is clear that a depression had fallen on her. Once again no help, no counselling existed to help bereaved children of the troubles. Instead Mum resolved that watching and monitoring her was all she could do.

Mum had always kept she and my Dad's plans in the back of her mind before he had been murdered they had resolved to move us somewhere else, somewhere more mixed. Yet the events of the last few years had left Mum insecure and afraid of all things new. So much so that she began to question whether uprooting us to a far of place would be the best solution. However her doubts were to be conquered very quickly. Immediately after Dad's death she had turned a blind eye to the remarks, stares and questions about her daughters but as time passed they were to become more and more difficult to ignore.

One day she came home from work to find Alison in convulsions; she was sobbing her heart out and was vehemently refusing to go back to school. On further examination the events of her day were unfolded. The children in Alison's class had been given an exercise to draw themselves. Alison, who believed she was quite the little artist, drew a picture of herself skipping. When the teacher had collected all the children's samples, she had stopped at Alison's and became outraged. She shouted at her the rest of her class the audience,

"That is not *you!*" she proceeded to draw an alternative picture on the board "*this* is you"

On the board the teacher had scrawled a child with big lips, fuzzy hair and bad posture, she pointed to the board telling Alison, "*You* are a negro and negro's look like this!"

Furious, Mum arranged cover for the following mornings work and with Alison in tow, reported to the school at nine am the next morning. She demanded to see the head mistress and found a voice she never knew she had. She described to the head the events of the previous day and informed her that her complaint would be taken to the education board if she didn't receive an immediate apology from the culprit. Mum was told this would not be possible, the teacher involved was busy. Yet Mum would not be brushed aside she was determined to receive her apology, *their* apology. So she continued her battle.

"Not be possible? But it is possible for your staff to humiliate a child in front of her contemporaries?" She had said, continuing "if she is busy I will wait whilst you arrange someone to cover her. I warn you though if she is not here in ten minutes I will begin instigating her dismissal." Mum looked at her watch, taking note of the time and sat down, making it clear she was going nowhere.

The head mistress clearly defeated left her office and Mum and Alison sat waiting. The standoff was successful and precisely ten minute later Alison's shamefaced, mortified teacher along with the headmistress entered the office.

Mum and Alison were given an apology and reassured that such an event would never happen again. Seizing her moment Mum assured them that she would take this no further if they honoured one more request. That the teacher involved would have no further contact with any of her children again. Alison was removed from her class that very day and Maxine and I were never taught or spoken to by that teacher in the future.

Mum left the school feeling a lot stronger, she had done Max proud. But seeing her child so upset had a profound effect on her. This time she had been resilient and had coped with the situation, but what about the next and the inevitable next? Single motherhood was gruelling at the best of times, but being a single mother to three mixed raced children in an all white town added even more complications.

The incident in the school was not the only incident, in only a few years in Strabane Mum had encountered more bigotry than she had thought possible. Even her mother had not been immune, she had once taken us to Mass and an old friend approached her at the end of the service and commended her on her charity work. By virtue of having little money her mother was never a big donator, she gave what she could, when she could, but she could never afford to give enough to have her generosity highlighted. Needless to say she was puzzled and asked the woman what she meant.

The woman explained saying that by taking in those African children and feeding and clothing them, she was highly admired and deserved a medal. In fact they all thought so. She had looked up to see the woman's cronies oohing and ahhing in agreement. Always known for her diplomacy she had quickly corrected them, but had been deeply upset at the incident.

I remember after that day in the church, it took Mum quite a while to convince Maxine and I that we weren't adopted and shipped in from some far away African country! Not for the first time I would look at myself and then at Mum, weigh up the older ladies comments and conclude that the ladies and their friends were right. Somehow Mum had gone all the way over to Africa and picked us to bring back to Strabane. Despite being told about my Dad I didn't remember him, adoption was a much more logical explanation.

One afternoon Mum had left us in the little red mini on the main street whilst she ran to the bank to cash her salary cheque. The three of us were excited as Mum had promised us a trip to 'Wellworths' were we could each select a small toy. As it was the end of the month the queue for the bank was long and Mum seemed to take an age. I remember we were singing silly songs and laughing when all of a sudden someone peered in the window, very soon we were surrounded by spectators, all mystified by the strange but cute creatures that inhabited the car. I felt like an animal in a zoo. To our audience the sight of us three children in that little mini was as if an alien spacecraft had descended right there on the main street. Thankfully Mum returned and quickly dispersed the crowds using a few choice words! When she climbed back into the car she turned to us and tried to make a joke at how they were admiring our nice hair yet she quickly saw that we were all in tears. Mum says it took her a long time to compose us. We never got our toy that day instead she took us home and closed the blinds.

Those days became littered with battles; Mum must have felt like the towns very own Martin Luther King championing race relations on an almost every day basis. She grew sick of telling them over and over again that we were all the same until eventually she gave up.

That was the day when Mum decided that she would cast her fears aside and take us to Nigeria. She would never expose us to such experiences again. She was not foolish enough to believe that she could escape racism there but she knew such experiences would be lesser if her girls blended in a bit more.

Chapter Thirty Eight

Whilst Mum was planning our relocation the political situation in Northern Ireland was as dire as ever. Mum had thought that our part in Northern Ireland's history was over however in some ways it had only just begun. A few years earlier Mum had outed herself as anti IRA when the train bomb had made headlines again. This time the bomb it was to make the headlines for different reasons. A priest who saw himself as a crusader for victims of British incarceration regardless of what they were guilty of, had decided to take up the bomber Patrick Flynn's case for release. He launched a ferocious press campaign throughout Northern Ireland to free my Dad's murderer. Father Faul would stop at nothing until he secured freedom for the man responsible for killing two innocents. He had an army of supporters who felt that the bomber who lost his best friend in the blast and had been injured so terribly meant that he deserved released from the terrors of the Maze.

On hearing and reading the priest's campaign Mum was devastated. What kind of man of God disregards the devaluation of human life and advocates murder? Mum wrote an open letter to the 'Belfast Telegraph' voicing her disgust but it was never printed. Instead people from far and wide right across Northern Ireland condemned Father Faul's actions and in some respect reassured Mum that decency existed. Regardless of the weight of support against Father Faul's intervention in the judicial system, he was still successful. He secured the release of my Dad's murderer after having served just a few years of his already light sentence. Mum was once again joined by Misery and thoroughly distraught. As was customary in bleak circumstances she took to her bed and her drugs were increased.

The increase in her prescription allowed her to function and got her through the early release and allowed her to concentrate on us. That was until one day when we ran out of milk. I remember that day like it was yesterday, it all started so well. Mum was off and feeling well and that morning she announced that we needed to get ready as we had to get milk and since she was off, we may as well go for a drive as well. As children we loved getting out for a drive and as Mum's days off and 'well' days were scarce we excitedly seized the opportunity. I remember my sisters and I playing paper, scissor and stone to decide who would get the privileged position of sitting in the front. Of course I choose stone so I was outwitted and relegated to the back beside Maxine. Alison was the winner that day so she would sit in the front. It didn't really matter though as Mum had promised us a long run and said we could listen to whatever tape we wanted on the journey. As Alison had won the race for the front seat Maxine and I could choose the tape. We choose Michael Jackson because he was cool.

For the most part Mum had taught us to ignore the town and its people. It was a staunchly republican town and IRA victims, catholic or not would never have been popular, not to mention black IRA victims. As such in those years we did most of our shopping in Derry, we only bought the very basic essentials in the town.

As I remember we certainly went for a run that day, but not the kind of run my sisters and I had in mind.

We got to the shop only to find that it was closed, the next shop and the next shop were too. Twenty four hour petrol stations didn't exist back then. But as this was a normal day there was no apparent reason why the shops would be closed. Mum and Alison double checked the time and according to them the shops should definitely be open. After all it was eleven o' clock. Baffled we moved on to the last shop we could think off, it too was closed. Mum made us all laugh when she suggested that we would have to drive out of the town altogether and find a cow. If we kept driving we would be in the country soon all we needed was a bucket and we could fill up. I remember giggling and giggling as if it was the funniest thing I had ever heard. I was quite looking forward to milking a cow! We were still squealing with laughter five minutes later as each of us proffered our parts in the milking process. We were a happy little bunch as we continued our drive around the town looking for a shop.

It didn't take long before Mum spotted a familiar face from the town walking his dogs. She pulled over beside him and asked him why all the shop were closed,

"What's going on" she enquired genuinely curious,

"It's the commemoration of the Easter rising" he replied perhaps a little too proudly.

It was then I noticed Mum staring ahead, I think we all did as soon we were all following her line of sight. Up ahead stood a gathering of people, no, more of a procession. A big man dressed from head to toe in black and wearing a mask raised his hand at Mum to stop the car until the procession had passed on.

The men in the march all had their faces covered and were all dressed in black. They carried a huge tricolour. I thought they looked like zombies because they walked so slowly. In response to the dog walker Mum said;

"IRA, you mean?"

"Yes the new commemorating the old" he proudly nodded.

I knew then that this was worse than walking into a zombie horde for the word IRA was a word that to my sisters and I was synonymous with death, bombs, bullets and of course tears. Our jovial little family outing was instantly transformed into one of utter fear. As Michael Jacksons 'Thriller' filled the car terror filled us. Mum became unrecognisable, she paled, she tensed and she swore. Mum's rage was palpable. When I remind her of that day she says that those 'bastards' holding up the road were murderers, and she was supposed to just sit there and idly let them pass by. There they were alive and breathing, walking and talking whilst the innocent rotted in their graves. She said she thought of my Dad at that moment his death was all the more reinforced by looking at his daughters sat in the back seat fatherless. She was reminded of my Dad's smiling face, she saw her mother telling us that our Daddy had gone and Anger took over her completely and utterly.

For once I was fortunate that I had not won the competition to sit in the front seat for all of a sudden my Mum pressed her foot to the accelerator and drove faster and harder than I had seen her or anyone else do before. As Michael Jackson sang I remember thinking of how all these men in balaclava's danced just like him. From my backseat vantage point it seemed their footwork was just as intricate as they dived for the pavement. They couldn't hear the music but they certainly must have heard Mums car because I could see them running and scattering in all directions. Yet that wasn't enough for Mum, she was adamant; she was on a mission to annihilate each and every one of them. Faster and faster she went not stopping until our car made contact with bodies, lots of them. I remember the thuds as one by one, they bounced of the boot, even those who sought refuge in the pavement could not escape Mum's little red mini.

As I peered behind me I could see men were scattered in various positions on the road behind. Even more alarming Mum had started to make the car go backwards; she was going to run over all the men strewn on the road. Luckily she decided against the idea and quickly made the cars go forward again; maybe she decided that hitting as many as she could, would be easier and more effective. I screamed, Maxine and Alison screamed, we had never seen anything as frightening before. It was as if the sound of our hysterics shook Mum back to reality for as she looked at us and her face changed, it started to register normality again, she was beginning to look like our Mum once more. Calm was restored as Mum appraised the situation around her; I think she saw what we saw. Our Mum, feral and dazed, wildly knocking down hordes of balaclava wearing men.

Mum simply turned the radio off, turned the now silent car around and drove us back home. She went straight to bed; I could have sworn I saw tears glisten in her eyes.

We didn't get the milk that day.

Over the next few weeks Mum worried about the repercussions as she had knocked down at least six men. The extent of their injuries was unknown. Yet for now with Misery by side I believe she hoped they were dead.

In Northern Ireland it was a well known fact that the IRA meted their own justice. From what my Mum had been told it was only a matter of time before they exercised it. We were once again barricaded in.

Chapter Thirty Nine

One thing the road rage incident did was spur Mum on to make concrete plans for the move to Nigeria. Our local priest Father Mulvey was instrumental in helping her make contacts. He had known a friend of a friend as Irish people generally do, who was working in Nigeria and slowly but surely she began to make arrangements. Mum saved as much she could. This would not be a cheap move, yet life in Nigeria seemed cheaper in comparison to here so we would save when we were there. The main thing for Mum was getting there and finding a job. She contacted some hospitals in and around the Lagos area and enquired if they had vacancies for nurses.

Slowly but surely the Nigerian plans began to take shape, in the meantime we continued to *exist* in the town. Mum had no friends a fact that I found so sad, if she had had friends perhaps her life would have been easier, they may have brought out the lively person she once was. Instead she simply had us, her work and Misery. Mum continued to have good days and bad days. The bad days tended to be the result of news of yet another terrorist atrocity or yet another bereaved family. Each new death compounded her own experiences.

To escape Misery befriended her and together in the darkness of her bedroom they shut out the world. She was a good friend to Mum and her friendship overtook everything else, us, work and her plans. We always prayed that the bad days would end and the good days would return. For it was on these good days that we caught a glimpse of what our mother could have been.

At this stage Mum worked in the towns health centre as a district nurse. The staff there got to know her well and had an understanding of her shattered life. Many of them were sympathetic. One of the doctors that Mum worked with was prompt to guess what was happening; that Mum was suffering from a deep depression. During one bout he called to our house and assessed Mum. Again Mum's drugs were increased and Misery not wanted to leave Mum completely released her hold enough to let Mum function.

It seemed that every time Mum got depressed, when she succumbed to Misery she was given more drugs. They succeeded in pushing Misery a little further away each time so she could work and focus her mind on us and the move. Mum admits that if she kept focused on something, anything at all, that she felt stronger.

Yet Mum didn't know then that the commemoration events that our little drive had interrupted, were only a prelude to the main parade. That year's main parade unbeknownst to Mum was the talk of the town. One day when she was calling at a patient's house to undertake the glamorous task of dressing yet another rotten bedsore, she became privy to the towns anticipation. The patient informed her that the parade would "honour the town's fallen heroes." She told Mum of how they had lost their lives at the hands of the "Brits". She delighted in informing her of how they had so bravely fought and thrown their own lives down for Ireland.

Mum didn't reply to the patient, but remembers thinking *'murderers you mean?... IRA bastards'*

The patient lost in her own romantic visions of Ireland's patriots went on to make the mistake of telling Mum that this year's day would be even more special than ever. The town could expect a special guest that day, one of the most heroic men of them all; Martin Mc Guinness. Mr Mc Guinness would even enjoy a short ceremony in the grave yard where he would fly the glorious tricolour high above all the graves as a mark of respect to all the heroes.

As soon as Mum had finished the patients dressing she drove straight to the parochial house. Mr Mc Guinness in those days was a known as an IRA commander. Mum was sure he would be made very welcome in Strabane, she was also sure that she would not let him fly his despicable flag in the grave yard. At the parochial house Mum met with Father Mulvey.

Father Mulvey was a nationalist priest but he was not a republican, he became famous during the troubles for condemning the IRA and their actions. As a child he was one of the few people who got across our front door. He and Mum got on well, mainly due to their shared political beliefs. He was a stern man, but a sensible man. He believed in right and wrong and had little time for the troubles. Father Mulvey spoke his mind and his beliefs were not always popular.

When Mum told him what she'd heard he confirmed that he also had heard the same. However, as far as he was concerned no one had sought his permission to fly any flag over the graveyard. He assured Mum that even if someone did ask for such permission it would never be permitted.

Chapter Forty

Soon the day of the parade was upon the town, a day I don't remember but I certainly remember the aftermath. Excited chatter hung in the air. As far as the townsfolk were concerned something *very* special was happening, someone *very* special was coming. Mr Mc Guinness would be gracing their streets. Their attention was so focussed on the VIP arrival that they came out in force. Unlike the procession of a few days ago this parade was on the town's main road, its length lined with supporters. The procession weaved its way through the town and stopped outside the grave yard. There the men said a few words and all heads bowed. They then were on the move again, this time preparing themselves to turn through the grave yards gates.

Martin Mc Guinness snaked through the road followed by legions of fans. Armed with a huge tricolour they were surprised encounter a priest standing in their path. They asked permission to fly the flag in the grave yard as a mark of respect to the town's heroes. Father Mulvey denied it. He knew of what had happened to Mum and many, many others as such he was not a supporter of their cause. Jesus said turn the other cheek, not to fight as they did. That was his philosophy and his reasons for refusing their entry.

Mum recalls his commanding voice booming through the crowd,

"You might want to honour your victims, but I have to bear in mind *their* victims, so I am sorry I do not and can not give you permission to fly anything political on consecrated ground."

He folded his arms and continued to block their path. Mum had never been a lover of the church, but today she found herself adoring it. A catholic priest standing up to the IRA was unheard of and a sense of justice pervaded her.

Jeers from protesters pelted Father Mulvey from every angle; he was heckled from far and wide. In the absence of any supporters for this brave man, Anger seized Mum and together stood beside him. Father

Mulvey called for others to join them, unsurprisingly no one did. Some stood in silence; others hung their heads, all were afraid to be seen confronting the public face of the IRA.

So it happened that there outside that little graveyard something utterly unheard of took place. A small but significant battle was unfolding, a tiny peace protest, where two stalwart campaigners faced an army that few dared to tackle. Side by side, a small town priest and a country victim stood together and openly against the IRA. I am so proud of my Mum for standing there that day; it must have taken every ounce of her courage.

"Murders" she remembers shouting as she made her way directly to Mr Mc Guinness. She doesn't remember the full content of the conversation but she knows that that was the day that she added a little Northern Irish French to her vocabulary! From that day on swear words became an integral part of her every day speech. Yet on that day she had a small victory, because Mr Mc Guinness and his hordes marched on by waving their flag behind them.

The following day my sisters and I greeted Mum after school with forlorn faces,

"What's wrong?" She had asked

"Mummy are you ill?" Alison replied.

"No, why?" Mum answered,

"Because everyone says you're sick"

That was how anyone who went against the consensus of this republican little town was viewed. As sick.

For a few months Mum heard nothing more about the event but inside she became worried, had she put her daughters at risk? These men were cold blooded killers; she doubted very much that killing a child would even tickle their conscience.

The plans for Nigeria soon became crucial and all consuming. Mum took to calling the hospitals and unlike before this time she spoke to staff about available jobs not possible jobs. Her plans were so advanced that she even put our house on the market. If a job or a sale came through then we would go, Mum would take us girls and run.

Chapter Forty One

Mum's actions boycotting the tricolour in the grave yard, confronting Martin McGuiness and knocking over a few IRA men meant that our family not only stood out because of our colour but also for being anti IRA. Mum in her bravado had made us potential targets. Which brings me to days I remember well; the days of the army raids which became a part and parcel of daily life in the town. On a regular basis the homes of many if not most of the town's residents were 'raided'. It became a common talking point amongst the locals usually concerning who was raided and what had been successfully hidden from the army glare. The raids involved the British army searching houses for weapons, explosives or any clues pertaining to terrorist connections. It seemed that at least one time or another, every house in the town had had a raid. All but ours.

Often we would arrive home to find every front door in the street wide open, many having been kicked down; personal effects would be strewn across hallways that were on open view to all. All of this was evidence that frantic searching had went on; that another no warning raid had taken place.

The people we lived next to would eye us with distrust; suspicions were high in those days. They must have wondered why we were being excluded, if we watching them or worse if we were we were some sort of informers. At this stage Mum was already running scared due to her previous stunts. She didn't need any more reasons to be targeted.

Soon the other children began making comments, calling us 'Brits' or what they took to be the ultimate insult 'Protestants'. It got so bad that in the end Mum went to the police and explained our predicament, how she was quite possibly the only non-sympathiser in the town. They swiftly informed her that they knew exactly who she was. They too had heard of her one woman mission to rid the country of IRA! An officer brought her into an interview room and told her that she had every reason to fear, these people were unscrupulous.

That day the police arranged for our house to be 'included' in any further raids. This simply meant that when the army raided our street that they would also come into our house. In practice it meant that whilst everyone else had their front doors kicked down, their possessions scattered and often destroyed we had our front door carefully opened, never would we find an item out of place. Sometimes a little note was left stating they walked through as requested!

I wondered now why no one noticed that our door was never damaged, that the contents of our house were never rummaged or destroyed. Yet the cunning rouse was successful and before long the natives believed that we too was subject to searches and enemy suspicion. We had successfully assimilated as far as the natives were concerned.

That day the police officer also gave Mum something which she found very valuable but which terrified me. She was furnished with a little mirror which she was instructed to use every morning before she left the house. The mirror was a means of scanning under the car before attempting to move it. It would alert Mum to any tampering and show up any devices that may have been planted. Mum was also given a quick vigilance brief in which she imparted to us, it told us what to look out for and contact numbers if anything, anything at all bothered us.

Even with the new devices Mum never felt entirely safe and our Nigerian plans became more and more real. When she found a buyer for the house, she knew it was time to make the move. I recall her sitting us three down and telling us the plans. She told us that she would always be there for us and we would be much happier there. Once again she told us about the bad man who killed our Dad and explained that the men that she had knocked down were his friends. She told us that the town was full of his friends.

I was so excited at the prospect of moving to the other side of the world, it would be such fun, never ending holiday. My sisters and I were happy to leave as we were young and adventure appealed to any child. Mum told us that we would be able to buy a new house there and that she would find a job. I was the most excited of all as apparently I was beginning to pick up some of my Dad's traits. I the one who never knew him was beginning to walk like him and worry like him. Yet one trait dominated above all the others; I loved animals like him.

Mum had described Nigeria as the land of milk and honey where dreams came true, so in my little mind I would have a dog or even better my very own pack of dogs. She agreed that when we got there I could have a pet; this was most likely to pacify me. I think I would have gladly moved to the moon if the promise of having a pet was fulfilled. Over the next few weeks, whilst my family were concentrating on Nigeria, I was naming my dog, pretending to walk it along with pointing out every waif and stray I saw. Mum really hoped this was a passing trait, she had enough on her plate and a four legged friend was not an addition she would relish.

Mum had arranged the big move for that summer thanks to the help of Father Mulvey she had several properties to see when we got there and a recommendation of a good boarding house where we could stay until we acquired a home .

Chapter Forty Two

When I asked Mum especially in later years why our move hadn't come to fruition, why it *really* hadn't occurred, she furnished me with what I then deemed to be a ludicrous tale.

She described sitting with her mother one afternoon over tea discussing the finer points of the trip when a knock came to the door. They hadn't been expecting anyone and it was strange to have a caller so early in the afternoon. Her mother answered the door and when she returned to the living room she was accompanied by some sort of priest. He was dressed from head to toe in white, and wore robes, robes like they had never seen before. He was swarthy and although not classical good looking he boasted a striking appearance. He had deeply tanned skin, dark brown hair and when Mum's eyes met his he had the kindest eyes she had ever seen.

"Gabrielle?" he inquired,

She nodded, looking from him to her mother trying to find some sort of answer as to why this man was here, to ascertain who this strange visitor was. Behind his back her mother shrugged and then as was customary for anyone who entered the house offered him a tea or coffee.

He declined anything and instead sat down when invited.

His eyes never left Mum's face and when they discussed his appearance afterwards they both felt that he seemed to glow, to radiate some sort of light. Her mother put it down to the bright day and his chair being positioned in the brightest corner of the room. That day the sun was blazing in and concentrated precisely on where he sat. Mum said nothing but as far as she was concerned she was in the presence of an extremely holy man.

When Mum was very young her grandmother used to tell her that when a priest was saying Mass that she was to not to look at him as a man. When a priest stood on the altar and uttered his sacred words he became far greater than man. Mum was to look beyond the man and see Jesus. Despite her Grandmothers words any Mass that Mum had ever attended or priest she had ever encountered had always been a mere man to her. She could see Jesus in them as much as she could see Jesus in a horse. Her grandmother would chuckle when she told her this, always careful to disguise her laughter and tell her off for being disrespectful.

That day this exotic man's presence instantly reminded Mum of her grandmother's words and for the first time ever, she saw Jesus in that beautiful priest in the living room. When she paid him the reverence she had been brought up to show any priest, this time she didn't do it to appease her family, she did because she meant it.

"I have had to travel to see you today" he said, his soft voice had no discernible accent, all that she remembers extracting from it was gentleness.

"Oh" she said utterly dumbfounded,

Her mother seeing her lost for words, was quick to intervene,

"Father, Gabrielle has been through a lot and is grateful for your visit; she's just a little quiet today"

He laughed revealing a smile that was as beautiful as the rest if him,

"I know, I know Mrs Caulfield" he leaned forward and was now sitting directly opposite Mum,

"Gabrielle I cannot stay long, but I come with a very important message for you"

"Oh" she said again, she really couldn't get any words out the whole experience was just so strange,

Smiling still he continued,

"Dear child, I know all about your plans, I know every one of them. I am telling you to cancel them"

"Oh" she said again, blatantly aware that a pattern was emerging on her side of the conversation. This man was going to think she was a complete fool!

Luckily for her, her mother again intervened.

"What plans father? She has quite a few"

"Nigeria" he said

"You're here about Gabrielle's plans for Nigeria?" her mother inquired,

"Yes" he said flatly, his smile vanished and was replaced with a look of intent as he placed his hands over Mums and said

"Do not go to Nigeria, you have my word that you and your children will be safe here"

"Oh" again words continued to fail her she felt such an eejit,

"Father she has arrangements in place" her mother said,

"Un-arrange them Gabrielle" he said, "Can you do that for me?" his eyes reaching into her very soul,

This time she surpassed herself and uttered a word rather than oh,

"Yes" she muttered,

"Do I have your assurance?" he asked still focussed intently on her face

She nodded.

"Good, then it is done" and with that he thanked her mother shaking her hand, gave Mum another dazzling smile and left.

Her mother saw him out and sat down in his place. She simply looked at Mum and said nothing, Mum simply looked back. They regarded each other for a while, before they both lit a cigarette and went over the incident.

The worst thing was that neither of them had seen him arrive or depart. Her mother admitted that she was every bit as baffled and stunned as Mum, she had just hidden it better. They never did get his name nor did they ever find out where he was from.

For Mum though she went home that day feeling a great sense of peace, waves of calm flowed through her and she slept. She slept for a long time and for the first time since Dad had died she didn't visualise the train. Mum kept her word and abandoned our move to Nigeria. Instead Mum found us a home in the outskirts of the town, a little more expensive than she could afford, but at least it us away from the majority of people. I was disappointed when Mum told us that our Nigerian adventure was cancelled, but as all the planes had been stopped we had little choice but to stay. Mum had said the only other way there was if we could by magic carpet and she couldn't find one. We were all so disappointed but I resolved to keep my eyes peeled for such a carpet and in the meantime I would try and get Mum to commit to her promise of a dog.

In a moment of weakness Mum relented. She claimed that without a father I had one less thing to love than my counterparts; maybe a dog wouldn't be such a bad idea. She must have rued the day she relented, because very soon every waif and stray from far and wide was collected. I spent my childhood days administering to creatures, seeing beauty in even motlest of mutts and driving my family mad in the process!

Chapter Forty Three

It didn't take long for us to move to our new house and settle in. Mum had furnished it with such attention to detail that it felt more like a show house than a home but it was nice that she had something to focus on. Mum still had her bad days but my sisters and I had learnt to accept them. She was working extra shifts to allow for the increased mortgage costs so we rarely saw her anyway. The house had needed to be purchased quickly as we had sold our last home for the move to Africa. It meant that Mum had to inject almost all of our savings for Nigeria to secure it. Mum was right though in that I didn't notice her absence or wasn't as needy when I had my dogs. All my spare time was fully occupied especially when much to my amusement one delivered a new litter of pups! I wasn't amused however when she ate two of them.

I loved it when Mum had a day off I used to count the days until her shifts finished. Although she would be tired and sometimes down at least she would be there. We may have had a beautiful home but we never really saw Mum. Mum had said that my Dad was extremely cautious with money he would have to justify the spending of each and every penny and always ensuring that we always had a contingency fund in the form of savings. He would tell her that saving for a rainy day kept crisis away. I'm sure the lack of savings did niggle Mum I remember her planning to build up new savings over the next few years.

Mum's second encounter with the woman in green or IT as she refers to her was to occur almost two years after our move to Nigeria was cancelled. Mum was still constantly improving the house and updating the decor. Cushions, curtains, new bed linens and pictures were changed frequently to match the going colour schemes of the time. To keep up with changing interior fashions Mum enlisted her mother to accompany her on a trip to Derry to finalise her needs once and for all. She recounts the events of that day as if it were yesterday; I suppose if I experienced them I would too.

The day began like any other trip to Derry they drove across distinctive blue and white Craigavon Bridge towards the city centre. The traffic lights ahead had turned red so Mum slowed the car to a stop. As they were waiting on the lights to change she looked at the river Foyle below musing that it seemed extra high that day.

Her thoughts on the height of the river Foyle were interrupted when she heard her mother mutter "Jesus, Mary and Saint Joseph." She saw her mother rustle in her handbag and extract rosary beads. When Mum looked up to see what had unsettled her so much she saw a familiar face. A face she last saw before her husband died. The green monster 'IT', who Mum had encountered on the 16th of January 1980 in the Europa train station, was standing in front of the car. Once again IT had appeared from nowhere.

This time it was to find Mum on the Craigavon Bridge in Derry. IT loomed over the bonnet and stared directly at her and like their previous encounter transfixed Mum to the point of paralysis. Her mother prayed and prayed. Mum now whiter than white clutched the steering wheel so tightly that her knuckles were transparent, her bones threatening to protrude through the flesh. Her mother shook her and said "Gabrielle drive".

Her words also shook Mum too, for she came out of trance and turned the car. She followed her mother's instructions and drove all the way back to the town and straight to the parochial house.

They recounted the incident to the new priest Father O' Kane and he left them for a moment. Father O'Kane ran a charismatic prayer group within the town and was known to be close to God. When he returned to the room he said he would pray over them. He spent a long time with Mum yet rather than take comfort in that it made her more afraid.

The last words Mum remembers him uttering to her that day send shivers down my spine,

"I believe Satan takes many forms, and I believe you encountered him today, you must pray Gabrielle, you must keep praying."

Shaken they thanked him and left. Her mother now remembering the previous encounter Mum had told her about before Max died looked utterly mystified. Yet her devotion to the church and faith in God was so strong that she kept believed whatever they had seen was no threat, she said that she would keep praying and reassured Mum that she would be okay.

In the weeks and months that followed the apparition Mum was extra vigilant keeping us close and taking extra precautions with the car and the house. She ensured that no bomb had been planted, that no gun man could break in and that every possible danger was removed. Yet nothing happened. I developed severe asthma a month later and Mum says that she convinced herself that this was the reason behind the appearance; that I was going to die. I always laugh as I remind her that this wouldn't have been possible, after all only good die young! I remember missing a lot of school but I was fine. Alison and Maxine were also fine. Mum just couldn't understand the reappearance of that thing.

Father O'Kane came and blessed our house scattering Holy Water in every nook and cranny of each room. He would sit and pray with Mum. Yet nothing untoward happened. Mum began to think that the visit that day was simply to serve as a reminder that she was cursed, to tell her that whatever vendetta IT had against her was still in force.

Chapter Forty Three

It was only when Maxine and I in particular started asking Mum about our Dad again when the mystery was solved. One cold evening we sat by the fire and Mum took out a sealed box, it contained Dad's personal effects. Things she had put away because she couldn't bear to look at them. Yet she kept them as she wanted to have some sort of memorial for us when we would be old enough to understand. I think on this night she decided that we were old enough. She took out a pair of scissors and cut the tape of the box, I remember it contained lots of newspapers articles, romantic letters he had written to Mum, sympathy cards and a photo album which I still retain today. We had seen pictures of our Dad in Northern Ireland before with Mum and his extended family; we used to pour over the pictures. Yet we had never seen the album from Nigeria, I remember its thick green leather cover and the fine paper between each page. I remember absorbing every minute detail.

The men wore funny clothes I had thought and laughed, I now know that they were wearing the Nigerian national costume. The women were so pretty. I was so taken with examining every detail of every picture, looking at these relatives that I didn't know. I was so engrossed that I didn't notice that Mum had stopped talking that she was silent and holding her breath. One of us asked her what was wrong for her reaction unsettled us, yet she shook her head and said she was fine. She picked up the album and put it back in the box.

A few years later I was to learn that in the back of the album Mum had seen a picture that at first looked like any other family gathering. It was only on closer inspection that she saw a familiar face smiling at the camera, a familiar set of eyes. It was the woman, the 'IT' the bearer of bad tidings, that had haunted Mum since 1980. When Mum looked at the names listed below the figures she confirmed what instinct was already telling her. That the strange sinister force she had been visited bore a striking resemblance to her mother in law. This was something she could never confirm but a suspicion she cannot shake. That day alongside the physical shelf where Dad's box was stored, Mum placed the conundrum of her mother in law, her possible uncanny ability to visit her on a metaphorical shelf in her head.

Whilst no one significant incident occurred to account for the visit, I do believe that many minor incidents were all somehow heralded by it. I remember Mum sending Alison initially to a Catholic secondary school, but when she came home talking in Irish she was removed and placed in the nearest Protestant School she could find. Her mother was furious and not for the first time they were at loggerheads. Under her mother's instruction priests were dragged to our door to enlighten Mum on the errors of her ways. Mum was absolutely raging; she would decide where her children would be educated. No one, not her mother, not the priests or even the pope himself would sway her.

Mum did not need to be dictated to again and to ensure this was the case her solitary disposition came to the fore and she retreated from her families fold.

Over the years Mum blew hot and cold with her parents. I remember not seeing them for years at a time. I think they grew used to Mums erratic behavioural patterns and left her to sulk. As far as they were concerned she knew where they were if she needed them. Mum's independent streak and her bond with misery made certain that she seldom came back.

Chapter Forty Four

It didn't take long, not more than a year after the visitation that Mum started to believe that the curse was alive and well. In stringent, merciless NHS cutbacks she lost her job. That job was all that kept us afloat; it was hard enough when Mum was working. I panicked; I just couldn't see how we would cope. I was now ten or eleven and was acutely aware that we still hadn't accumulated any savings, every penny that came in was needed, there simply wasn't enough left to put away. It took three months for Mum to succeed in finding a new post, as Mum was paid at the end of the month it would be four months before we hit the all important pay day. The other problem was that even though the hospital was geographically less than a mile away it was in the Republic of Ireland; to the tax man this was a different country. Strabane was a border town and considered a part of Northern Ireland whilst Lifford where Mum's new post was, was considered to be in Ireland. In reality all that physically separated Ireland and Northern Ireland for residents of border towns was a mere footstep. Yet each country, neighbouring or not had different systems and governments, which had the implication that Mum would be paid in punts and that her tax rates would be different than what she had been used to.

As it transpired when Mum received her pay slip it looked great, yet due to heavier tax in Ireland she would lose almost than half of her earnings and even more again in the exchange of currency. Even though Mum worked, in effect we weren't much better off. The result being that she had to take on more shifts just to keep us afloat, until she was working what seemed to be continuously.

As we grew older we grew more expensive, secondary school uniforms, keeping up with our peers and even feeding us all required bigger budgets. A budget Mum no matter how hard she worked could not fulfil. When she did it was to the detriment of something else. Now on Mum's days off I would come home from school and find her staring at nothing, rather than being in bed. She would have a pile of unopened letters in front of her and the phone would be off the hook. It was as if she was cutting herself from all communication, what she didn't know couldn't harm her. Sometimes she would cry, she would say that it's hard to believe she was married to a chartered accountant yet all alone in this. I knew she was scared but remember a cruel part of me thinking 'get over it' and worse 'get on with it'.

I was eleven by this stage and being so young my life span was my eternity, I couldn't imagine anything gone before. I knew my dad had died nine years earlier but to my young mind that may as well have been ninety years earlier. Now I know that such a time frame is a blink of an eye.

One day after Mum had left for work (I knew she would be away for twelve hours) I resolved to get to grips with the situation myself. My sisters were at secondary school and out more and more with their friends, the repercussion being that I had lots of time to myself. I may as well make myself useful I mused. I came home from school and as usual lit the fire, peeled the spuds and put the dinner on. This day though was different for rather than retreat to the table to do my homework I went to the drawer in the living room where Mum had stashed the letters from the last fortnight. I took the heap out and worked my through the pile. There were bank statements, final demands and numerous bills. Some emblazoned with capital red letters and marked urgent.

Even then and as young as I was I knew the situation was dire. In the four months between pay checks we had lost almost everything and with Mum's pay being lower I just didn't know how we could regain it. I sat up late that evening trying to work something out to create a new budget based on clearing overheads and somehow getting us out of debt. It was much later that I remember it being said that most people are never more than three months away from the streets, when I look back on those times I know how true that saying is.

I tried my best to work out a solution but it seemed unworkable to my young mind. Mum's bond with her parents had been severed by her own accord. She had no one to turn to for help, despite searching everywhere it seemed that no financial assistance was available and losing our home was unfortunately inevitable. Mum began to crumble. I would shout at her that we needed money; she would shout back that she couldn't do any more. It was a dreadful time and Mum became depressed again. She found her old friend Misery and retreated to bed. All the letters and phone calls in the world couldn't find her there.

One day I had had enough, I was so upset and afraid that I confronted Mum bearing a cup of coffee and begging her to get up.

Mum's new drugs induced a trance like state so for the most part my pleas were ignored. My sisters were now accustomed to Mum's unpredictable behaviour so tended to avoid being home where possible. Yet somehow Mum listened to me this time, she saw her GP who introduced her to a new drug to keep her nerves and anxiety at bay: Diazepam. Misery retreated back from Mum a little and only tried to gain entrance when she wasn't busy.

After a few weeks the Diazepam and other drugs had taken their effect. Gone was Mum's trance like state and at last we were able to sit down and look at the letters,

"Mum, I've used all the money there's nothing left"

"It's ok," she reassured me "I'll get something organised"

"I spoke to the bank" I said afraid of Mums reaction "they're taking the house" bawling now I wailed "I tried to pay them as much as I could, but we ran out, I'm so sorry," I think my distress shook Mum into action.

The gravity of the situation confronted her; there was no going back on the banks decision. As all the letters and communication attempts were ignored we now had just twenty eight days to leave. Our last day in the house would be Christmas Eve.

"Right young lady" Mum said "it looks like, we're homeless, I suppose we'll be needing boxes to live in, there's four of us so one each perhaps? Or would you like to share?"

Her joke was lost on me and I wailed even more by this stage my understanding of the predicament was too strong. I even reminded Mum that this was no laughing matter.

That was the day that my proud Mum threw herself at the mercy of the state. Since Dad's death she had struggled alone, she had sought help from no one until now. Hesitantly and dripping in shame, she claimed social security and put her name down on the councils housing list. The man in the council offices had said that the timeframe she had given him was tight and it would be unlikely that a home would arise at such short notice, especially with Christmas coming up. Mum says that she panicked inwardly, but came home and told us to pack up, that she had secured a home.

The next few weeks were a waiting game; we had packed up our belongings but had nowhere to go. Homelessness loomed. Then when least expected with only three days to Christmas Mum received a call from the council.

A house had become available, enormous relief washed through her and she had to sit down to continue the call. Lighting a cigarette she braced herself to take in the good news. It was a good thing that she had sat down, for it seemed the only house that the council could find us, the only way we could avoid homelessness was to accept a house in the town's largest and most republican estate.

The estate was notorious, a large brown and grey sprawling development that housed many known terrorists, it was the hiding place for IRA arms and the meeting place for IRA campaigns. It was flooded with army on a daily basis. It had such a name that when we heard that someone lived there it was assumed that they were *in it up to their eyeballs*.

Mum used to warn us against befriending the children from the estate, as she feared ever coming into contact with their parents. Now we would be *from* the estate. Mum's stomach plunged and she begged the council to find something else, anywhere else. Unfortunately they could not. And so it became that the woman who had made a stand against the IRA, one of the town's only victims was left with no alternative but to live amongst them. It was a very unhappy Christmas that year.

Chapter Forty Five

Reluctantly we moved into the unknown enclave, only this time we were stony broke. We needed to carpet the house from top to bottom, get curtains and paint throughout. Council houses weren't left decorated and pretty like houses on the private market. The house had all necessary safety fixtures and fittings but it hadn't seen a coat of paint in many years. How we were to get the money in the wake of our Christmas repossession was a conundrum but one I soon solved by looking in the local paper.

A local car garage was paying cash at 'best' rates for cars and since that was about the only thing we had managed to cling onto I asked Mum if she would be prepared to sell ours. Like me she thought that this was a great idea, however she didn't relish the idea of selling the car locally. Instead she instructed me to go and get the 'Belfast Telegraph' where we could scan the classifieds for a garage further away, one that offered similar promises. Low and behold we found one, Mum gave them a ring and they agreed to buy our car on inspection and even replace it with another cheaper model, thus providing us with cash in hand whilst still having a means of transport. How they were going to do this was beyond me as our current car was far from new and worth little. Yet miracles did happen so Mum and I arranged to go to Enniskillen to meet the amazing car dealer.

Alison was cynical and preferred to stay at home whilst Maxine going through the awkward teenage stage preferred to mope to romantic music in her room. It would be just Mum and I on this journey.

After what seemed like an endless drive we arrived in Enniskillen and found the garage easily enough. The man Mum had spoken to on the phone met us and looked over our car; he nodded all the while seemingly happy with what he saw. He brought us into his office and told Mum he would take the car of our hands; he would give her £500 cash and another cheaper car. I was delighted and although Mum sat poker faced I knew she was too.

When everything was signed and sealed the salesman brought Mum and I out to the back of the garage, a place not seen by his regular customers. There he presented us with our new car. It was gorgeous red and so shiny, a four door Nissan Sunny a model that was all the rage back then. This car was better than the car we had traded in! Mum nudged me excitedly and eagerly took the keys from the sales man and we made our way towards our new car.

"Where are you going?" The sales man asked bemused,

"To the car" Mum replied,

"Sorry love I know we pride ourselves with value but we're not magicians" he said shaking his head laughing,

"Your cars against the wall there" He pointed to the very back of the yard.

Eclipsed by the shinning Nissan was our car. It was parked tightly against the wall in the furthest most reaches of the garage; it was as if even they were ashamed to have it. I can honestly say it was a banger like no other. A brown fiesta so old it looked like if you touched it, even sneezed beside it, it would disintegrate. It was difficult to determine if its unique colour was rust or paint. It wasn't difficult to determine the colour of our faces however, for both our faces burned red with shame.

Ten minutes later still red faced we both clambered in, we couldn't get out of the yard quick enough; the cars slow pace did not help in our efforts. When we got round the corner Mum pulled over at a cafe and said we may as well get our tea. We entered the cafe and sat down laughing so hard that we didn't get a chance to look around us. When we did it was too late. The cafe was straight out of a time warp. It consisted of two tables with little blue and yellow (formerly white) checked table cloths, locals gossiping in the corner and 1950's decor. The waitress was upon us before we could escape or even comment,

"Just two teas" Mum said

"Auck is that all? We have good specials on today too" she said "two for the price of one"

Mum sighed and asked what they had; we were hungry after all,

"Stew or beef burgers" she said,

"Maybe the burgers, do you want one Jayne?" Mum asked.

The waitress looked at me with such pleading eyes that I was afraid I would offend her if I said no, so I reluctantly agreed to have a burger and nodded my answer to Mum.

"Two burgers then" Mum said

We anxiously awaited our burgers rather frightened at what we would presented with, all the while watching as the oldest lady I had ever seen tucked into a bowl of stew.

Eventually our burgers arrived delivered by the smiling and as we discovered to our horror, toothless waitress. A smile is always a pleasant sight but when one smiles with no teeth the overall picture is not at oil painting to put it mildly.

When she left us Mum looked at her burger then at me, in the middle of the baps was a meat ball it clearly hadn't been flattened or had undergone any attempt at being shaped like a burger. We dissolved into giggles much to the distaste of the clientele. Afraid for our lives we quickly composed ourselves and ate around the baps.

Just like in the garage half an hour earlier we couldn't get out quick enough and as Mum went to pay for our interesting dinner I watched as the stew eating old lady scraped her bowl clean, her spoon clattering against the dish as she scooped up every drop. Clearly not satisfied that every morsel was gone, she removed her false teeth and with her forefinger she scarped the remainders of her stew from the rim and sucked it. The image stayed with me for a long time.

Once we paid we readied ourselves for our journey home. We climbed into the car and began the trip back to Strabane, it was a long trip not helped by the fact that the car shuddered when it reached more than thirty miles per hour. Yet the journey gave us time to count the holes on the floor. In true Flintstone style we slowly made our way back laughing all the way. We decided that we would have been home quicker if we'd walked! I always remember that in the absence of a disguise I ducked as low as I could on entering Strabane. That was how I spent any journey I was ever forced to go on in that car.

Now we lived in a council estate and drove a banger, I wondered could we get any lower. On the plus side we had had a hilarious day and had secured enough to get the house decorated so I supposed it wasn't all bad.

Chapter Forty Six

Gradually we settled into the estate, our immediate neighbours were an elderly couple and we grew very fond of them. Directly behind our house was the back of another house. As this house was elevated slightly more than ours, it meant that its residents could see into our bedrooms with ease. As our house was lower than theirs we could only see into their kitchen and gardens. We tried not to look, the same way we tried to ignore the residents hiding guns in the manhole and the comings and goings of shady figures in the night.

This was going on right across the estate, right across the town right and right across the country. In light of the enormity of such dealings, Mum warned us all to ignore anything we had seen or heard. It was like living in a gold fish bowl and like goldfish we would have to have very short memories if we were to survive here. Yet I knew Mum was seething; if pride comes before a fall then she must have been the proudest of them all, for she had certainly fallen not just once but over and over again. Everything my Dad had aspired to, every dream he had, Mum was unwillingly doing the opposite.

To make matters worse, a thousand times worse Mum's kindly grandmother, Dad's main champion, began to take ill. She started to become confused and disorientated and no one needed to tell Mum that she was suffering from dementia. The symptoms grew and grew until she no longer recognised her family. Within two years of their onset she had died. I was young at the time so don't remember much about Nanny taking ill I just remember how upset Mum was and that she cried and cried.

Every month when Mum exchanged her month's punts into sterling, we would watch what looked like a decent salary fade to a pittance. We were still being pursued by the bank on what was left of the mortgage and found that many other bills were falling behind. This was when I remember Mums shifts really increasing. Now that we were all a little older Mum nursed around the clock. To access Mum these days it was easier to phone the hospital because when she was at home she was so tired she just slept. When I asked Mum about those days she says she was angry, angry that we were growing and just as in our early years she was missing out on us. She would watch other woman working normal hours if working at all and she grew bitter. She was working so much she barely had time to live; she worked to support us the irony being that in supporting us she never saw us.

It was in those early days that I remember having my first thoughts on my weight. I began to worry about my normal body shape and in some sort of dysmorphic mind-set I saw myself as obese. I started to skip the occasional meal; after all who no one was ever there so no one would notice. As long as I had the dinner ready and the house tidy no one was around to see if I ate. Besides which I had more important things to deal with than food, I had to make sure we kept afloat.

Mum used to allow me to go and cash her salary cheque, this was especially essential when she worked nights. When I cashed the cheque I dished out the money to the various creditors and would spend hours trying to work out how to make it elastic so it would stretch until the end of the month. It was a puzzle I never solved.

Maxine at the time was getting in with a bad a crowd, I remember Mum trying her best to dissuade her, but with the hours she worked she just wasn't there long enough to check up.

Alison now eighteen had shunned the academic route and travelled down the route of beauty. She entered beauty contests province wide and even made it into the finals in Miss Northern Ireland. She had started courting a young man from the country and when not posing for the camera, she spent all her free time with him.

It would have been hard on two parents having three teenage girls but for Mum she had to exercise the role of both mother and father and become a tight disciplinarian. That was when she got the time. I'm sure she needed support in these days more than ever, a husband, someone to help her with us. She says that she was painfully aware of our dad's absence during our teens. All we were painfully aware of was a presence rather than an absence; the stick! Mum had introduced her childhood nemeses to us in order to retain control.

Chapter Forty Seven

After years of working full time and then some, Mum grew tired of nursing she simply had nothing more to give. Once she had compassion and respect for each and every patient, but now she viewed them all as great big time consuming *lumps*. She began to resent her patients and feared that they resented her too. She did her best to plaster a smile on her face when she was treating them and for the most part it worked.

Mum often told me about the day when she finally had enough. She had been asked by a colleague to draw blood from a lady in the hospital. Mum had always been expert in finding veins, where none seemed available. If any of her colleagues had difficulty in extracting blood they would call her. After struggling to find a vein in the old ladies paper like skin, the young nurse whom Mum was on duty with called for her assistance. Mum tied the lady's arm and for the first time in almost twenty years of nursing failed to find a vein.

She apologised to the patient telling her that she would try her other arm. The woman was old and the situation could be seen as traumatic for her, so she was as gentle as she could be.

Just as she was tying her other arm, the woman said,

"I'm not surprised really,"

"Oh?" Mum said, not really listening to her, so intent she was on not hurting her,

"Sure you can do nothing right"

"Pardon?" Mum was all ears now.

"You couldn't even have children right; didn't you end up with three black bastards?"

Mum dropped everything and turned her back on the horrible woman. She didn't care if they had to enlist Count Dracula himself to take her blood. In fact she hoped they did! Her colleagues were also disgusted and the woman was despatched to a different ward where Mum wouldn't have to see her hideous face again.

Of course Mum had had racist jibes before, especially working in the small towns in and around Strabane, but never had they made her want to pack the whole thing in. If it wasn't for our dire financial mess, she would have turned her back on nursing there and then but unfortunately she couldn't. She was tied to the job, to big *lumps* forever, it seemed.

Even with all Mum's hours our cupboards were still bare, Mum still didn't have any friends it seemed her life revolved around work and rest. I felt sorry for her then as to me she was so pretty yet she never had any fun or even a fragment of a life; all she had was worry.

Alison helped as best she could but her low wage barely skimmed the edges of our debts. She was at secretarial training college and got paid a trainee wage enough to get her to and from work. Maxine was in her final year at school and I was only thirteen. We were useless to Mum. I used to tell her how useless I felt and she would say even if we were millionaires she would not expect anything from her children. All she expected from us was for us to be happy. If only she knew that with the situation as bleak as it was, we never could be. How could we be happy when she was so sad?

Maxine and I didn't have any clothes and shopping became a distant memory. Mum began wearing her uniform even on her day off. One of my saddest memories was Mum dividing one beef burger, all that remained in our freezer between four and serving it up for dinner. No one complained, this was just how it was. We all lived for the end of the month, when we could stock the cupboards again.

We fell into a feast or famine pattern, when Mum got paid she would stock up the cupboards, heat the house and even get us small gifts. The result was that for three weeks out of four we had no food, no heat and often no electric. Things appeared so grim that I feared Misery returning. Mum pre-empted her though and went to the doctors who instantly increased her drugs

I was now fourteen and I remember Mum buying the 'Belfast Telegraph' more often than usual. I guess she was assessing our current predicament, she seen that she didn't have any friends or money, in fact the only thing that held her to the town was her job. She contemplated what she was doing there after all she hated it and we hated it. It was then she realised that nothing, absolutely nothing was holding us there. Mum made a decision then, a decision that pains me most of all because it shows me that Mum tried, she wanted happiness and she wanted a chance. There was still something in her then.

She had been happy once, she had been happy in Belfast. Mum would chase that happiness and put this gloomy town behind her, she would return to where she once had a life. We would all be happy; we would blend in more in a city. Mum reasoned that it was 1993, and the world had moved on from the 1970's, racism was generally condemned and we could make a fresh start. By now Belfast would have changed, Mum was sure that by now it would be home to more families from different ethnicities. Our family would no longer stand out; we would no longer be oddities.

All the horrible incidents of Mum's past were firmly placed on her shelf; she had a glimmer of hope on the horizon and we were all swayed by her enthusiasm. I was not so keen on moving to Belfast but Mum's optimism was contagious and at last for the first time in my life it seemed Misery was a friend Mum wanted to dump. To me Mum was filled with hope; her new plans may just make the disposal of Misery possible. It was therefore settled that we would all move back to Belfast.

Chapter Forty Eight

We moved to Belfast in March 1994, we began our time in the city full of hope and gullibility. For Mum the move heralded a new start, just what her family needed. Just as twenty years before the big city lights beaconed to her once again.

Mum didn't have any friends in Strabane she had resolutely stayed away from the townsfolk and once again was on bad terms with her family, so we had few goodbyes to say.

Mum's now thoroughly blackened credit rating ensured that buying a house was out of the question, the Housing Executive had nothing available on its transfer list so the only option we had was to find a rental. Every day we scoured the Telegraph for something within our measly price bracket. Mum was astounded to find that we were priced out of South Belfast area. The rents there were alarmingly high. Even if she worked twenty- four- seven, her wallet would just not be big enough.

This didn't discourage her though; instead she said we would have to consider new unknown parts of the city. We knew form the daily news bulletins that the West was predominately Catholic and the East predominately Protestant. Coming from a small town that was entirely Catholic Mum wanted to live in a mixed area. She said she couldn't cope with the thought of a religiously segregated area again. Where segregation existed bigotry was bred. So we took a risk and went with the only other part of Belfast that was left, the North.

It was a fun time as we searched for houses; we would scroll through the small print of the Telegraph's classified and put a big circle around the houses that we could afford. Then we would phone the landlords and ask questions about the smaller details, what type of heat it had, were pets allowed etc.

It didn't take long before we found a house that seemed ideal, it was a good price and the landlord claimed it was in a quiet family area. Google didn't exist in those days so Mum went on trust; he seemed a genuine man. Over the next year he would be working on a series of repairs, but for now it was clean and comfortable. When he assured her that the house would be a long-term let and that we could have it for as long as we wanted it she was sold. Rather than make the two hour journey to Belfast to view Mum took him at his word and signed all the relevant paperwork from home. She wrote a cheque for the deposit, a month in advance and the next month's rent. She paled at the amount of money it had cost but all the furniture was included and we had nothing to do but move in. We could sell our current furniture and gain some of the money back. In that respect it could be viewed it as a saving; she would just have to find a job as soon as we arrived to ensure further rent instalments were made. Within five days the keys arrived in the post and we were good to move.

Naivety was always one of Mum's strong points and on seeing the new home she knew her strong point had not let her down!

I will never forget it; it was the most dilapidated house I had ever seen. Before we even set foot in the door I knew that Mum had made a huge mistake. I think she did too I knew by her face which was clamped into a tight frown. I wanted to run back to the grim council estate but even then at fourteen I knew it was too late. Anywhere would be better than this ramshackle excuse for a house.

As the removal men moved what little furniture we had brought in I cringed, this was Mum's good clean furniture, furniture that I remember her struggling to buy. After a week in here it would surely be destroyed. The windows were paper thin, some were even cracked. If I had applied any pressure to them I knew they would shatter. The walls were decorated with little blue black splodges that could only be damp. On opening the kitchen cupboard I encountered an army of ants.

We were all horrified, but there was nothing for it we were here now, so we got stuck in and began to help Mum attempt to clean the place up. As soon as our phone was connected Mum called the landlord and told him of her concerns that his house was not as described. He reassured her that he knew there was work to be done and that it was his top priority. Mum called him every week at the start, soon she gave up.

The move meant that I had missed a considerable amount of school and I was keen to escape the damp house. I asked Mum if we could find a school over the next few weeks, she agreed and together we sat over a map of Belfast to find the nearest grammar. Low and behold it seemed that we were within a mile of a school, we called it and they were happy to see me. Within two weeks I was ensconced in Belfast Royal Academy (BRA).

There I had my eyes opened, I had come from a small country convent school and all of a sudden was faced with a school with over a thousand pupils and things I had never encountered; boys and Protestants. I can honestly say that prior to BRA I had spent my life surrounded solely by Catholics, Protestants were few and far between where I had grown up. The school meant that I mixed with people from all walks of life and religions and I found that this was a good life lesson, perhaps the only thing I can be thankful to the school for. In those first few years I hated it, I hated the uniform a long sweeping grey ankle length skirt, I hated the pretentiousness and I hated the city children with their mature ways. The school had a certain coldness to it and from my perspective seemed to value the more affluent children.

I knew I wanted to go to university, I knew to do so I would have to be at school. Reluctantly I spent four years in that school; most of which involved polishing up my maths skills as I counted down how many days I had left before I could leave!

Chapter Forty Nine

A month into life in Belfast we all had plans or knew what we were intending to do. I was now in school and Maxine and Alison were looking for work. Alison quickly found an office job and Maxine a place in the local technical college. Mum too found work, for it seemed the city was littered with nursing homes; it wasn't long before she was once again buried in rigorous twenty-four hour shifts alternating her weeks between day and night duty.

I could see little difference in our daily life in Belfast but Mum had wanted to move here so much I decided to give it more of a chance, I was sure that the city must have some merits. Very quickly it emerged that Belfast wasn't what Mum had thought it would be either. The people she encountered in Belfast were not what she had remembered. She didn't approach her old friends; she had lost touch with them when we had been moved back to Strabane. When I asked her why she wouldn't contact them she would say she couldn't let any of them see her living like this. Rather than give up though she tried to make contact with the locals, Mum wanted friends, she had lacked them for so long, yet no matter how friendly she was they clearly weren't interested in befriending her.

I feared she would reach out for her old friend Misery again but luckily enough Mum had found a new GP in Belfast. This doctor seemed more promising than Strabane's doctor when Mum explained her symptoms he had Mum assessed by a psychiatrist and even secured a diagnosis. Mum had severe depression a result of two factors; nursing carnage victims of the troubles and of course Dad's murder. Mum had been experiencing flashbacks for many years along with extreme depression and suicidal thoughts. She could never function normally with such a condition. Unfortunately, no treatment existed and the doctor believed that counselling at this stage twelve years after the bomb would be futile, instead based on the psychiatrists' recommendations Mum was started on a new course of drugs. These would help her; they would keep Misery away I thought.

When Mum received her first pay cheque, I was a little shocked to see how little the private nursing homes paid, I didn't voice my thoughts but I can remember panicking a little wondering how we would cope on it. I knew what had happened before in the absence of savings and I worried about a repeat performance. I worried so much that I began to become introverted as my mind ran over all the possible scenarios. I remember going to schools friends houses and being acutely aware of how differently they lived of how their Mum's were so *normal*, of how they stayed awake all day and of how they had fathers. My response was to stop eating. It gave me a chance to concentrate on something other than our current predicament, on my Mum who even then I knew was just not right.

My overwhelming memory of the time was being so unhappy. I had been swept up by Mum's enthusiasm to move, yet the city was now an unknown entity. We had gone for a walk around on our first weekend here and every street was scarred, the Antrim Road, the Limestone Road, Cliftonville Road and the Shore road. It didn't matter which for as we walked along them Mum listed the atrocities that had occurred on them. A shooting on this one, a bombing on the other, the streets of this city she had said are like little memorials, each one had its own part to play in the troubles.

That was the day when she asked me,

"How could any place be good when all this bloodshed has occurred?"

My stomach plunged as I knew Mum hadn't moved any further forward. In fact Belfast seemed to take her right back. The move hadn't made everything okay like I had thought, that was when I had a shiver of dread, of knowing. What if moving back to Belfast had make things worse? What if the move was an even bigger mistake than I had initially thought? I was slowly realising that by moving Mum had simply been chasing a past.

A past that like my Dad was dead.

I really looked forward to our first trip to the city centre Mum had said that we all deserved a day out and that she would give us a tour. In the absence of our fiesta, or the 'brown bomber' as I had dubbed it (it had fallen apart before the move) we got a taxi into the city centre rather than brave the buses. I sat quietly in the back seat looking around me, Belfast then seemed so huge, the buildings were taller and the streets wider than anything I had been used to. When we reached the back of Castlecourt we got out of the taxi. Alison and I rushed ahead eager to experience the thrill of the big shops that the 'Clothes Show' and 'Mizz' magazine ranted on about. It was a great day at first; everything was so new, glossy and modern. We were so busy taking in the sights that it was only when we were walking along the upstairs of the shopping centre that I noticed all eyes were on us,

"Mum look" I said feeling my face reddening under the harsh lights.

Mum looked around for what I saw and could clearly find nothing out of the ordinary. It was then she noticed that things were very ordinary, too ordinary. She saw what we always saw when we were out. People were staring, heads whirled around as we passed, eyes directed towards us, taking us up and down. It was horrendous, I stared back, hoping they would avert their eyes but they continued to gawp. It was then that I looked at the scene surrounding us and noted that yet again, my sisters and I were the solitary black faces in the whole centre.

I wanted to cry Mum had promised that things would be different here, that city life was perfect for us; instead my sisters and I were the subject of curiosity, oddities once again. People believed they could stare openly at us if because our skin was brown, as if it wouldn't hurt us. Our shopping trip ended quickly that day and I became resigned that in Northern Ireland, the place where I was born and bred, that my sisters and I would always stand out like sore thumbs.

Chapter Fifty

After three months, twelve long weeks in the damp miserable dwelling the landlord hadn't darkened the door. We were wasting our money even phoning him. I knew that the promised repairs were never going to be carried out. I could see Mum's eyes beginning to go vague, she was seeing but not seeing. I knew Misery was approaching. My sisters and I managed to block her just in time before she sunk her claws into Mum. We had Mum seen by her friendly GP who topped up her medication again. It is only now that I am older that I can definitively say that Mum's condition was to worsen in my teens because she had more time to think about her past.

The treatment offered by any doctor Mum had ever seen was more drugs, she became like a walking pharmacy yet they kept prescribing more. I used to tell her that she would rattle if shook. A link with post-traumatic stress and victims of the troubles was an abstract tentative notion back then. Unfortunately it has only recently been discovered as a valid illness for people in Northern Ireland. The late link between the illness and victims meant destruction for Mum and the bulk of her adult life and as a direct result the lives of her children.

However at fifteen I found Mum's doctor a God send, I knew little about mental illness back then. All I knew was that Mum's doctors willingly dispensed her any drug she felt would be of use. It was easier for them, easier to ignore the root of her problems. For me it meant that the drugs kept Misery away or at least held her back a little, it meant I had my Mum back.

Having Mum's full attention was crucial in that house; with no success with the household repairs it was time for us to move again. We were fortunate in that we found a little home that was clean and fresh and in an area that was wonderfully friendly. We all liked the house and after living in such a hovel the basic little terrace felt palatial. We didn't get our deposit back from our old landlord but no one complained, not even Mum who had to work on her days off to build a new deposit, and instead we were just relieved to be on the move.

Not that I saw much of my sisters these days. Alison had become engaged to a man she had met in her beauty queen days. She was constantly accompanied by her new fiancée. Maxine had become even more withdrawn and independent than ever and took advantage of Mum's working patterns.

Much to my annoyance my abnormal eating patterns began to get noticed. I had thought I had hid my new slim-lined self well, obviously not well enough. My baggy tee-shirts and jeans failed to conceal the bones that now poked through my skin. I was skeletal. Soon my Mum and sisters were constantly ranting and wailing at me. One day they would be cross, the next sympathetic but on all days they tried to make me eat.

In the meantime I continued making the dinners, cleaning, cooking and looking after the household bills. It took my sudden collapse before the doctor who had tired of getting dragged to make a diagnosis. I had developed anorexia and bulimia. A lethal combination one that I would carry with me into early adulthood, any time the going got tough from that point on my eating patterns became peculiar.

Mt fifteenth and sixteenth years were spent avoiding everything to do with food. Mum had Misery and I had my eating disorder, everyone had their coping mechanisms I would reason, mine was just more noticeable than others.

Now Mum tells me that she was so desperate for me to get well that she began praying again, she would pray to my Dad imploring him to help. She knew she needed to spend time with me but she also needed to work if we were to have a roof over our heads.

She said she needed him for so many things, to give her the okay on Alison's fiancée and to bring Maxine back within the fold. Yet Mum faced the problems alone.

I was taken to the Mater hospitals A&E after a further collapse; they could do little but recommended some sort of counselling. Mum remembers leaving the hospital that day feeling totally useless. She blamed herself she spent what little free time she had monitoring me and gradually I gained weight, although even now I can say that I never fully recovered.

Meanwhile life went on as it tends to do and the public holidays were approaching. This particular holiday, was celebrated nowhere in the world but Northern Ireland. As the glorious twelfth of July loomed our friendly little street soon was a little less friendly. It became littered in red white and blue flags and sectarian connotations. The stones on the pavements were painted to match the flags. We never had to deal with this particular holiday in Strabane so watched the spectacle with interest.

On the night before the holiday, 'the eleventh' the festivities began. Revellers lit a huge bonfire and partied around it until the small hours. The bonfire was stacked high. I was ashamed to admit that Mum had contributed to it! In a bid to get rid of some pieces of old rickety furniture that had come with our house, we had given it to children who collected wood from the doors in the weeks before the twelfth. I remember how delighted Mum was; giving them the wardrobes saved us the hassle of getting rid of them ourselves.

On the top of the bonfire stood an effigy of a famous IRA politician, Mum laughed when she saw it and decided then and there that she was born into the wrong side of the fence. If only the effigy were real she thought! That night I listened to them condemn the IRA, show their strength by shooting bullets into the air. It was their final actions that sent a chill through my core, they condemned each and every Catholic, they tarred all Catholics with the terrorist brush. I think Mum was taken aback by the levels of hatred they showed as well and she told me to come away from the window and go to bed.

The bitterness emanating from their words presented Mum with another side to Northern Ireland, a side just as bitter as the side she hated. This place was poisoned she would say, one sides as bad as the other, there will never be peace here. I understand her reasoning because the parents of the entrenched on both sides would infect their children and on and on it would go. Hatred and suspicion would always remain and with it other families would be shattered like mine.

It didn't take long for the locals to discover that they had Catholics in their midst, I really believe they smelt us! Little threats came through the letter box and once again we were on the move.

This time we choose a Catholic area, again in North Belfast. Yet soon IRA supporters discovered; they always had their ways, exactly who we were. A few years later we were to try living in North Belfast again, we got a reasonably priced rental on Alliance Avenue. We didn't stay there long.

Chapter Fifty One

I began to notice that Mum was growing tired, more tired than I had ever seen weariness was etched on her face. We had been in Belfast now for three years and moved five times. In the background the peace process had began. The news that peace had been delivered was broken to Mum and I by a jubilant crowds in a chemist shop. She was collecting her prescription when the hugging and celebrating began. We asked them what the occasion was? We were told we had peace; Northern Ireland was at peace at last.

"Well it's come too late for us" Mum said, but her voice was drowned out by their cries of jubilation.

We had moved back to South Belfast, the rents were higher but at least the areas were mixed. None of us could stand living in one sided areas. More to the point the last few years proved that these areas couldn't stand us either! So to cope with the rents Mum took on even more hours and now worked seventy two hour weeks. She was paying a high price to live in this area so much that ironically she never saw our house.

I was doing my A- Levels at the time, I remember the days passing in a whirl of essays and exams. The only real thing that stands out for me during those years was meeting Mum on her way home from work one day. She had left me a fiver to get some provisions after school, which I had done so I took my little dog to the park. The dog became over excited and ran off and then I noticed that he was running in the direction of someone in the distance, as I got closer I saw it was Mum. She looked all done in but I remember she smiled pleased to see me and my crazy dog. I remember remarking what she was doing walking; she normally caught the bus or got a lift. She muttered something about it being a dry day. We began to walk home together when I noticed that Mum wasn't keeping up, she was a good six steps behind. I looked at her puzzled saying "get a move on" when my eyes were drawn down.

Mum's heels were bleeding, her red blood a stark contrast against her white nurses shoes.

"Mum what happened?" I asked

Then it occurred to me, before she could even answer I said,

"Please don't tell me you walked"

"Okay I won't" she laughed

Mum had given me her last that morning, she had known she couldn't make it home from work yet she said nothing. Instead she walked all the way from the Sanddown Road to the Lisburn Road.

I was lost for words and she and I made our way home in silence.

Luckily Mum soon found another nursing home nearby, it was during her time working there that she once again came home worse for wear. It transpired that a colleague approached her and told her that a younger nurse working there was also from Strabane. Apparently she had been talking about Mum.

It took a while for me to extract the full story but it seemed that the younger nurse took great delight in telling all Mum's colleagues that Gabrielle horror *of horrors* had three black daughters! She took great delight in running my sisters and I down it seemed. The nurse was snobbish and spoke of her background as if she stemmed directly from royalty. Mum just couldn't work out who she was. The country girl in Mum came out, as her small town habits came to the fore. Hailing from a small town everyone knew everyone or they knew someone who knew someone! Yet Mum could not place her.

It was only when she discovered that she was married, that things began to click. Mum had been trying to establish exactly who she was using her married name, no wonder all her leads ended nowhere. As soon as she discovered her maiden name she established exactly who she was. Mum also learned exactly what she had been saying about our family. She looked down on us and Mum in particular all because we were black. Now that Mum knew who she was however, it wasn't long until she turned the tables. This nurse, this snobbish creature had been the offspring of one of the town's most working class families; in fact working class was too high a title, rather than coming from great things Mum claimed that this girl had come from the gutter.

When Mum revealed the younger girls true background and her surprise at her newly acquired plumy tones, the rumours soon stopped. Yet Mum was horrified that someone at the bottom, the very bottom of the social heap, felt that because she had black daughters that she was someone to be looked down upon. The staff were supportive and told her to take it with a pinch of salt. Even though Mum had felt she had brought an end to the situation and that it wouldn't happen again I remember feeling awful, I was so upset that someone could talk about my Mum like that.

All because of us.

After hearing Mum's experience it was reinforced to me that racism was everywhere and I think Mum realised that it was something she would always have to cope with. Just because my Mum had married the man that she loved and had his children she would forever be tarred. Mum had done nothing but follow her heart I still fail to understand how that was so wrong. Even years later, people still believed that Mum was guilty of a heinous crime. My Mum would always be punished for falling in love.

I think that incident where Mum was made to feel bad about meeting and marrying my Dad was when his box that she had tucked far away in her mind, began to rumble. She would voice more often that she wanted him here so much. If he were here she wouldn't be in this mean place, she wouldn't have to listen to such remarks, to be judged. My parents could have faced these people together. If my Dad were here, my sisters and I wouldn't have needed our incessant questions. If Dad were here Misery and Mum would never have been acquainted.

Chapter Fifty Two

One night after a few drinks Alison's boyfriend picked up his car keys to prepare for his journey home. He was drunk so Mum promptly snatched the car keys from him and demanded that he slept on the sofa. His reaction came from nowhere. He pushed Mum with such force that he slammed her into a wall; he even kicked one of my dogs, so hard that he broke her tiny rib. Inside Mum says she screamed for Dad as she knew she couldn't take this man on alone. She didn't have to. Maxine and I were screaming at him to leave her alone, we pulled at him and eventually restrained him. Alison just sat there, she was in shock.

Alison ran out after him and the pair drove off into the night. That night he had a car crash. Alison who didn't drive was said to have been behind the wheel. Yet eye witness accounts claimed otherwise. Mum banned my sister then in her early twenties from seeing that man ever again. If a man could show that type of violence to his mother in law then what could she expect. Alison ignored Mums warnings and within a year they were married. We did not attend the ceremony.

Maxine was the next to fly the nest; she had been in the city centre one day when someone asked her the question that my sisters and I were often asked,

"Where are you from?"

"Belfast, then Strabane, and then Belfast again!" She had replied

"But where were you from before that?"

"The only other place I've lived in was Strabane "she had said

"Aye, but where were you born?"

"Belfast" she replied,

The woman had laughed asking her what age she was, when Maxine told her she was twenty, the woman had responded,

"People like you aren't born here; there was no one like you here twenty years ago."

That week she had a few more racist jibes and came home in tears.

"Mum I can't listen to these people anymore; they won't allow me to say I'm from here"

She had no answer for her.

Two months later my sister and my best friend moved to London. She said she would never be back. To date bar one special occasion she has kept her promise.

Mum was growing more and more tired and once again falling behind on the bills, I did my best to pay them but A–Levels took priority. Then a rent increase left us in severe trouble. Our cupboards held half a bag of sugar and a tin of beans. After my previous bout with eating disorders I wasn't a big eater, nor was Mum but we were so hungry a tin of beans would barely take the edge of it.

Mum was working so hard that on the face of it we should have been surviving, holding things together but all the moving took its toll, each new house we got required some sort of furniture, some sort of improvement whether it was furnished or not. Each house required a removal van for our personal effects we had no car, and most expensive of all each house required a month's rent in advance and a deposit. We never saw our deposits again there was always an excuse for not fulfilling them. We grew tired of filling other peoples oil tanks, carpeting their floors, painting their walls and carrying out repairs that were not our duty to do. Eventually we were spent out; we were left with the choice pay the rent or eat.

For the first month after the rent increase, we choose to pay the rent. That month I remember being poorer than ever before and knowing no solution. I would tell Mum I would leave school get a job but she always steadfastly refused. My Dad wanted us to have an education, she would never force one on us like his parents did, but when one of us was interested she would never and could never take that option from us. If she made me give up on my university dream she would have failed me and more importantly my Dad's wishes. We made a loaf of bread last for a week and raised £1, which we used to buy a bag of potatoes.

When I peeled the first potato I discovered it was off; I had inkling when a rancid odour wafted my way when I opened the bag. I bundled the bag up, receipt in hand and went to the shop keeper who I had just bought them from. He had told me he hadn't sold me those. I pointed out to him that he had, showing him the pile I had gotten them from and he chased me away, saying,

"You blacks are always trying to take the hand". We did without our potatoes that week and had thrown away our precious pound.

Chapter Fifty Three

I had always aspired to go off to university and would turn eighteen soon. It would nearly be time for my compensation payment awarded to me by the state on Dad's death. Mum and I were in a mess so I promised her that whatever funds the state had awarded would be used to help us out. Our spirits were lifted as we knew we only had to endure this situation for a few more months.

It was during this time that Mum received a call from home, her father had become unwell. He would be treated in Belvior hospital in Belfast. She was able to see him every day as he was being treated in the city. The nurse in Mum had seen his diagnosis many times before and therefore knew his prognosis was not good. Her father had lung cancer. He deteriorated quickly, it was so, so sad. Her father loved a yarn, he would talk to whoever would listen yet he was left with a disease that took away his breath, it had rendered him speechless.

It wasn't long before we received another call; her father who had returned back to his home town in a break from treatment, had taken a turn for the worst. Mum had to get to the hospital in Derry that night. Yet we had no funds. We had nothing and no one to ask. Mum called the hospital in Derry and asked them to phone her with any news, if he got worse or if he became stable. That night my Mum received a call from her sibling.

"Your fathers dead" she said and disconnected the call. I watched as Mum sunk to the floor, she remained there for many hours.

Alison was informed and with her fiancée we made the trip to his wake and his funeral. We were ignored by most and lambasted by others. No one cared why my Mum couldn't make it that night; she wasn't there, that was all that mattered.

Yet she carried her father, the other great man in her life with her and thought of him daily.

Chapter Fifty Four

Mum must have gone to work and listened to her colleagues' talk of holidays, socialising and nights out as I do now. Even if they spoke of something as basic as shopping, she must have felt about an inch high. She had an empty cupboard, empty wardrobe and empty stomach. For the pleasure of living in South Belfast, the only place we were *allowed* to live, the rent was strangling us. At the end of that month she asked me not to pay the rent. Instead she said we would phone the landlord and tell him we were struggling, he seemed an affable man. Maybe we could arrange some sort of repayment plan with him. We would buy some food, even get an outfit each and have a nice day out. That's what we did and again on the next month and the next.

Therefore our eviction came as no surprise; once again we began a search for another house. This time we were back at the mercy of the council. They found us a house on Belfast's Ormeau road, and we tried our best to make a home of it. Unfortunately we faced the usual dilemma; we had no money and no furniture. Privately renting didn't allow us to accumulate furniture as the landlords used their own. The house had recently been renovated, bare walls and cement floors were its main features. For the first few months we slept on bundles of the few clothes we had.

Then at last my money came through and like my sisters before me Mum expressed her disappointment. In her grief stricken state 16 years earlier she had trusted the state to invest the money awarded on the death of our Dad with care. Since mine had been held the longest, Mum assumed that I would attain a good sum. Instead I received £150 more than Maxine, who received £150 more than Alison. My sisters and I began 16 years ago with £2000 each and we all finished with just under £5000.

Yet neither Mum nor I were in a position to complain, how we needed that money. To me it seemed liked millions! I had hoped to attend Trinity University to study Law if my A level results were good enough and intended this money to fund my studies. I had second thoughts when I compared what I received with the price of a degree in Dublin. Instead I decided that I would spend her university years here in Belfast and stay at home to save funds.

Mum admits now that inside she seethed. My Dad had considered education his top priority. Mum couldn't help she could barely support us as it was. Had my Dad been alive I knew I could have attended ten universities fully funded if it meant I was pursuing an education. The box marked Max in Mum's head had begun to rumble again and she could feel her old friend Misery approach. This time I believe she struggled to push her aside.

Chapter Fifty Five

The TV was now full of news about the victims of the troubles; I watched keenly and thought that maybe we would be okay after all. There were over three thousand victims and something was to be put in place to help them. Maybe these new incentives could help Mum? I thanked the heavens, Mum had shouldered too much alone. The new Labour government with the bright young Tony Blair at the Helm was forward thinking and committed to devolving the country. It seemed we would get some sort of recognition for those who had been lost.

Mum and I didn't get time to dwell on the news as yet again we had another house to furnish and fix. Mum had to do this between her long shifts and me between A–Level revision. I wondered where we would get the time. With my money we did what we could with the house and created a comfortable home.

By some miracle I got the grades in my A- Levels I needed to attend the Law course in Trinity, Mum was so proud, she said Dad would have been too. Mum cried that day, although she was elated she was saddened too because my Dad wasn't there. In the end the Trinity course was too expensive and that was before we had even looked into Dublin accommodation. Mum and I agreed that Queen's was a good choice and that a university was a university (within reason).

I started Queen's in September 1997, as I hadn't applied there for law I couldn't study law that year and would have to wait for the following year's intake. One year seemed so long to my eighteen year old self, so I got a place reading my next favourite subject; History. Mum was still working away and a routine was gradually taking shape. Until late one night we had a visitor.

Alison who we hadn't seen in over a year came to the door. My sister was a married woman now and had coincidentally moved around the corner. Mum was so glad to see her that she immediately reached out and embraced her. She may not have agreed with her choice of husband, but it was her bed so she could lie on it. In the meantime she appeared happy. We were just so glad to see her.

It felt like our family was reunited and I would even say happy for a while. Mum even tried again with Alison's husband, if he was going to be a part of her daughter's life, then she may as well get used to him.

Alison and her husband became regular fixtures at our house and Mum and I went to theirs each week. In between all that I squeezed in my university career in which I loved. I had started a part time job in Mum's nursing home and was enjoying a social life, frequenting the 'Bot' and the 'Egg' like my parents many years before. I was enjoying my freedom, alcohol and men and more than anything being open about my smoking hobby which I had managed to conceal for years! An announcement over a family dinner one evening made things even better. Alison declared she had something to say and hushed us all before she said,

"Mum I'm pregnant"

It was like music to Mum's ears; she loved children and was excited already. She must have been like my Dad on hearing the news of his daughter's conception all those years ago. It wasn't until a day or so later that realisation struck Mum. It is a true to say that for Mum every silver lining has a cloud, and this new sure had a cloud; for she would be a granny!

"Surely I'm too young for that?" she exclaimed!

On a sadder note she said she had not imagined facing the news of her first grandchild alone and thought wistfully of how my Dad would have reacted to his daughter's announcement. She only hoped he was looking down on Alison and making sure that everything to do with this little one was as it should be.

Nine months later I sat (admittedly slightly hung-over) in the Royal Hospital in Belfast and waited as Mum's first granddaughter and my niece came into the world. Maxine had come over from London especially for the occasion. I remember the combination of the previous night's drink and the idea of childbirth made me feel positively green, I was disgusted by the whole thing. Yet Mum was overjoyed.

On the 6th of September 1998, my niece Sarah-Jayne was born. She was a beautiful baby; if you liked that sort of thing that was! Mum said she reminded her so much of her little ones when we were at that stage.

To me Sarah-Jayne was a strange little thing, she was white and on checking her little fingers as Mum had told us to do with all mixed race children, no pigmentation existed. It seemed she would stay white. Sarah-Jayne had a head full of black hair and a little African nose. She reminded Mum of Alison and of course her grandfather. It was then that it really struck Mum that this child would never know her grandfather. Mum's shelf began to shake a little more furiously than usual. Yet she ignored the tremors and told her doctor of them. Once again her drugs were upped and her shelf was stabilised. Now Mum had a new reason for living; her little granddaughter.

Mum spent all her free time at Alison and her husband's home. She really could not get enough of this little girl. Mum loved her as much as she loved her own and discovered that a grandchild was just another child to worry about. For me it was great that Mum had something more in her life, she deserved some joy and Sarah-Jayne brought it to her by the bucketful.

That winter was a lovely one, the new baby injecting some sparkle into our dull world. She brought so much laughter into our house that we spent that Christmas smiling and for once filled with hope. Yet in the February of that year the sparkle turned to ash, when once again our door knocked late in the night. Just like the year before Alison was on the doorstep, this time with a baby.

"Mum I've left him" she said,

Mum brought them in as it was so cold outside and through her tears Alison explained how unhappy she had been.

This was no place for '*I told you so's*', instead Alison was taken in and once again under Mum's roof. In the months that followed Alison and her husband fought a bitter, acrimonious battle. Dragging their marriage through the courts as both of them fought for custody of the baby.

Mum wanted no part in the battle and ignored it where possible; with the exception of Dad's trial no one in her family had ever been to court. "What on earth would Max have thought?" she asked me on one occasion. Even though Mum felt she should have supported my sister more she said she was empty, she had nothing left to give.

Instead we concentrated on immediate concerns such as the need for a bigger home. If Alison and Sarah-Jayne were to remain with us we would need at least one extra bedroom. So when the courts decided that Sarah-Jayne would stay with her mother, we were once again searching for another home.

As Sarah-Jayne grew she took to calling Mum granny Bumba, she couldn't pronounce Olorunda no matter how hard she tired. I couldn't really blame her as most adults I met couldn't! The name stuck and for a while Mum became known to us all as Granny Bumba.

If Sarah-Jayne needed anything or if Mum was mentioned in a conversation with Sarah-Jayne she was referred to as Granny Bumba. I would hear her ask for Granny Bumba every day and found amusement in how such a little child could change the name that my Mum had been known by for fifty years.

It didn't take long to find a house to hold us all and one that we could afford. This house was again in North Belfast but had a nice layout. It didn't need much more than a few coats of paint. We moved in and made it our home. We seemed to settle in well, that was until that summer when riots broke out. I had never seen riots before and it seemed that all hell had been unleashed! The world's media descended at the top of our street. They watched crowds of men, women and in many cases children fighting bitter battles. Every night, Catholics faced Protestants and fought across a peace wall. Our side of the wall was on the Catholic side. It was just our luck that the wall that divided the two communities was right behind our house.

Each night fell petrol bombs were launched over our house; we crammed into a room in the middle to avoid being struck and to drown out the voices of the angry mob.

One night they needed to get through our row of houses to the other side,

"Go through the Niger's house" they cried.

We were terrified not to mention shocked, when we first moved there the community boasted of its anti-racist attitude, the poor Catholics faced similar plights and claimed to empathise with the many black communities around the world. I lost count of how many taxi drivers and locals told us we would be perfectly safe here. That was until their true opinions emerged, as my Mum always maintained scratch the surface and you'll find a bigot. In times of tension in Northern Ireland this surface was well and truly scratched. For once Mum had nothing to say instead of taking her usual stance and defending us she passed out. I think her shelf rumbled more than ever before shaking her to the core.

We moved from that house within a week, loosing another deposit in the process and I believe a large chunk of Mum. I graduated during these years gaining a 2:1, Mum was proud but she cried on the news because Dad wouldn't be there to hear. We made a decision then that due to his absence we would miss the graduation and have a quiet family dinner instead.

Chapter Fifty Six

Belfast was changing with more and more black faces; who as far as many locals were concerned, were blotting the landscape. Yet Mum said these faces weren't like our Dad, these new people on the whole were not professionals they weren't middle class. They were refugees and asylum seekers. They had come here out of sheer distress; many had nowhere to go. Within a few months they filled out the many rentals in Belfast. Some of the houses housed so many that they were full to overflowing.

I would hear remarks of the locals, "they're everywhere", or "they're coming here to steal our jobs, our benefits and our houses". Suddenly Alison and I found ourselves labelled; what little individualism we had was gone, we were simply immigrants. So far we had been asked if our cousin or brother or sister lived down the road, had been in the same shop as us or had been on our bus. It seemed that to the

Northern Irish all black people were related, regardless if they resembled each other or spoke in the same tongue or even came from the same country! I was once asked if a lady from Thailand was my sister, despite the fact that our ancestors hail from different parts of the Globe. Mum would tell us if they were to ask again, to point out a random white person and ask the person enquiring, what their relation to them was.

Even though Mum began to depend on me more and more she still had her mothering instinct and Mum grew scared for us. Her fears didn't go unfounded. They materialised one day when I was walking my dog in the local park.

I was attacked. I remember that a black man had jogged past me; he was simply out for a run harming no one. After he had passed a white man approached me. It was all too much for his little mind to have a black man passing him followed in quick succession by a black girl. He exploded and took his disgust out on me. He had grabbed my shoulders his fingers digging roughly into my bones and shook me. He spat at me to go back home and "Get the fuck out of his country". His explosion finished with a punch.

I returned home shaken and bruised and told Mum of my ordeal. We didn't go to the police, instead Mum meted out her own justice. She dragged me to the park every day at the same time until we finally ran into the attacker. I identified a large man in his late fifties as the culprit. Mum approached him and he continued his rant to her. She gave him an opportunity to apologise, but when she saw that none was forthcoming, she did what I least expected. She called on her old friend Anger, and together they attacked him. Mum says she didn't know where her strength came from that day; perhaps he received every blow that every racist she had encountered deserved. It wasn't long before he screamed for mercy. He apologised frantically and I believe sincerely to me. He reassured me that he would never, ever utter another racist word again. When I looked at how he groped his neither regions after Mum's kicks, something told me to believe him!

Dealing with the attacker unfortunately did not put an end to the racial tensions that were unfolding all over Belfast. The locals were none too happy at having something new in their midst and being Northern

Irish weren't afraid to express themselves. Their opinions didn't surprise me; these people couldn't live with each other, so it was no revelation when they struggled to live with anyone else!

One day I went out to our back yard to find it splashed with a swastika, the following morning the tires on my little banger, my pride and joy were slashed. A brash warning was thrown in our letter box. We packed our belongings and fled.

Chapter Fifty Seven

Our fourteenth house was just outside Belfast in the village of Holywood, and Mum loved it. She said in an alternative world had she and Dad decided to settle in Northern Ireland this was where she would have chosen. It was in this house that Mum's tiredness reached epic proportions and I pleaded with her to give up work. I was beginning a Master's degree but was also working part time, Alison was working full time. My sisters and I weren't high earners but we combined my part time income with her wage from temping and decided we would cope. Mum was worn out she needed a break and this new house in this pretty village was the perfect place for her to recuperate, to allow her to regain strength.

Recently Mum just had no strength; she was tiny and began to look so frail. Her hands shook and her conversation became fragmented. There was some benefits for Mum though because whilst Alison was working Sarah-Jayne and her Granny Bumba spent their days together. They would go to the local beach, the park and make all manner of buns and cakes. Mum would say that she was doing what she missed out on with us.

We spent a year in that house until our rent fell behind. Alison's contract came to an end and my job had to go, the final stages of my masters were becoming intensive. Once again we were faced with pay the rent or eat.

We ate, we were evicted and we were faced with moving to house number fifteen.

We moved into house number fifteen on a Tuesday and we were evicted on the Friday. Things were worse than ever, this time we really had struck rock bottom, we were homeless. I couldn't take any more yet alone Mum. She was collapsing more and more I can only liken it to a powerful blow hitting her head, I imagine her skull reverberating in pain, as she felt the hinges that supported her shelf being ripped one by one from the wall. Dust and debris filled her consciousness and the wall shook. Painful remnants of her past, shelved neatly away until now assaulted her, striking her from every direction. Her childhood, nursing during the troubles, my Dad, racism, endless moves and poverty all came back to her. I believe Mum's shelf collapsed.

2005 -2010

Chapter Fifty Eight

From a very early age I remember suffering from a recurring dream. I used to wake at night shivering and terrified. Some dreams are forgotten when consciousness returns yet the frequency of this one meant that it always stayed fresh. I used to dream that I was standing outside Melmount Church in Strabane, and looking for Mum amongst the crowds leaving the Mass. I would see her standing near the doors and make my way towards her. When I would get near the crowds would disappear and I would look up to find three people who all looked like my Mum. I knew that only one was the real her and that the other two were bad. Yet I had no way of telling them apart, they were all identical.

Each one would be beckoning me and I never knew who to go to. I would eventually make up my mind and approach the one that I felt was Mum. Then I would wake just knowing that I had made the wrong decision. Now I look at my dream with an uneducated interpretation, I think I was always seeking the good Mum, the one who I saw now and again, the one who wasn't depressed, angry or tired.

After our eviction and Mum's complete breakdown I was on my own. I couldn't fathom why our landlady had suddenly asked us to leave and could only assume Mum had said something wrong, pushed her too far. I was furious my only thoughts at the time were 'what *has she done now?*' or '*that's another fine mess she's got us into*'. I had used every last penny of my final wages and then some to secure this house and Mum had just bloody told me that the landlady wants us out.

The mortification of it all! How would I ever begin to explain this one? The few friends that I had clearly assumed I was from a travelling background, as no sooner had we moved into one house were we packing up for another.

Recently Mum had become a law onto herself. She had been acting so strangely. She would forget her phone number, her date of birth and even more scarily her name. I worried about her all the time.

For the most part though, Mum made me laugh. She had begun to say the most terrible and inappropriate things, she would comment on strangers' right to their faces, telling them they were fat or worse point out features like big noses or their general ugliness (as she perceived it). I spent my days silencing her; she really was going to get herself into trouble.

I began to take her everywhere over those years, she was behaving so oddly I feared she might get lost. Or worse and more likely, that she would say the wrong thing to the wrong person. I had taken her to the doctors one week and two ladies were talking amongst themselves in the waiting room. Mum began to show signs of irritation and eventually looked at me and asked,

"Are they ever going to shut up?"

I invariably shushed her, looking over my shoulder to ensure they hadn't heard. They hadn't and went on with their talking. This was unfortunate; for them. As they continued talking Mum turned to them and bellowed,

"Would you fucking shut up" they looked at her aghast, as did I, "this is a doctor's I have a headache and your droning is making it worse, now if you want a social gathering why don't you go elsewhere? Instead of sitting here making the sick sicker" she had tutted.

I put my head in my hands and chastised myself; *I should have seen this coming.* Mum had been getting agitated. This was my fault.

The doctor must have heard the commotion, and realised what its source was because within seconds, Mum was ushered into the office. If nothing else Mum certainly knew how to beat the queue!

When the door closed, I looked at the two stunned ladies and apologised, they smiled and nodded. I assumed my apology had been accepted, yet they never regained their conversation. Well I mused inwardly if they hadn't needed a doctor before, they certainly needed one now, so at least they were in the right place.

It transpired that Mum had asked the Landlady to fix the electric cable that connected the cooker to the mains and for new flooring in the living room, these demands were too much. Within ten minutes of Mum's request, we had been blamed for tampering with her oil boiler; 'something we often did as a family pastime', and an eviction statement rather than notice was administered.

I was so angry, the thought of another move and one so soon made me feel sick. How could I have been so silly and not predicted this? It's not as though we hadn't experienced landlords before. Good grief I had known more landlords in this town than I had hot dinners and I meant that literally. I should be able to see a scoundrel by now. I had done most of the dealings with this one, Mum was loose cannon these days and Alison was out and about with her new boyfriend. This eviction was therefore all down to me.

With some regret I let myself wallow for a while, if only we could have some permanency, just some time to plant roots. I wished we could just stay in one place long enough, if we could save something, have something behind us so we could be prepared for crisis. We could be proactive for once. In all my years it seemed that Mum had done her best, but circumstances had driven her to be reactive.

Hearing that we had set a new family record, perhaps even a world record in having the shortest tenancy in history, I became enraged. The house had once been a student house and looked like one. At least three slovenly young lads had lived in it. Not only had we just moved back to bloody Belfast, we were stuck with yet another hovel. The coastal town that Mum adored had few private rentals at our asking price. I had scoured the papers and shop windows searching for something, anything that could keep her there, nothing had been available. As we were once again behind on the rent we had little time to find this house, as usual we had no time to plan.

We had packed up all our things and moved in; for the umpteenth time I arranged the transfer of electric and phones and re-directed the post. Alison arranged for Sarah-Jayne to attend yet another unfamiliar school.

Chapter Fifty Nine

We were expert at this moving business, I couldn't do a lot of things but hand me a tenancy and a new set of keys and I excelled. Mum and I with the help of Sarah-Jayne, in reality the hindrance of Sarah-Jayne had spent three days cleaning before we could unpack.

Many houses can be described as bursting with life, this was one was positively exploding with it. The kitchen looked like it could walk away all by itself, and the bathroom nurtured its very own species.

For the umpteenth time since our move to this city, we started to clean the kitchen first and then worked our way through the house. We scrubbed the house and it's furnishings down from top to bottom, our hands were red raw and blistered. At least the place now smelt clean and fresh and we could begin to unpack.

We had no furniture of our own anymore, over the years anything we had accumulated we had lost in our many moves. Sometimes we hadn't lost anything at all, but it was easier to think that we did. The reality was we had had to sell even the chairs we had sat on, money was tight it had always been, but these moves were taking it out of us.

As usual each house needed a deposit, a month's advance rent and removal vans. They all needed a cash injection. To raise funds we borrowed and when that option was exhausted we sold something. The loan repayments grew so high that we were working for nothing, at the end of each month when everyone was paid back there was barely enough to buy a few food items. A trip to the pawn merchant became a part of the monthly cycle.

This time though we were spent out and had nothing left to sell. For the previous move, Mum had parted with the remains of her jewellery. The last item left in a once impressive collection was her wedding ring, to my shame this too had to be pawned. I was glad she had pawned it rather than sell it; I wanted so much to buy it back for her and was until now making good progress towards that goal.

Our new landlady had other ideas; she was intent on throwing us out. I knew then that I could forget the promise I had made of retrieving the ring, it was like everything else we ever had of value, a thing of the past. On the positive side I had just received the news that I had achieved my Master's degree, I was elated. It also meant that I was no longer a student; I could now look for proper work. I could support Mum. This next move although unplanned would be easier I would secure a job and I would ensure that the rent was paid. Mum was even cheered by the news of my Masters; she seemed to liven up a little and even promised to attend my graduation. I had missed my first graduation so was looking forward to attending this one. First though I had to secure a house.

Chapter Sixty

Mum briefly displayed signs of life on hearing I had gained my Masters, yet ten minutes later she was sitting on the armchair absorbing the news that we would be moving again,

"How long have we got here four or five days Mum?" I asked her, I needed to know what time frame I was working on.

She didn't answer. I asked her again and still no answer was forthcoming. She was upset I supposed, so I left her and went to our newly installed phone and called the landlady. She was nasty and angry and when pressed for the reasons behind our eviction she told me that she couldn't cope with a tenant who was so demanding. I tried to persuade her to let us stay but she was having none of it. No contracts had been signed, our low budget rentals rarely came with any contracts and she would like us out in a week.

There wasn't any point in wallowing; the cow obviously wasn't going to change her mind, there was no persuading her. With great difficulty I swallowed my pride and asked about our deposit. The cow went on to confirm that if the house was in good condition we could have our deposit back on the day we left. I bit my tongue, wondering if she was talking about a different house than the one we had got. The house had never been in good condition! Due to our hard work and back breaking labour she should be paying us. We would be debt free if she refunded us for the price of cleaning products alone. She had had the place intensively cleaned for free. We had lifted the used condoms from under the filthy beds, cleaned the strange smelling items of the kitchen floor and scrubbed her bathroom that was sprouting glorious green algae.

Putting down the phone I turned to Mum again. I called her but she was just sitting there, a cigarette in her hand staring into the distance. I followed her gaze to see what she was looking at. The wall held nothing of interest to me.

She looked so pitiful, her little hands shaking, as they had started to do recently. My heart went out to her and I gave her a little hug,

"You sit tight, and I'll get a paper, don't worry we'll find something and when we do we'll have a lovely day at Queen's for my graduation". I grabbed my coat and went to the shop. On the way there it occurred to me that Mum hadn't answered me, in fact, she hadn't responded at all. That was the day that I really noticed that my Mum's had taken a turn for the worst.

I couldn't dwell on Mums' predicament though; I had four days to find us a new house. Plenty of rentals were available but not many were available the following week.

In the end I found one. A dark ugly terrace, in the heart of an area that left a lot to be desired. Yet for now it had a roof, so it fulfilled the basic function of any home; shelter. I would clean it up as best I could before Mum saw it and hope for the best.

One week later we had moved into our seventeenth home. My knowledge of Belfast was extensive at this stage, not a wonder I supposed considering we had lived all over it. I laughed to myself thinking that if all else fails I could always become a taxi driver.

This new house was the same as most of the others, smelly and damp. When I asked the electric board to come and connect us, the electrician told me that the little box that housed the electric meter was filled with woodworm. If there was woodworm there, then I could expect the place to be riddled with it he'd said. I cringed inwardly slightly embarrassed but thanked him for his observations.

In the meantime I had a deposit to collect, so returned to the old house to meet the landlady. I was so angry I would have done anything to avoid her, but if we wanted to retain our new roof I needed the money. The cow knew we had paid royally to arrange the move and had arranged all our affairs around this address. Yet to her she felt giving a family one weeks' notice to pack up their belongings was reasonable. That being the case I dreaded confronting her.

I knocked the door of the house that had been our home for one week and she greeted me, coolly. I knew that we had left it cleaner than we had found it. We had even made a few alterations, hanging a new shower curtain to replace the old mouldy one and to lesson our removal costs left a solid mahogany fire place in the living room. We had even left a little vase of flowers on the top.

The cow trotted through the house ensuring I was following behind her. I could see she was looking for a reason, any reason to refuse repaying the deposit. So far she had found none. Then we got to the living room. She appraised the room, then me from head to toe. I don't know what was stronger her disgust at the fireplace we had left, or her disgust at me. As she chewed her cud and took in all seven stone of me, I knew something was coming that I wouldn't like.

I was right, for the cow went on to swallow her cud and say,

"I want that gone" and pointed at the fireplace "then we can discuss deposits"

A cough came from the door behind us and I looked around to see a man standing, he smiled and informed me that he was this barnyard creature's husband.

"Hello" I said to him, then to her "okay I'll have that arranged"

"No dear" she moooed, "you will move it now, I'm going today so won't be back and I want this house cleared"

"Okay" I said gulping as I looked at the girth of the fireplace; it took two men to carry it in. I just wondered how I was going to carry it out.

I looked at her looking at me and saw she wanted action immediately. Well I thought, we needed the money so by hook or crook I would have to remove this bloody fireplace. She stood back and watched me push and push, her only remark was "mind my floor dear".

I continued pulling, pushing and tugging and managed to move the beast out of the living room and down the front steps. I was exhausted already and decided if I could get the heavy piece of furniture just to the back-lane a stone's throw away I could arrange for it to be moved later.

Tears pricked my eyes as I assessed my strength; even to get this moved around the corner right now seemed an epic task. I could hear talking from inside and glanced up in time to see her restraining her husband, who was coming to help,

That's when the tears really came. How was I going to move this thing another inch? The cow noticed my intent seeing the direction I was angling the piece.

"I hope you're not taking that to the back-lane"

"Yes" I panted "just until I can get it lifted. I can call the council and they can collect it"

"Well in the meantime, you're not leaving that outside my back, take it to the other side of the lane"

I looked up the long terraced street at least one hundred houses in length and knew what she wanted. She wanted me to drag this deadweight of a fireplace all the way down there. On my own, I had no choice; I ignored the glances of those walking and driving by and began dragging the lead like piece of furniture down the street. When I was halfway down, her husband must have been granted permission to assist and he helped me. He struggled himself even with my assistance, to drag and push the fireplace to the other side of the back lane.

I walked back to the house, the cow was now satisfied that I had been thoroughly humiliated and her tramps palace was now in order. She gave me back my deposit.

I looked at the envelope in my hand and thought, I may have lost any sense of pride I ever had and completely mortified myself in the process, but at least we would eat this week. To that end it had been worth it.

Chapter Sixty One

The day of my graduation dawned and I was so excited, Alison and little Sarah-Jayne and most importantly Mum would be attending. We made our way to Queens' University and I donned my black graduation gown. Mum had a little tear in her eye but didn't say much. Sarah-Jayne on the other hand said lots! She laughed at all the people dressed like ghosts and was shushed too many times to remember during the ceremony.

It was only after the ceremony that Alison told me that Mum had bawled, she had said that someone was missing. We didn't go for a meal that night but we did have an Iceland party! Alison had bought lots of little party treats and we all sat together and had a lovely night. Mum talked of Dad a few times and of how proud he would have been but other than that she didn't say much.

I knew Mum was not improving; she was spending more days than usual in her bed. It was often just she and I in the house so conversation was scarce.

I coaxed her awake one day and dragged her with me to approach the Housing Executive. She hated doing anything like that, but by this stage she was so far gone I didn't believe she was aware of what she was doing. Together we sat in their offices and applied for a house. We joined the housing waiting list in 2007.

Sarah-Jayne was growing up fast, our succession of moves ensured that by the age of seven she had attending four different schools. I often wondered how this would affect her, but she was such a bubbly child she seemed she seemed to take everything on the nose.

As luck would have it I found a job and as my luck had it I swiftly lost it. Mum needed more and more care, concentrating on work and home became too much and something had to go. I let the job go. Alison was always out with her new boyfriend so she was rarely around. I didn't blame her, I knew that happiness was a scarcity and believed that it should be clung to when found.

Mum and I were once again plunged deeper into debt. I laughed when people admired my slim figure, for it was not through choice my dieting days had long gone. Instead I was slim because I existed on the few basics we could afford. We could no longer heat the home and had long ago made the choice that we would eat rather than heat.

I had my Mum and two little dogs and they became the focus of my shrinking world. As long as they were fed and watered it didn't matter about me. As a child Mum routinely gave up her meals for us, I had vivid memories of counting out what scraps we had, when I would cut them between four and Mum would say,

"Split it three ways. I'm not hungry"

Well now it was my turn, I was now splitting the food between them and if I was fortunate I even managed some myself.

Yet I held true to what I had been taught, Mum always said hold your head high. No one ever has to know what you live like, we may not be have much but we have our pride. Our father didn't plan for this life for us. He came here and faced his adversaries with his head in the air; he never let them see that they hurt him. Mum would say, "Never let this place see its beaten us Jayne, hold your head in the air too and remember this was not how things were meant to be".

Chapter Sixty Two

Race relations in Belfast had gotten worse; many families from different ethnicities were being burnt out of their homes. I got scared; really sacred. In that that year I was spat on, called some horrendous names and accustomed to being greeted with "Go back home". Some really funny people showed more creative uses for their jibes, one day in a crowded bus stop, two sober men approached and sang me a little song,

"Consider yourself at home; consider yourself one of the family".

I didn't get the bus that day instead I walked home and hung my head in shame. Their serenade rang in my ears even hours later. I *was* at home yet these people would never see it that way. Despite the fact that I had been born here, educated here, worked here, paid taxes here and spoke in an accent from here, my skin was brown. That meant to them that I would never be truly from here.

I broke down a little that day and cried, I wanted out and for the first time ever I began to hate them as much as they hated me.

Mum who was in bed got up that day to ask me what was wrong, I told her and she just nodded. I didn't leave the house much after that. Instead I focussed my attention on Mum, who in between her increasing prescriptions was acting strangely. She claimed she couldn't sleep yet spent her days in a darkened room, only really becoming animated when little Sarah-Jayne would come up saying in her sing-songy voice "Granny Bumba".

Mum would sit with Sarah-Jayne and tell her all sorts of stories and for those moments our house was happy.

"Why is Granny Bumba so sad?" Sarah Jayne would ask and I would reply with the only answer that came to me, "because the world made her that way."

Mum went steadily downhill. She refused to get out of bed and started to talk in a strange gibberish, I lost count of the many times I took her to the doctors in despair. Eventually after a few years we found ourselves at the Royal Hospital where Mum was to see a psychiatrist.

I waited a long time for her whilst she seen by him, I was worried sick but she came out bright and breezy. She had entered his office removed and remote and I wondered what had brought about this sudden change. This man must have been a miracle worker; I began to think I would like an appointment too! Whatever medicine he had administered had worked because Mum was looking more like her former self than she had done in years.

It was the thought of medicine that triggered a little alarm bell in my head. It stopped me in my tracks. I looked at Mum's hand to see if she had a prescription; sure enough she did. Mum hadn't been cured; no problem had been solved. As always when Mum got depressed they solved the problem by giving her yet more drugs.

Chapter Sixty Three

We left the hospital and crossed onto Belfast's busy Falls road. We needed to get a taxi home and with no taxi's in sight I called into a local shop and asked for directions to the nearest taxi depot. As luck would have it there was one just around the corner.

We followed the directions the helpful shopkeeper had given us and quickly found the taxi depot. It was a dark office in a residential terraced street. We walked from the light into the gloom and I approached the grid in the wall. It served as a divider between the waiting room and the office. I ordered our taxi and looked up. At a games machine in the corner was a man who was badly scarred. He was staring at me like I was a ghost. I was used to be stared at so shot him a filthy look, yet something in this man's demeanour made me take another look.

He looked like he *knew* me. I racked my mind trying to pull something or some point from my past where this man familiar. No, nothing came to the fore. Mum on noticing my reaction followed my stare, she instantly tensed.

The growing silence in the room was interrupted when Mum spoke,

"Jayne meet the man who killed your father"

That was it. That was why this man was staring at me. He may not have been familiar to me, but I was certainly familiar to him.

I was a bit flummoxed and thought what am I supposed to say to this one?

As always when in doubt I remembered my manners. I stepped forward, held out my hand and said "Hello"

The man was surprised, yet he took my hand and shook it.

"I've followed you girls" he said "I know you went to Queens', did you finish your degree?"

"Yes" I replied and "and my Masters"

"What about the other two? I know one had a baby"

I told him about both my sisters. Mum stood there, she just stood there.

We had discussed what we would do if ever this situation arose and I knew that Mum would not be thinking along the lines that I was. I knew that if this man valued his life he should flee, but he remained.

Okay, it was over to me. I did my best Archbishop Tutu impersonation and decided there was nothing else for it but to become mediator.

"Mr Flynn, how do you feel about it all now?" I asked

"I was a soldier" he said,

Mum was coiled so tight that on hearing his reply I was waited for her to unravel and pounce. I had to act fast,

"Yes" I said, "I don't agree with that or with any war, but funnily enough I studied Irish history, so I can see your cause" I said full of fake bravado, "but do you regret, my Dad?"

Everything hung on his answer and part of me expected the worst. World War III was about to break out in this tiny west Belfast taxi office. I braced myself to duck from the inevitable carnage.

He didn't reply, instead he did something I least expected, he cried. His answer was there in those tears running down his scarred cheek.

I turned to look at my Mum and found that she was crying too. The pair embraced, him expressing his regret and my Mum saying one poignant line which will always remain with me,

"I will never forget what you did, but I forgive you. I forgive you"

We all stood there for a while in that dark taxi office in West Belfast. Time became irrelevant, because a miniature ceasefire had taken place. The victim and the terrorist united in pain, the pain that this Godforsaken land produced.

That day I realised that we were all victims, victim of our past, victims of evil circumstances and misfortune. The carnage, the bloodshed and the tears destroyed not only the innocent's lives, but also the lives of those who were unfortunate enough to carry life threatening weapons. Not all involved in Northern Ireland's struggle have souls; many of the murderers still do not repent. Those who repented, those who stood up and regretted their actions proved they possessed souls and that their souls felt hurt and suffering like everyone else's. They were victims too, their lives were also destroyed.

Chapter Sixty Four

After the encounter in the taxi depot Mum released a lot of her bitterness. I could never say she loved the IRA, but she had reached some sort of acceptance within herself. She had reconciled her differences with the man of her nightmares and clearly felt some relief. This relief opened new doors for her; she began to tell me all about my father. I would hear the same stories over and over until I felt that I knew him too. Stories would pour out of her, more than I had ever heard before. It was as if her meeting with Mr Flynn had opened the floodgates and nothing or no one could close them.

She still had trouble sleeping and I asked her why, she was on so many drugs that such a cocktail would literally knock a donkey out. Her reply was to tell me about the aftermath of the bomb all those years ago, of how she had reached out for the coffin, to make sure Max was still with her.

"Every time I go to sleep, Jayne I see the coffin, I still reach for it. I wake up and it's gone, he's gone. I go back to sleep again and wake up and go through the same process over and over."

My heart reached out to her like most people, I had known love before and I had lost it. Yet I had lost love naturally, none of my relationships had been serious so they had simply faded and died. The relationships that I had experienced had died a metaphorical death, no lives were lost and no one was hurt. Mum had known such a greater love, her one true love, this had been taken from her and her life had been spent trying to ascertain why and of course putting the pieces back together. She cried again that day,

"I loved him Jayne...... I still do"

I cried too, it was hard to conceive that someone could know such pain and loss and carry this around every waking day. The years had not diminished my parents love, instead they had simply created questions, another world of what ifs. She would never see this other world; she would never see how her love would progress.

Chapter Sixty Five

We spent those years freezing and for the most part hungry. I could see no solutions. Then one night the First Minister filled our TV screen as his party gave its party political message. He informed the nation that Northern Ireland had reconciled with its past. Its victims had been taken care off. The country could move on in the security that it had done right by all.

I thought of Mum's tears and wondered how she had been taken care off. She had been waiting three years for a council house. I had told the Housing Executive of her situation, of how she had suffered from Post-Traumatic stress and why, yet they had no policies in place to help victims. She had watched the wives of my Dad's colleagues grow into very wealthy ladies, as their husbands became partners or opened their own firms. Yet here she was husbandless and in a ghetto.

Since my Dad's death she had never had a permanent home or stability. The 17th of January 1980 had ruined her life and it had never been repaired.

I rarely grew angry, but on seeing the First Minister broadcasting his delight to the nation I saw red. All my mother had asked for was a council house. She had not moved an inch on the waiting list in the three years since she had went on it. From all accounts Northern Ireland's intuitions were now recognising its victims; I could see no proof of this.

That was when my campaign began. I tried to speak to the first minister but he was too busy. Even his PA had little time for me. I spoke to every victims group that the millions of pounds allocated to help the victims had been ploughed into. They could offer Mum some acupuncture or even some art lessons, but they couldn't help with housing or her mental illness. Surely these issues were the real issues? Why plough millions of pounds into victims, create numerous jobs yet leave the victims with useless help. One victims group headed by Willie Frazer was the only group that bothered to help my Mum. I wondered was it because its founder however militant, was a victim that he actually understood. A stark contrast from the numerous civil servants and third sector employees, who knew as much about being a victim as they did about nuclear physics. Unfortunately for us Mr Frazer's group were unable to help in the end, but at least they provided some support. With no one left to turn to I went to the newly installed victim's commissioners.

Now they held promise. We no longer had an interim victim's commissioner, who had used Mum's story in her report, Mum being covered under a pseudo name of Anne. We now had four commissioners, they had been appointed by the government tasked to work on behalf of the counties victims. I was so excited at last Mum would be saved; she wouldn't be ignored any more. I ran up to Mums room and told her of their establishment. I jotted down the address and left it on the mantel piece. We would go to them, they would help.

Over the next months we had spoken to them on the phone, but never formally met them. I had started a new job in the city centre and was based close to their offices. I planned on booking an appointment right away.

Mums condition continued to deteriorate. Once a woman who had once taken such pride in her appearance, she now thought nothing about stepping out with her night dress under her coat. Her shaky hands meant that the buttons were never matched right, always some were missed or in the wrong place, the result was that her nightdress was visible to all. I did not worry about this too much, as Mum rarely went out. She would panic when I left her in the house alone.

Every day when I left for work I would leave her a little note listing some tasks, some things she could do with the day. The tasks were always basic, wash the dishes, read a magazine or watch a certain programme on TV. Sometimes she even rang the commissioner's office asking for help with housing, my entrance to teacher training, whatever she could think of at the time. I knew if Mum had something to do, no matter how minor she would panic less.

Most of the time my lists were never read, instead Mum would retreat to her room. There I would hear her engaged in conversation, so deep and fluid that sometimes I believed that someone was actually there with her. She would talk to and answer her invisible friends with such accuracy that it was difficult to imagine she was alone.

One day, like Lazarus my Mum rose and decided to come down the stairs. I had left for work already and left her a list, but she had other ideas. She ignored my list and instead found the details of the Victims Commissioners I had left out. She had something to focus on a grain of hope. Somehow she made it to the city centre and to their offices. I received a call in work from my Mum, she was in the city centre and she was stuck. Could I come and get her?

I left my desk immediately and rushed out to meet her. She was in tears, she had called to their office, a huge glossy building, had even passed a commissioner on his way out of the office wearing an exquisite linen suit and carrying a bunch of flowers. She had made her way to the opulent reception and asked to speak to a commissioner. She was told to take a seat and she had waited. After a while she was told that no one could see her. She begged and pleaded with the staff and dissolved into tears. Still no one could see her. She left the office and a kind lady had enquired if she was okay, she had extracted my work place from Mum and called it to reach me. I took her home and she went back to her bed. Not even Sarah Jayne could rouse her from this depression.

Shortly after, maybe on having enough Alison and Sarah Jayne moved out, leaving me alone with my Mum.

The incident in the victim's commissioner's office roused anger in me. I had exhausted every avenue I could to try and get my Mum some help, and even those who were put in place because of people like my

Mum could not help. I called them and arranged a proper appointment for Mum and I this time to meet with a commissioner. I secured an appointment with Bertha Mac Dougal and remember cringing as Mum and I sat in her office on the day. Mum was pouring her heart out, all the while the office door remained open, everyone could hear.

I had had enough and decided I would take matters into my own hands. I began a campaign bombarding every politician in the country. I started with telephoning Stormont in 2008. Speaking to them first, then emailing. What follows is one of my first emails to the First Ministers office;

Friday, 7 November 2008, 13:42
Hi David,

My Mum has asked me to email you I only hope that she has taken your address down correctly.

I don't know where exactly to start but I'll try to summarise her case.
My Dad was murdered by the IRA in 1980 and ever since then she has never been settled. We honestly have never had a permanent home. After Dad who was a chartered accountant died my Mum was unable to maintain the mortgage (though working full time as a nurse her salary was just not enough) and unfortunately had the home repossessed.
We then moved in with my grandparents and had lived there until 14 years ago when my Mum decided to move to Belfast. As a mixed race, mixed religion family it was difficult to find affordable rents in 'mixed' areas and as a result rents were always beyond our means. We have never had a permanent home something my Mum lost on Dad's death and never regained. Since moving to Belfast we have lived in 18 homes 2 off which we were forced to leave on the basis of my colour.
When a few years ago victims issued hit the headlines I think we felt so hopeful and my Mum thought that now at last she could get a permanent home. Talk then was of Northern Ireland's institutions addressing victims and their issues so we naively thought that the Housing Executive would be one of them and sought the help of the then victim's commissioner to help us.
Mrs McDougall was then full of hope and stated that as soon as she was instated properly we would be her top priority. She even used us in her interim commissioner's draft - my Mum under a pseudo name as Anne.
So when the victims commissioners were appointed this year my Mum contacted Bertha right away and in my opinion was more or less told she was no longer top priority and that the commissioners had no remit to deal with the Housing Executive.
My Mum broke down in their offices, something which as her daughter I am accustomed too but find it hard to bare.
Bertha wrote my Mum a letter and rather than address her as a victim to the executive simply went through to the executive using the same procedure as one would use for any applicant - a request for an appeal. Her letter implied that we should seek another landlord and didn't state that she was a victim and that she should have some kind of concession for that (which was what she had previously stated).
My mother has also been banned from the NI memorial fund. She got a grant from them 4 years ago to furnish yet another house. Because she did not supply receipts they have banned her permanently. On appealing to Bertha to help her with this once again it wasn't in her remit. Unless my mother could get receipts then she would not be helped by the memorial fund. My mother suffers from post traumatic stress a common illness suffered by victims, effecting memory, nerves etc how on earth is she to even remember what she purchased or even where. After 18 homes things become a blur even for me! So as for the last 3 years my Mum has not been allowed to apply even for the hardship grant a grant to help victims and not shame them and once again the commissioners could not assist with this. In a way that's

£3000 that the state has set aside for victims that she is not entitled to, to me that is unfair especially for a system set up to help, not to make her feel like
a beggar. Again the commissioners were unsympathetic and could not help.

In the meantime my Mum, my niece and I live in a house without Central heating, mould growing on the kitchen ceiling and walls slick with damp. On seeing Mr Robinson's Party political broadcast he mentioned human rights for victims, and I would ask why hasn't my Mum been helped? She is no longer coping and I fear that I will lose my Mum as well and am quite frankly sick when I see or hear people mention victims' rights, because as a victim myself, growing up and now looking after my Mum I feel we have been stripped of any dignity we once had, and if our Dad were to see how we now live he would turn in his grave.
Why can no one seem to help and is my Mum to be left living like this because it is not in the commissioners remit? after 5 years on the waiting list for a 3 bed house, it is clear that NI cares no more about its victims then it does about its rubbish.

Jayne Olorunda Bssc, Msc

I waited and waited for a response and finally I approached them for one.

Hi David,

My Mum contacted the office of the first minister early November and was told someone would look into her case. Unfortunately no one has gotten back to her. I'm assuming the matter was investigated by now?

Regards

Jayne Olorunda

--- On Mon, 10/11/08,

The response they sent looked promising;

> To: jayneolorunda
> Date: Monday, 10 November, 2008, 3:21 PM
> Jayne,
>
> Confirmation that I received your email, at long last! The
> First Minister has instructed officials within his
> Department to investigate your Mum's case with a view to
> getting back to you as soon as possible.
>
> Kind regards,
>
> David.

Nothing ever came of these 'investigations' and I would phone regularly to find out what had happened.

No one was ever available to take my calls. It looked like I was being ignored by the First Minister.

With no other option I bypassed him and went to the then Prime Minister Gordon Brown, from him I went to the secretary of state for Northern Ireland. Victim's issues were on the news every day, to the stranger to Northern Ireland it would appear that our First Minister had been right, the victims were dealt with. Their presence in the headlines every night confirmed this. Yet upstairs in our pitiful accommodation lay one victim who was completely ignored. It seemed that Gordon Brown and the secretary of state were busy as well, but at least they bothered to respond. So I went to BBCNI and then re-approached.

The emails between the secretary of state and I are documented below,

---Original Message-----
From: jayne olorunda
Sent: 25 February 2009 17:58
To: SOS
Subject: Urgent help required! BBC E-mail: Victims' 15 year search for home

Dear Mr Woodward,

As you are the secretary of state for Northern Ireland I have decided to ask you for assistance. I have tried various victims groups, the victim's commissioners and the First minister, all to no avail.
My problem is summarised in the BBC link below, however since that date our situation has escalated. By bringing the BBC team into our house we have now been evicted and are to leave here in approx 12 days. All the Housing Executive could offer is temporary accommodation in the form of a hostel.
My mother has severe post traumatic stress and my sister and her daughter are vulnerable. We cannot live in a hostel. We have been on the Housing Executive list for 5 years and still no permanent home has been found.
Essentially on our imminent eviction we will go into temporary accommodation, until such times when a permanent home can be found. This will mean another two moves bringing out total houses moves to 17 in 15 years. I know this will kill my mother, this country has taken my Dad and I don't want to to take my Mum too.
I dislike having to do write to you as I'm sure you have more pressing matters to deal with, but let me assure you my family and I never aspired to an executive house. Yet this is what we have been reduced to and now after 5 years on the list are having to beg.
We are victims of the troubles, my reasoning for putting my Mum on the Housing Executive list was that Northern Ireland had pledged to look after it's victims. The victims commissioners in their draft report even claimed to have the remit to intervene in government bodies when it could make the lives of victims easier (Bertha Mac Dougall even used my Mum's case in her interim commissioners draft proposals, Mum under a pseudo name as Anne. She promised her that when she was instated properly we would be top of her list and that wheels would be set into motion to make the housing executive make concessions for victims in its point allocation system). Instead when my Mum sought their help she was left so feeling so insignificant that she was reduced to tears in their office. They suddenly did not have the 'remit' to help her. No one showed her any sympathy, they just sent her home for me to pick up the pieces.

The first minister also pledged to help, his PA alluding (I have copies of the emails)that the first minister was investigating matters to find the best possible solution for my Mum. It took him four months to tell us he could do nothing.
My second issue is the Northern Ireland Memorial fund, again I have approached the first minister and the commissioners for help with them. Four years ago my Mum got a discretionary grant from the Northern Ireland Memorial fund to furnish yet another house. Six months later she was asked to provide receipts,

unfortunately due to racial abuse we had left that house and receipts were not provided. At which point due to Mum's condition Post Traumatic Stress she couldn't remember what she'd bought anyway! Memory loss is common with suffers of PTS, which surely even the memorial fund will appreciate. Or so I thought as it claims to help such sufferers.

When my Mum applied again last year (victims should be entitled to this grant on an annual basis) she was turned down again for the grant, something that all spouses of victims - especially those suffering from Post Traumatic Stress are entitled to, all because she didn't submit receipts.

Now we are homeless, well we will be in 10 days and in desperation I explained to the Memorial fund our plight. Again they could not help unless receipts were provided. Frankly I feel this is ridiculous and unjust, this money was set aside for victims in hardship, which is exactly what my poor Mum is facing now, yet she can't have it. Once again she has been sidelined.

What right do they have to deny her her basic entitlement, we have suffered enough over the years and all we have ever asked for is a home (something we lost when my Dad was murdered) and a discretionary grant. All the recent efforts to help victims are not working, they are surrounded by red tape and not getting to those who need them. They are not help and shouldn't be classed as such, they are more of a hindrance, essentially prolong the suffering which they were established to alleviate.

Again I am sorry Mr Woodward for such a rant, but I keep hitting brick walls. We are now in DESPERATE need (we have 10 days and it seems no one can/is prepared to assist) and I am hoping that you could find the time to intercede for us, something which the various institutions to help victims could not do.
My contact details are xxxxxxxxx or mobile xxxxxxxxxx, my email address is above.
I would also appreciate it if my message to you could be passed to Mr Brown, as I believe victims here, well the people who have not raised scenes are being ignored.

Please see report below for a brief description of our story.

The response I got reduced me to tears – we were being passed from pillar to post

FROM: SOS
TO:

- jayneolorunda@yahoo.co.uk

Message flagged
Friday, 27 February 2009, 13:52
Dear Jayne

Thank you for your e-mail addressed to the Secretary of State.

I note your concerns over housing and the NI Memorial Fund. In respect of the former, as you are probably aware, responsibility for the NI Housing Executive has been devolved to a local Minister, Margaret Ritchie MLA and you may wish to contact her office regarding any issues you have on your housing problems.

The Minister can be contacted by the following means:-

By post

email:

Telephone:

In relation to your issues with the Northern Ireland Memorial Fund, the Fund is an independent charity governed by a Board of Directors. In light of this I have passed your correspondence on to Mr Dennis Licence, Fund Chairman and have asked him to investigate the issues you have raised and respond to you directly.

I understand that this may not be the response that you were seeking but I hope that you will find the information contained in my e-mail to be of some assistance to you.

Assistant Private Secretary
Secretary of State's Private Office (Belfast)

In the end it was the BBC's coverage that secured us help, shortly after we got a house.

In February 2009, our story made headline news across Northern Ireland, Alison (who was now back home) and I took up most of the interview as Mums footage for the most part was incoherent. Our absent landlady evicted us the next day, concerned about the state of disrepair her home had fallen into. Not once in four years had she checked the house, she never fulfilled her promises of annual decoration, instead she sat back month after month and extracted the rent. The last time the electrics were safety tested was in 1990, after a succession of electric shocks and fungal infections from, the mould we had long ago had the house condemned as being unfit for human habitation. When my Mum and I went to the council offices almost four years earlier they had viewed our current dwelling and had on the spot registered us as homeless.

The day after our eviction notice a housing officer called and within a week Mum was given her first permanent home, one she could afford and even better one in an area that was neither Catholic nor Protestant. It was the first time she had had this since losing our Dad in 1980.

Of course we were given a home but no funds to furnish it and once again were faced with the prospect of moving house with no money and no furniture. I pulled together every penny I could selling every last non-essential we had and got us moved. We moved in with three new beds and sat on cushions in the living room.

Over the next few months I again did the rounds of the various victims groups for help. One of whom, the 'Northern Ireland Memorial fund' promised assistance to victims in need; perfect I thought, I called them and was dumbstruck to find that I was treated like a beggar. In fact that was exactly what I had become, their need for evidence of our poverty and sending someone out to the house to prove it, simply reinforced this. It was bad enough having to ask for help, but to have an organisation requesting proof was humiliating. The organisation in question had been set up to help victims not to strip them of what remained of their dignity. As far as I was concerned the only criteria they should have needed was central to their being; that those asking for help were victims.

Well I would take what they gave because we would need it. They awarded us £750 and I did my best to buy as many essentials as I could, they demanded receipts for every purchase which I sent to them but vowed never again.

It was a well-known fact that those who had been released from prison early during the peace process were given houses immediately and given finds to decorate and buy basics. Yet here I was trying to furnish my Mum's house and being made to beg for droplets of help. I remember thinking that this country really did have an upside down way of dealing with things, by rewarding its guilty and penalising its victims.

Chapter Sixty Six

On being given the home after years in the no-man's land Mum changed. Unlike in fairytales where happy endings are guaranteed in real life this was not the case. If only it was. If I thought Mum was bad before, her behaviour in this home showed me what deteriorating really meant. She became angry and confused. Everything angered her, she would sit scowling at the TV, swearing at whoever's poor face happened to grace the screen.

Her tablets once again were increased, but this time even they didn't help. Every time I would wander up the stairs I would find her talking. What was more alarmingly was the fact that she often invited me in to join her and her acquaintance. Or worse, she would be talking to me and I hadn't even opened my mouth yet; there she would lie responding to my every non-existent comment.

Often she would talk as if she lived in the 1970's, as if she were my age and talk about her three little girls. Once she ran downstairs and asked me why the police were in the living room, who had died?

I would laugh and ask her what she was talking about, sometimes she would even laugh back, quickly realising her error, reacting to the concern in my eyes.

She then turned nasty criticising Alison's every move, so much so that Alison fled the house with Sarah-Jayne in tow, seeking sanctuary in Women's Aid. When they left the strange behaviour continued and intensified.

Mum would talk to a little grey haired woman who appeared at the end of her bed. She loved her visits and the pair of them talked for hours. When I came in, the grey haired woman disappeared because she was 'shy'. Mum even watched TV in her room and would tell me all about the great film she had seen. She didn't have a TV in her room.

Then the suicide attempts began, I had started another job and wasn't at home with her as often as I should have been. Every job I started, I had to give up; Mum's condition whatever it was, demanded that she had someone with her constantly. It was difficult as I needed to work to support us but I couldn't work if I wanted to support her.

In one suicide attempt Mum had slashed her wrists. This was followed by a succession of overdoses and yet more strange behaviour. Most worryingly of all were the falls. I couldn't leave her unattended; she was so unsteady on her feet. She would get up from her chair and fall, overnight she would try to go down the stairs and fall, or she would simply pass out. I was at my wits end and had no one to turn to.

In the end it was on yet another trip to A&E, where she had worked many years before, that seen the doctors eventually recognise that something was amiss. They kept her in overnight, concerned about her falls but they quickly released her. I began to worry so much so that I began to wonder if I too would become ill. I would take strange headaches and wake to find that hours had passed that I wasn't aware off. I wondered what would become of us both. I prayed that God would bring my Mum back, but she got progressively worse.

Chapter Sixty Seven

One evening I had fed her and got her to bed, I was watching TV with my dogs when the smoke alarm erupted. The dogs went mad at the high pitched sound and I ran upstairs to investigate. Outside Mum's room a fire raged, it climbed up her door eating at the wood. I ran for a towel from the bathroom and frantically swotted it. When I checked if she was ok, I found her sitting in her bed waiting for the flames to take her.

She knew me that night and she cried sore, she wanted it to end; she had had enough of struggling, of being alone, of the poverty and she wanted Max. I didn't know what to do; at my wits end I called the doctor and went with Mum to the hospital.

That night Mum was taken to a secure mental health unit. Here she could no longer hurt herself or inadvertently hurt others. My mother had been driven insane and I couldn't help her.

The nurses interviewed me for a brief history and one question they asked saddened me,

"She claims to be a nurse where does that come from?"

I nodded sadly, "she is, or was" I said. My mother had been a nurse and whatever else they choose to believe about this new patient that fact remained. Mum had nursed until she could nurse no more; she had worked long and hard on the wards, so hard that just thinking of nursing sickened her. It was a career she had once loved, but fates intervention had made her a prisoner of the wards and turned this love into hate. Nevertheless her work had kept us sustained through childhood and beyond, it had kept a roof over our heads. It was one title that I would not let her lose.

Mum had always been a good storyteller; I had grown up fed on tales of her past, from voodoo curses delivered by a green woman all the way from Nigeria, to visitations from mysterious Christ like priests. Mum had loved nothing more than a good yarn and in me she found a captive audience. Now as she sat in this bleak hospital I wondered if I would ever hear her tales again, I wondered if they were true.

I left the hospital that night with an image of my Mum that would stay with me forever. A once strong and courageous woman who had stood up against racism and the IRA had been broken. She had admitted defeat. She had fought her hardest against poverty, she had loved us and she had loved Max. As she sat on her bed in a mental health ward; all that remained was a frail, scared, shrunken woman. Her empty eyes and twisting hands had become despair itself.

On my way out of the ward, the nurse gave me a bag of Mum's effects. So many everyday things were viewed as hazardous and removed from the patients. Even her nightgown strap was viewed as a danger. That night I would put them away for her, she would have them for when she came home.

As I drove home I passed a famous cemetery in Belfast. I had visited there once and curiosity drove me to the republican section. This section was the hero's part of the cemetery, a section of the cemetery devoted to Ireland's greatest fighters, to the heroes of the republican struggle. It has its own dedicated marble pathway and each grave in the section is elaborately finished. All the graves lay in the shadow of a patriotic speech inscribed on the wall. People come from far and wide to pay their respects and it remains on the tourist trail to this very day. In this section of the graveyard lies the man who killed my Dad, forever glorified for his brave actions furthered Ireland's cause.

As I passed, I wondered who was paying their respects to these hero's right now and in the back of my mind I was reminded of another grave one hundred miles away. A grave which marks the life of an innocent man; a family man, guilty of nothing but boarding a train. This grave is unmarked and unattended, as I have been told that this grave lies empty, that nothing of this man was left. All that remains of him lives on in his family, his granddaughter, his daughters and his wife, who incidentally now sits in a little mental health unit in Belfast. That night was one of the saddest of my life I felt so alone. I placed my feelings about the two very different graves and Mum's illness a little shelf I had created in my mind.

Epilogue

Now Mum is doing better, she is still being treated by drugs but at last it has been discovered that there is a definite link between victims of the troubles and post-traumatic stress. Many of those who worked in the emergency services during those years were severely affected. Mum's nursing combined with Dad's death dealt her a double blow. Now Mum has good days and I think for the most part they outweigh the bad and that is all I can hope for. Throughout it all Mum had her friend Misery.

Northern Ireland today is a partially changed place, unfortunately we still see the occasional terrorist murder and more grieving families, but not on the scale of many years ago. Yet Northern Ireland's future is a very delicate balance, now and again tensions simmering beneath the surface boil up and threaten to overflow. Luckily enough they are quickly cooled, before any additional bloodshed occurs. This little country although beautiful has an ugly side, a side that always runs parallel with progression.

As for Northern Ireland's victims I still see no evidence of any tangible help. No-one is out there to treat post-traumatic stress, no-one is there to prevent families falling into the abyss that mine fell into. Above all no one is there to help the children of the struggle. Certainly some groups do exist, the legacy of the troubles meant that a myriad of victims groups were set up. Each group, third sector or government has paid members of staff; each being paid and benefiting from others misfortune, hurt and loss. The millions of pounds set up for victims doesn't reach them all, instead it reaches only the very few, the rest is pumped into the pockets of too many people. To some extent Northern Ireland has benefited from its victims but who are the real winners? Those who need it? Or those who prey on innocents? To me countless victims are being exploited for the gain of a few.

Money allocated to victims would be better spent on training doctors, medical staff, government institutions and private institutions. These people would have been instrumental in preventing my Mum's suffering and countless others. Northern Ireland should ensure its institutions recognise its victims and provide them with some sort of dispensation for what they have suffered at the hands of their country, the place they call home. No-one should have suffered like my Mum and mechanisms should be put in place to ensure such suffering like the troubles is a thing of the past.

Mum still plays a song from her youth and often I listen to it and think how true it's lyrics are and I feel they sum up my Mum's life and how some things can never be changed. We can only move forward.

'For what's done is done

And what's won is won

And what's lost is lost forever'. (Phil Coulter)

THE END